# SANDINISTAS

ROBERT J. SIERAKOWSKI

# SANDINISTAS

A MORAL HISTORY

University of Notre Dame Press
Notre Dame, Indiana

Published in the United States of America

Names: Sierakowski, Robert J., 1983– author.
Title: Sandinistas : a moral history / Robert J. Sierakowski.
Description: Notre Dame, Indiana : University of Notre Dame Press, [2019] |
Includes bibliographical references and index.
Identifiers: LCCN 2019037145 (print) | LCCN 2019037146 (ebook) |
ISBN 9780268106898 (hardback) | ISBN 9780268106928 (pdf) |
ISBN 9780268106911 (epub)
Subjects: LCSH: Nicaragua—Politics and government—1979–1990. |
Frente Sandinista de Liberación Nacional—History. | Nicaragua—
History—Revolution, 1979—Moral and ethical aspects. | Nicaragua—
Politics and government—1937–1979. | Nicaragua—Social conditions. |
Nicaragua—Politics and government—1990-
Classification: LCC F1528 .S54 2019 (print) | LCC F1528 (ebook) |
DDC 972.8505—dc23
LC record available at https://lccn.loc.gov/2019037145
LC ebook record available at https://lccn.loc.gov/2019037146

*Dedicated to my mother and father,
John and Margaret Sierakowski, my siblings,
Chris Sierakowski and Cindy Tamburri,
and their wonderful families*

CONTENTS

ILLUSTRATIONS

## ACKNOWLEDGMENTS

Researching and writing this book has been one of the most incredible experiences of my life and much of it was thanks to the hundreds of Nicaraguans who gave so willingly of themselves to bring this project to fruition. From rural hamlets to provincial towns to the archives of Managua, I experienced great warmth, charity of spirit, and selfless openness to my efforts to document their country's experiences. As a foreigner, from a nation whose historical treatment of Nicaragua has been largely negative, these innumerable interactions of support taught me much about the character of the people, which doubtlessly shined through in the dark era that I was researching. It also provided a lesson as to how all of us in the United States could and should treat those who come from abroad to our country. Given the caliber of the human beings I encountered on a daily basis, I have no doubt that Nicaragua will find its way through its current difficulties to a better and brighter future.

This work owes everything to the women and men who opened their homes and their hearts to a stranger in Estelí, La Trinidad, Condega, Pueblo Nuevo, El Regadío, La Montañita, Santa Cruz, Somoto, San Lucas, Cusmapa, Palacagüina, Yalagüina, Telpaneca, Totogalpa, and Ocotal. In particular, I would like to recognize the family of Otilia Casco Cruz and Anastasio Rivas Cruz, who provided hours of conversation, meals, and a place to sleep in El Regadío when I was first beginning this project. Waking up in the early hours of the morning to the crisp mountain air, a cool misty drizzle, and the smell of freshly made warm tortillas and sweet coffee is a moment that encapsulates my experiences doing fieldwork.

This project would have been impossible without the guidance of the various academic mentors I have had over the years. My undergraduate advisor at Tufts University, the brilliant Peter Winn, first sparked my love of Latin American history and a deep appreciation for the experiences and role of the region's everyday people. At the University of California, Los Angeles, I could not have asked for a better dissertation advisor than Robin Derby, an academic innovator with a huge heart and a boundless intellect. She provided encouragement, constructive criticism, and steadfast support during challenging moments. Not only did she carefully guide me through the research and writing process, but she also taught me to expand my horizons and take on new roles inside and outside of the classroom.

I carried out my research in Nicaragua thanks to the generous support of the Fulbright-Hays Fellowship and to the Graduate Summer Research Mentorship grant provided by UCLA. While in Nicaragua, I was based at the Institute of Nicaraguan and Central American History (Instituto de Historia de Nicaragua y Centroamérica, IHNCA) at the Central American University (Universidad Centroamericana, UCA) in Managua. Headed by Margarita Vannini, the IHNCA houses a treasure trove of historical documentation and a staff of caring professionals. I remain grateful for the daily assistance I received from María Auxiliadora Estrada, Lissette Ruiz, Annabelle Jerez, and María Ligia Garay. During my early days in Managua, the younger cohort at UCA—Victor Daniel Rodríguez, Allinson Somarriba, Karelia Mendoza, and Carolina Mercenaro—made me feel at home, whether by sharing a lunch in the archive or attending the Agüizotes festival in Masaya.

At the General Archive of the Nation (Archivo General de la Nación, AGN) located in the former National Palace, I am appreciative to the staff of Luis Latino, Ivania Paladino, Aracelly Ramos, Evelia Rivas, Teresa Castro, Mauricio Flores, and Allan Vargas. At the Nicaraguan Army's Center of Military History (Centro de Historia Militar), the knowledgeable archivist Soraya Sánchez was an invaluable resource and consummate host while I conducted research on the base.

My first day in Estelí I gained the help and friendship of César Álvarez and Catriona Knappman, who—sight unseen—helped me situate myself, find housing, attend a housewarming fiesta, and begin research the very next day. In Managua, I am grateful to the relationships I formed through the NGO Witness for Peace (WFP) with Rachel Anderson, Kevin Glidden, Galen Cohee Baynes, Brenda Molina, and Gustavo Flores Molina. The WFP house was not only a space of recreation but also of important conversations. My Bello Horizonte housemates, Luis and Annie Barberena, and also Jorge and Robeyra Raudez (whose wedding I attended in Boaco), taught me much about Nicaraguan life and culture. Patricia Lorente, whose family lineage runs deep in Santa Cruz, Estelí, provided a link between the north and Managua. While in Cusmapa, Las Sabanas, and Estelí, my participation with the Fundación Fabretto brought me into contact with committed and supportive people, such as Octavio González, Jordi de Miras, Nuria Roig Vicens, Claudia Nadal, Peter Schaller, Anajhensi Gutiérrez, Mariela Robles, Zenia Ramírez, Geneli Quiroz, Francys Vindell, and Wilmer Lagos Reyes.

At UCLA, Geoffrey Robinson and Kevin Terraciano played integral roles in the development of my project, while seminars with Bill Summerhill, Herman Ooms, Michael Salman, Lynn Hunt, César Ayala, Bonnie Taub, Ana Maria Goldani, and Edward Telles proved formative experiences. In Los Angeles, I benefited greatly from the intellectual support and cordiality of fellow graduate students, such as Xochitl Flores-Marcial, Melanie Arias, Pablo Sierra, Molly Ball, Ben Cowan, Brad Benton, Liz Jones, Mir Yarfitz, Dana Velasco Murillo, Diana Schwartz, Aaron Olivas, and Miriam Melton-Villanueva. Writing my dissertation, I also had the opportunity to spend time with Gil Joseph's excellent cohort of graduate students at Yale University, including Jennifer Lambe, Erika Helgen, and Marian Schlotterbeck.

I look back fondly on those days thanks to the friendships I made through UCLA, such as with Jean El Khoury, Pavel Torea-Villegas, Fredy Arias, the Contreras family, Eowyn Williamson, Noah Ebner, Lorna Apper, and Babken DerGregorian. My wife's family, Arnoldo and Lilian, Nereida, Arli, and Nestor, provided a home away from home on too many occasions to recall.

During my years at the Department of History and Archaeology at the University of the West Indies (UWI), Mona, in Kingston, Jamaica, I enjoyed the collegial support and academic engagement of colleagues Matthew Smith, Kathleen Monteith, Veront Satchell, Swithin

Wilmot, James Robertson, Julian Cresser, Jenny Jemmott, Aleric Josephs, Enrique Okenve, and Zachary Beier. Through UWI, I had the chance to meet Jeb Sprague and Lloyd D'Aguilar, with whom I have shared many hours debating about human rights and political activism in Central America and the Caribbean. At Trevor Day School, I have benefited from the camaraderie of David Thomas, Nina Rosenblatt, Bert McCutcheon, Dan Feigin, and Scott Reisinger, who have helped me in my development as an educator.

In developing this project, scholars who have worked on Nicaraguan history were an amazing resource and willing to lend a hand or provide feedback whenever I reached out. In particular, I want to highlight the assistance of Knut Walter, Michael Schroeder, Victoria González-Rivera, Jeffrey Gould, Richard Grossman, Frances Kinloch Tijerino, Ligia Peña Torres, Alejandro Bendaña, Jaime Wheelock, Dora María Téllez, Justin Wolfe, Hilary Francis, Claudia Rueda, and Yuridia Mendoza.

At University of Notre Dame Press, I would like to thank Editor in Chief Eli Bortz for lending his support for this project and shepherding it through the publication process. I am also grateful to Matthew Dowd, Susan Berger, Wendy McMillen, and Kathryn Pitts for their assistance. Special thanks go to Scott Barker for his thoughtful copyediting of the manuscript, which greatly improved the text. The two anonymous readers provided useful feedback, which helped make this book into a much stronger work.

My most important acknowledgment goes to Ingrid Sierakowski, my partner in all endeavors, a brilliant scholar and thinker, and simply one of the kindest people that I have ever met. She has pushed me to go further, read countless drafts, and offered me innumerable ideas, many of which are reflected in this book. Our ongoing conversation and journey that began thirteen years ago have been the great joy of my life. Thank you for absolutely everything.

Credit to everyone who contributed their *granito de arena* to this book, but—as the saying goes—the errors are mine alone.

Robert Sierakowski
New York City, February 1, 2019

# ABBREVIATIONS

| | |
|---|---|
| AA | Alcohólicos Anónimos/Alcoholics Anonymous |
| AGN | Archivo General de la Nación/General Archive of the Nation |
| AMNLAE | Asociación de Mujeres Nicaragüenses Luisa Amanda Espinoza/Luisa Amanda Espinoza Association of Nicaraguan Women |
| AMPRONAC | Asociación de Mujeres ante la Problemática Nacional/Association of Women Facing the Nation's Problems |
| AMROCS | Asociación de Militares Retirados, Obreros y Campesinos Somocistas/ Association of Somocista Workers, Peasants, and Retired Soldiers |
| CDC | Comités de Defensa Civil/Civil Defense Committees |
| CDS | Comités de Defensa Sandinista/Sandinista Defense Committees |
| CEB | Comunidades Eclesiales de Base/Christian Base Communities |
| CELAM | Conferencia Episcopal Latinoamericana/Latin American Episcopal Conference |
| CGT-I | Confederación General de Trabajo-Independiente/ General Labor Confederation-Independent |
| CHM | Centro de Historia Militar/Center of Military History |
| CIA | Central Intelligence Agency |
| CNA | Cruzada Nacional de Alfabetización/National Literacy Crusade |

| | |
|---|---|
| CONDECA | Consejo de Defensa Centroamericana/Central American Defense Council |
| CPDH | Comisión Permanente de Derechos Humanos/ Permanent Human Rights Commission |
| EDSN | Ejército Defensor de la Soberanía Nacional de Nicaragua/Army in Defense of the National Sovereignty of Nicaragua |
| EEBI | Escuela de Entrenamiento Básico de Infantería/ Basic Infantry Training School |
| EPS | Ejército Popular Sandinista/Sandinista People's Army |
| ERN | Escuelas Radiofónicas de Nicaragua/Radio Schools of Nicaragua |
| FAO | Frente Amplio Opositor/Broad Opposition Front |
| FER | Frente Estudiantil Revolucionario/Revolutionary Student Front |
| FES | Federación de Estudiantes de Secundaria/High School Student Federation |
| FLN | Frente de Liberación Nacional/National Liberation Front |
| FSLN | Frente Sandinista de Liberación Nacional/Sandinista National Liberation Front |
| FTE | Federación de Trabajadores de Estelí/Federation of Workers of Estelí |
| GN | Guardia Nacional/National Guard |
| GPP | Guerra Popular Prolongada/Prolonged Popular War |
| IHNCA | Instituto de Historia de Nicaragua y Centroamérica/Institute of Nicaraguan and Central American History |
| IMF | International Monetary Fund |
| INFONAC | Instituto de Fomento Nacional/National Development Institute |
| JPN | Juventud Patriótica Nicaragüense/Nicaraguan Patriotic Youth |
| JSN | Juventud Socialista Nicaragüense/Nicaraguan Socialist Youth |
| *LP* | *La Prensa* |

| | |
|---|---|
| MDN | Movimiento Democrático Nicaragüense/Nicaraguan Democratic Movement |
| MES | Movimiento de Estudiantes de Secundaria/Movement of High School Students |
| MNN | Movimiento Nueva Nicaragua/New Nicaragua Movement |
| MPU | Movimiento Pueblo Unido/United People's Movement |
| MR | Movilización Republicana/Republican Mobilization |
| OAS | Organization of American States |
| OLAS | Organización Latinoamericana de Solidaridad/ Organization of Latin American Solidarity |
| OSN | Oficina de Seguridad Nacional/Office of National Security |
| PGR | Procuraduría General de la República/Attorney General's Office |
| PLI | Partido Liberal Independiente/Independent Liberal Party |
| PLN | Partido Liberal Nacionalista/Nationalist Liberal Party |
| PS | Policía Sandinista/Sandinista Police |
| PSC | Partido Social Cristiano/Social Christian Party |
| PSN | Partido Socialista Nicaragüense/Nicaraguan Socialist Party |
| SAC | Servicio Anticomunista/Anticommunist Service |
| TP | Tendencia Proletaria/Proletarian Tendency |
| UCA | Universidad Centroamericana/Central American University |
| UDEL | Unión Democrática de Liberación/Democratic Liberation Union |
| UNAN | Universidad Nacional Autónoma de Nicaragua/ National Autonomous University of Nicaragua |
| UNO | Unión Nacional Opositora/National Opposition Union |

# INTRODUCTION

My government guarantees order, peace, and social stability, despite the fact that outside forces promote disorder by attacking the tranquility and well-being of the Nicaraguan people.
— Gen. Anastasio Somoza Debayle, July 1979

One morning in early March 1979, an excited report from Comandante Francisco Rivera crackled over the guerrillas' clandestine transmitter, Radio Sandino. Rivera, the top rebel commander in Nicaragua's rural north, detailed numerous skirmishes against the armed forces of the dictatorship of Gen. Anastasio Somoza, and also a recent raid his young troops had carried out in the city of Estelí. "Various brothels owned by Somocista elements in league with military officers of the National Guard were burned down," he explained. He emphasized that the destruction of this property was "yet another sign of our willingness to eradicate prostitution from our country once and for all."[1] At age twenty-five, Rivera was already an experienced leader in the Sandinista National Liberation Front (Frente Sandinista de Liberación Nacional, FSLN), a leftist armed group vying to overthrow the Somozas, whose family had ruled the country for more than four decades. The regime's loyal military and police force, the National Guard (Guardia Nacional, GN), stood accused of committing numerous atrocities

1

against the civilian population in their efforts to defeat the insurgency. As the repression expanded, membership in the Sandinistas ballooned, and guerrilla encampments overflowed with scrappily armed youths clad in olive green fatigues eager to fight back. After nearly a decade and a half of clandestine struggle against the Somozas, the FSLN finally began to threaten the regime's survival.

Rather than marginal-to-guerrilla efforts, the destruction of these government-backed businesses fulfilled a decade-long pledge to their Catholic civilian base of support, which saw such locales as destructive to family stability. Elsewhere in the rural north over the coming weeks, the Sandinistas declared "liberated zones" free from regime control where they similarly "set about burning down centers of vice," such as cantinas, brothels, and gambling joints.[2] The guerrillas' most recent manifesto proudly stated that not only would their victory bring an end to the dictatorship and expand social rights for the poor, but also that "organized crime will disappear forever: sex trafficking, prostitution, dice tables, 'illegal' gaming, the red-light districts, and all those businesses controlled by the military and the accomplices of Somocismo . . . will be swept away by the Frente Sandinista."[3] Despite legal proscription, a vast network of vice and social corruption had long been fostered by the government and the National Guard through a system of kickbacks and impunity. The rebel sabotage reported by Francisco Rivera sought to reduce to ashes not only their physical structures but also the immoral and unjust system that they believed these establishments embodied.

As the FSLN evolved over the previous decade and a half, the regional population had pressed their concerns about morality and family breakdown to the heart of the revolutionary agenda. Conservative-sounding calls to end social and political corruption and impose "law and order" drew the population of the rural north to the Sandinista movement, which proved undogmatic and willing to take up issues often spurned by the Left. Opposition activists argued that the Somoza dictatorship encouraged family breakdown and dysfunctional male sociability through its permissive attitude toward criminality. Such efforts, aided by Catholic liberation theology, crystalized in a mass protest movement of working-class and peasant families that called for an end to social injustice. However, it was the GN's chaotic repression and atrocities that exposed the utter lawlessness and moral depravity of the regime and drove thousands of families into the arms of the Sandinistas. Through the process of collective defense, the revolutionaries constructed their own practical visions of insurgent morality, incorporating solidarity, egalitarianism, and sacrifice. In the eyes of the population, Somoza's claim in the epigraph above was exactly inverted: from their stance, *his regime* threatened "the tranquility and well-being of the Nicaraguan people," while an insurgent victory promised "order, peace, and social stability."

After months of open civil war, the Sandinistas captured Managua on July 19, 1979, sending the remnants of the GN scrambling and initiating a decade of change that would catapult this small country to the frontlines of the global Cold War. The Sandinistas became the only guerrilla organization in all of Latin America to successfully follow in the footsteps of the Cuban Revolution, which had inspired a generation across the hemisphere. *Sandinistas: A Moral History* offers a reinterpretation of the origins of the Nicaraguan revolution from the perspective of popular mobilization and the personal experiences of the countless women and men who helped construct its ideals. Drawing on a wealth of previously untapped archival and oral sources, I show that the armed FSLN guerrillas formed only the tip of the iceberg of a mass movement for social and cultural change that developed in direct reaction to the regime's seedier aspects. Centering the contributions of these local actors—from artisan trade unionists and Catholic peasants to high school students and middle-class housewives—suggests the limited utility of the 1980s debate over whether the Nicaraguan revolution was primarily nationalist or communist in nature. Although it is confounding to the classic stereotype of a left-wing insurgency, the destruction of "centers of vice" and popular demands for law and order indicate how revolutionary aims went beyond demands for mere political or even social change, aiming instead for a deeper moral renewal. Armed insurgency emerged out of a broader—yet less visible—history of consciousness-raising and popular protest through which working-class and rural Nicaraguans stretched the definition of *Sandinismo* to new limits by incorporating their own aspirations for personal and social transformation. The Sandinistas' singular success, I argue, was due to their distinctive radical politics that married a traditional, moralizing conservative discourse of family breakdown and vice with a revolutionary critique of social inequality, political corruption, and state violence.

## A View from the Revolutionary Heartland

To uncover the historical trajectory of the Sandinista Revolution, this book focuses on the Segovias, considered the country's most quintessentially "revolutionary" zone and the veritable heartland of the Sandinista movement. According to Michael Schroeder, the Segovias are "a rugged, mountainous frontier region with a bewilderingly complex physical and human geography," with a "uniquely violent" place in Nicaraguan history. This borderland region near Honduras had witnessed cycles of armed gangs and political violence dating back to the civil wars of the nineteenth and early twentieth centuries between Conservatives and Liberals.[4] Drawing on these traditions, a rebel army led by Augusto César Sandino rose up in the Segovias against the U.S. military occupation of Nicaragua during the 1920s and 30s. The peasant guerrillas of his Army in Defense of the National Sovereignty of Nicaragua (Ejército Defensor de la Soberanía Nacional de Nicaragua, EDSN) carried out a nearly seven-year-long "David and Goliath" war against one of the most powerful countries in the world and their local clients. The U.S. marines responded with aerial bombings and other atrocities throughout the mountainous north, but they were never able to defeat the nationalist rebels.

Decades later, during the 1960s and 70s, the Segovias once again served as a primary locus of action for the young revolutionaries who revived Sandino's name and took up the red-and-black flag of his rebel army. The region's major urban center, Estelí, gained international fame for being "three times heroic" (*tres veces heroica*), with insurgents receiving widespread civilian support during three urban insurrections against the dictatorship in 1978 and 1979. In explaining the reasons for such heightened participation in the upheaval, FSLN leader Humberto Ortega claimed, "Ever since the time of Sandino, Estelí was the scene of battles. . . . As such, there was a tradition of struggle."[5] Political scientist Timothy Wickham-Crowley similarly postulated a "preexisting rebellious culture" in northern Nicaragua that permitted the Sandinistas to thrive in the very areas where Sandino's EDSN had once been active.[6] Many academic observers have thought likewise, erroneously casting the FSLN guerrillas of the 1960s as emerging almost seamlessly from Sandino's nationalist struggle of the 1920s and 30s. As a hotbed of rebellion that bridged these two eras, the Segovias became a lynchpin in official Sandinista discourse and the revolutionaries' appeals to historical legitimacy.

This account, I show, is largely FSLN political mythology that homogenizes two sharply divergent historical moments. Rather than the isolated borderland of the years of U.S. occupation, the Segovias region underwent a profound economic transformation during the decades of Somoza rule, with flourishing exports of agricultural goods, such as coffee, beef, and tobacco. The construction the Pan-American Highway and rapid urbanization transformed the landscape, while commercial agriculture increasingly replaced subsistence farming. However, despite superficial signs of modernization, this growth fostered galloping social inequality between an increasingly opulent elite and the impoverished peasants and townspeople, who had limited access to education, health care, or decent wages. Much of the new wealth produced found its way directly into the pockets of the Somoza family and their large landowner allies at the regional level. Even with growing social tensions, the emergence of an armed insurgency with significant civilian backing was never preordained. Contrary to the romantic Sandinista narrative, the Segovias, in fact, developed a solid reputation as a dependable base of support for the Somoza regime. This was true of the city of Estelí and many towns and villages that had once supported Sandino.[7] In fact, many of the region's peasants (*campesinos*)— desperately poor and often indigenous—were the prime recruitment pool for the National Guard for almost half a century.

In light of its centrality to both sides of the conflict, the Segovias provides the perfect locale for a close historical investigation of the roots of the revolution and the political violence of the 1960s and 70s. The Segovias region consists of the present-day departments (provinces) of Estelí, Madriz, Nueva Segovia, Matagalpa, and Jinotega. However, in this book I mostly focus on the first two departments, given the fascinating contrast that they provide. Though contiguous, neighboring provinces, Estelí and Madriz experienced strikingly divergent trajectories over the decades of Somoza rule. Estelí developed into a

guerrilla stronghold deeply identified with the FSLN, but poverty-stricken Madriz and its capital, Somoto, remained a bastion of Somocismo and a prime recruiting ground for the GN until the
dictatorship's final days. *"Madriz liberal, el pueblo más leal"* — "Liberal
Madriz, the most loyal people," went a popular saying.

Where standard explanations fail to account for these contradictory developments, I demonstrate that the previous history of guerrilla
warfare did not spontaneously draw Nicaraguans to the red-and-black
banner of the FSLN. Rather than the "inevitable" resurrection of Augusto César Sandino's anti-imperialism, the key to the rebels' subsequent success was the manner in which they framed their struggle as
an effort to extirpate vice, violence, corruption, and glaring inequality
from everyday life. The Sandinistas, driven by grassroots protest move-

*Map 1.* Map of the Republic of Nicaragua, with political divisions during the
Somoza period. Departments of Estelí and Madriz shaded.

*Map 2.* Map of the departments of Estelí and Madriz during the Somoza period.

ments, projected themselves as answering family breakdown and social disorder with moral regeneration. They offered a durable critique of the Somozas' cascading web of impunity, which had enmeshed the regime within the fabric of Nicaragua's patriarchal society from wealthy landowning elite families down to the National Guard and other grassroots agents. In response to this defiance, the government met suspected FSLN militants and those civilians accused of supporting the rebels with ever-increasing violence. Repression, however, only enhanced the moral critique of the Somoza regime, further invigorating calls for wholesale social renewal. Rather than a destabilizing force, the insurgency appeared to offer the restoration of order and justice in the face of chaotic state terror. The FSLN achieved their aim in 1979, precisely by bringing an end to the GN attacks unleashed against the civilian population and by promising an end to the everyday, interpersonal violence long present in Nicaraguan society.

## A State of Disorder: The Somoza Regime through a New Lens

Conventional accounts cast the Somoza government as a brutal regime that "maintained law and order through control of the National Guard, a well-trained force thanks to the occupation of the United States Marines earlier in the twentieth century."[8] However, I contend, rather than the imposition of "law and order," the longevity of the Somoza regime was due precisely to its willingness to countenance criminal disorder. In this way, the Nicaraguan government differed greatly from the brutally efficient 1970s military dictatorships of South America. Some scholars have insisted that unlike these institutional and ideologically oriented military dictatorships, the Somozas' "sultanistic" and personalistic regime remained isolated from society and, thus, structurally prone to popular upheaval.[9] Historians Jeffrey Gould, Victoria González-Rivera, and Knut Walter have definitively refuted the claim that the Somozas ruled solely through political repression. In their work, they demonstrate how the Somozas at strategic moments mobilized working-class support via clientelism and populist appeals to campesinos, organized labor, and women, while negotiating power-sharing pacts with wealthy political adversaries in the private sector.[10] Despite these important revisionist accounts, however, we still lack a clear understanding of the local dynamics that allowed the dictatorship to perpetuate itself in power for so many decades.

Like the legendary symbol of Sandino, the Somoza dictatorship (1936–79) itself also dated back to the period of U.S. military occupation of the 1920s and 30s. Following the 1927 invasion of the country—the third intervention since 1909—the U.S. government organized and armed a new military and police force, the National Guard of Nicaragua. They later handpicked a relatively obscure military officer, Gen. Anastasio Somoza García, to serve as the first Nicaraguan commander of this constabulary force. With the U.S. withdrawal in 1933, Sandino negotiated a provisional peace treaty with the Nicaraguan government. In an act of betrayal, Somoza had the unarmed rebel leader treacherously assassinated the following year. With his major challenger for national power eliminated, he soon carried out a coup against the elected president and began ruling as the country's strongman in 1936. After

two decades of personal dictatorial rule, Somoza himself was assassinated in 1956 by a young poet in the city of León. Following his murder, Somoza García was succeeded in power by two of his sons, Luis
and Anastasio Somoza Debayle.

Throughout the long decades of Somocista family rule, government policies overwhelmingly benefited large landowners with access
to state resources, many of whom came to serve as *caciques* (political
chieftains) at the regional level. These landowning families benefited at
the expense of the peasant families whose land they dispossessed and
whose wages were kept down with the aid of state repression. In parallel, the Somozas constructed a loyal popular base among the poor by
offering social mobility and impunity to its military and its civilian
agents to engage in widespread small-scale illegal activities. In this way,
the GN—the very institution responsible for policing—fostered an entire underground "amoral economy" based on male sociability, vice,
and criminality, including prostitution, gambling, and alcohol sales.
These illegal practices helped link middling local agents, many of
whom owned bars (those I call *cantina caciques*), to the Somoza regime
and the GN. Though consumers were largely male, a significant number of women loyal to the regime also participated in the trade at the
community level. When the time came for one of the regime's sham
elections, this web of local operatives publicly dished out cash, food,
and copious hard liquor to campesino and working-class Nicaraguans,
who duly cast their vote for Somoza.

The regime could also rely on the security forces to repress any political threat. Historians have often analyzed the National Guard in its
structural role as a ballast for the Somoza family and a proxy for U.S.
interests in Central America.[11] My work moves beyond previous ap-
proaches by closely examining for the first time the role played by
average soldiers, many of them recruited from among the impoverished
indigenous peasantry of the Segovias. Ironically, in search of social
mobility, the country's poorest peasants came to fight, kill, and die in
defense of the Somozas and other elite families that dominated the government. By considering the *machista* internal culture of the National
Guard, which gave free reign to abusive masculine behavior, we gain
great insight into both the nature of the regime and the widespread
backlash it provoked.[12]

Far from "order, peace, and social stability" (as Somoza put it), I show, the GN fostered only a veneer of stability, while chaotic disorder increasingly defined much of everyday life. During the years of Somoza rule—and well before the rise of guerrilla warfare—the nation was one of the most violent in the world. During the late 1950s and early 1960s, for example, the country's homicide rate was often only surpassed by Colombia and Mexico. Between 1964 and 1967 (at which point the Somoza regime stopped providing data to the United Nations), Nicaragua took the lead with the world's highest homicide rate.[13] This disastrous rise in crime and murder was recognized even by the dictatorship's primary international sponsor. A U.S. embassy employee wrote in 1967 that the GN was "no good at all as policemen. Law and order is non-existent in Nicaragua . . . it is officially recommended that one carry a gun if one go[es] out of the city of Managua."[14] U.S. State Department experts three years later continued to sound the alarm regarding rising levels of violence: "Murder and aggravated assault appear to be the major criminal threat in all parts of the country. . . . There has been an increase in geometric proportions of common crime of an increasingly brutal character. . . . A very large proportion of the population regularly go armed."[15]

Much of the violence of the Somoza years was not political in essence but instead social and interpersonal. Many homicides were the product of conflicts between men of all ages armed with machetes and pistols in rural areas, particularly in quarrels over family feuds, women, plots of land, and cattle. Widespread access to *aguardiente* or *guaro* (cane alcohol) at local cantinas, political rallies, polling stations, and religious festivals only added further fuel to the fire. The government kept no official statistics, but domestic violence, sexual abuse, and rape were also widespread and correlated with popular perceptions of family breakdown. Alcohol and quotidian violence had long been salient features of the country's social landscape, but under Somoza they came to play a central role in the regime's operations on the level of cities, towns, and villages. Partly as a result of the official encouragement of both vice and male sociability, Nicaragua in the late 1960s had the highest rates of hard-liquor consumption (three times as much as El Salvador or Guatemala) and alcoholism in all of Central America.[16] The atmosphere fostered during these years would also provide the context for the grassroots movements for social and moral regeneration that later coalesced around the FSLN.

## Sandinismo: Breaking with Old Dichotomies

This new conceptualization of the Somoza dictatorship helps us to re-think traditional understandings of the revolutionary movement that overthrew the regime in 1979. Many early accounts of the rise of the Sandinistas were colored by the polarized Cold War discourse fostered by the administration of Ronald Reagan (1981–89). Opponents of the Sandinistas in the U.S. government often presented the events in Nicaragua as the latest expansion of Soviet communism into Latin America ("America's backyard"), shoehorning complex national dynamics into a simplistic geopolitical framework. Official State Department and CIA statements cast the Nicaraguan revolutionaries as mere Cuban-backed Marxist-Leninist proxies, who had cynically seized their country in the name of international communism. This claim served as the justification for the unrelenting U.S. campaign of sabotage, economic strangulation, and a counterrevolutionary proxy war, at the cost of tens of thousands of Nicaraguan lives. The actual roots of the revolutionary upheaval against the Somoza dictatorship were, however, obscured by this conspiratorial, superficial explanation.

The revolution's defenders, on the other hand, embraced the FSLN's own "origin story," downplaying the organization's Marxist roots and casting the movement as the latest iteration of a long-standing nationalist struggle against U.S. domination. *Sandinistas* contests the now almost commonsense notion that the FSLN succeeded merely by resuscitating Sandino's struggle and drawing on Nicaraguans' deep-seated anti-imperialist sentiments.[17] Though a critique of U.S. imperialism was certainly of importance to FSLN leaders, anti-Yankee sentiment was almost never the spark that led to rank-and-file participation.[18] Instead, the widespread popular nationalism we affiliate with the revolution was largely a *consequence* of the Sandinistas' decade in power (1979–90) and not the initial *cause* of the insurgent fervor. Throughout the 1980s, the country found itself under violent siege by the "Contras," armed and trained by the United States, which laid bare the nature of U.S. intervention in Nicaragua. Taking the Sandinista account at face value, sympathetic foreign observers reimagined the insurrection in light of these later developments. Even in the Segovias with their storied history, however, issues of nationalism and anti-imperialism were almost never the impetus for joining the revolutionary movement.

Neither of these two competing paradigms—communism from abroad or anti-imperialism at home—captures the appeal of the anti-Somoza insurgency to its supporters. The FSLN itself was founded in the early 1960s as a political-military organization by a small group of leftist university students inspired by the 1959 Cuban Revolution and frustrated by the social and political ills of their country. Scholars have shown how official FSLN ideology was primarily the creation of the group's most significant founder, Carlos Fonseca, who selectively read (and reinvented) the symbolic figure of Sandino in light of the Cuban experience and his own Marxist politics.[19] In her masterful biography of Fonseca, Matilde Zimmermann documents how the group's philosophy arose out of nearly two decades of "zigzags, debates, and rejection of failed strategies."[20] Her account historicizes this complex evolution, but my work looks beyond the FSLN leadership to help us understand how their ideas were ignored, embraced, and transformed at the level of everyday politics.

I break definitively with earlier accounts by reconstructing the history of the revolution from the perspective of families, neighborhoods, villages, and towns, rather than focusing solely at the level of international geopolitics or top guerrilla commanders. Behind the armed militants, and integral to their success, was a broad and diverse coalition of civilian supporters who collectively sought to bring an end to the dictatorship. By hiding guerrilla fighters in their homes, building barricades, or selflessly providing food, water, and shelter, each member of this vast, clandestine network of noncombatants contributed "their grain of sand" toward the Sandinista victory, risking their lives in the process. Indeed, the struggle was waged not only in the mountains or behind the barricades, but also in the homes and churches of Estelí and other towns and villages. The hopes and aspirations of these women and men, we will see, went well beyond the one-dimensional framing offered by competing Cold War paradigms on the right and the left.

Popular participation in the revolutionary movement remains understudied by historians. The principal account is Jeffrey Gould's now-classic history of campesino land rights mobilizations in western Nicaragua, *To Lead as Equals: Rural Protest and Political Consciousness in Chinandega, Nicaragua, 1912–1979*. Gould documents the evolution of peasants' and rural workers' political consciousness as they dealt with the consequences of expanding cotton plantations in the western departments of Chinandega and León. He argues that these rural communities began their struggle within the institutions of the Somoza government, before increasing their autonomy, developing class consciousness, and coming to cooperate with the revolutionaries by the late 1970s. In laying out this lengthy process, Gould sought to challenge previous accounts, which assumed "that somehow support for the FSLN emerged naturally out of the workers' and peasants' innate hostility toward the regime," an approach that simplified "the regionally varied, complex process through which the popular classes came to support the FSLN."[21] Gould emphasized the role of rural Nicaraguans in efforts against the dictatorship, arguing that in "the key agro-export departments of Chinandega, León, and Matagalpa, a 20-year-old agrarian movement created the conditions for a campesino-FSLN alliance, thus providing a large political and military base for the revolutionaries."[22] Though his work delivered a much-needed corrective, the lack of comparative research into other regions of Nicaragua has allowed these unique experiences to be extrapolated onto the nation as a whole by many observers. In fact, most of the country did not experience mass peasant movements for land reform similar to those described by Gould in his work on the cotton-producing zone and his later work on indigenous communities in Matagalpa's coffee-growing regions.[23]

In addition to Gould's writing on peasant land mobilization, the works of Lynn Horton and Timothy Brown briefly consider peasant participation in the Sandinista insurrection as a backstory to the CIA-backed Contra war of the 1980s.[24] Both studies suggest rather limited support for the FSLN among the peasants of the isolated eastern Segovias region (Sandino's onetime center of operations) during the war against Somoza and the GN. Horton argues that the Sandinista insurgency did not organize around class lines in the mountainous municipality of Quilalí. They instead formed links with wealthy landowners, who in turn mobilized poorer campesinos through traditional patronage networks. Following the revolution's triumph, this cross-class highlands alliance quickly turned against the FSLN and joined the Contras. Brown emphasizes a speculative longue durée argument of regional ethnic difference and resistance, but Horton closely tracks the continuing patron–client relations between rich and poor. Though similarly focused on Nicaragua's rural north, they describe events in the thinly populated agricultural frontier that bear little resemblance to the developments that took place in Estelí and Madriz.

## FAMILY, GENDER, AND THE SUBVERSION OF VICE

In its response to Nicaragua's patriarchal social milieu, I contend, the anti-Somoza movement garnered support through its calls for an end to quotidian violence and vice and the restoration of law, order, and family harmony. In the Segovias and elsewhere in Nicaragua, most of the population did not conceive of their society as divided into utility-maximizing individuals or even competing social classes, but rather as organized around families and extended kinship networks. As Carlos Vilas notes, both the Somoza family dynasty and their elite opponents among the traditional landowning classes epitomized the dominance of patriarchal family groups that maintained prominence even after the revolution.[25] In her overview of studies centered on the family in Latin America, Nara Milanich writes that "family history has morphed into a relatively self-contained subfield disengaged from scholarship beyond its immediate thematic purview. The central challenge facing the field is to link the family to broader narratives of historical change."[26] The Sandinista struggle demonstrates the contributions of the gendered insights of family history to events that went well beyond the bounds of "private life." Again and again, the question of family and kinship proved vital to political developments: from the elite families' systems of vice, patronage, and corruption, to activists' critique of "family breakdown" among the poor caused by male consumption of vice, to the guerrillas' search for alternative masculinities outside of the machista sociability embraced by the dictatorship.[27] Although the census data is unclear, there appears to have been a rise in the rate of impoverished, female-headed households over the years of Somoza rule, particularly with urbanization.[28] The idea of a stable, male-headed "traditional family" at risk of "breaking down" and "threatening stability" served as a powerful perception in Nicaragua, as it did elsewhere in Latin America. However, as Elizabeth Dore shows, female-headed households had long formed part of the family landscape, while the "ideal" two-parent nuclear family, married in the eyes of both the Church and the state, was only universal among the wealthiest, land-owning families.[29]

Given this emphasis on vice, honor, virtue, and familial harmony, understandings of gender played contradictory roles in the movement, both disrupting and reinforcing preexisting norms. Compared to earlier social revolutions, the Sandinista Revolution was notable for the high level of female participation in both armed and unarmed roles. The academic literature on female combatants has consistently provided a rank-and-file view of everyday life not found in the wider historical literature. Studies have ranged from Margaret Randall's early testimonial work on female Sandinistas to Karen Kampwirth's comparative study of *guerrilleras* throughout Latin America, which foregrounds women's motivations for joining guerrilla movements and their significant contributions to these efforts.[30] Lorraine Bayard de Volo examines the important contribution, in addition to combat roles, of the "Mothers of the Heroes and Martyrs," who lost their children in the struggle and mobilized around a gendered image of maternal suffering to "win hearts and minds" for the new Sandinista government of the 1980s.[31] Many feminist scholars have critically engaged with the legacy of the FSLN discourse regarding traditional gender roles, emphasizing sharp limitations to feminist gains and the failure of the FSLN to transcend patriarchy and sexism.[32] As Rosario Montoya notes in her study of gender relations in rural Nicaragua, the ambiguities of Sandinista discourse later allowed men "to legitimize their opposition to women's participation" and helped to perpetuate privileged masculinity.[33] Building on the insights of these gendered accounts, I move beyond a focus on men or women to emphasize family identities, masculinity and femininity, and how the household became—in many cases—the fundamental cell of revolutionary activity.

These notions of family and gender helped to shape the movement's discourse and focus on moral regeneration. In other Latin American contexts, moralistic calls for the eradication or regulation of vice— defined as prostitution, drinking, and gambling—have often served as a tool of social control and nation-building, as elites and middle-class reformers imposed their norms upon stigmatized working-class women and men.[34] Similarly, campaigns to excise vice were central to revolutions in France, Russia, China, Mexico, and Cuba, and were cast as part of a transformation of the social order under the new governments.[35] An effort for moral regeneration was integral to all of these major revolutions, often noted solely for their political and social transformations. As Sean Quinlan noted for the French Revolution, "moral regeneration . . . was one of the great aspirations. . . . Revolutionaries fashioned new cultural practices to emphasize collective rebirth and the individual citizen's own break with a degenerate past."[36]

The Nicaraguan movement proves quite distinct from all of these cases. Unlike the top-down projects, whether launched by conservative, reformist, or revolutionary governments, the demand for moral regeneration emerged directly from working-class and marginalized Nicaraguans in the process of a revolutionary struggle to improve their families' lives. Revolutionaries framed all of their efforts within the realm of the possible: a moral world imagined in reaction to quotidian violence, vice, and state repression. Rather than utopianism, they foregrounded practical needs: higher wages, access to social services, public infrastructure (electricity, running water, plumbing), and an end to high rates of alcoholism, absentee fatherhood, and crime. Through protest, female and male activists denounced government corruption at the local level and demanded that schools and health centers replace the innumerable cantinas, brothels, and gambling dens that marred the landscape of the Segovias and tore at the fabric of family life. Activist men sought out new models of manhood as a way to temper the machista male sociability structured around hard drinking and vice, while women increasingly took on prominent leadership roles within grassroots organizations.

Particularly catalytic to the emergence of the Sandinistas' insurgent morality in northern Nicaragua was the advent of Catholic liberation theology across Latin America during the 1970s. This new, more accessible Christian current promised a "preferential option for the poor," reimagined Jesus Christ as a persecuted revolutionary, and denounced social inequality.[37] I trace how deeply held religious beliefs that had long bolstered the status quo now helped to galvanize opposition. Linking everyday family life to national politics, priests, laypeople, and guerrillas all denounced vice as a product of the lack of education, poverty, and violence—termed "ignorance," "injustice," and "slavery"—which were to be expunged from society. Rather than chaos, the insurgents seemed to promise the imposition of "God, Order, and Justice," the vague electoral slogan of Somoza's Conservative Party opposition. Though at times paternalistic and even patriarchal in their approach, local activists and guerrillas pushed this conservative critique beyond mere moralism to the necessity of profound social change to achieve moral regeneration. The peculiar fusion of radicalism and conservative morality allowed Nicaraguans from all walks of life to identify with the revolutionary movement and participate actively in the rebellion, even if they personally did not take up arms.

## "A Single Family": Insurgent Morality amid State Terror

The revolutionary movement had long insisted that violence undergirded the entire order of vice and corruption, but the repression of the late 1970s cast the regime's moral degeneracy and its threat to family life into stark relief. The National Guard was responsible for state terror, including attacks against protesters of all ages, and the torture and killing of political prisoners. During the civil war of 1978–79, this violence culminated in summary executions, indiscriminate aerial bombardment of cities, the use of sexual violence as a weapon of war, and massacres of entire families in rural villages throughout the countryside (many documented in this book for the first time).

The transformation of the National Guard during the 1970s prepared the military to carry out harsh violence as the decade came to a close. In analyzing this shift, my work contributes to the emerging literature on political violence and what Gilbert Joseph characterizes as "the grassroots dynamics and meanings of the Latin American Cold War" and "the conflict's domestic and foreign dimensions."[38] With the advent of the guerrilla challenge in the wake of the Cuban Revolution, the dictatorship and its U.S. backers sought to modernize the antiquated and vice-ridden military and intelligence apparatus for the needs of counterinsurgency. Yet all of these efforts of training and reorganization failed to "professionalize" the army but instead burnished new forms of military masculinity and techniques of mass killing. These efforts served to neutralize what philosopher Jonathan Glover describes as "moral resources," such as sympathy, respect, and a sense of moral identity, and thus permitted average soldiers to commit atrocities.[39]

Such disproportionate state violence effectively left many with no option but to take up arms and head to the mountains, or risk almost certain death. Building on earlier Catholic networks, communities organized "as a single family" for self-defense. *Madres* (mothers) provided food, water, shelter, and information to young *muchachos* (teenage boys) who joined in the heat of the battle. As the numbers of rebels ballooned because of the threat of state violence, activists refashioned the constellation of concepts that I term "insurgent morality" through their resistance. Moving beyond protest and denunciation, insurgent morality called on participants to put their values into practice. They set about creating—in incipient form—the very sort of society of "tranquility and well-being" (to use Somoza's words) that they hoped to build after the triumph of the revolution.

This vision of insurgent morality imagined Nicaragua as a renovated and idealized family unit built via an alliance between mothers and youthful combatants. As a result of their struggle, social barriers came crashing down: between young and old, rich and poor, urban and rural, male and female, educated and unlettered. Within the ranks of the FSLN, Nicaraguans gained an everyday experience of social leveling, order, and solidarity to replace the hierarchy, chaos, and selfishness that they identified with Somocismo. Such a vision was not utopian but instead emerged directly from the practical experience of egalitarianism and a life without vice that was forged in the struggle. As the regime's violence reached the level of full-scale massacres of entire unarmed families, such experiences became the fundamental building blocks of this emerging identity for the survivors. Importantly, accounts of massacres at the hands of the Guardia are almost never narrated in the register of victimhood but are instead interpreted as virtuous sacrifice, projecting each life lost as a contribution to the final defeat of the Somoza regime on July 19, 1979.

A WORD ON SOURCES AND METHODOLOGIES

Unlike the many studies of the Sandinista Revolution written before the dust settled and while the Contra war of the 1980s was underway, *Sandinistas: A Moral History* has benefited from the passage of time and the opportunity to look at these events with new eyes, less clouded by the political passions of the era. At the same time, the events studied were still recent enough to gather richly detailed ethnographic data and oral history material. This reevaluation of the revolution was largely made possible through my access to several major archival sources not used by earlier historians.

First, I was able to draw upon a vast collection of thousands of interviews carried out shortly after the revolution with Nicaraguans from all walks of life who lived through the period of guerrilla warfare and insurrection. The collection of 7,000 cassette tapes—currently being digitized for use by future historians—is housed at the Institute of Nicaraguan and Central American History (Instituto de Historia de Nicaragua y Centroamérica, IHNCA) at the Central American University (Universidad Centroamericana, UCA) in Managua. These oral histories were produced during the National Literacy Crusade (Cruzada Nacional de Alfabetización, CNA), which saw thousands of high school and university students dispatched to live in working-class barrios and rural villages from March to August 1980 to teach Nicaraguans how to read and write. Over those five months of concerted effort, the literacy brigades dramatically reduced the high illiteracy rate bequeathed by the Somoza government. Some of the young teachers were additionally chosen to form part of the Germán Pomares Ordóñez Historical Rescue Brigade (Brigada de Rescate Histórico), a select group responsible for collecting local experiences for a project called History of the Sandinista Popular Insurrection. Virtually untapped by scholars, these recordings provide a unique primary source for the study of the grassroots dynamics of revolution.[40]

With tape recorders donated from abroad, some brief training, and a carefully designed questionnaire, the 215 amateur oral historians spread out to the four corners of the republic and began interviewing all those willing to share their stories. Carefully organized in the archive by department, municipality, city/town, neighborhood, and village, these interviews provide a fascinating and unparalleled portrait of the experience of regular men and women in the uprising. The teenagers who recorded the interviews and asked the questions from the official questionnaire are identified by their initials in the citations. For my research, I reviewed more than 300 of the interviews from across the Segovias. Despite their unique "history from below" perspective, the CNA testimonies also present some obvious difficulties for the historian. Because they were working in a state-building project of the new revolutionary government during a particularly heady moment of social change, the interviewers and their questions often steered participants toward the emerging official narrative of the events that foregrounded and celebrated FSLN leadership. The young people conducting the interviews largely stuck to the script provided and rarely asked follow-up questions. At times, some Brigade members even corrected interview subjects who gave "politically incorrect" answers to questions. Anti-Sandinista perspectives—or even ambivalence about the guerrillas' role—were completely excluded from the CNA recordings. These silences, as I shall explain, helped to inspire further research.

The second major archival source that made this project possible were the 180 boxes of case files from the thousands of trials held against former members of Somoza's National Guard following the Sandinista Revolution. This collection of court documents is housed at the General Archive of the Nation (Archivo General de la Nación, AGN) in Managua. As the first scholar permitted access to these documents, I was able to chart out the events of the 1960s and 70s from the perspective of those fighting to keep Somoza in power. These Special Tribunals (Tribunales Especiales) were organized in 1980–81 by the Office of the Attorney General (Procuraduría General de la República). Capital punishment was banned, but membership in the GN or the secret police at the time of the insurrection all but guaranteed a lengthy prison sentence. The trial transcripts provide a rich collection of interrogations, testimonies, denunciations, and documentary evidence, which together offer a rather comprehensive vision of the National Guard's internal structure and its repressive actions. Interestingly, these fascinating court documents not only expose GN terror but also provide a far more nuanced understanding of the soldiers' personal lives and motivations in their own voices.

I built upon this vast array of accounts collected in the immediate wake of the revolution with many traditional historical sources. At the AGN, I consulted the sizable archival collection of internal government documents from the Somoza period. Most fruitful were the many folios of correspondence between Somoza, the National Guard, the Ministry of the Interior (Gobernación), and local political officials throughout the Segovias. These letters and telegrams provided insight into how the dictatorship functioned at the regional level and its responses to the growing opposition of the 1960s and 70s. The Nicaraguan Army's Center of Military History (Centro de Historia Militar, CHM) granted me access to the rich and virtually unstudied documents from the clandestine guerrilla army, including its pamphlets, manuals, mimeographed communiqués, and reams of handwritten internal correspondence. Because today's Nicaraguan army is the direct institutional descendant of the guerrilla FSLN of the 1970s, its collection offers an insider's view of the struggle as it unfolded.

Finally, taking into account the lacunae found in all of these sources, I spent close to two years carrying out 200 original oral history interviews and ethnographic fieldwork in Northern Nicaragua. I interviewed individuals who experienced the events from different vantage points, such as campesino families, indigenous community elders, trade union pioneers, guerrilla organizers, former student activists, and Catholic priests. I also spoke with many mothers, widows, and surviving family members of those struck down decades earlier in state violence, and also former guerrillas permanently disabled by injuries they suffered during the insurrection and civil war. Some of those I spoke to were the very same women and men who had been interviewed thirty years earlier in 1980 during the Literacy Crusade and whose earlier accounts I had listened to on cassette in the air-conditioned archive in Managua.

To understand both sides of the conflict, I also searched out those who were not sympathetic to the guerrillas and had opposed the Sandinistas during the 1980s. I tracked down numerous members of the Somoza government and conducted dozens of oral histories with former Guardias and alleged secret police informants (orejas). For many, their interview with me marked one of the very few times they had ever spoken publicly of the period. Throughout, I have left some interviewees anonymous (or used aliases) because of the sensitive nature of the information they provided. A vast set of conflicting discourses, memories, and perspectives, these oral histories allowed me to fill in the silences in the Literacy Crusade interviews and trial transcripts from 1980 and to foster a rewarding dialogue between interview subjects and the documentary record in the archives.

Building Insurgent Morality: Structure of the Book

*Sandinistas* follows a narrative that is mostly chronological. However, there is some temporal overlap between thematic chapters, which helps facilitate a more in-depth analysis of processes spread over several decades. In chapter 1, I map out the webs of kinship, corruption, and patronage that held the regime together, and the criminal and vice-related underground economy fostered by its grassroots agents and National Guard officers. In chapters 2 and 3, I consider the opposition movements that formed in direct response to the dictatorship during the 1960s and 70s, including labor unions, high school students, and Catholic organizations. In each of these, I emphasize the contributions of these grassroots activists in redefining the meaning of the nascent Sandinismo as a critique of vice, violence, and social inequality.

I then turn to the period of revolutionary upheaval and state terror. Chapter 4 considers the institution responsible for this repression, Somoza's National Guard, from the perspective of its grassroots agents, recruited from among the poor and desperate population of the Segovias. Chapters 5 and 6 zoom in on Somoza's final two years in power, with a close consideration of the development of notions of insurgent morality amid a period of protest, insurrection, and civil war. Chapter 5 examines the widespread participation of a grassroots family alliance during the 1978 uprising and its aftermath; chapter 6 provides a close reading of numerous massacres against those accused of supporting the FSLN, analyzing how survivors folded personal experiences of political violence into community narratives and popular understandings of insurgent morality. In my epilogue, I consider the events that followed the fall of Somoza in light of this new interpretation of the Sandinista Revolution.

CHAPTER ONE

# STATE OF DISORDER

Vice, Corruption, and the Somoza Dictatorship

In February 1970, Pedro Cardoza, the municipal magistrate of the small, rural town of La Trinidad, Estelí, closed an illegal brothel as stipulated by Nicaraguan law. In a letter explaining his action, Cardoza wrote that "El Buen Gusto" ("The Good Taste") had been "open until the wee hours of the morning and was the scene of scandals and complaints: people were robbed, drunken women harassed young people on their way to school, and drunks fired their guns in the presence of Sergeant Fuentes, the comandante of this town."[1] The man expected to enforce the laws, National Guard commander Fuentes, in fact, was co-owner of the cantina with a local woman. By attempting to eliminate a public nuisance, Cardoza brought the weight of local powerbrokers down upon himself. A petition signed by thirty-nine La Trinidad residents (including a large number of women) was sent to the minister of the interior (*gobernación*), demanding the brothel resume operations. The signatories declared the bar's female owner a "true asset in the ranks of the Liberal Party" and insisted that the town's young men needed "a place for physiological recreation."[2] The GN comandante of nearby Estelí wrote to Managua saying that the illegal establishment had paid all of its taxes—and, implicitly, its bribes to the GN—and was not bothering anyone.[3]

The owner herself dashed off a missive to the minister explaining, in telling language, that she and her family were "Somocista Liberals that cooperate in everything within our reach. Right now, I have a jeep in which I am installing loudspeakers to dedicate to propaganda

23

supporting His Excellency Señor President General Don Anastasio Somoza Debayle. Please believe that our commitment is sincere and we
would make any sacrifice necessary for the cause of General Somoza."[4]
Not surprisingly, several days later, the official order came back from
the ministry. El Buen Gusto was reopened and the sex workers were
sent back to work, despite the fact that prostitution had been outlawed
fifteen years earlier.[5] This episode represented politics as usual in small-
town Nicaragua under the Somoza dictatorship, where well-connected
families were given carte blanche to violate the law. Rather than marginal to politics, criminality and vice were the very glue that held the
regime together.

These maladies were the direct result of the "disorder" that the regime had imposed on Nicaragua and of the destabilizing social changes
underway since World War II. From the 1950s, rapid export-led growth
and substantial public works transformed the country. Never before
had Nicaragua experienced such fantastic economic modernization.
With their complete control of the National Guard and the uncondi-
tional backing of the United States, the Somoza family dominated the
government and the economy. At the provincial and municipal level,
prominent landowning families used their political offices to channel
public resources for their own benefit. The majority of the population,
however, was largely left out of the economic bonanza and continued
to experience truly dismal living conditions. Elites gained access to un-
told riches (public lands, government contracts, and bottomless credit
from financial institutions), but further down the food chain, the regime offered only poorly paid employment and an arbitrary application of laws and regulations, as exemplified in the case of El Buen
Gusto.

On these lower rungs of the hierarchy, National Guard officers
and grassroots government backers tapped into the Somozas' political
machine through an expansive web of illicit businesses, including
brothels, cantinas, gambling halls, bootlegging, marijuana growing, and
cattle rustling. The cantina served as the fundamental social institution
through which the regime articulated with its grassroots supporters,
embedding itself within popular notions of masculinity. Such inebriated male sociability was often linked to violence, through which men
enacted their personal frustrations upon each other—and on members

of their families. Machismo in the Nicaraguan context, writes anthropologist Roger Lancaster, has several "core practices: hard drinking, excessive gambling, womanizing, wife beating."[6] Over the years of Somoza rule, these stereotypically masculine attributes were not challenged but fostered and co-opted by the government, while the rates of alcoholism, domestic violence, and homicide rose to historic highs. Wives and daughters from poor families were the primary victims of this expansion of vice. However, specific politically loyal female Somocistas, often single mothers—and, in the case of brothel owners, former prostitutes—were among the most identifiable facilitators of vice and family tension at the community level.[7] As we will see in later chapters, the Somoza regime's success fostered the very tensions and contradictions that later spurred an opposition movement calling for the redemption of familial harmony and society's moral regeneration.

## DYNASTIC POLITICS AND ECONOMIC MODERNIZATION IN THE RURAL NORTH

From the rise of the Somozas to power in 1936, the Segovias region in northern Nicaragua had been considered a bastion of support for the dictatorship. Within days of nationalist rebel Augusto César Sandino's murder at the hands of the GN in 1934, provincial newspapers celebrated his demise: "Sandino, as the head of Sandinismo and its system, represented anarchy, disorder, war, pillage, murder; that is to say chaos. . . . Somoza and the National Guard represented order and peace."[8] Accounts defaming Sandino and casting Somoza as imposing law and order became a trope to justify strongman rule. Estelian *diputado* (congressman) and Pueblo Nuevo landowner Esteban Midence Irías, for instance, denounced the nationalist rebels in similar terms. "I know and have felt the work of Sandino's bandit hordes," he told Congress. "They put me on their hit list, and I had to flee my home. There are no words to describe the crimes they committed."[9] Somoza soon moved to impose a personal dictatorship on the nation, overthrowing President Juan Bautista Sacasa two years later. In elections held to legitimate his new regime in 1936, Somoza knew he could count on the ranchers and planters of the north to deliver the votes of

their peasant subordinates: "I have a profound feeling of having provided the greatest good for Nicaragua: peace. The Segovias belong to
me as a single bloc."[10] Indeed, many people from all social classes in the
north now praised Somoza García as *"el Pacificador de las Segovias"*
(The Peacemaker of the Segovias).[11]

Following his seizure of power, Somoza García and his family
came to dominate Nicaraguan politics for nearly a half century, controlling the National Guard and amassing vast landholdings and an
immense fortune. For twenty years, Somoza García served as the country's *caudillo* (political strongman) who ruled Nicaragua on behalf of
his clientelistic network. With the dictator's assassination at the hands
of a poet in 1956, Somoza García's children took the reins of power.
His son Luis Somoza Debayle replaced him as president (1956–63),
and Luis's younger brother, Anastasio Somoza Debayle, headed the
National Guard and later acceded to the presidency himself (1967–79).
The Somozas oversaw a boom in agricultural production in the country, with growing exports of coffee, cotton, beef, and tobacco, sent
largely to the U.S. market. With the production of food crops — such as
corn, rice, beans, and sorghum — the Somozas took to touting Nicaragua as the once and future "granary of Central America."[12] The family's
economic empire quickly swelled with their acquisition of sugar
plantations, cattle ranches, and coffee haciendas. From these agrarian
holdings, they branched out, investing in factories, ports, mines, slaughterhouses, a shipping line, an airline, and car dealerships. They also
owned newspapers, radio stations, and all manner of other businesses
large and small — even a barbershop![13] Benefiting from government
control over hard-liquor distilling and distribution, the Somozas also
became leading producers of aguardiente or guaro, an intoxicating bev-
erage that proved fundamental to their methods of rule.[14]

As a political scientist observed in 1963, "the phenomenal growth
of Nicaragua's agricultural export trade was largely due to the government's intense determination to expand national roads."[15] The Pan-
American Highway transformed the landscape of the Segovias during
the Somoza period. *La Panamericana* was a transnational network of
roads linking the Latin American republics to the U.S. southern border
and integrating the regional economies. "Estelí is a small department,"
observed René Molina Valenzuela, the Segovias' preeminent Somocista

politician and landowner. "It does not have very rich lands; it doesn't have anything good for agriculture. What Estelí did have was the luck that the Pan-American Highway came to practically divide the department in two."[16] In the wake of this development, Estelí became a point of convergence for all of northern Nicaragua. Municipalities in Estelí, Madriz, Nueva Segovia, Matagalpa, Chinandega, and Jinotega all came to funnel their commercial traffic through the city. With increasing demands for agricultural credit, numerous banks opened in the town beginning in the 1940s.[17] Estelí came to function as a booming "Mediterranean Port" during these decades, leading some to speak of "the Estelian miracle" (*"el milagro esteliano"*).[18]

Estelí's traditional landowning class quickly attached themselves to the Somoza regime, attaining lucrative posts within the government and the ruling Nationalist Liberal Party (Partido Liberal Nacionalista, PLN).[19] With several notable exceptions, the same wealthy cattle-ranching families that had founded Estelí in the early nineteenth century continued to monopolize regional power. As late as the 1950s, wrote one resident, Estelí "still conserved a patriarchal structure, in which kinship ties functioned as a heritage of the colonial order."[20] Power was held at the provincial level by the *diputados* (congressmen), *senadores* (senators), *jefes políticos* (governors), and *alcaldes* (mayors), all of whom were handpicked by the regime.[21] A small number of well-known *apellidos* (surnames) filled the registers of government appointees and business associates of the Somozas. Before the arrival of women into political office, these positions were solely under the control of male patriarchs from powerful kinship networks. For prominent families in Estelí, María Dolores Álvarez Arzate writes, marriage through the Catholic Church, and at city hall, assured the legal "union of their property—particularly their haciendas—and the consolidation of social and economic relations between family groups."[22]

Political power in the rural north also passed from father to son, paralleling the perpetual rule of the Somozas. One of the leading political dynasties in Estelí was the Molina family, led by longtime jefe político Antonio Molina, a leading cattle rancher and owner of the hacienda Rodeo Grande. His tenure began in the time of Somoza García, and his son René rose to prominence as a diputado during the rule of Anastasio Somoza Debayle.[23] In this role, René Molina came to wield supreme influence over both the political and economic life of Nicaragua's north, particularly after he and General Somoza Debayle became business partners. Another respected family was the Briones clan, whose patriarch, José María Briones, served in the Senate from 1946 and later as jefe político of Estelí. Similarly, the Castillo family fielded several political figures in the national government, including Minister of Public Health Dr. Doroteo Castillo and his son, Minister of Agriculture Dr. José María "Chema" Castillo. José Indalecio Rodríguez, from another Estelian lineage, served as jefe político of Estelí during much of the regime's later period. In the smaller towns of the department, locally dominant ranchers and coffee growers likewise figured as the political chiefs of Somoza's PLN. Among some of the best-known Liberal leaders were landowners, such as the Midences in Pueblo Nuevo, Salvador Castellón in San Juan de Limay, and Juan María Pérez in Condega.

For these landowning families, these were years of phenomenal economic growth, with rising production and increased access to foreign markets. One of the most successful coffee producers was another Molina—Filemón—the owner of Darailí and San Jerónimo, two large estates located in the cool, humid highlands to the east of Condega.[24] In warmer, lowland climes, on the other hand, landowners converted their haciendas into efficient commercial cattle ranches. Beef exports were given a boost with the opening of the EMPANICSA slaughterhouse and meatpacking facility in Condega. Among the principal shareholders were the Somoza family and former diputado Sebastián Pinell. In 1962, EMPANICSA was granted USDA approval for export to the United States and began offering lucrative lines of credit to politically connected ranchers throughout the Segovias.[25] In the departments of Madriz and Nueva Segovia to the north of Estelí, Somocista political operatives began clear-cutting the rich pine forests that indigenous communities had used as their commons for centuries. Logging companies such as EMAGON and YODECO signed contracts with government officials and began chopping down the trees to sell to North American corporations.[26]

Over the long years of the Somoza dictatorship, local *hacendados* (landowners) consistently used their political office to gain access to previously public lands, such as *ejidos* (municipal lands) or indigenous community holdings. The few privileged families built up their own economic strength on the backs of the peasantry's precariousness. In depriving them of access to land, wealthy planters and ranchers shattered the integrity of the family unit for countless poor Nicaraguans and cast many campesinos adrift. As early as 1939, a dismayed jefe político in Estelí complained that diputado Leonte Alfaro, the owner of the hacienda El Guaylo, had "used his money to force out his neighbors living on ejido lands, leaving them without work and forcing them to migrate to other places so that they and their families can survive."[27] In El Robledalito, Condega, a campesino family accused PLN leader Romeo González of seizing lands where they had previously planted coffee. When the family's children went to pick beans on their farm, González called on the GN to throw them in jail.[28] In another instance in San Lucas in the department of Madriz, indigenous community leaders denounced diputado Dr. Pedro Joaquín Ríos of trying to strip them of 200 *manzanas* (lots) of land. Shortly after their sixteenth-century land titles went missing, they learned that congressman Ríos, a lawyer, had been overheard bragging of a "donation" he had received from the community.[29] Similarly, in San Juan del Río Coco, alcalde Mauricio "Nicho" Portillo was accused of fraudulently encroaching on the holdings of the indigenous community of Telpaneca and felling their forests to sell the lumber to the American company Plywood.[30] Community members alleged that Portillo, a major cattle rancher with ties to EMPANICSA, was dispossessing the community of 140 manzanas, where thirty families already lived.[31] Cases like these showcase the widespread pattern of land grabs by the politically connected throughout the Segovias during the years of economic growth. One of the strategies hacendados deployed, as Jeffrey Gould has shown for elsewhere in Nicaragua, was to deny the very existence of indigenous communities in order to gain control of their land and resources.[32]

While peasant family structure and social stability was seen as breaking down, elite families solidified their patriarchal dominance through ever-expanding business ventures. At the pinnacle of the pyramid and indicative of this pattern, of course, was the Somoza family itself. As with the meatpacking plant, the Somozas' hands were ever present in the new agricultural initiatives in the Segovias and throughout Nicaragua. In the 1960s, hacendados began planting tobacco for cigars as a new export crop in the valleys of Estelí, Condega, and Jalapa.

The project began as a joint venture between Anastasio Somoza De-bayle, René Molina, and a group of Cuban cigar producers who had fled the 1959 Cuban Revolution. The government's newly created National Development Institute (Instituto de Fomento Nacional, IN-FONAC), in turn, provided seed, technical assistance, and financing. Molina was impressed with the generous terms Somoza offered: "I was to participate in thirty percent of the partnership without investing a cent; he would assume all of the risk. I would get thirty percent just for putting up the land."[33] With official backing, tobacco plantings tripled during the 1960s.[34] With their connections to foreign markets and the technical know-how of their Cuban associates, Molina and Somoza made millions on the project, while smaller Nicaraguan tobacco growers who attempted to get in on the business went belly-up and declared bankruptcy after the first failed harvest.[35] Unlike coffee or cotton, tobacco required laborers year-round for planting, irrigating, fertilizing, picking, and drying the leaves, and for rolling the cigars. The new plantations and factories, however, gained notoriety for refusing to pay the minimum wage to the largely female workforce and for calling in machine-gun-toting National Guards to intimidate workers attempting unionization.[36]

## Campesino Labor and Social Inequality

The expanding wealth of the region's elite lineages found its mirror image in the poor households subject to family disintegration. The *Area Handbook for Nicaragua*, published in 1979, described the country's "vertical or hierarchical social structure" as the product of elite families with "strong paternal and maternal blood and marriage ties," which contrasted with "the so-called 'grandmother family' or mother-centered family" among "lower-class urban and rural sectors . . . which consists of a woman, her children by one or more men, and her mother."[37] Many poor campesino families lived in common-law marriages, eventually consecrated by the Catholic Church but rarely appearing in the civil registry.[38] Peasant families in many cases maintained "the masculine logic, culturally accepted as custom, in which men reaffirm their virility through the procreation of children with various women at the same time, as well as the residency of several of these in the house of the main wife."[39] Unlike wealthy families, marriage alliances were not about unifying properties but merely having additional hands to work the fields. In earlier years, peasants could rely on better-off distant cousins (*primos*) as a support network. As the regional population grew and families became much larger, many campesinos had trouble gaining access to patronage simply by sharing an apellido and a home village with a leading hacendado or political boss.

Given the differential effect of economic growth on elite and working-class families, "the persistent maldistribution of income" was identified by the early 1960s as "the most glaring drawback in Nicaragua's economic development."[40] With private haciendas gobbling up the best fields and the population ever expanding, campesinos were increasingly forced into low-paid wage labor to supplement their meager subsistence production.[41] The 1963 census, conducted outside of harvest time, found a third of Estelí's population employed as day laborers (*jornaleros*).[42] "When Somoza came to power," recalled Antonio Centeno from Condega, "there was peace and lots of work. In everything: sugarcane, rice, cotton . . . the coffee haciendas grew. But there was no respect for the worker. There was what the *patrón* (boss) said and nothing more."[43] Child labor had long been a mainstay of Nicaraguan agriculture, but ever-increasing numbers of boys were regularly expected to leave the family farm to work for wages on large, purportedly "modern" estates. Many peasants recall the exploitation and abuse they received on these farms, working long hours at the will of the hacendado and his at-times abusive foremen.[44] As we will see in chapter 2, the GN stifled all efforts to organize rural labor unions.

Large haciendas focused on export crops, but small and midsize farms mainly planted food for local consumption (beans, corn, sorghum). Campesinos without sufficient land worked as sharecroppers (*medieros*) on large landowners' fields, giving the owners half of what they produced. In fact, the department of Estelí had among the highest rates of *mediería* in the country, ranging from 40 to 50 percent in densely populated Estelí and La Trinidad, and between 30 to 40 percent in Condega.[45] "One was obligated to hand over half of the production," noted former campesino Salvador Loza Talavera from Rodeo Grande, Estelí. "It was an unjust mediería because it was at the cost of our sweat. . . . We were the ones who worked the land and contributed everything: the seeds, the water, the harvest, the tools, and the risk."[46]

An American researcher who visited Estelí in 1963 noted that share-cropping relations virtually compelled campesinos into wage labor. Their cut of the production was so low that many had to work for the same landowner during the *zafra* (harvest).[47]

Campesino producers often fell into debt by selling their produce to local merchants and wholesalers in advance (*adelantado*) for usurious prices. Marco Orozco Espinoza from Santa Cruz, to the south of Estelí, described the situation:

> The majority of the country was exploited. Those with money were fine and we, the campesinos, were poor. Due to a lack of food and money for clothes and shoes, we had to enter into contracts with them. Later, they paid the prices they wanted. That's to say, if we borrowed 100 pesos to pay it off later, we had to work twenty days here as a campesino because they paid us five *córdobas* [per day]. Later, there was an increase, and they said they were going to pay the campesinos eleven córdobas, but they kept on paying us eight. And we couldn't protest at all because that brought down the butt of the Garand [rifles used by the National Guard]. Those three pesos they took from the campesino every day were to pay off the Guard colonels so they would pressure us. If we said anything, they beat us with their gun butts or sent us to jail.[48]

In El Regadío, working conditions were quite similar and land ownership highly concentrated. Campesino Anastasio Rivas Cruz explained:

> Those that lived here in the time of Somoza were the workers of José María Briones, Daniel Moncada, Hilario Montenegro, and a couple of others. It was just these three or four people [that owned all of the land]. We were the workers in the sugar mills; others worked cleaning the cane or milking their cows. This community was small, and there were no big factories to create jobs. We started at four or five in the morning and left at four in the afternoon. They were long workdays! There were two National Guards who were in the service of [the landowners] and not us. We were terrified of them. One Guardia could capture ten or twenty men at a time. The poor were always the most punished by the laws of earth; the most

oppressed. There was a Ministry of Labor, but the poor never won a dispute. It was just to have there, not to defend the rights of the little guy.[49]

As both accounts illustrate, campesinos were forced by poverty and landlessness to work for long hours and low wages. Notably, both men referred to the failure of the government to apply its own laws, such as the 1945 Labor Code and the 1963 minimum wage. As was often the case during the Somoza regime, these laws were dead letter. In addition, both accounts emphasized the coercive role that the National Guard played in their communities, helping to bolster the power of the hacendados over their workforce and silence any complaints.

Even when opportunities to earn higher wages appeared with the construction of the Pan-American Highway, Estelian landowners were said to have conspired with U.S. contractors to keep salaries low. "Nicaraguan workers," they allegedly told the Americans, were "lazy, cunning, crafty, roguish, thieving, vulgar scoundrels" and not worth more than 50 cents an hour. Instead, the patrones offered to send 500 of "their campesinos" to the Thompson Cornwall Company at a rate of just two córdobas per day.[50] In other parts of the Segovias with fewer employment alternatives, landless campesinos or impoverished subsistence farmers often found work enlisting as soldiers in the National Guard.[51] With such low incomes, the deprivations of average working people stood in glaring contrast to the wealth of the small group that benefited stupendously from the export economy.

This growing inequality was most apparent in the flourishing provincial capital of Estelí. The department's urban population more than quadrupled between 1930 and 1974, reaching 36,000 out of a total population of 88,000.[52] Artisanal production grew, with numerous workshops producing bricks, furniture, shingles, soda, candy, bread, and shoes.[53] The downtown was dramatically transformed with the installation of paved boulevards, running water, sewage, and electricity during the 1950s and 60s.[54] On the main thoroughfares, one saw new department stores, pharmacies, hotels, movie theaters, banks, and doctors' offices. Along the highway, gas stations, mechanics' workshops, restaurants, and motels now catered to travelers and truck drivers. For most of the population, though, the glittering town center stood in stark contrast to their villages and the swelling shanties. As future guerrilla commander Francisco Rivera put it, the city of Estelí now contained "two different worlds."[55]

As a counterpoint to the progressive veneer, shantytowns sprang up on the town's outskirts as migrants arrived from the rural hinterland. These "miserable, inhumane houses" had little access to clean water, with sewage overflowing and dirt roads flooded during the rainy months of winter.[56] Despite the growing economy and increased public spending, statistics on social indicators remained rather abysmal throughout the Somoza period. Tropical diseases remained common, and few had access to a doctor. Public hospitals were underfunded and constantly lacking in basic supplies and medicines.[57] Thousands of men, women, and children died of curable sicknesses each year from the lack of health care. With medical treatment too expensive, charlatan *curanderos* (folk healers) wandered the Segovias, doing bogus bacteriological testing, selling "medicines," and even reading tarot cards in some cases.[58]

In terms of education, the period witnessed a rapid expansion in some areas and neglect elsewhere. The Somoza government opened many small schoolhouses over its decades of rule, but most were located in larger towns and villages alongside major highways.[59] In some parts of the Segovias, enterprising priests and nuns established several prominent learning centers, including the first public high schools and even a regional extension center of the Catholic university in Estelí in 1969.[60] Despite this, less than 38 percent of men and 44 percent of women could read by 1963, according to the regime's own statistics.[61] Increasingly, girls were more likely to be educated, especially as many campesino boys dropped out before finishing primary school to find work on the plantations to contribute to household income. These conditions of poverty and inequality allowed the government to manipulate and co-opt a needy population and perpetuate itself in power for decades on end.

NACATAMALES AND CIRCUSES: ELECTIONS UNDER THE SOMOZAS

Throughout this period, the political system combined military authoritarianism with a pro forma nod to democratic procedure.[62] Somoza loyalists held a total monopoly over government institutions, and the regime reaffirmed its dominance every few years through the ballot box.[63] Though observers ridiculed these show elections for their utter falseness (see table 1.1 for the official vote counts; always a landslide for the Somocista candidate), they nonetheless served an essential role in legitimating the regime, while allowing government opponents to let off steam and bargain for inclusion. The electoral system functioned as a well-rehearsed script in which various sectors—landowners, the GN, the Catholic Church, and public employees—worked in concert to showcase the dictatorship's stability. Victoria González-Rivera has rightly described the elections held under the Somozas as "both commemorative events and rituals."[64]

Rather than staid democratic contests, the regime's electoral campaigns, political rallies, and voting days instead mimicked the ambiance of traditional *fiestas patronales*. During these annual festivals, entire towns celebrated the local patron saint with great fanfare, including religious processions, gambling, a county fair, and a rodeo. These religious festivities became "a pretext for collective drunkenness," as men imbibed copious amounts of alcohol.[65] Electoral campaigning was carried out in a similarly celebratory manner, with regime agents handing out cash, food, and guaro. During the frenzy of presidential elections, politics under the Somozas became widely associated with this culture

*Table 1.1.* Percentage of Votes for PLN in Presidential Election Results

| Year | Estelí | Madriz | National |
|------|--------|--------|----------|
| 1936 | 76.00 | 77.50 | 79.41 |
| 1947 | 67.20 | 84.60 | 61.80 |
| 1950 | 82.53 | 89.88 | 75.63 |
| 1957 | 85.00 | 94.99 | 88.73 |
| 1963 | 96.32 | 99.27 | 90.48 |
| 1967 | 83.59 | 90.29 | 73.62 |

*Source*: AGN, Fondo Presidencial, Sección Consejo Nacional de Elecciones, 1.20.1, folder "Actas."

of public intoxication and open vote-buying. This chaotic and disorderly form of popular mobilization projected the sense that the regime flowed seamlessly from the body politic itself.

When Somoza Debayle traveled to regional towns to campaign, local officials festooned town buildings with red Liberal Party flags in preparation. Scores of campesinos waited—often on horseback and in their finest clothing—on the road leading to their town's entrance. These *jinetes* (jockeys) were Liberal Party loyalists who received free food and drink for serving as part of the *caballería*. Upon his arrival, Somoza donned a cowboy hat and red bandana and triumphantly entered the city on horseback alongside the jinetes as a man of the people. The presence of the caudillo symbolically brought the campesinos into close contact with the center of power. Somoza's speech to the assembled crowd, including peasants trucked in from distant villages, served as the day's main event (see fig. 1.1). Even for those with few political ties, the atmosphere of revelry broke the dreary monotony of everyday rural life. Campaigning saw "large mobilizations of the population under the influence of alcohol and *nacatamales*" and a "processional and folkloric attitude that mixed with political fervor."[66] Nacatamales, a traditional Nicaraguan food made of cornmeal and meat steamed in a banana leaf, were distributed by the thousands to Somocista voters during the election season.

Contributing to the façade of democratic competition was the continuing Liberal/Conservative political division that often broke out into violence at election time. The two main political parties—Somoza's dominant Liberals represented by a red flag, the minor Conservatives by a green flag—were less ideologically driven parties than rival patron–client groupings. These mapped directly onto different family networks through a binary logic: those tacked into the government's system of patronage, employment, and recognition, and those that were not. In this way, family feuds and factional disputes within communities going back decades took on the mask of party competition. Very often in the Segovias and elsewhere, the party affiliation of one's father was inherited and passed down between generations.[67] At the national level, the Conservative Party historically represented the interests of the traditional, colonial-era landed elite based in Granada. At the level of political discourse, Conservatives appealed to religious traditionalism with their vague slogan of "God, Order, and Justice."

*Figure 1.1.* Anastasio Somoza Debayle campaign rally in Somoto, Madriz, May 2, 1974. Courtesy of Instituto de Historia de Nicaragua y Centroamérica.

Their moralistic rhetoric harangued uncouth, nouveau riche Somocista politicians for their large-scale corruption and Liberal voters for their involvement in illegal vices and lack of Catholic virtue. This language was later repurposed by more radical government opponents. Over the decades, numerous Conservative Party bosses signed unseemly pacts with Somoza, permitting them a quota of power and a share of the spoils.[68] On the grassroots level in the rural north, however, many Conservative families considered themselves fervently in opposition to the regime. They closely followed *La Prensa*, the stridently anti-Somoza national newspaper edited by Pedro Joaquín Chamorro, scion of the country's most prominent Conservative dynasty and a critic of his own party's regular collaboration with Somoza. In addition, minor political parties, such as the Independent Liberal Party (Partido Liberal Independiente, PLI) gained a following among anti-Somoza Liberals in Estelí from the 1940s onward.

In the run-up to election day, the government assembled numerous pro-Somoza "organizations" practically overnight to mobilize different groups of voters. The *Ala Femenina* (Feminine Wing) of the PLN was often led by schoolteachers and the wives of prominent Somocistas, and it rallied women to the polling stations. Women were first granted the vote in 1955 and were widely said to have contributed to the electoral "victory" of Luis Somoza two years later.[69] Other "fronts," "associations," and "unions" enlisted public employees and *jueces de mesta* (village-level microauthorities) in shoring up the vote for the regime or harassing the opposition.[70] In 1946, the opposition accused Estelí's jefe político Antonio Molina of distributing cash to jueces de mesta with which to pay campesinos—three córdobas each—to register and vote for Somoza's PLN.[71] Another group was the GN's Civil Reserve, made up "largely of campesinos and laborers and led by retired officers or local politicians," which functioned as "a government claque at political rallies and similar government functions."[72]

The campaign atmosphere of chaotic revelry often carried over into election day itself. According to the daughter of one Somocista politician, the elections were "very beautiful . . . a party and a very happy day."[73] From early morning, voters were roused to polling stations often located in front of Liberal Party members' homes or on the haciendas of Somocista landowners. A secret ballot (introduced in 1963) was a mere formality. Poll workers doled out rewards to those who duly cast their vote for the official candidate: a nacatamal, some guaro, and five córdobas in cash. Using state and party resources to buy votes with money and liquor had long been traditional practice in Nicaragua, but the Somozas took it to new heights.[74] For example, voters were presented with red cards bearing the photo of the caudillo, Anastasio Somoza (García or Debayle, depending on the era), declaring them members of the ruling PLN. This document, known as *la Magnífica*, was required for access to government services and public employment.[75] Given the incentives, some Nicaraguans cast votes for Somoza at multiple polling stations, and some Honduran campesinos were even said to have crossed the border to participate. Diputado René Molina observed, "Whether they like it or not, the campesinos were always the main bastion of support of the Liberal Party. . . . We had at least eighty percent support. The campesinos are very smart: they go with the party that they think is going to win. And the Liberal Party controlled the state and controlled the army, so they always voted for it."[76] Indeed, Somoza's PLN was by far the largest and wealthiest party machine, financed by a 5 percent "contribution" from all government employees' salaries.[77] If the vote was close on election day, Lib-

erals could stuff ballot boxes and falsify vote tallies to assure that the
official candidate won. Ironically, the Somozas' own constitution denied citizenship rights for "habitual drunkenness" and to anyone
involved in "violence, coercion, corruption or fraud in elections."[78] As
so often in Somocista Nicaragua, the reality was the exact inverse of
what was dictated by law.

The rowdy atmosphere often led to violent incidents, fueled by the
regime's use of free-flowing alcohol to ply the crowd.[79] During elections, chaotic—often alcohol-lubricated—violence broke out between
Conservatives and Liberals in the Segovias. The quotidian violence that
made up so much of day-to-day life now took on a political hue. On
election day 1963, for example, there were numerous clashes between
Liberals and anti-Somocistas. In La Trinidad, the remains of a man
hacked to death with a machete were discovered in the woods in the
morning, and another corpse was found in Monte Verde in the after-
noon, allegedly the victim of seven attackers.[80]

Such violent confrontations—almost exclusively between men—
were not limited to partisan divisions. Similar fights even broke out
between Somocistas at the guaro-soaked celebratory events sponsored
by the government. At a Somoza rally held in Estelí in October 1971,
the chaotic merriment left at least three men dead. The first victim was
a campesino jinete awaiting the dictator's arrival, who—in his apparently inebriated state—lost control of his horse and fell to his death. In
the city itself, another man was murdered by a fellow campesino in a
conflict over a disputed piece of land. The shooting took place mere
blocks from where the dictator had just finished giving his speech. Finally, an argument broke out in a pickup truck returning to Condega
after the rally with several drunken revelers on board. Suddenly, the
truck's driver shot a campesino passenger dead (strangely, seconds after
the victim had shouted "Viva Somoza").[81] Just a month later, another
Somocista celebration in Estelí again led to violence. The PLN held
a dance with free food, plentiful aguardiente, and three bands hired
to play for the crowd. Once again, a brawl broke out, and a pistol was
drawn, precipitating "a human avalanche" that injured dozens and
crushed the bands' instruments in its path.[82]

Regional politicians also exploited preexisting social divisions, at
times leading to violence. In parts of the Madriz department divided
between indigenous people and *ladinos* (nonindigenous), the regime

stoked long-standing ethnic hostility. Given the degree of race-mixing and cultural assimilation in the Segovias, these ethnic divisions were not based on language or clothing, as elsewhere in Central America. Physical appearance (such as hair texture, skin color, and facial features) was not always a clear marker. Instead, ethnicity was a product of one's family lineage—immediately denoted by their apellidos—which either traced its origin to the indigenous communities of Madriz or to ladino families that had migrated from outside. Come election time, one Somocista postured as pro-ladino and anti-indigenous, while another PLN candidate was said to be the defender of indigenous community lands. Eulogio Hernández, an indigenous campesino from Cusmapa, recalled the scene:

> They had us so blindfolded that they were able to trick us. And as we didn't know any better and didn't know how to read, they told us: Camilo López is in favor of the whites; Victor Manuel Talavera is in favor of the indigenous. And they were the same shit. So the fierce little Indian said: "Camilo López is with the ladinos, we aren't going to support him because he's with the ladinos!" Or they said, "We're going with Talavera, he's with the indigenous!" And they were the same thing. They even fought over this with their machetes and killed each other. One said, "I'm with Camilo López!" "But you're not ladino, you son-of-a . . .," said the other one. But really, López and Talavera were the same thing. . . . Camilo López won and got to be senator for four years, and Victor Manuel got to be congressman for four years. I said to myself: What a scam, right? [laughs] And these son-of-a-guns were in office for life. Old Camilo López died, his son replaced him. Old Talavera died, his son replaced him. How they tricked us![83]

Because both factions represented the Liberal Party and given the nepotism of provincial family dynasties, indigenous communities and ladino peasants came out losing either way.

The regime also publicly distributed patronage in the months and weeks prior to an election. Consider a photo (fig. 1.2) from Somoza's newspaper *Novedades* in which diputado René Molina poses while ritually handing out loans, insecticide, seeds, and fertilizer (in bags marked "Somoza") to the all-male members of a peasant cooperative

*Figure 1.2.* Diputado René Molina Valenzuela provides fertilizer for the Guasuyuca Cooperative in Pueblo Nuevo, Estelí. *Novedades*, May 21, 1968.

of bean producers in Pueblo Nuevo. The beneficiaries, it is worth noting, were likely among those whose access to land had been negatively affected by the expansion of the haciendas in the region. Accompanying Molina are smiling representatives of the GN, the National Bank, and the local leader of the Ala Femenina. The power dynamics of shame and obeisance are visible in the facial expressions of the recipients paraded before the flash of the cameras.

One of the most hotly contested elections of the Somoza period took place in 1967. Gen. Anastasio Somoza Debayle, the West Point–educated head of the National Guard, ran for the presidency against popular Conservative caudillo Dr. Fernando Agüero Rocha, the candidate of the National Opposition Union (Unión Nacional Opositora, UNO), an alliance of the Conservative Party and the PLI. In late 1966, the anti-Somoza parties held well-attended rallies in favor of the UNO in Estelí and other cities.[84] In order to prevent Conservative peasants from voting, the regime consciously manipulated the locations of polling stations. For instance, Liberal stronghold San Juan de Limay was assigned sixteen voting centers, including ten in rural locations on Somocista haciendas, while in "the valleys close to Estelí populated by large nuclei of hamlets where the majority are opposition supporters, not a single polling station was opened."[85]

In light of the rising support for the candidacy of Agüero, the regime formed a new paramilitary group known as the Association of
Somocista Workers, Peasants, and Retired Soldiers (Asociación de Militares Retirados, Obreros y Campesinos Somocistas, AMROCS) in
1966 to strike fear into the opposition. In Managua, Victoria González-
Rivera has shown, AMROCS' membership overlapped with the so-
called *turbas* (mobs) of Nicolasa Sevilla, an alleged onetime prostitute
who organized mobs from the poor barrios to attack opposition political activists.[86] In the Segovias, members included former Guardias,
unemployed young men, Somocista campesinos, and several wives and
daughters of Guardias.[87] In rural Estelí, AMROCS stood accused of
distributing alcohol and registering the same Liberal voters each weekend under different names, blatant violations of electoral law.[88] Armed
AMROCS posses were said to have patrolled the streets of Estelí, using
"exaggerated pressure to impede members of the opposition from registering" and provoking "grave tension" in the city. The opposition
newspaper even claimed that these militias were led by René Molina
and Aniceto Rodríguez, "prominent figures of Somocismo . . . who,
showing weapons, harass the opposition at polling stations, provoking
a dangerous situation."[89] The preelection violence—taking place across
the country—reached a fevered pitch during the final UNO rally held
in Managua on January 22, 1967, for which Conservative peasants were
bused in from around the country. In circumstances still shrouded in
mystery, many opposition demonstrators were gunned down in the
streets as the National Guard fired into the crowd.[90] Many present that
day blamed the bloody events not only on the Somoza regime but also
on the Conservative bigwigs, who, it was claimed, hoped to spark a
coup d'état or a U.S. military intervention by using the misled peasant
throngs as cannon fodder. Predictably, Anastasio Somoza Debayle was
declared the winner in the election held just two weeks later.

### "Outrageous Personal Family Ambitions": Corruption and Kinship Networks

Governors, congressmen, and senators from prominent families were
the caciques—political bosses—who flexed what Somoza termed "he-

gemony" throughout the country, with substantial political, judicial, and economic power. U.S. ambassador Turner Shelton informed the State Department: "At the departmental level, the PLN is headed by 'geographic caciques' who in many respects are 'little Somozas' of the provinces, although they are not permitted to become prominent enough to rival Somoza."[91] These officials, such as René Molina, had access to a relative cornucopia of state funds, employment opportunities, and government contracts to hand out. In Somoto, one resident criticized these party bosses with a gendered, familial metaphor: "In addition to their big salaries," politicians were "given the honorable title of Padres de la Patria, but these leaders are . . . the opposite. . . . They are the most disobedient sons who suck on the big, long, and juicy teats of the Madre Patria."[92] One of the best-known leaders in northern Nicaragua was Hector Mairena, a diputado and later senator for Estelí. In his stronghold of La Trinidad, Mairena was, by and large, a well-loved "miniature cacique." To this day, residents of the town recount stories of how he was able to get local men freed from prison as long as they agreed to work as sharecroppers on his sprawling El Guasimal estate in recompense. In addition to this impunity for regime supporters, opponents also accused him of "ordering the imprisonment of any citizen who does not follow his orders."[93]

Caciques applied laws with great favoritism toward their family members and business partners. In 1959, for instance, it was claimed that Estelí's diputado Sebastián Pinell and jefe político José María Briones had selected 40 percent of the city's juror pool from workers on Pinell's hacienda, including some who were illiterate and expected to deliver the verdicts that the Somocista bosses ordered. Just days later, campesinos denounced Briones for allegedly diverting water from his poorer neighbors' cattle ranches to his own sugar and grain fields.[94] In Somoto, peasants complained that diputado Camilo López Nuñez allowed a wealthy landowner to illegally cut off road access through his property to "humble campesinos." López Nuñez—whose father had been Sen. Camilo López Irías and whose wife, Tula Baca, had become jefe político—stood accused of favoritism toward his close friend and fellow cockfighting aficionado Sebastián Corrales.[95]

Given this arbitrary power, there was an intense struggle over the control of municipal governments and their financial resources.

Somoza García replaced municipal autonomy in 1937 with the direct appointment of mayors, but he reintroduced a limited measure of local control in 1950.[96] Five years later, the Somoza government granted women the right to vote, doubling the electorate and bringing numerous women into political office at the regional level. With the return of partial competition for municipal office, at times there was more internal division *within* the Liberal Party in Estelí than *between* Liberals and their Conservative adversaries. Insiders attributed the heightened conflict to the "lack of a true leader in the Estelian Somocista ranks, as each one wants that position. Between members of the governing party, between each municipality and town, there is such division that it damages the interests of each place."[97]

The battle for spoils often followed family lines, and the election of Somocista women to political office took place largely on terms that strengthened the "patriarchal structure" of the dominant kinship networks. Though municipal law banned members of a single family from serving in multiple government positions, nepotism was the very essence of small-town politics.[98] In San Juan de Limay, for example, an excluded PLN supporter fired off a complaint to the minister of the interior that one of the alderwomen was the first cousin of the mayor and the mayor's son held the job of town secretary. He signed off by stating that he had only raised such criticisms in order to contribute to the "brilliant administration of the Great Nationalist Liberal Party, led by our great leader General Anastasio Somoza Debayle." Interestingly, he also took the opportunity to castigate the Somocista landowners for permitting these abuses: "The leader of this town, Salvador Castellón Guevara, doesn't see these things. He doesn't care about this at all because he only cares about his capital."[99]

Factional struggles between rival coteries had the unintended effect of exposing the degree of graft permeating the entire administrative apparatus. In 1967, Romeo González—a large landowner and Liberal leader—became mayor of Condega and found the town's finances deeply in the red. Hoping to restore fiscal control to a disastrously mismanaged town, González began surveying the public ejido lands to assess the debt prominent families owed in back taxes. Among those using the town's land for free was Juan María Pérez, the local colonel of the Civil Reserve, tax collector, aguardiente concessionary, and González's longtime challenger for control of the municipal PLN. Others in debt to the town hall included a former mayor, the owner of the movie theater, and other prominent hacendados and businessmen, including even diputado René Molina himself.[100]

As a result of his efforts to get them to pay their back taxes, these elites practically rose up in rebellion against the new mayor. José Indalecio Rodríguez, the jefe político, was sent from Estelí to investigate González's alleged "abuses" and reported to the Ministry of the Interior that there was no solution in sight. "He has the majority of the population against him," Rodríguez wrote, "particularly the Liberal Leaders of the zone."[101] González, in his defense, responded:

> Those that the jefe político calls "leaders," of course, feel defrauded because my authority is for the citizenry, and in my office, there are neither privileged people nor those who, due to their economic position or political influence, get to give orders to the authorities. . . . The truth is there is a marked interest that I leave my position as soon as possible. The complainants are the owners of lands or renters of lands and, as we are working to measure these lands and apply the respective fees, they think that when I leave office, this process will not take place.[102]

By challenging these powerful families, González quickly hit a wall in his efforts at reform. He was removed from office a few months later, effectively ending the attempt to charge local elites for their use of public resources.

Similar problems of municipal misgovernment tormented the regional capital of Estelí, with its much more sizable budget. In 1967, Lilliam Vílchez de Benavides, the local PLN party secretary, became the first female mayor of Estelí in the city's history and attempted to impose order. Refusing to serve as a puppet of the city's male bosses, she showed an independent streak that challenged the deep-rooted corruption of her own political party. Immediately upon reviewing the ledger left by her predecessor, she—much like González in Condega—found the town millions of córdobas in debt and called for an official audit.[103] City finances were in a "chaotic state," she wrote in an open letter, as "goods belonging to the municipality had been treated as though they were private. . . . It is time the representatives of the people make their voices heard . . . and forget about their outrageous personal family ambitions that are known to all the citizens."[104] She publicly alleged that the Electric Company of Estelí (*Empresa de Luz Eléctrica de Estelí*)—privately owned by Somocistas René Molina and Francisco Moreno—had charged exorbitant rates to the municipality, transferring vast sums from municipal coffers to private bank accounts. She demanded an end to this "anachronistic contract" and a "substantial decrease in the price of these services," which provided the owners with profits of "C$5 million tax-free córdobas a year."[105]

Much like the alcalde in Condega or the municipal magistrate who tried to shut down the brothel in La Trinidad, Vílchez quickly provoked the fury of powerful stakeholders who benefited from the "chaotic" status quo. Party leaders withdrew their support for her administration and threatened to purge her from the PLN if she did not step down immediately. A campaign of paid radio advertising accused *her* of criminal behavior and corruption as a ploy to confuse the public. Vílchez responded that the propaganda was the work of those who "owe great sums of money" to the municipal government.[106] "The situation is getting dangerous for the *alcaldesa*," a confidential report explained. "A woman of firm character, honorable and inflexible, she could be forced from office by the politicians."[107] Soon, dubious judicial proceedings began against her for alleged embezzlement, and Vílchez insisted she was the "victim of dirty intrigues on behalf of local politicians, including the current diputado René Molina Valenzuela and the jefe político Señor José Indalecio Rodríguez."[108] All of her denunciations of the usual suspects were to no avail. A miniature "coup d'état" was carried out in the town council, with Vílchez officially stripped of her position and subject to arrest. Rumors spread that when the National Guard encircled her house to arrest her, she escaped out of her window and across the rooftop, clutching her four-year-old son in her arms.[109] This image captures the violent threat facing the town's sole female mayor—as a politician and a mother—for challenging the leading patriarchal family networks' stranglehold on power and trying to bring about some sense of order. Even from the mayor's office, she had fought city hall and lost.

Cantina Caciques: Grassroots Somocismo and Impunity

Below these political intrigues over provincial offices and state resources, the regime maintained a dense network of lower-class adherents, whom I refer to as "cantina caciques." U.S. ambassador Shelton
described them as the PLN's "ward heelers who do the real legwork of
turning out the masses . . . effectively rounding up the voters, hauling
them to the polls and giving them food, drink, and small cash payments."[110] Through their links to the GN and the Liberal Party, these
government supporters at the barrio or village level gained virtual impunity before the law. These Somocistas engaged in numerous illegal—
yet commonplace—economic activities, establishing cantinas, brothels,
and gambling halls, and also bootlegging, planting marijuana, and cattle
rustling. As interstitial figures, they served as brokers linking the state
to the community, paying bribes, informing on opposition members,
and backing Somoza and the PLN in the elections. Though rarely officeholders themselves, cantina caciques attached themselves to such
figures, paying their dues during election season and expecting privileges in return.

With official backing, cantinas spread like wildfire during the Somoza period. As Estelí grew in the 1950s, such working-class neighborhoods as Venecia, El Tanque, and El Bajío (also known as Barrio Los
Placeres, or "the pleasures") virtually overflowed with bars and brothels. As has been noted about other Latin American contexts, these hypermasculine spaces were a central locus of male sociability.[111] Much
of the academic literature, however, treats cantinas as targets of government bureaucrats (taxes, regulation, etc.) and moralist reformers
who aimed to police working-class male behavior. However, as can
be seen from the Nicaraguan case, cantinas were fostered by the state
and played a vital role in bolstering a corrupt political system. Particularly on weekends and holidays, men flooded the cantinas, and public
drunkenness was widespread. For impoverished campesinos, cantinas
provided a place to spend time with friends and drown their sorrows
in guaro. Even from a very young age, Nicaraguan boys and young
men were encouraged to begin drinking to prove their masculinity,
for as a popular saying had it, "Guaro is for men" (*el guaro es para los*

*hombres*).[112] Even though cantinas as such were legal establishments, they functioned as the focal points around which a whole slew of illegal vices and criminal practices took place.

The National Guard was responsible for controlling "vices," such as prostitution, gambling, and bootleg liquor, by directly levying fines on offenders.[113] In practice, however, the Guardia stimulated rather than suppressed these illicit activities, with commanding officers profiting from tens of thousands of córdobas each month in kickbacks from illegal enterprises.[114] Some cantina caciques aligned with the regime also engaged in sex trafficking, bringing teenaged girls from the countryside under false pretenses to work as prostitutes and splitting their profits with Guardia officers.[115] Many illicit businesses even came to be directly owned by GN officers, as we saw in this chapter's opening vignette. Within a decade of Somoza's rise to power, public health studies noted a direct connection between growing hard liquor consumption and the country's rising homicide rate: "The little money which, at the cost of hard work, the peasant earns, is almost entirely dissipated in one night of drinking, which is repeated frequently. The majority of these drinks have a terrible effect, and produce dangerous alcohol poisoning or intoxication. The peasant, drunken in this manner, becomes aggressive and belligerent. The majority of the homicides are committed under such intoxications."[116]

Drunken shoot-outs and stabbings became so prevalent in the red-light district of Estelí, an observer noted, that on "Saturday and Sunday, this city lives like the days of the American West from the movies."[117] This atmosphere of violence found in the cantina and the street consistently found its way back into working-class households in the form of domestic abuse against wives and children as men stumbled home under the influence in the wee hours of the morning. Though statistics are impossible to come by for the Somoza period, as early as 1937 intellectual Carlos Cuadra Pasos claimed that family abandonment and drunken abuse led many working-class and peasant women to avoid marriage.[118]

Thus, widespread access to alcohol became the lubricant for a wide range of vices, criminal practices, and quotidian acts of violence. Given the state monopoly over aguardiente distribution for tax purposes, the government granted vendor concessions only to loyal Somocista families.[119] These concessionaries purchased taxed guaro by the barrel and then doled it out to locals who arrived with empty bottles. As we have seen, the very same liquor was also sold at cantinas and used to ply voters during PLN rallies, registration drives, and on election day. Bootlegging remained pervasive in the rural north, with dangerous and poisonous moonshine sold not only on the black market but even at government dispensaries. "Clandestine aguardiente was found to exist in various places, but things continue the same," the shocked mayor of Condega wrote to the Ministry of the Interior in 1967. "They found altered guaro in the aguardiente depository in this town and in the revenue administration of Estelí, mixed with *casusa* (pure alcohol). It is terrible that such a thing is happening in a government institution."[120] When state inspectors came to apply the law, however, it seems that an under-the-table payment to the GN allowed the responsible parties to escape punishment.[121]

Jueces de mesta, peasant Somocistas in each village appointed to their post by the jefe político, played a similar role in fostering disorder and vice in rural areas. Though not directly paid for their work, the government granted these (often illiterate) peasants relatively arbitrary power over their neighbors and the ability to fine and jail those committing any of a long list of infractions.[122] As village patriarch, the juez de mesta could be an abusive "miniature dictator" or a relatively anodyne community leader, depending on his individual personality and relationship with his neighbors. Rather than upholding the law, some ran small-scale illegal cantinas and gaming tables of their own. Other jueces protected family members who produced illicit *chicha* (moonshine made from corn), grew clandestine stalks of marijuana, or poached animals from neighbors' lands. In some extreme cases, jueces even covered up violent crimes, such as rape, assault, and murder. Jueces de mesta were also a part of the apparatus responsible for mobilizing campesinos to the voting booths on election day.

As was the case in the regime's upper echelons, there was a perpetual incongruence between the law as written and its application in practice. Technically illegal gambling enterprises became widespread with the complicity of the GN, fleecing peasant men of their meager earnings and denying those much-needed funds to their wives and children. In 1943, for instance, a member of Pueblo Nuevo's municipal council wrote to the minister of the interior complaining that "despite your clear orders," dice games continued to be openly played in the town, damaging family harmony by promoting "demoralization among the youth and fathers. The owners of the game tables are laughing at and annulling your orders."[123] A decade later, in 1954, the problem persisted. The vice minister wrote to the jefe político of Madriz that he had forwarded his complaints about illegal gambling to General Somoza. If the GN refused to apply the law and act against them, the minister told the jefe político, the mayor could instead order the jueces de mesta to capture and punish the owners of the gaming tables.[124] In Santa Cruz three years later, residents complained of a gambling hall operating directly in front of the local elementary school. Children ("future citizens"), they said, were being corrupted by these habits "due to a regime that has not only been unable to stop them but instead tolerates and manages them."[125] A 1960 letter to the editor of *La Prensa* complained that "DICE GAMES, POKER, BINGO, COCKFIGHTING and CANTINAS" functioned with total impunity in Estelí, and "the words of the President of the Republic were ignored by those with an obligation to carry them out."[126] Of course, the GN's guilt was often one of commission rather than merely omission.

Like illegal gambling and alcohol production, by the 1960s, prostitution had also become a lucrative and pervasive business for those allied with the regime. Though officially outlawed in 1955, the very time at which women gained the right to vote, the number of brothels ironically grew exponentially thereafter, mainly thanks to GN encouragement and complicity.[127] One of the towns most criticized for its "low morality" was Somoto, said to be teeming with brothels and cantinas where "the worker and campesino leave not only their money but also their health."[128] Neighbors complained of the drunken violence of the cantinas and the presence of scantily clad prostitutes in the town's streets. Responding to these accusations, jefe político Tula Baca de López, one of the few women governing an entire department and daughter-in-law of a Somocista patriarch, confirmed to her superiors that such businesses did in fact exist. However, she wrote, "If we follow the law, I am sure that we won't be heard. Because the same thing happened to me when I explained the complaints of citizens of this municipality in which eighteen brothels are in business and merely raising the issue provoked the anger of the Señor Comandante [of the National Guard]."[129] The appeals of even this prominent female office-holder could not compel the National Guard to crack down on brothels, given their economic and political importance.

While thousands of impoverished peasant girls were being lured and entrapped within the scores of cantinas scattered throughout the Segovias, older working-class women (often onetime prostitutes themselves) served as the madams who sold the young women's bodies to paying male customers. The ultimate beneficiaries of this illicit trade, though, were the GN officers who demanded regular bribes from the brothels. One cantina owner and matron, Antonia G., wrote directly to President Somoza in 1968, complaining that "the new comandante . . . has prohibited me from running my business, a cantina with women. He wants to charge me C$35.00 for each woman while I used to pay C$25.00. These women don't cause any problems. I am a poor woman without resources. I beg you to give me the permission to have women, and they won't cause any problems." Her plea was signed "your dear, dear friend, and Somocista Liberal."[130] That party members could write to the president of the Republic demanding the right to run an illegal brothel reveals again how laws were rendered meaningless and superseded by political loyalty.[131] The human trafficking and sexual exploitation of the young women and girls, it is worth noting, went completely unmentioned by the brothels' defenders, and by those conservative critics worried about "low morality" and the presence of "drunken women."

An additional area of criminal activity and disorder that plagued the rural north during the Somoza period was cattle rustling (*abigeato*). Rather than the isolated action of individuals, cattle theft was a coordinated effort that often had the tacit complicity of political and military authorities. The government was responsible for ensuring sanitary conditions of slaughterhouses and collecting taxes from the buying and selling of cattle. In addition to generating tax revenue from the industry, the government also monitored slaughterhouse sales aiming to prevent rustling. However, these regulations were spottily applied, and black market sales of meat were widespread.[132] In the 1940s, Estelí rancher Dr. Alejandro Briones denounced the GN's lack of interest in catching the "well-organized group" that had stolen more than thirty head of cattle from his hacienda.[133] By the 1960s, rustling had become "constant and systematic" with perpetrators armed with shotguns and rifles, dressed in khaki and using motor vehicles to ferry away their loot.[134] Details such as the khaki uniforms and armament strongly suggested the direct participation of off-duty Guardias in the crime spree. The Association of Cattle Ranchers of Estelí (Asociación de Ganaderos de Estelí) complained of more than one hundred cows stolen and held meetings with both the mayor and the GN comandante. They emphasized the authorities' unwillingness to act when the thieves figured as members of the politicians' extended families or patronage networks. The Association demanded that "cattle rustlers not be released until they are punished, as some politicians have freed these individuals, thus avoiding punishment for their crime."[135]

During moments of political tension and chaos, the cattle of regime opponents were considered fair game in the eyes of the local GN, which directly or indirectly encouraged their theft. When the president of the ranchers' association, Dr. Alejandro Briones (son of the Dr. Briones mentioned above), wrote to the government in 1972 demanding action against the latest wave of thefts, the GN comandante responded to President Somoza: "The doctor, like the other members of the Association of Cattle Ranchers of Estelí, are inveterate Chamorristas [Conservative Party supporters]—I even have the list of when they held a celebration for Pedro Joaquín Chamorro . . . and, thus, are enemies of Somoza and the National Guard . . . but either way, I am willing to give them support [if ordered to do so]."[136] The GN refused to protect even wealthy landowners who were political "enemies" of the dictator from the disorder and criminality.

In the case of those bandits without the requisite political connections or who dared to steal from powerful Somocistas, however, the National Guard responded with brute force. "I remember they found a band of thieves that went around stealing cows," one former Guardia bragged, "The Guardia didn't take them prisoner; it just killed all of them. This made it so everyone would reflect a thousand times before thinking of stealing."[137] Likewise, in 1971, the local GN comandante in San Juan de Limay allegedly murdered two accused cattle thieves, seizing their "money and other belongings." The family of the deceased demanded an investigation into the deaths and into the whereabouts of the missing cash and the stolen "cattle that had supposedly been recovered."[138]

Making up a further layer of the system of organized rustling were the local butchers (*destazadores*) and tanners, who knowingly processed and sold the cheaper stolen goods. Again, this was an area of the illicit economy in which working-class, female Somocistas played a fundamental role. Engracia J. was a butcher who lost her license for slaughtering rustled livestock after complaints by the ranchers. She wrote to the minister of the interior requesting that her license be immediately restored, given that she "had helped the Nationalist Liberal Party in the elections by voting and distributing campaign propaganda. . . . I am a poor, single Liberal woman with a big family to take care of."[139] Similarly, another woman, Yolanda L., accused of the same crime, wrote indignantly to Somoza himself, explaining that she had "been a faithful collaborator in political campaigns and within the Party, as you can verify with the entire town of Estelí. I am a leader in Santa Cruz and have always moved hundreds of people in favor of yourself and the rest of the Liberal Party." Yolanda not only asked for the right to return to her business ("for the needs of my family which is facing increasing poverty"), but she also took the opportunity to ask "you, our maximum leader and boss . . . for your understanding and human sentiments to help me out in some way—in other words, monetarily."[140] As we saw with brothel owners, she based her claim to impunity before the law on political loyalty and personal participation in electoral mobilization.

Those engaged in the same activity as these women (but with even closer ties to the authorities) did not have their licenses revoked at all. "They don't even mention the truly guilty," Estelí mayor Lilliam Vílchez wrote privately, "those that didn't spend even a single day in jail for being related to people with political influence in this city." Among the culpable, she wrote, was a "Señor E. Molina"—still in business—"in whose tannery stolen animals were butchered in the late hours of the night and from whose jeep they sold the meat of these animals clandestinely."[141] Based on his last name, it is not difficult to imagine to which political boss the tanner was directly related. The female mayor who made this accusation was unceremoniously thrown from office by the department's elite families and chased from Estelí by the GN.

## CONCLUSION

The Somoza regime's decades of rule witnessed an upsurge of export agriculture, vast projects of economic modernization, and significant social transformations. In the Segovias, the commercial and agricultural boom centered on Estelí dramatically upended local life. This sparkling chimera of progress and modernization came at a substantial cost, though, as ballooning inequality exacerbated class tensions and social instability. With landowning political bosses capturing much of the post–World War II export boom, the gap between themselves and average Nicaraguan families grew ever larger. Corruption and impunity before the law were not incidental aspects of everyday life, but the very beating heart of the social order (or disorder), and the Somoza family and its millionaire business associates were its most spectacular beneficiaries. The regime's longevity was the result of its ability to weave dense webs of rewards, privilege, and punishment from the national to the family level. To secure the consent of those social classes left out of the economic bonanza, the Somoza regime countenanced a vast array of illegal activities by its grassroots agents.

By embracing popular notions of male sociability and commercialized vice, Somocismo sought neither to police nor reform peasant and working-class masculinity but to co-opt these aspects of everyday life to serve its political purposes. Men dominated the political order at all levels, but women also became integrated into these webs of corruption (though to a lesser extent) as politicians and cantina caciques. Despite the regime's rhetorical claim to have restored "peace" and "stability" to Nicaragua, through its very permissiveness, the GN fanned the flames of quotidian violence, social disorder, and crime. Cantinas, brothels, and gambling halls proliferated in cities and villages alike, while Nicaragua's homicide and alcoholism rates spiked ever upward. These developments increasingly jeopardized the familial harmony of poor and working-class Nicaraguans. As we will see in the coming chapters, this atmosphere of illicit behavior and social chaos soon became a key target of regime opponents, who sought to uproot the very structures that had made Somoza government so durable. The inchoate popular opposition would project their vision for moral regeneration onto the Sandinistas, which they came to define as the antithesis of all that Somocismo embodied.

# CHAPTER TWO

# BURNING DOWN THE BROTHELS

Moral Regeneration and the
Emergence of Sandinismo, 1956–1970

It was just after six in the evening on Good Friday 1965 when the flames began tearing through Estelí. While the local fire department was busy assisting with the religious procession of the Holy Burial, a loud blast echoed through the city. One blaze engulfed the home of political boss René Molina and, in the melee that followed, thousands of dollars' worth of jewelry allegedly disappeared from the house. For anyone who thought the fire had been accidental, other explosions soon went off across the town, and the smell of diesel hung heavy in the air. Though Guardias, armed reservists, and secret police agents flooded into Estelí, the arson continued unabated. Over the coming nights, gambling dens, cantinas, brothels, and the opulent homes of the city's influential families and GN officers accused of corruption, continued to go up in flames. The attacks did not seriously injure anyone—their sole aim was to raze the property of the city's agents of corruption and vice.[1]

The arson that occurred throughout the week followed a definite pattern, targeting what many perceived as morally deviant enterprises linked to the Somoza dictatorship. The fires also cast a bright light on the hypocrisy and false morality of the Catholic Church, as seen during religious holidays, such as patron saint celebrations and Holy Week (*Semana Santa*), which were entwined with alcohol-infused revelry in practice. Some conservative Christians whispered that the fires sought

to extinguish the sinful depravity of this modern-day Sodom and Go-
morrah; this twentieth-century Babylon, "mother of all prostitutes and
obscenities in the world" (Rev. 17:5). Regional politicians and large
landowners, instead, quickly fingered the perpetrators of the arson as
"communist" activists who had built labor unions in the city in recent
years. Trade unionists, for their part, responded that the fires were actually a plot by regional elites hoping to justify a crackdown against
organized labor. In the weeks and months ahead, the Guardia arrested,
jailed, and tortured Estelí's top activists, and the labor movement was
left decimated. To this day, there are still conflicting accounts as to who
was responsible for the property destruction of that sweltering Holy
Week in 1965.

This event—so charged with political and religious connotations—
proves highly revealing to our understanding of the emergence of the
Sandinista National Liberation Front (FSLN). Still veiled in mystery
even decades later, it helps explain how the people of the Segovias came
to reject the conditions they were forced to endure under the Somoza
regime and then projected their vision of "the good society" onto the
Sandinistas. I argue that the FSLN garnered force in the rural north
precisely through its attempts to purge Nicaragua of growing moral
decay and societal breakdown. Nationalism and anti-imperialism may
have driven FSLN leaders and cadres, but on the grassroots level in the
Segovias, revolutionary sentiment drew strength through its calls for
moral regeneration and a break with the gaping economic inequality
and widespread masculine vice fostered by the regime. To many, the
brothels, cantinas, and gambling halls set aflame represented the deca-
dence that had damaged the male breadwinner, fostered absentee fatherhood and quotidian violence, and torn at the fabric of working-class
families. Rebels launched numerous unsuccessful armed movements
against the regime from the late 1950s, but Carlos Fonseca's FSLN
uniquely linked the anti-Somoza cause with a political program attuned to these grassroots anxieties. The Sandinistas' radical politics
took this conservative critique of vice to its ultimate conclusion, moving
beyond moralistic pieties and paternalism, and calling for social transformation through militant armed insurgency.

Numerous critics of the Sandinistas have agreed with David Nolan
that "objectively, the Sandinismo of the FSLN . . . was never a lower-
class phenomenon" and instead found its only base of support among

middle- and upper-class youth.[2] But, in fact, in the Segovias the FSLN clearly emerged as a "lower-class phenomenon," spearheaded by impoverished artisan workers and rural wage laborers in the workshops and farming zones adjacent to the growing towns. Although slighted in previous accounts of the Sandinistas' origins, these working-class activists helped to initiate the guerrilla effort in the north, which only later drew lower- and middle-class high school students into its orbit. These young people, the second generation of FSLN activists at the regional level, were galled by the social inequalities and corruption of Somocista Nicaragua. Many student activists were drawn to the revolutionary vision of the "New Man," as a new model of masculinity, purified of vice and self-sacrificing for the cause of the downtrodden and marginalized. Rather than seeking to burn down Babylon to liberate working-class men from vice, some young men among this new generation foregrounded the exploitation of sex workers by Somocismo. These revolutionaries grasped for alternative revolutionary models of manhood, including Augusto César Sandino, Ernesto "Che" Guevara, and Pavel, the lead character in Maxim Gorky's 1906 novel *The Mother.* Though the National Guard brutally attacked all those identified with the FSLN, the spark of popular indignation could not be swiftly contained once unleashed, much like the fires that consumed Estelí.

### RED-AND-BLACK: GUERRILLA WARFARE AND THE ORIGINS OF THE FSLN

On March 25, 1958, Estelí awoke to find a red-and-black flag draped from the town's cathedral, placed during the night by an unknown person. It was described by observers as a "Castro flag," but locals well knew that the very same colors had flown decades earlier in the Segovias as the herald of Augusto César Sandino's rebel army.[3] Since December 1956, many in Nicaragua had been following news from Cuba, where a guerrilla army led by Fidel Castro had been battling it out with the military of Fulgencio Batista, the corrupt dictator who controlled the island with U.S. backing. As occurred across Latin America, the Cuban example breathed new life and a sense of urgency into oppositional politics in Nicaragua. Government opponents saw parallels between Batista's regime and that of the Somozas and Castro's 26th of

July Movement as an example to replicate. With the victory of the Cuban Revolution in January 1959, ever greater numbers of idealistic Nicaraguan youths were willing to take up arms against the state.

Following the September 1956 assassination of Gen. Anastasio Somoza García and the assumption of power by the dictator's sons, the country had entered an era of acute political instability. With Luis Somoza Debayle named president after yet another fraudulent election, members of the opposition began trying to topple the government with small-scale invasions from neighboring countries. Almost every month brought tales of new plots by armed anti-Somocistas. Many of these military incursions took place across the border from Honduras into the mountains of the Segovias, Sandino's former stomping ground. These makeshift armies brought together varied coalitions of Independent Liberals, Conservatives, leftists, and even some aging former Sandinistas from the 1930s. In September 1958, Ramón Raudales, a white-haired, elderly onetime officer in Sandino's army, led an invasion attempt from Honduras that was quickly crushed by the GN after crossing into the country.[4] Several of Raudales's followers later formed a group called the Sandino Revolutionary Front (Frente Revolucionario Sandino), which again attempted to carry out similar actions in the Segovias, but to no avail. The triumph of Castro's guerrilla army in Cuba in January 1959 only gave further impetus to the armed movements. In July of that year, another group of oppositionists, planning an invasion in El Chaparral in Honduras, was ambushed by the Nicaraguan and Honduran militaries.[5] In September, yet another armed expedition from Honduras, led by anti-Somocista journalist Manuel Díaz y Sotelo, was severely repressed by the GN and the jueces de mesta near Pueblo Nuevo in rural Estelí.[6]

In each of these short-lived efforts, the armed men found little popular support and the GN quickly squelched their rebellions. Despite their hopes to resurrect Sandino's struggle, the Somoza regime had penetrated down to the town and village level. Time after time, local campesinos immediately denounced the rebels to the GN. When Colonel Santos López, who had fought alongside Sandino in his youth, arrived in Estelí in early 1958 seeking support, the secret police tracked his every movement. According to reports from the GN's Office of National Security (Oficina de Seguridad Nacional, OSN), López trav-

eled to La Trinidad and "invited all of the men to participate in a revolution against the government of Nicaragua, saying that the arms had
already arrived from Honduras by truck and mule."[7] In Somoto, the
secret police learned, he held clandestine meetings at the hacienda San
Luis, whose aged foreman was also a former member of Sandino's
army.[8] These armed groups were, however, unsuccessful in garnering
support from the local population, partly because of their circum-
scribed social origins. In the Segovias, the few locals who did participate in these movements were from Estelí's city center, rather than the
working-class shanties or the rural hinterland. They were, as Salvador
Loza Talavera put it, "people from the so-called middle class or the
wealthy class. Many of them were professionals and generals, and they
were organized in the traditional political parties."[9] Despite Loza's interest in joining these armed uprisings, as an urban worker of campesino background he was an outsider to the social circles of the city's
prominent families. These armed movements and their support base
were almost solely male affairs. Unlike the Cuban insurrectionary
war, as analyzed by Lorraine Bayard de Volo and Michelle Chase, the
Nicaraguan invasions of the 1950s (and even the early Sandinista efforts
of the 1960s) rarely included women in noncombat roles.[10] For the
movement to attract greater numbers of adherents, it would need to
take a far more inclusive approach in terms of both gender and social class.

   The Nicaraguan Patriotic Youth (Juventud Patriótica Nicaragüense, JPN) was another organization founded in the heady period
after the triumph of the Cuban Revolution. According to the Somoza
government, the group was financed and directed by the recently appointed Cuban ambassador to Managua.[11] The JPN held its first provincial meetings in July 1960, with its local representative, Armindo
Valenzuela, putting a call out to all the young people "of Estelí without
distinguishing political party, sex or class, etc."[12] Many of those who
joined the JPN were male scions of the traditional opposition families
who had tired of their elders' willingness to participate in the dictatorship's farcical elections. With the wave of armed invasions as his pretext, Luis Somoza quickly struck against the youth group. Only a
month after its founding, the National Guard sprung into action,
arresting all of the JPN's members in Estelí and other cities.[13] JPN

activists went on to play leading roles in other organizations, but the heavy-handed crackdown left the organization defunct in Estelí by the end of the year.

Amidst the increased repression, Estelí began to witness its first mysterious acts of violent sabotage of the sort that would become a defining feature of the social and political struggle. On August 31, a makeshift bomb exploded outside the home of Salomón Gómez, the Somocista mayor, destroying his door and shattering his neighbors' windows. No one was hurt, but the explosion was said to have shocked the "tranquil city" and "its peaceful inhabitants."[14] The local GN co-mandante, writing to Somoza, blamed the blast on a leftist "exiled various times from the country for his radical ideas and [trained] at Patrice Lumumba University in Moscow."[15] Despite such accusations, suspicious information complicated these claims. The bomb, it was al-leged, had been assembled in the workshop of Sen. José María Briones and placed on the mayor's doorstep by a campesino who worked for another member of the local elite.[16] The closeness of these prominent landowners to the event led some to believe that the government was merely using the explosion as a "false flag" pretext to "impede all or-ganizing activity among parties and opposition groups."[17]

The FSLN was the longest-lasting political group that emerged out of this period of political effervescence. The FSLN's founders had been young militants in the small Nicaraguan Socialist Party (Partido Social-ista Nicaragüense, PSN), established in 1944. The Marxist-Leninist PSN, like other pro-Moscow communist parties in Latin America at the time, had taken a moderate position when it came to social revo-lution, supporting electoral politics and opposing guerrilla warfare as "adventurism."[18] Along with other young people, some PSN activists saw the Cuban Revolution as a clear model of how to topple a well-armed, U.S.-backed dictatorship, and carry out radical change. PSN's go-slow approach now seemed hopelessly outdated and ineffective compared to the courageous actions of Castro and his celebrated Ar-gentine colleague Ernesto "Che" Guevara.[19]

The leading voice for armed struggle in Nicaragua was Carlos Fon-seca Amador, a Marxist university student and young PSN and JPN member from Matagalpa. After being seriously wounded in the 1959 El Chaparral attack, Fonseca argued that these earlier invasion attempts had failed because of a lack of internal support for the exile-based movements.[20] Fonseca, inspired by Castro and Che, insisted that guerrillas needed to link their armed struggle to a program of far-reaching transformation that would benefit the country's poor majority. In its statutes, Fonseca's New Nicaragua Movement (Movimiento Nueva Nicaragua, MNN) called for "a true revolution" to bring about "material and spiritual progress" and "to end the tremendous misery and suffering of the people and the criminal wastefulness of the oligarchy."[21] Based across the border in Honduras, the MNN established its third clandestine cell (after Managua and the university city of León) in Estelí. Using mimeograph machines, the MNN printed numerous documents propagandizing Cuban accomplishments, such as land reform for peasants, higher wages for workers, and free public health care and education for all. "This literature spread a great deal at the regional level, especially in Estelí," Fonseca later reflected. "We have to take into account that Estelí was an intermediate point between the capital and the border. So, often these materials stayed some time in Estelí and never arrived in Managua but spread in Estelí itself. We have to consider the role that the diffusion of these materials played, especially in the general unrest in this zone."[22] Estelí's emerging labor movement would prove particularly receptive to the vision of "material and spiritual progress" described in these pamphlets.

Fonseca and his associates later formed the National Liberation Front (Frente de Liberación Nacional, FLN) and, after a time, added an additional letter to the acronym in tribute to Sandino (FSLN).[23] The organization was referred to as a "front" because it aimed to bring together various opposition factions into a united coalition, including the few remaining original Sandinistas from the 1930s, militant trade unionists, and young activists from various organizations.[24] Interestingly, the decision to assume the mantle of Sandinismo was controversial at the time. Some members felt that using his name would exclude all those unconnected with the earlier movement. Others, however, complained that Sandino—neither a Marxist nor a socialist—had ignored the need for class struggle against Nicaraguan elites in his war against U.S. occupation. Indeed, Sandino had constantly emphasized that his effort was based purely on nationalism and that social revolution and land reform were not high on his agenda.[25]

Fonseca, on the other hand, cast Sandino as not only a Nicaraguan patriot who fought against foreign occupation, but also a "proletarian guerrilla" who epitomized masculine virtue and selflessness.[26] This claim meshed with ideas then in vogue on the Latin American Left in the wake of the Cuban Revolution. In his essay *Socialism and the New Man in Cuba*, Che Guevara had posited that the aim of revolution was not merely economic redistribution but the fashioning of a new consciousness freed from the personal corruption and greed of capitalist society.[27] Unlike the Somozas, Fonseca claimed, Sandino had eschewed corruption and held his followers to an exacting ethical standard, opposing vices such as alcohol and teaching his peasant troops to read. "In his personal conduct," Fonseca wrote, "he had an air of sobriety. On one occasion when he was offered a shot of liquor to make a toast, he refused, saying: 'The clear water of the mountain is the only thing that I have drank in these last few years.'"[28] Even Pedro Joaquín Chamorro, the Conservative editor of *La Prensa* and an opponent of the Left, embraced this image of Sandino, writing in 1965, "It would be enough to note that he prohibited guaro in the territory controlled by his forces to conclude that there was something exceptional about him that contrasts completely with those in the [Somoza] government, who are the enemies of literacy, the greatest promoters of guaro, and the protectors of all of the vices."[29] Chamorro's recognition of Sandino's antivice crusade among his peasant and working-class soldiers demonstrates the conservative appeal of such a message. However, that is as far as Conservatives were willing to go in their denunciation of the regime's seedier underbelly. Over time, the Sandinistas took this moralizing critique of state-sanctioned vice to its ultimate conclusion, linking it to their militant insurgency.

At the same time, the FSLN saw Sandino's rebellion as a model of guerrilla warfare.[30] Aiming to learn from those earlier experiences, Fonseca made contact with surviving former combatants from Sandino's army in both Nicaragua and Honduras. Particularly noteworthy was Santos López, who was exiled in Cuba and now headed back to the mountains of the Segovias to teach the young men the basics of guerrilla tactics.[31] Combining the examples of both Sandino and Che, the FSLN aimed to forge a rebel army in alliance with the campesinos not only to force Somoza from power but also to carry out a socialist revo-

lution.[32] In his study of the earlier struggles, Fonseca found that Sandino's army (as with Castro's in Cuba) had won over the support of
the civilian population through its methods of warfare. As Michael
Schroeder explains, Sandino often used brutal tactics against opponents, but he aimed to fight the war as a "moral revolution as much as
a political and social one; . . . strict moral codes against rape, for instance, sharply distinguished Sandinista violence" from the National
Guard.[33] Che Guevara likewise agreed that "a fundamental part of
guerrilla tactics is the treatment accorded to the people of the zone."[34]
He insisted that revolutionaries "demonstrate effectively, with deeds,
the moral superiority of the guerrilla fighter over the oppressing soldier" by banning alcohol and gambling among fighters and providing
just treatment to captured enemies.[35]

During the 1960s and 70s, the FSLN established numerous guerrilla bases, or *focos*, in isolated regions in the country's northeast (such
as Bocay and Río Coco, Pancasán, Waslala, and Zinica). Estelí came to
play a major role in these new efforts. Not only did it serve as an intermediary point between the capital and the Honduran border, but it
also functioned as a jumping-off point for guerrillas' efforts in the
mountainous north. With Che and Sandino in mind, Fonseca privileged
military organizing in rural areas over the towns, believing that Nicaragua's revolutionary tradition was "more alive in the countryside and
the mountains than in the city. . . . Sandino is a thing of the past in the
city. In the countryside, and above all the mountain, Sandino is — to a
large extent — of the present."[36] As time went on, however, Fonseca
came to understand that a successful guerrilla movement could not
merely base itself on the furtive remnants of that earlier nationalist
struggle. Instead, the FSLN learned to embrace the needs and concerns
of the Segovian present to garner widespread support in the north.

## SANDINISMO, LABOR UNIONS, AND NEIGHBORHOOD ORGANIZING

Despite the FSLN's orientation toward rural warfare, Estelí's nascent
artisan trade unions were the first to embrace the incipient revolutionary movement. With Somoza García's promulgation of the Labor

Code in 1945, workers gained the right to organize labor unions (*sindi-catos*). Unions not aligned with the government, however, faced constant harassment by the GN at the behest of the bosses. In the period after the assassination of Somoza García, Estelí's workers led a new wave of labor organizing. As artisans, their conception of "workers" at times included both hired craftsmen and workshop owner-operator employers sympathetic to their cause.[37] The town's shoemakers (*zapateros*), a trade with a long history of combative politics, led unionization efforts in the early 1960s. At that time, there were around thirty shoe workshops in Estelí, using local leather to produce large amounts of basic footwear for use by campesinos on nearby coffee plantations. In 1960, the young zapateros Adrián Gutiérrez, Filemón Rivera, Fausto Garcia, and Froylán Cruz founded the Shoemakers' Union of Estelí (Sindicato de Zapateros de Estelí). These young men lived in the muddy and oft-flooded shantytowns that had sprung up alongside the river on the town's western edge. Many of them came from rural families, had worked on the haciendas as children, and only attended elementary school as teenagers at a recently formed night school. After a conflict with the principal, however, the group was kicked out of the school and found work at El Zapatón, a shoe workshop that proved an amenable locale for union organizing. Its owner, Ramón Altamirano, was himself an active member of the anti-Somocista PLI and had even taken up arms in Raudales's failed invasion attempt two years earlier.[38]

Guiding the workers' political education was Altamirano's friend, Dr. Alejandro Dávila Bolaños, a medical doctor from Masaya who had moved north years earlier.[39] Dávila Bolaños gained a national reputation for his research into indigenous mythology, language, and medicine, and was well loved by Estelí's campesinos for providing free medical treatment.[40] Though briefly the president of the PLI in Estelí in the 1950s, Dávila Bolaños with his recognizable hat and glasses was also a Marxist and longtime member of the PSN. As the city's leading public oppositionist, he was routinely tossed in jail by the National Guard at the slightest sign of political turmoil or instability anywhere in the country.[41] He, along with the shoemakers, became part of the first concerted effort to articulate a radical critique of the social inequality that beset Estelí.

With up to twenty men seated alongside one another pounding the shoes together, the workshops became hotspots for political conversation. Dávila Bolaños assisted by giving lectures on a range of historical topics. With a piece of chalk and a blackboard, a student recalled, he taught the zapateros about "the class struggle in a nice and simple way. He explained to them that the history of Nicaragua since the beginning of the Spanish colony has always involved the oppressors above—the owners of the wealth—and the oppressed always below, accepting the yoke, as was happening in the Somoza dictatorship in present times."[42] He taught them about those men he considered "the great liberators of Latin America": Simón Bolívar, José Martí, and Augusto César Sandino.[43] Another of the doctor's protégés, trade unionist Dámaso Picado, recalled lessons on "Marxism, but they were clandestine because you couldn't speak publicly about such things. He taught us world history, European history, the parties that existed in Europe during the time of Marx, the nineteenth century, and in the United States—which was very interesting—the first of May of 1886. We had a great leader. He was a man that helped in all senses. We saw he was a real leader with heart. A real leader is one who feels the pain of the worker. And he wasn't a worker, he was a doctor."[44] Dávila Bolaños's importance is reflected in the high esteem in which he was held by his former students even decades later.

One of Dávila Bolaños's primary teaching tools was Maxim Gorky's 1906 novel *The Mother*, the Russian socialist realist novel about an impoverished working-class family in the years before the Russian Revolution.[45] This work of propaganda told the story of a female factory worker, Pelageya, who suffered years of domestic abuse at the hands of her often absent and drunkard husband before his untimely death in a factory accident. Her teenaged son, Pavel, begins working at the factory to support the family, falling into the same trap of alcoholism and despair as his father. He is soon personally transformed by his interactions with socialist comrades, completely abandoning drink and wholeheartedly embracing the labor movement, the fight for better wages, and the cause of workers' revolution. As Pavel suffers persecution and imprisonment at the hands of the Tsarist government, his initially timorous mother likewise becomes convinced of the cause. She supports her son's radical activism to its ultimate consequences, becoming a class-conscious militant herself. The central event in the novel is a May Day march in which the mother and son participate together and which is violently crushed by the authorities. The half-century-old work of literature from the other side of the world seemed to capture so much of the reality in which the young trade unionists were living in northern Nicaragua: poverty, repression, exploitation, vice, domestic violence, family breakdown, absentee fathers, and struggling mothers, who survived thanks to the financial contributions from their hard-working sons. The novel's promise of moral regeneration and familial unity through self-sacrifice and revolutionary commitment struck a chord inside those who heard Gorky's tale explained aloud in the workshops.

Some of Dávila Bolaños's young followers joined the PSN's youth wing, the Nicaraguan Socialist Youth (Juventud Socialista Nicaragüense, JSN) and campaigned for Republican Mobilization (Movilización Republicana, MR), a legal political front for the PSN.[46] In its electoral efforts, MR called for land reform, workers' rights, neighborhood improvement, and social equality. In the eyes of Estelí's political and economic elite, Dávila Bolaños was considered an evil genius who single-handedly converted once happy workers into violent rebels. Ironically, as a loyal PSN cadre and bookish intellectual, on strategic grounds he strongly opposed the use of armed struggle to overthrow the Somoza regime. Unbeknownst to the doctor, however, a number of his pupils soon made direct contact with clandestine guerrilla organizers from the FSLN.

The shoemakers' union quickly began gaining affiliates. The zapateros demanded higher wages and better conditions in the shoe workshops owned by local Somocista bosses, such as Sen. José María Briones and former diputado Adolfo Urrutia. Incrementally, the movement began bearing fruit as unions exerted pressure on Labor Ministry authorities that usually acquiesced to the patrones. For instance, when shop owner Victor Manuel Ubau fired fifteen workers, refusing to pay back wages, vacation pay, and other social benefits required by law, they publicized his abuses. After dragging Ubau to court, they won their jobs back. The workers announced that if Ubau did not fulfill his obligations, they would go on strike and could "count on the solidarity of all of the workshops in Estelí."[47]

The *sindicalistas* were able to organize more freely during the political opening under Luis Somoza's successor, President René Schick (1963–66), a Liberal politician widely considered a puppet of the Somoza family. During his nominally civilian presidency, the National Guard remained firmly in the hands of Gen. Anastasio Somoza Debayle. Despite this, Nicaragua experienced a modest degree of political liberalization under Schick. These were the years of the Alliance for Progress, developed by the United States in response to the Cuban Revolution, a short-lived effort to promote social programs and democratization to prevent "more Cubas" in the Americas. It did not take long for the United States to return to its traditional role in the region of backing openly military regimes. During this brief opening, the government began implementing the regime's Labor Code in the Segovias. Estelí's trade unionists sprang into action, expanding their efforts beyond the shoe workshops, helping form trade unions for construction workers and truck drivers, and also the Sindicato de Oficios Varios, bringing together various artisan trades. By 1963, there were five officially registered unions in the city, which came together as the Federation of Workers of Estelí (Federación de Trabajadores de Estelí, FTE).[48] The federation affiliated at the national level with the General Labor Confederation-Independent (Confederación General de Trabajo-Independiente, CGT-I), a PSN-led grouping that had broken with the traditional Somocista CGT after a brief period of cooperation.[49]

Public demonstrations and protests often helped the unions display their growing clout during this period. Each first of May, the labor unions organized marches commemorating International Workers' Day, which the National Guard often dissolved with violent force. At one of the sindicalistas' early May Day rallies, shoemaker leader Filemón Rivera and Dávila Bolaños delivered rabble-rousing speeches from the steps of the health clinic next to the central park. In response, the workers followed their speakers' cue, shouting "¡*Viva la clase obrera!*" (Long live the working class!) and "¡*Viva el primero de Mayo!*" Suddenly, the GN and secret police agents rushed the crowd, beating them with gun butts and fists.[50] These fierce attacks on demonstrators, however, further heightened the leaders' reputations as speaking on behalf of the people. Many unionists earned respect in their neighborhoods as brave fighters willing to stand up to the bosses and the Guardia.

The FTE's organizing activities went well beyond the struggle for better wages and working conditions, as labor unionists attempted to forge a new sense of community and personal transformation. They began promoting alternatives for male recreation in the city, which had long revolved around hard drinking and escapades to the brothels and gambling dens of the red-light district. Trade unionists organized a baseball league with teams of different trades (including the zapateros' team, Los Salvajes), turning the popular pastime into a recruitment tool and opportunity for conversation beyond the reach of the employers' ears.[51] The trade unionists also rented a building for the FTE offices, where they hosted parties to raise funds and bring together people of all ages. From their perspective, these sports leagues and festivities were healthy alternatives to the "immoral" male activities that sapped workers' earnings and promoted a stifling apathy among "the proletariat." The red-light district with its plethora of vice and social corruption, they believed, damaged working-class families, siphoning off much-needed funds on payday, keeping fathers outside of their homes, numbing laborers to the pain of their exploitation through escapism, and providing a significant obstacle to lower-class empowerment.[52] Women were still primarily cast as objects of protection rather than fellow protagonists in the project of social transformation.

Aiming to foster community well-being and familial tranquility, the unionists began forming neighborhood improvement groups in marginal barrios. These "defense committees" expanded the sindicalistas' influence beyond the shop floor by calling for public services, accountability for the powerful, and an end to government-fostered moral corruption. As their model, Estelí's activists pointed to recent events in Cuba. They were particularly impressed with how Castro's revolutionary government had quickly closed Mafia-run casinos and banned prostitution in Havana, long infamous as the Caribbean's "tropical sin city" for American tourists. In widely touted episodes, slot machines were smashed in the streets, brothels shuttered, and former prostitutes taught new skills and provided with employment.[53] Trade unionists dreamed of a revolution that would bring an end to the vice and quotidian violence that enveloped the lives of the poor in Somoza's Nicaragua. However, such stories out of Cuba had great appeal even for traditionalists and conservatives, who held no brief for Castro's communism.

Alcohol abuse was rampant in Nicaragua in the early 1960s. Somocista president René Schick, himself a recovering alcoholic, personally promoted Alcoholics Anonymous (Alcohólicos Anónimos, AA) to inspire people to battle their vices through abstinence, parental responsibility, and new models of male sociability.[54] AA chapters spread widely throughout the country beginning in 1964 as the group's success stories multiplied. However, given Schick's utter dependence on Somoza and the Guardia, he proved unwilling to carry out a full frontal attack against state-sponsored production and distribution of guaro. Whatever his personal desire, the country's omnipresent "centers of vice" were largely left untouched under his watch. Local organizations formed with union assistance were less muted in their approach. In 1964, residents of Venecia and Los Placeres — Estelí's red-light district — formed the Committee in Defense of Morality (Comité Pro-Defensa de la Moralidad), publicly criticizing "the constant violations of morality by individuals of lowly conduct, due to the excessive consumption of aguardiente and the numerous brothels and cantinas that have been installed in this area, so that in a sector of barely two blocks, there are 15 of these businesses that on a daily basis witness scandals and acts that conflict with morality."[55] The committee's entirely male membership spoke from a place of wounded working-class masculine honor, complaining that their "wives, daughters, and sisters" were unable to go outside after six in the evening without being harassed by thugs (*maleantes*). Unable to convince the National Guard, the community organization promised to bring their demands to the bishop of Estelí, given the Catholic Church's ostensible role as a protector of traditional morality and family harmony.[56] Even anticlerical PSN members did not depart from culturally dominant Christian concepts of sin in their challenges to the Somocista status quo, using terminology that appealed to the broader population. In these efforts, neighborhood groups pressed a conservative cause into the service of political opposition.

This paternalistic and limited vision, however, continued to cast men in their traditional gender roles as benign patriarchs and protectors of the virtue of female dependents. Their discourse was not that far removed from Conservative newspaper publisher Pedro Joaquín Chamorro, who described Somocismo as "the total inversion of the moral values of Nicaraguan life: prostitutes against mothers, alcohol against civic duty, blackmail against honesty, lowlifes against citizenry."[57] Despite this oppositional rhetoric, a heavy dose of bourgeois moralism infused these efforts, such as the emphasis on prostitution (and by extension, prostitutes) as a threat to the family and motherhood.[58] They showed little concern with the voices and conditions of those women and girls—sometimes young mothers themselves—forced into sex work, whether by traffickers or poverty.

The sindicalistas also denounced the almost total lack of social services in the city's shantytowns and emphasized the obligation to help the poor in their efforts to build stable family homes and orderly communities. In doing so, they emphasized the detrimental effect of wealthy landowners on the social stability of impoverished families. The Committee in Defense of the El Rosario Neighborhood (Comité Pro-Defensa del Barrio El Rosario) was founded by the Labor Federation and residents of that neighborhood, located on the city's periphery on the other side of the Estelí River. The committee wrote an open letter to President Schick appealing for a medical center and an elementary school for the shanty's "300 children who have never entered a classroom." They concluded their letter by denouncing "four big capitalists, who want to evict us from our poor little shacks, just because they don't want to see the misery in which we live. The landowners that are threatening us have properties in the area around the neighborhood." Among those that they claimed were harassing them was prominent Somocista businessman René Molina.[59] Unlike the Defense of Morality Committee, the Defense of El Rosario Committee included both male and female members, and its public statement contained the signature of both Máxima Peralta, the group's female secretary, and Dionisio Mendoza, its secretary-general. The leader was male, but Peralta's powerful prose captured the moral indignation of working-class mothers denied a decent future for their children and the fundamentals of a dignified family life.

Given the labor unions' emphasis on the male breadwinner, they never actively organized the city's female service workers into sindicatos. However, many working women adopted the language of class struggle and social injustice proffered by the activists. The sindicalistas' distribution of the PSN newspaper *Orientación Popular* helped to disseminate their message of workers' rights. The paper, zapatero Dámaso Picado recalled, "sold like hotcakes" (*como pan caliente*) and gained a wide readership, even among female domestic workers. The city's wealthy families were particularly perturbed when their housemaids began demanding their long-denied labor rights.[60] In 1963, Rosalina Valdivia Sánchez, a young hairdresser in Estelí, publicly denounced beauty salon owner Celso Asencio for firing her without warning and not providing back pay. This, she said, was a "social injustice," only possible because the government's labor inspector was firmly "on the side of the *patrones*."[61] To quash the burgeoning movement, the National Guard directed their ire against the labor leadership. In November of the following year, the GN arrested Filemón Rivera and a fellow activist for distributing *Orientación Popular*, which the government termed a "subversive" and "communistic" publication. When fellow zapatero Adrián Gutiérrez arrived at the station to petition for their release, he was allegedly beaten by former Somocista diputado and zapatería workshop owner Adolfo Urrutia in plain view of the GN.[62] It was only under threat of prison or murder, Picado remembered, that the unionists agreed to stop distributing the newspaper.[63] The labor movement faced violent harassment against their legal activism, but all manner of illicit activities by government supporters, including state-sanctioned vice, continued unabated. To many labor activists, the Sandinistas' call for armed struggle appeared ever-more legitimate.

CHANGING THE RULES: CAMPESINO UNIONS AND
RURAL MOBILIZATION

By the 1960s, graffiti began appearing on the once bare walls of the city center, with strange new acronyms spray-painted on buildings: "JPN," "MR," "MNN," and, soon, "FSLN." When student activists in the National University (Universidad Nacional Autónoma de Nicaragua, UNAN) in León began searching out potential guerrilla fighters and civilian backers in Estelí, they found the labor movement sympathetic to their calls. Those unionists who had been arrested and beaten by the GN simply for organizing against the patrones were especially receptive. "The compañeros Filemón and Adrián started to make contacts and connections with people from León," zapatero Salvador Loza Talavera noted. "These people were following us trying to see who we were because they had heard of our history. So they tried to get close and talk to us. They tried to raise our consciousness. In those days, it was hard because you couldn't trust anyone. They couldn't trust us, and we couldn't trust them. But we started getting to know each other in depth."[64] The "people from León"—university militants such as Carlos Fonseca—saw the Segovias with its Sandinista heritage as a potentially fruitful setting for revolutionary struggle. Estelí was to serve as the launch pad for all of their rural activities. Interestingly, the FSLN soon formed a brief alliance with the PSN (from which its leadership had earlier split) in efforts to establish rural unions in the country's north.[65]

With Estelí's economy dominated by low-wage agricultural production, the threat of unionized campesinos struck great fear into the hearts of the hacendados. Indeed, in 1965 more than two-thirds of the department's 71,000 inhabitants lived and worked in the countryside.[66] During his last months in office, Luis Somoza reformed the Labor Code to facilitate the creation of rural unions and introduced the country's first rural minimum wage.[67] Despite this promise, however, far less than 1 percent of all campesinos in Nicaragua joined labor unions in the first year of the law's enforcement.[68] Even though it was legally applicable to all farmworkers, landowners still refused to pay the minimum wage even years after its passage. For the sindicalistas, payment of six córdobas became a rallying cry and the regime's own unenforced law a tool in their hands.

To investigate working and living conditions in the Segovias, the trade unionists' newly formed Rural Union of Estelí (Sindicato Agrario de Estelí) carried out research with the assistance of university students from León. In an unpublished report, they claimed:

> Nicaraguan agriculture has not emerged from feudal relations of production, and all of the campesinos suffer the most brutal exploitation. The northern zone of the country is one of the richest in Nicaragua, and yet, the peasants from this region live in total pauperism, which contrasts with the immense riches of the landlords and traders that dedicate themselves to the productive business of fleecing the peasants. These men only have to figure out how to take away the lands and harvests from the campesinos, adding them to their own, while robbing rural workers of their labor power through the payment of miserable salaries.[69]

They also condemned the use of exploitative practices, such as buying in advance (*adelantado*) and sharecropping (*mediería*), that took advantage of the desperately poor peasant families. In Palacagüina, Madriz, the unionists wrote, landowners paid two and five córdobas in advance for each *arroba* of corn and beans, only to turn around and sell them after the harvest for twenty and forty córdobas, respectively. "Worst of all," the sindicalistas noted, "campesinos only have the opportunity to work two months a year during the coffee harvest for a salary of five córdobas a day." In another village in Pueblo Nuevo, Estelí, the local juez de mesta (considered "the terror of the campesinos") was a member of the progovernment paramilitary AMROCS organization and owned a lucrative gambling den in league with the GN comandante.[70]

The trade unionists also documented the effect of low salaries and prices on the social welfare of campesino families. Many subsisted solely on a diet of beans, tortillas, and "coffee" made from toasted corn. In one hamlet they visited, dysentery and malaria were common, and the nearest health center was located fourteen leagues away. Meanwhile, less than half of the village's fifty school-age children attended classes in the dilapidated schoolhouse.[71] According to the unionists' survey, even in a significant cattle-ranching area such as Estelí, many campesinos were unable to consume beef regularly.[72] Socialist trade union leader Domingo Sánchez Salgado described the situation of rural workers on the haciendas of the north as "depressing," noting that in addition to landlessness, low wages, and poor housing, campesinos were "the victims of alcohol, gamblers, peddlers, ruffians, and prostitutes."[73] Notably, in his telling, prostitutes were once again couched as *aggressors* targeting male campesino breadwinners, rather than fellow victims of exploitation worthy of empathy and solidarity. Such a conservative perspective was quite typical for the era, but younger FSLN members attempted to push beyond such male-centric views. A foreign observer used strikingly similar language to comment on the lack of access to education in rural Nicaragua, noting that "campesinos have to work from sunup to sundown while the children of their exploiters go to the best high schools in the city. They are condemned to ignorance, superstition, and fanaticism, which leads to all forms of social ills, from alcoholism and gambling to prostitution and crime."[74] As they had previously done in the city, sindicalistas linked their immediate demands for better wages to a program of social and moral regeneration.

The guerrilla organizers advised trade unionists to avoid the PSN's dogmatic and abstract rhetoric when reaching out to rural folk. Through their interactions with the peasantry, Carlos Fonseca and other Sandinistas were attuned to the fact that the countryside was a culturally conservative milieu. Rather than use words such as "capitalism," "socialism," "surplus value," "modes of production," and "dialectical materialism," the unionists instead spoke a straightforward language grounded in campesino experiences and sense of fairness. An appeal to morality took precedence over ideological arguments. Zapatero unionist Adrián Gutiérrez recalled:

> Carlos told us . . . . that we're going to change the rules. We're not going to preach philosophical things because that is what the Socialist Party did. They trained you to say mechanical and philosophical things from Marxist theory. So Carlos told us, we're not going to do that, we're going to talk to the people in a simple and clear way, with no theory. We're going to explain, especially to the campesino, how much they got paid and how much goes to the patrón and ask the campesino if that was fair. Ask if he could send his kids to school and who it was that made the landowners into millionaires. Ask the campesinos if they could go to the doctor and explain that the children of the landowners went to study abroad to come back later and keep exploiting the campesinos.[75]

Young workers such as Gutiérrez, born in rural Estelí and familiar with the techniques of labor organizing, met the campesinos on their own terms, foregrounding the most visible social inequalities between Segovian families.

As part of their campaign, the unionists replicated the strategy they had carried out among urban workers, using the Somozas' own patchily enforced labor laws to their advantage. The sindicalistas headed to the countryside on weekends to organize campesinos in rural areas outside of Estelí and Condega. They made inroads, notably where large estates had expanded at the expense of neighboring peasant homesteads, converting family farmers into wage laborers.[76] "In Condega, there was lots of work and lots of injustice," explained Gutiérrez, mentioning that most coffee haciendas still refused to pay the minimum wage. "So we started to penetrate there and advise the people and help with lawyers. We started to fight with lots of consciousness. I told the Frente that we would go and investigate the situation. So we came, made a demand, and when the landowner found out, he fired all of the workers. But when new workers were hired, they had to pay the legal amount."[77]

The activists also cast into stark relief the utter immorality of the hacendados' continued exploitation of vulnerable child labor. During the 1964 May Day demonstration, the unions marched behind Dávila Bolaños along with a mass of children carrying placards calling for "an end to the custom of employing underage people," glaring evidence of the state's failure to protect society's most vulnerable.[78] As the government boasted of new schools, many children continued to work in the countryside, condemning them to a lifetime of illiteracy and abuse at the hands of the hacendados. A few months after the May Day march, a dozen child coffee-pickers—boys between the ages of seven and twelve—filed a complaint at the Labor Court in Estelí against their employer, Filemón Molina, the well-connected owner of the hacienda San Jerónimo in Condega. They demanded the rural minimum wage, as they were only receiving three córdobas for a full eight-hour workday. According to the news report of the incident, the children had walked thirty kilometers from the farm to the city and did not have money to get back to the hacienda or food to eat.[79]

In response to their attempts to assert their rights, campesinos faced a backlash from wealthy landowning families and local officials (often, as we have seen, the same people). A group of union-backed campesinos, for instance, protested when Condega's mayor Romeo González, owner of the coffee hacienda next to San Jerónimo, cut off access to a road through his property. The mayor speedily dashed off a telegram to the local GN office calling the peasants' leader "an enemy of the regime, a declared communist and a disciple of Dávila [Bolaños]."[80] In another letter, the mayor stated that his opponents had "brought the departmental leader of the extremists [Dávila Bolaños] to the hamlet to hand out communist pamphlets and excite their spirits in order to establish a climate of instability."[81] When the government's own labor inspector in Estelí, Carlos Talavera, attempted to apply the Labor Code as written, even he was "accused of being a communist by the hacendados," who allegedly warned him he "could lose his job for attacking the rich (*la parte adinerada*)."[82] As we saw in chapter 1, those who attempted to follow the letter of the law were quickly booted from office by the city's powerful families. At times, populist tactics were also used by the government to stave off the rising tide of rural mobilization in the Segovias. In December 1964, President Schick authorized the government's Agrarian Institute to hand out more than 4,000 manzanas of land to eighty campesino families in San Juan de Limay "so that they can work and no one will bother them."[83]

Given its integration into the status quo and hatred of leftist politics, the Catholic Church also came out very strongly in opposition to organized labor's activities in the countryside. Estelí's first bishop, appointed in 1963, Monseñor Clemente Carranza y López, was a close friend of the town's leading families, who—thanks to their generous donations—reserved the elegant pews nearest to the pulpit for them. He also, it was said, served as a commissioned chaplain-major in the National Guard.[84] Another priest, Monseñor Emilio Santiago Chavarría, hosted a weekly radio show on which he decried the "atheistic communism" creeping into Estelí and the "red infiltration among the peasantry."[85] In a highly religious country town, such an accusation from a respected figure was enough to tarnish the unionists' reputation in the eyes of much of the public.

The National Guard was often called in to suppress their activities and arrest sindicalistas at the behest of the hacendados. In Cofradías in Pueblo Nuevo, for instance, a labor union was established among the workers of Pastor Midence, the local Somocista boss. According to zapatero Filemón Moncada, the GN captured one sindicalista, stripped him of his shoes, and forced him to walk fifty kilometers barefoot back to Estelí. "They told him that if he couldn't walk anymore, they would kill him," Moncada explained. "He was able to make it to the city, where they put him in jail." After six months—the legal limit for detention without charge—he was released and immediately rearrested for another six months, a technique known as *pisa y corre*.[86] By the mid-1960s, simmering tensions between the labor movement (the emerging representative of peasant and working-class families in their demands for a more significant share of the economic boom) and the regional power structure came to a head.

## "To Set All of Nicaragua on Fire": Holy Week 1965

The major turning point in the already fraught relationship between the trade unionists and local elites occurred during Holy Week a few months later. The mysterious rash of arson attacks described in this chapter's opening vignette damaged the homes of diputado René Molina and GN captain Fermín Meneses, two prominent Somocistas widely accused of illegal enrichment. Unknown hands similarly set ablaze the gambling dens, cantinas, and brothels owned by the regime's grassroots agents.[87] Symbolically, the fires seemed to implicate government officials in the spread of vice and corruption. Through their activism, sindicalistas had exposed this link by helping urban and rural workers assert their rights and by organizing "Committees for the Defense of Morality."

The fires gave the GN an excuse to begin an all-out assault against the trade unions. By Easter Sunday, a climate of tension and fear had settled over the city. The National Guard, true to script, immediately arrested Dávila Bolaños, along with a number of the young unionists. On the local radio station, La Voz de las Segovias, a roundtable was organized with Somocista politicians, landowners, and businesspeople, along with the GN comandante and the bishop. These leaders took a highly aggressive and threatening tone, with Francisco Moreno, the owner of the Electric Company of Estelí, declaring that "we have to fight fire with fire" by attacking "the communists with the same weapons."[88]

The unions were quick to respond to accusations that they were behind the attacks, declaring their innocence and blaming the fires instead on a conspiracy orchestrated by the city's leading families. Dámaso Picado, then serving as secretary of culture for the FTE, told the press that the events were "a plot that the landowners have carried out in cahoots with the army and the bishop, to wipe out our groups for the mere fact of demanding better salaries and benefits. These fires are nothing but a plot by these men to create disorder and to provoke the persecution of the workers because what they want to do here in Estelí is something similar to what occurred in Chinandega." [89] Picado referred here to the murder of activists at the hands of the National Guard in the cotton-producing department of Chinandega.[90] He also claimed that the unionists "knew in advance that the landowners were going to unleash a wave of terror to blame the workers because someone present at a meeting held in the church rectory with the military, the landowners, and el Señor Bishop had told us that they had set up a plot involving fires to finish off the workers because they said we were communists."[91]

The bombings reminded the activists of what Dávila Bolaños had taught them of the history of the 1886 Haymarket affair, in which the U.S. government persecuted labor leaders for a bomb thrown at the police during a Chicago rally for the eight-hour workday. Using the explosion as a justification, the courts convicted eight labor leaders on scant evidence and sentenced seven to death by hanging (four of whom were later hanged). To Estelí's sindicalistas, that far-off history of struggle seemed to be repeating itself. According to Dávila Bolaños, the aim of the secret meeting at the bishop's home before the fires had been "to put a price on my life and the lives of others affiliated with MR or who work for the labor unions of the working class and campesinos." Fearing for his safety, he declared that "if anything happens to me," Somocistas such as René Molina and Francisco Moreno would be to blame, given their inflammatory declarations broadcast on the radio.[92]

The political, military, and ecclesiastical authorities accused by Picado and Dávila Bolaños roundly rejected the unionists' allegations. The bishop asserted that the meeting held at his rectory had not been to target the labor unions but rather to "bring together and achieve understanding between workers and employers," while the head of the fire department, Dr. Manuel Munguía, claimed they had met in order "to help the poor."[93] Both statements betray a keen awareness by elites that the city's yawning economic inequality was the primary source of tension. The National Guard, for its part, appeared unable to find those responsible for the arson despite an intense search for the culprits. Reflecting on the incident, the opposition newspaper *La Prensa* asked, "What is happening in Estelí? Why is one house after another burning in this city? Is it true that some right-wing gentlemen, converted into

Neros, burn their own town to place the blame for the fires on innocent members of the extremist parties? Or is it the other way around and, along with terrorist fires, they are lighting the flames of criminal libel? The inversion of values is reaching the point of chaos. . . . We are playing—literally—with fire!"[94]

The origin of this spate of fires remained a contested memory among former unionists. Dámaso Picado maintained decades later that his accusations of a conspiracy had been truthful, but Adrián Gutiérrez, a founder of the zapatero union, claimed that the fires were, in fact, the work of a secret Sandinista "morality squad." According to Gutiérrez, this group aimed to destroy "the scandalous centers of vice owned by the bourgeoisie. . . . They found locales where they played cards, dice, and roulette, which were owned by the government. They investigated them and then set them on fire. The National Guard blamed [Dávila Bolaños], but he didn't know. He was no lover of violence. Later, we learned that terrorism was not with the thinking of the revolution. Because terrorism—Carlos Fonseca said—is reactionary. So this calmed down. If not, they would have had to set all of Nicaragua on fire."[95] For organizers such as Gutiérrez, the regime's corruption, its fostering of vice, and the exploitation of workers formed part of the same web of injustice that gave Somocismo its strength. Such vigilantism may have drawn upon popular notions of morality, but, as Fonseca acknowledged, the fires were conspiratorial actions isolated from the broader population. Not only did the arson put innocent lives at risk, but they also provided a pretext for a witch hunt against the labor movement, truncating its progress in both the workshops and on the haciendas.

Following the Holy Week events, labor organizing became increasingly impossible in Estelí. Filemón Rivera and three other unionists were again thrown in jail in July for merely selling the MR statutes in the park. Though released after just twenty-four hours, Filemón soon got into a fistfight with a member of the National Guard at one of the zapateros' baseball games. In fear of arrest, he decided to go underground, directly joining the guerrillas.[96] Years later, behind bars for participating in FSLN activities and suffering from poor health, Rivera noted that he "first began to work with the campesinos by way of the labor unions," but when the Guardia began accusing him of crimes he "got scared and joined the Frente" for protection. He explained to the reporters: "I only joined the Frente so that we workers and campesinos could earn better wages. I did what I could."[97]

The arrests continued apace, with union founder Adrián Gutiérrez captured in a zapatería workshop and accused of possessing several sticks of dynamite.[98] When a shootout erupted between the National Guard and three individuals "of left-wing tendencies" near the market, yet another wave of captures took place.[99] Though not involved in the clash, the GN again arrested Adrián Gutiérrez. "They started to beat me savagely," he described, with great pain. "They took me to a farm near Mina La India and beat me until I was unconscious. Then they urinated on me. I infuriated them because they asked where Carlos Fonseca was and I answered that I didn't know that *señor*. So they told me, 'He's not a señor, he's a young guy like you.' And I responded, 'To me, Carlos Fonseca is a señor.' So they beat me even more." When he was brought to the prison in León and thrown into a cell for female prisoners, he recalled, "my body was so inflamed from all of the beatings that the women began screaming like crazy."[100]

Gutiérrez claimed he was personally visited in his cell by Anastasio Somoza Debayle—apparently accompanied by a U.S. advisor—to request the shoemaker work as a secret police informant. He says that he swallowed his pride and anger, calmly declining the invitation by explaining that he feared reprisal by Fonseca. After promising to leave labor organizing forever, Gutiérrez said that Somoza told him: "You're going to go free but I'm going to recommend one thing: you need to walk on eggshells (*con pies de plomo*) because if you work against me, you will be back in jail or the hospital . . . or the cemetery."[101] Others captured during this period, Gutiérrez claimed, were more willing to challenge the dictator to his face and, as a result, lost their lives. As his friend Filemón before him, Adrián joined the FSLN guerrillas in the mountains immediately following his release from prison. He saw no alternatives but to seek protection in the FSLN or risk murder at the hands of the Guardia.

The year 1967 marked a crucial point in Nicaragua's historical trajectory. With the ascension of General Somoza Debayle—head of the National Guard—to the presidency, he jettisoned the civilian veneer and liberalization of the Schick interlude and adopted a more openly authoritarian posture. The GN's bloody repression of opposition demonstrators in Managua on January 22, 1967, mentioned in chapter 1, presaged the nature of Somoza Debayle's rule. The sindicalistas attempted to revive the momentum of the early 1960s but had little success. The Drivers' Union (Sindicato de Motoristas) was denied a permit for their annual May Day march, with the explanation that Somoza's inauguration was that very day.[102] Eventually, the workers' demonstration went forward in a context of heightened tension. Union leader Filemón Moncada recalled that the FTE decorated a flatbed truck with an elaborate float depicting the hanging of the 1886 Haymarket martyrs of Chicago, the historical event commemorated by International Workers' Day. The sindicalistas saw a strong parallel between the persecution of their union leaders in the aftermath of the April 1965 fires and that historical episode, which sent prominent American labor activists to the gallows. Moncada described the response, "The Guardia came, and they didn't understand. They asked what were we doing acting like we were going to hang the rich people of Estelí! Because they didn't know the history of labor struggles. So they took the trucks from us. The National Guard stood on the other side of the sidewalk with their guns aimed at us in firing position, and all of us were on the other side together."[103] In the melee that followed, the GN dissolved the crowd by beating several workers with their gun butts. The demonstrators found refuge at the union office where Dávila Bolaños and Moncada gave speeches, while the Guardia patrolled the blocks outside.[104] With legal organizing increasingly impossible under the rule of Somoza Debayle, the appeal of armed struggle grew among local activists.

Between May and August 1967, the FSLN launched a guerrilla campaign in the Pancasán region in the northern mountains of Matagalpa.[105] Among those involved were three former zapatero leaders from Estelí: Filemón Rivera, Froylán Cruz, and Fausto García.[106] Numerous Sandinistas—including García—lost their lives in bloody, one-sided combat against the well-armed GN. The surviving members of the guerrilla columns fled abroad or to Managua safe houses, seeking to reconstitute their support network and recruit new fighters. The zapateros' former mentor Dávila Bolaños was himself arrested in June and again in October, following a trip abroad for allegedly "violating the Constitution" by traveling to Havana and Moscow. While in Cuba, he attended the inaugural meeting of the Organization of Latin American Solidarity (Organización Latinoamericana de Solidaridad, OLAS) held under a massive image of the recently murdered Che Guevara and featuring numerous speeches in favor of armed struggle. Upon his return to Nicaragua, he only secured his release following hunger strikes by both him and his wife, Mercedes.[107] It was clear that the margins for above ground political action had now been severely limited.

### "To Live Like the Saints": High School Students and a New Masculinity

With the union leadership decimated, the clandestine Sandinista cadres now responsible for organizing in Estelí—Enrique Lorente and José Benito Escobar—directed their attention after 1967 to high school students. Estelí's school system had expanded rapidly over the previous decade, and by 1969 the city had more than 15,000 children and young adults attending primary and secondary schools, both public and parochial. These enrollment figures gave Estelí the second largest student population in the country after the capital Managua.[108] This delayed entrance into adulthood and paid employment for many young people, allowing for a new sort of youth culture to form among high school students. Recognizing the importance of this growing social group, the FSLN established the High School Student Federation (Federación de Estudiantes de Secundaria, FES) as an extension of the Sandinista university student movement based in León, known as the Revolutionary Student Front (Frente Estudiantil Revolucionario, FER). "Given their youth," Carlos Fonseca wrote during this period, students were still relatively free of the "vices engendered by corrupted capitalist society."[109] Fonseca believed that by taking up arms and heading to the mountains, urban youth could be morally purified and "proletarianized."[110]

FSLN organizers capitalized on the student strikes already underway in Estelí high schools since the early 1960s, pushing them in an increasingly radical direction. As one former student activist recalled:

The high school students' demands were mostly things like to get rid of a teacher, to offer better food in the dormitories, or to change the math teacher. Things like that. They were not political demands, but instead student demands disconnected from the realities of most of the population. When the student movement started to carry out strikes and occupations, the students started gaining a more direct vision of what the Frente Sandinista was. We started to realize that the student demands had an origin: that the compañeros that were members of the Frente were, through the student leaders, beginning to organize us . . . to give a more political character to the student struggles.[111]

Just as the city's labor movement itself began independently of FSLN influence, student activism likewise emerged in a somewhat spontaneous manner, but gradually became more strategic and militant.

Each year on July 23, students across the country commemorated the 1959 deaths of four university students shot by the GN during a demonstration in León.[112] These annual mass meetings played a similar role in the development of the student movement to what May Day marches had done for the labor movement. In Estelí, high school students attended memorial masses at the cathedral and staged symbolic burials in memory of the fallen young men. The authorities often attempted to deter these acts of protest. In 1964, for instance, the Guardia surrounded the marching students, giving them five minutes to disperse and return to their homes. If they did not comply, GN officer Franklin Montenegro allegedly threatened that "the same thing will happen as five years ago in León." It took the mediation of the bishop to assure that the students would be allowed to leave unharmed and continue their memorial inside the Instituto San Francisco.[113]

By 1968, a year of youth upheaval around the globe, student mobilization had reached a significant scale, surpassing that of labor unions, who now found themselves severely repressed. In May, for instance, 1,000 students—male and female—went on strike to protest the replacement of the high school's beloved founder, Padre Francisco "Chico" Luis Espinoza, with a more pliant Somocista director.[114] Additionally, when the student leaders later solicited a permit to march in memory of the 1959 massacre, the jefe político denied the request.

José Indalecio Rodríguez explained in a patronizing tone that such a march "would be taken advantage of by elements opposed to the National Government and at the same time by . . . leftist elements that want to use this day for their own benefit (*para llevar agua a su molino*)."[115] Following the memorial mass held that day, the GN arrested numerous young men and women "day and night" over the following weeks.[116] For many Estelian families, the arrests of their teenaged sons and daughters contributed to a growing current of anger against the government.

Many of the new generation of student Sandinistas were middle-class youths with a modicum of privilege and social mobility, and yet felt they could not live comfortably in a morally debased and unequal society. Though empathetic, deep thinkers and not stereotypically "macho" young men, they were driven by a sense of male duty to act on behalf of others. These were the select few who joined the guerrilla army during the years when it promised almost sure death. One of the FSLN's main student contacts in Estelí during this period was Leonel Rugama, a nationally recognized poet even at his young age. Rugama's mother was a schoolteacher, who was related to the city's prominent Briones family, and his father a carpenter she had met while teaching in a rural village outside of Estelí. Leonel was noted for his sharp intelligence, graduating at the top of his class, and he had published poetry both nationally and abroad.[117] He wore thick glasses for his myopia and was often spotted playing chess with friends. Commenting on his poetry, Carlos Fonseca later wrote that Leonel's "creative achievement is best measured by noting that he came from a working-class family from Estelí, a predominantly rural Nicaraguan region, in which only a tiny number of young people reach the sixth grade."[118]

Relatives recalled that from a young age, Leonel had been disturbed by the living conditions in his father's village.[119] He had initially joined the seminary with plans of becoming a priest, but Rugama tired of the hypocrisy and corruption he witnessed in the Church, including a Somocista priest who ran a brothel with government approval.[120] This cross-pollination between corrupt religious authorities, sexual exploitation, and government malfeasance was the other side of Nicaraguan Catholicism that Leonel knew well from Estelí. Friends believed that the asceticism he embraced in the seminary predisposed Rugama to many of the ideals of self-sacrifice of the revolutionary movement.

The poet returned to Estelí and, given his academic acumen, he also taught mathematics to younger students while completing his high school diploma. Under an assumed name, he registered at UNAN in León in 1969 and continued his organizing activities as part of the FER and the FSLN.

Although—as with other young men his age—he regularly frequented Estelí's red-light district, friends noted that Leonel was distressed by the regime's blatant promotion of sex trafficking and prostitution. Friends recall that he rarely touched a drop of aguardiente and spent much of his time chatting up the women and asking about their lives. Many of these penniless campesinas had been promised jobs as domestic workers in the city only to find themselves entrapped in sex work upon arriving in Estelí. Others had been booted from their homes by their parents for getting pregnant at a young age. His friend Donaldo Altamirano emphasized that Leonel expressed a great appreciation and personal warmth toward "the beggars, the prostitutes, the drunks, all of those who were at the bottom of the social scale from a moral perspective . . . . [He felt] a profound human acceptance of these people; despite all of the prejudices that you could have against those usually defined as morally degraded, they had real value [and] that the supposed degradation of these people was a superficial and false judgment. Despite the undignified occupation that they were forced to perform, they were people with value as human beings."[121] Leonel's vision was doubtlessly linked to the biblical narratives of Jesus as a defender of the oppressed that he heard at the seminary. In political terms, his view marked a significant shift from both Conservative and leftist discourse of the early 1960s with their emphasis on the male breadwinner and the effect of brothels and cantinas upon the moral standing of working-class families. Rejecting the moralistic judgments of "upstanding citizens" and duplicitous Catholic discourse about the "morally degraded" women, Rugama's empathy extended beyond his own family unit and social circle.

Over time, what he witnessed and learned from the women in the brothels of Estelí's red-light district became a virtual obsession for Leonel. He placed their circumstances at the very center of his political action, as the clearest example of the need to uproot Somocismo. Fellow Sandinista Doris Tijerino Haslam, one of the first young women to join the FSLN's armed struggle, recalled: "We spoke a lot about women. He was greatly bothered by the situation of the prostitutes. . . . He felt responsible for their problems as a human being. He spoke a lot about them; a lot. He was pained by their situation; it really bothered him. He didn't reject them because of their condition; rather, he felt a great deal of understanding for their situation."[122] For Leonel, the essence of radical politics was the hope it held out for moral regeneration and the uplift of the exploited and marginalized. Rather than scapegoating the sex workers themselves for the ills of society, as some earlier dissidents had done, Rugama understood the broader system of subjugation under the Somoza regime as responsible for their oppression. Prostitution had turned the very bodies of young women and teenaged girls into commodities. Only a socialist revolution, he felt, could genuinely liberate women from this treatment.

Armed revolution quickly replaced religion in Rugama's worldview, as he consciously upended the masculine expectations of his surrounding environment. Rather than imitate the male behavior of older generations, identified with vice, interpersonal violence, and absentee fatherhood, FER youths sought alternative forms of manhood. Rugama soon became a fervent admirer of guerrilla fighter Che Guevara, teaching his FSLN recruits to "be like Che" and that it was a "man's duty to raise up others out of poverty and exploitation and to rise to a higher level on the revolutionary scale."[123] Rugama often spoke of Guevara's concept of the "New Man," and the claim that revolution meant bringing about a transformation of values, both personal and societal. For Rugama and other young men of his generation, this paralleled what he had learned from the Catholic Church he now saw as hypocritical. "Now We Are Going to Live Like the Saints" (*Ahora vamos a vivir como los santos*), Rugama entitled one of his poems, which spoke to the downtrodden, emphasizing the totalizing sacrifice, puritanical moral rectitude, and selfless commitment expected of guerrilla fighters.[124] Rugama's example showcases what Luisa María Dietrich Ortega has argued regarding the multiple expressions of militarized masculinity among the Latin American Left, which included "repertoires of tenderness."[125] Rugama's empathetic vision restored humanity to sex workers and others disparaged by traditional morality and societal judgment. At the same time, his conception of political agency remained overwhelmingly defined by individual acts of male solidarity— "a man's duty"—toward the downtrodden. As Rosario Montoya argues, the Sandinista "figure of the New Man" remained a highly gendered and patriarchal construct: "a proper family man, free of vices and excesses such as drinking and womanizing."[126]

Unlike the working-class trade unionists who had led the first wave of activism in Estelí, student revolutionaries were often from more established families in the town center, rather than the shanty-towns on the periphery. Another young student from Estelí who followed Rugama into the FSLN underground and would become a prominent revolutionary in his own right was eighteen-year-old Igor Úbeda. Though related through marriage to Sen. José María Briones, the Úbedas were certainly not wealthy, but they had a more comfortable existence than the town's impoverished masses. For instance, though Igor was still in high school, he already owned a stylish black Triumph motorcycle, a purchase beyond the reach of younger workers even after they had won wage concessions from the workshop owners. This class difference also manifested itself in the student activists' preference for soccer (a sport at which both Rugama and Úbeda excelled) rather than baseball, the organizing tool of the working-class trade unionists from the shanties.[127] Despite his access to the social advantages and trappings that many newly minted "middle-class" Estelianos wore with excessive pride and disdain for their social "inferiors," Igor remained "very humble, very country-like (acampesinado)," his mother, Isidora Herrera de Úbeda, recalled. "Even though he studied here in the city, rather than having only friends in the city, he liked to make friends with kids from the countryside (campo)."[128] Like Rugama, Igor had one foot in the social mobility promised by higher education and another in the vast rural hinterland of poverty and destitution that lay just beyond the confines of the schoolhouse and the walls of his family household.

Whereas the trade unionists saw themselves as fighting for the social well-being of their immediate families and impoverished communities, the new generation of student revolutionaries conceptualized their struggle as one waged *on behalf of* the marginalized from a position of relative privilege. In 1968, Rugama penned a prize-winning essay, "The Student and the Revolution," in which he remarked that students "despite their theoretical vision of the situation, have a restricted knowledge of it. Because of this, it is necessary to live for a time among the oppressed class and thus learn of its problems."[129] He wrote that if the struggle "requires that we give our lives, we will give them without hoping that we be mentioned by future generations. But let us assure that our bones will be the columns of that future."[130] Shortly after his attempts to obtain a scholarship to study abroad in Germany proved unsuccessful, Rugama vanished from Estelí and threw himself wholeheartedly into the armed struggle.

Rugama waxed poetic about the masculine figure of Che Guevara and the "New Man," but for Úbeda the figure of Augusto César Sandino became an all-encompassing male symbol of personal sacrifice and moral rectitude. Knowing his grandparents had helped the rebel army of the 1920s and 30s, he often quizzed his mother about this history. At age twelve, she recalled:

> He started to ask me to tell him about the war of Sandino. I told him, if you had lived in those times, you wouldn't ask me about it because it was horrible. For me as a child, it was horrible. I didn't know what it was about; I just knew that my father was at risk of being killed. He could be killed by one side or by the Guard. But, [Igor] told me, "I like this sort of thing. I want to know more about Sandino's life." He didn't stop asking; he wanted to write down all the things I told him. He kept growing, and I could see this was something natural for him: revolution and social change. I suspected something, but I didn't know his unease was so great. He was very reserved. He didn't say anything about this except to certain compañeros that he could trust. To be honest, many youths joined, but they didn't like it and quickly quit. But Igor didn't quit. When he left our home, it was because he was being persecuted.[131]

Such ambiguous family memories of the earlier struggle passed down by his parents and grandparents did not provide the clear-cut historical continuities he hoped to discover. Igor instead contextualized these recollections within the new construction of Sandino found in Fonseca's FSLN manifestos and the study circles that he and Leonel attended at the home of Dávila Bolaños, where they (like the earlier generation of activists) also read Gorky's *The Mother*. For organizing students and speaking out for the underdog, student activists soon found themselves squarely in the Guard's crosshairs. In January, the GN arrested one of

Úbeda's peers in Estelí after being denounced by a government informant for shouting "Viva Sandino!"[132] The stakes were continually rising, leaving young men such as Úbeda increasingly vulnerable to state
repression.

The single most serious incident of violence in Estelí against the
student movement of the 1960s took place on July 16, 1969. The previous day, four young student guerrillas had been killed in an all-out
military assault against a Managua safe house by hundreds of well-
armed Guardias. Among the dead was Estelí high school graduate and
former student activist Alesio Blandón.[133] The deaths sparked the indignation of university students in León, who traveled in a caravan to
Blandón's hometown to protest. They carried a mock casket aloft in a
funeral march, demanding that Blandón's body be returned immediately by the government to his family for burial. The National Guard
attempted to block the angry demonstrators, meeting the crowd with
brute force. As scuffles broke out, the GN opened fire, killing two local
students, the young journalist René Barrantes and Manuel Herrera. In
the chaotic clashes that followed the shootings, many locals claimed to
have seen Leonel Rugama lobbing a Molotov cocktail at the soldiers.[134]

The march had commemorated the youths killed in Managua, but
now the GN's attack against the unarmed protesters brought the violence home and shocked the city's population. *La Prensa* commented
the following day: "It is tragic to think that to impede a symbolic
burial, the authorities have produced two real burials that will surely
lead to more agitation than the first."[135] In intensifying demonstrations,
massive crowds turned out for the funerals of the two young men,
while schoolteachers, administrators, and even the Catholic Church
condemned the shootings. A letter signed by the relatively conservative bishop of Estelí critiqued the "imprudent behavior of those
called to maintain order and respect life who instead provoke reactions damaging to national peace. We are against violence wherever it
comes from."[136] Because of intense public outrage, the GN was forced
to carry out a court-martial of the commanding officer, Capt. Fermín
Meneses, and one of his subordinates. Their punishments were predictably mild.[137] In the aftermath, the anniversary of the killings became
another date for student mobilization, while the GN continued to
attempt to prevent public protests and to block the arrival of students
from other cities.[138]

State violence against demonstrations effectively derailed the student movement in Estelí, but it had the unintended consequence of increasing recruitment to the FSLN. At risk of arrest for their participation in protests, the Sandinistas dispatched numerous student activists to safe houses in Managua or to encampments in the mountains of the northeast for training as guerrillas.[139] Following the defeat of the 1967 Pancasán expedition, the FSLN began shifting the focus of their armed actions to the cities, mounting urban campaigns in which former student activists such as Rugama and Úbeda would participate. Throughout late 1969 and early 1970, the FSLN targeted banks in armed robberies, which they euphemistically referred to as "economic recuperation actions." The National Guard, however, proved effective at tracking down and murdering many young Sandinistas. In January 1970, Leonel Rugama was shot dead after a pitched battle in an eastern Managua neighborhood where he had been hiding. The GN attacked a building that it deemed a "Sandinista nest" with a massive military operation and overwhelming firepower, killing the three suspected guerrillas inside. When they were called on to give themselves up, Rugama shouted his infamous last words of masculine defiance to the Guardias: "¡Que se rinda tu madre!" (Tell your mother to surrender!).[140] Just months later in early May, Igor Úbeda attempted to carry out a "recuperation" at a National Bank branch in downtown Managua with four other guerrilleros and was gunned down in the process.[141] The deaths of these young men, whether during protests or in armed combat, marked the closing of the protest cycle in which the Frente Sandinista gained a solid foothold in Nicaragua's northern region. The struggles in the streets and the period of consciousness-raising, however, would not be soon forgotten.

With its reputation as a hotbed of Sandinismo, Estelí lived under "almost a state of siege" during 1970, with the population subject to "extreme surveillance," "constant patrols, day and night," and secret police interrogations of suspected guerrillas and their families.[142] Despite the ban on open expressions of political dissidence, there were multiple signs that righteous indignation still seethed beneath the surface. When President Somoza came to Estelí to hold a rally in March, for instance, former shoemaker Adrián Gutiérrez and a fellow guerrillero were—by coincidence—entering the city on an expedition. Having been incommunicado in the mountains, they were unaware that the dictator was visiting at that exact time and the GN had saturated the city with military patrols. At the bridge near El Rosario, the men crossed paths with a group of secret police agents there to provide security for the president. After a shootout commenced, two agents were shot dead, and Adrián escaped with serious wounds. Unwilling to admit that the FSLN had gotten so close to Somoza himself, the government diverted blame, claiming that an elite squad of Cuban agents had been behind the attack.[143]

Against this tense backdrop, mysterious fires and suspected acts of sabotage began to break out across Estelí, much as they had during the 1960s. Rather than merely destroying "centers of vice," the fires consumed key symbols of the economic inequality and corruption. Blazes "of extraordinary proportions" decimated millions of córdobas worth of tobacco belonging to Somoza associates, including René Molina and the Cuban exiles.[144] Though it may have merely been the hot, dry March weather that caused the warehouses to ignite, Estelí's landed elite now saw plots and a subversive hand wherever they looked. Gone were the days when they could expect to reign over a quiescent and apathetic population.

## Conclusion

Surveying the events of recent years, *La Prensa* noted shortly after Igor's death that Estelí had emerged as a focal point of guerrilla insurgency in Nicaragua. "Taking into account the population of this city and that of the whole country," the Conservative newspaper wrote, "the percentage of young men from the FSLN that have died at the hands of the military is very high. This suggests that this leftist extremist organization held a school or training center here."[145] In fact, the Sandinistas' roots in the region went far deeper. Over the previous decade, Estelí had been integral to the emergence of the FSLN, providing its earliest recruits and helping to galvanize a powerful message of moral regeneration with mass appeal. The Sandinistas in the Segovias emerged directly out of the militant artisan labor and high school student movements formed during the moment of political upheaval of the 1960s.

Even though socialist ideology and anti-imperialism were of vital importance to the FSLN leadership, grassroots activists succeeded by appealing to the people on their own terms and blending radical calls for social transformation with a moralistic language critical of vice, inequality, and family breakdown. The state's violent response scared many into submission but lent further legitimacy to the Sandinista call for armed struggle in the eyes of some activists. Unable to protest openly, many young men from Estelí enlisted in the FSLN and vanished into the mountains of the north or the clandestine underground of Managua to become full-fledged guerrilleros. With Gen. Anastasio Somoza Debayle installed in the presidency from 1967, the authorities proved ever-more willing to countenance aggressive repression of opposition activities. In the 1970s, as the revolutionary energies of the Sandinistas merged with new forms of Catholic mobilization, anti-Somocismo in Estelí increasingly took the form of a genuine mass movement.

CHAPTER THREE

# PERSECUTING THE LIVING CHRIST

Guerrillas, Catholics, and Repression, 1968–1976

A large procession of religious folk marched through the hot, parched streets of Estelí on Good Friday 1976, re-creating the Passion of Christ. "From the mass of people, they brought out a 'Living Christ,'" campesina María Briones recalled. "It was my brother, Juan Ramón Briones . . . he participated as the Living Christ. Padre Julio came and prepared this person with the cross, made him look all dirty and disheveled, shoeless with a broken *sombrero*, and brought him into the procession. . . . Even in our village of La Montañita, we didn't know who he was because they made him look so haggard."[1] Along the procession route, GN soldiers followed close behind, apparently hoping to arrest the filthy vagrant who was shuffling alongside the parishioners decked out in their Sunday best. Briones continued:

I guess [the Guard] didn't understand what was going on. Then Padre Julio came and took the cross from the Living Christ and brought him close and said in his prayers: "¡Viva el 'Cristo Vivo!'" In the Stations of the Cross, Padre Julio spoke of slavery, of the rich, of the bourgeoisie, and of those who had nothing. . . . They saved him from the Guardias who were persecuting him because he was so filthy. . . . On [Easter] Sunday, Padre Julio brought this up in Mass and said that we knew that this image was well adored. . . . He called on the parishioners to see the needs of the people, the situation of the Living Christ, and how Somoza

93

was treating him. The parishioners always spoke about this moment. . . . Well, those who agreed with it. Those who didn't, well, they didn't want to hear what he was saying.[2]

This anecdote suggests the tectonic shifts underway in Nicaraguan religious life during the 1970s. Labor activists had considered the religious processions of Holy Week symbolic of a hypocritical Catholic Church complicit in the Somoza regime's moral depravity. Many men who would have spent Semana Santa in the cantinas and brothels a decade earlier now marched alongside their wives and daughters as members of the congregation. During the early 1970s, the Sandinistas found a well of support for their revolutionary efforts by embracing the religious transformation underway in Latin America. Known as liberation theology (*teología de liberación*), the new interpretation of Catholicism promised a "preferential option for the poor" and conceptualized Jesus Christ as a persecuted revolutionary who fought on behalf of the have-nots. The influence of this new Christian current cannot be understood by theological analysis alone, but instead through the ways in which religious ideas were drawn upon and reformulated by grassroots activists to address their everyday lives.[3]

Much like the secular movements of the previous decade, Catholic groups in the Segovias succeeded by linking personal and social change to popular visions of moral regeneration and challenging family breakdown. By participating in Christian retreats, seminars, Bible study circles, and radio schools, many men withdrew from the machista popular culture on which the regime had based itself, abandoning drink, philandering, and interpersonal violence. Women were not only drawn to the movement by the personal asceticism and "reformation of machismo" they witnessed in their husbands, but they also took on prominent leadership roles in community-based organizations for consciousness-raising and protest.[4] Partially because of this Christian influence, the FSLN would soon develop into what Karen Kampwirth describes as "the first guerrilla movement in Latin America that was truly a dual-gender coalition."[5] To purify themselves of sin and begin suturing the tattered fabric of the family, Nicaraguans of different backgrounds became convinced that they needed to overturn a social structure marked by vice, violence, and inequality. In addition to calling for the closure of brothels, cantinas, and gambling dens, Christian activists also sought access to education and health care, all of which would permit the "restoration" of order and familial harmony.[6]

The traditional conservative, moralizing discourse was thus channeled into the broader program of radical transformation, which aimed to inspire change at a personal, familial, and societal level. During the 1970s, many of those active in the Catholic movement came to work with the FSLN, offering food and shelter to the rebels. Sandinista organizers promised them a future in which they would be "treated as human beings," and schools and hospitals would be open to all. Their alliance with segments of the Church blunted claims that the FSLN were atheistic communists, drawing together diverse groups of religious and secular activists around an agenda of moral regeneration, rather than left-wing ideological purity. Even when state violence targeted the fragile networks the Sandinistas had built, many came to understand the role of the GN in "persecuting the Living Christ," bequeathing a depth of support and commitment that would prove essential to the Sandinistas' eventual triumph.

The opposition increasingly identified the National Guard as the fundamental lynchpin of Somocismo and its vice and violence. Rather than cowing the movement into helplessness, the regime's wanton torture and killing of unarmed dissidents inadvertently had an empowering effect on those who witnessed its crimes. Just as Jesus had died on the cross for sinners, members of the Catholic movement came to believe that the sacrifices of the persecuted would bring redemption and vindication in the future. The promise of moral regeneration and greater equality helped many imagine a different and better future, rather than to feel hopeless in the face of repression. The FSLN's armed revolution, many came to believe, was the only viable way to achieve that vision.

## "Goodness, Order, and Morality": Cursillos and the Emergence of Liberation Theology

During the many decades of Somoza rule, the Catholic Church had played an integral role in affirming its structures of power and privilege. In its liturgy, the clergy had long taught that all that came to pass was God's plan for mankind and that poverty was the product of his will.[7] The Church hierarchy often eagerly aligned itself with the land-owners in the Segovias and opposed trade unions. Some priests even served as chaplains in the GN and conspired with the political elite. Only following the GN's killing of student activists during the late 1960s did they begin to speak out against state violence. Despite the Church's dominant social standing in rural Nicaragua, it had not suc-cessfully imposed Catholic orthodoxy in either practice or belief. In-deed, relatively few Christians had regular contact with clergymen or access to sacred texts before the 1960s. Having spent many decades under the distant Diocese of León, spiritual life in the Segovias still included traditional syncretic forms of worship with little oversight from the official Church hierarchy.[8] Even years after the creation of the Diocese of Estelí in 1963, there were still only fourteen priests serving a nominally Catholic population of 250,000.[9] Though baptized into the faith as infants, Segovian campesinos continued to appeal in daily reli-gious practice to local myths, saint cults, and magical objects not en-dorsed by the Church. This popular religiosity often found expression in the annual processions for patron saints.[10] Christian holidays with their days off from work drew the rural population to the towns for acts of religious devotion, generalized bacchanalia, and copious alcohol consumption. For campesinos, in particular, these celebrations offered an escape from the drudgeries of rural life.

During the 1960s and 70s, changes occurring within the Catholic Church at the international level significantly affected religious prac-tice in Nicaragua. The Council of Vatican II, held in Rome from 1962 to 1965, aimed to bring the Church into the modern world, and it spurred reform across Latin America. Among other modifications, priests would now conduct Mass in Spanish rather than Latin. Popes John XXIII and Paul VI published encyclicals in the 1960s calling for human rights, health care, education, and housing for all. At the 1968 meeting of the Latin American Episcopal Conference (Conferencia Episcopal Latinoamericana, CELAM) held in Medellín, Colombia, progressive Church intellectuals had many of their proposals accepted as regional policy by the bishops.[11] Defined as a "preferential option for the poor," the emerging liberation theology argued for rereading the Bible from the perspective of the struggling Latin American masses. Many in the Church now spoke of "sinful" social structures, which

Christians had an obligation to challenge. In addition, the bishops called for the training of laypeople to assist in the evangelization of large rural populations. In Nicaragua, a national pastoral congress held in early 1969 saw a fierce debate between traditionalists and reformers over how to adapt the CELAM platform to local conditions.[12]

In the Estelí region, the clergy disseminated ideas of liberation theology through the *Cursillos de Cristiandad*. Cursillos were short-term Bible study seminars based on a Spanish model brought to Nicaragua by Jesuits at the Central American University (Universidad Centroamericana, UCA) in Managua. Many of these weekend activities were part of the Christian Family Movement (Movimiento Familiar Cristiano, MFC), an organization of the laity that sought to improve the broader social milieu by fortifying married couples in their Catholic faith. With spousal abandonment and marital separation on the rise, the cursillos conceptualized family breakdown as one of the primary roots of the country's social ills. Cursillos began with an initial three-day retreat (*retiro*), in which a group of ten couples spent a weekend studying the importance of the sacrament of marriage and the family.[13] Rather than an elaborate theological exegesis, cursillos aimed to foster community through a direct experience of faith.[14] Early retreats showed little influence of liberation theology, foregrounding instead what one observer called a "mystical worldview" of prayer, song, and ritual.[15]

The first cursillos held in the Diocese of Estelí also focused exclusively on middle- and upper-class citizens, drawing in doctors, lawyers, dentists, and other professionals. The clergy explicitly hoped to incorporate only those they termed "the elite" so that they would serve as a "vertebrae" for moral renovation and the paternalistic uplift of the poor, orphaned, and sick.[16] Local businessman Felipe Barreda, owner of a watch shop, and his wife, Mary, joined one of the retreats on a whim in the late 1960s. Their participation in the retiro served as a spiritual "rebirth" for the couple, strengthening their marriage and leading them to participate actively in Church activities over the coming decade. The Barredas later invited their close friends, schoolteacher Josefa Ruiz Lorente ("la Chepita") and her husband, Rodolfo Rodríguez ("Chilo Negro"), to join in. This couple also came to play a guiding role among the laity as the cursillos moved beyond their initial emphasis on matrimony.[17] The cursillos, Chepita recalled, served as both a social and a political awakening:

We started to study the documents of the Church, the new documents. For example, Vatican II and Medellín. . . . And the Bible,
too, of course; all of this was based on the Bible. So this awoke in
us a consciousness: the renovation of the Church. On the one hand,
we were getting together to raise consciousness and, at the same
time, these Church documents were inviting us to participate in
changing the structures. We couldn't say we were Christians if
we were living in structures of injustice and crime and remaining
quiet. We couldn't. So in these groups, we were able to raise critical
consciousness but also to participate in changing things.[18]

Through dialogue between Christian men and women, moral problems
such as family disintegration, alcoholism, domestic violence, and prostitution were increasingly identified not as mere personal failings but
themselves the products of "structures of injustice and crime." This recognition would increase over the coming years as the cursillos cast an
ever-wider net in terms of participation.

The GN quickly perceived the cursillo movement as a threat,
stressing some participants' links to small opposition parties such as
the PLI and the new Social Christian Party (Partido Social Cristiano,
PSC).[19] For instance, even though Felipe Barreda was a successful businessman and a member of the local Lion's Club and Chamber of Commerce, he was outside of the Somocista networks of corruption. Estelí's
GN comandante, Lt. Col. Ricardo López, wrote to President Somoza
in 1969 explaining that they had determined the cursillistas were "a new
front group established with the unquestionable goal of taking power
by any means possible," in the service of "communism disguised with
an exotic name whose ideas cannot compete with those of the Nationalist Liberal Party."[20] Given the Catholic Church's traditional power in
Nicaragua, however, the GN could not prevent the religious meetings
from taking place. Over the coming years, the cursillo movement grew
so rapidly that even a local GN comandante eventually joined in their
prayer circles.[21]

Driving the cursillos' success during this period was a younger
generation of priests, many of them from abroad, who were highly
critical of the Nicaraguan Church's complicity with the dictatorship.[22]
The most prominent was Padre Julio López, a native of Medellín, Co-

lombia, who had entered the priesthood amidst the atmospherics of the CELAM conference held in that city. Known for his longish hair and boundless enthusiasm, Julio made his mark in the parish of El Calvario, a working-class neighborhood to the southwest of the city center, just blocks from where the Sandinista cells had formed a decade earlier. El Calvario's residents had participated in the neighborhood committees of the 1960s, demanding electricity, running water, plumbing, and sidewalks. Locals even joined together to fund-raise for and collectively build a parish church.[23] This chapel would be the site of intense mobilization during the 1970s, building on the earlier experience of community organizing. Padre Julio arrived in Estelí just before the devastating December 1972 earthquake that hit Managua, killing thousands and decimating the capital city. In the aftermath of the earthquake, the opposition denounced Somoza and the Guardia for misappropriating international disaster aid funds and personally profiteering in the reconstruction efforts.[24] The Diocese of Estelí was responsible for aiding 5,000 desperate refugees (*terremoteados*) who arrived in the city without food, shelter, or employment. Providing aid to those fleeing the devastation in the capital helped bound the parishioners together in a project of solidarity. This collaboration between the clergy, churchgoers, and refugees from Managua proved a fruitful beginning for Padre Julio.[25]

As we saw in the opening of this chapter, Padre Julio soon gained a dedicated following in the town, as many parishioners hung on every word of his sermons. López and community members soon turned their attention to El Calvario's social problems, focusing mainly on manifestations of moral degradation and hypermasculine behavior. With a large and growing female membership, the Catholic movement particularly emphasized the issue of alcohol abuse and interpersonal violence, linking the eradication of vice to both individual transformation and the broader social structure. The pastoral team, for instance, presented a photograph of a drunken man passed out in the street and asked parishioners what they saw, how many cantinas existed in their neighborhood, who benefited from the sale of alcohol, and what were the consequences of this vice on the Nicaraguan family. They referred to guaro as "the idol of escapism . . . adored by those who don't know how to please themselves with ordinary or simple things in life or who don't have the opportunity for wholesome entertainment where they live, those who don't know how to confront a problem (failure at work, in the family, lack of valor to say what they think, resentment, etc.), those irresponsible people who don't care about wasting their household sustenance on alcohol."[26] As we have seen, the processions of patron saints, religious holidays, election campaigns, and voting were among the many community interactions that featured hard drinking by men. Under López's leadership, the Christian circles launched a protest movement to close the Guard-supported cantinas, gambling dens, and brothels that blighted their neighborhoods, damaging community and familial harmony. With the backing of the Church, these campaigns were somewhat more successful than similar efforts spearheaded by the labor unions in the 1960s.

Many of Padre Julio's early supporters included a number of female schoolteachers who had clashed with the Somoza government a couple of years earlier in a labor dispute. When Somoza had declared the 1970 school year over two months early rather than concede to any of the teachers' demands, the women of Estelí denounced how the government "closed schools when it had never ordered closed any of the brothels, cantinas, and gambling dens, of which there are so many in the city."[27] Teachers such as Chepita Ruiz attempted to keep the schools running with the support of Bishop Clemente Carranza y López and the diocese's priests, but the GN forced them from the bishop's residence.[28] With these women now taking leadership roles among the Christian organizations, the popular movement's critique of vice continued to evolve from its patriarchal form. Rather than judging prostitutes as depraved sinners for their social status, many activists now defined sex workers as part of the community of the oppressed: sisters and daughters to be liberated from exploitation by male customers, Somocista brothel owners, the GN, and broader structures of poverty and marginalization. The congregants still marched behind the city's patron saint, la Virgen del Rosario, but the redemption of Mary Magdalene was increasingly present through their reading of the Bible. As Leonel Rugama before them, the women challenged entrenched cultural prejudice and patriarchal Catholic dogma, while successfully closing many of the hated locales.[29] Even a Marxist such as Dávila Bolaños—no admirer of the Catholic hierarchy—praised Padre Julio for the shuttering of the cantinas and the brothels, and for nurturing a sense of "brotherhood and friendship that existed between all of the people of his parish. . . . His words, full of wisdom and love, inspired the residents to take the path of goodness, order, and morality."[30] To mitigate the social roots of the city's problems, the Christian activists also established a new office of Caritas (the Church's aid program), an apostolate for the sick, and a credit and savings cooperative for residents.[31]

## CHALLENGING THE "GOD ON EARTH":
### CURSILLOS IN THE VILLAGES

From their home base in El Calvario, the cursillistas began incorporating other neighborhoods and large numbers of impoverished campesinos in rural areas outside of the town. Padre Julio noted in retrospect:

> The cursillos began with the idea and had the mentality that they would bring in people of a certain cultural and economic status because they believed that the people above were going to change the atmosphere. It was a good idea because all social sectors have good people. But it didn't expand beyond something for very few people. There was a great feeling, but we left a lot of folks out. That was when I had the idea that, instead of using these criteria, we should bring people from the countryside to the cursillo and do it in a much simpler way.[32]

This strategy used by the Church paralleled Carlos Fonseca's admonition to early FSLN organizers to "change the rules" and "talk to the people in a simple and clear way." Following the cursillos, urban laypeople divided up responsibility for different villages, where they organized fasts, vigils, and prayer circles.[33] In this manner, they built new links between town and country, with Christians heading out on the weekends to rural locales, such as Santa Cruz, El Regadío, Tomabú, El Pastoreo, La Montañita, and San Roque.

Campesinos selected from each rural community were taken to weekend retreats at the Center for Pastoral Formation in San Ramón to the north of the Estelí. These retreats were led by Padre Julio, who came to be cherished by attendees for both his warmth and the new perspective he brought to Catholicism. "He was a very beloved man and very friendly," recalled Abelardo Velásquez Laguna, a campesino from Santa Cruz. "He put the gospel into true practice; he took the gospel of Christ and compared it to the situation in which we lived. When he came, he identified with the poor. He told us that Christ came for the poor."[34] Participants described the harmonious sense of community at San Ramón with great nostalgia and as a turning point in their lives. Don Filiberto Cruz Casco from El Regadío, for instance, explained:

> The retreats were beautiful. We went from El Calvario to San Ramón, and we were there for three days participating with the Bible and talking about God and brotherhood. Maybe eight of us from here went to the retiro, but they didn't put us all in the same group. Instead, we participated with *hermanos* [brothers and sisters] from other places whom we didn't know yet, to get to know each other, to learn each other's names. While we were there, we felt a great sense of relief and were rather devoted to God. They started telling us that as Christians we had to find a way to untie ourselves; that we were tied up. And that we had to feel the pain of our brothers.[35]

In the villages on Estelí's outskirts, participation in the cursillos held out a new promise of moral regeneration and a rejection of the machista culture of violence that had been nurtured by the regime. One such locale was La Montañita, a village infamous for its high rates of poverty, illiteracy, and alcoholism. It also had a fearsome reputation as a violent community in which, *La Prensa* claimed, "all men are armed with machetes, and all are aggressive people—to such an extreme that there doesn't exist a man above the age of ten without a machete scar on his body."[36] Against the stern advice of some parishioners, Padre Julio decided to bring the campesinos of La Montañita into the cursillo movement. On his way to the village for the first time, he came across a drunken man unconscious on the side of the road and carried him home on horseback. "It was practically a miracle," Julio explained, incredulous decades later. "From that moment, they were rather affectionate with me and became very close to the Church. Later on [the village] began changing"[37] (see fig. 3.1).

*Figure 3.1.* Padre Julio López conducts a baptism in the rural community of Las Ruedas, 1980. Courtesy of María Jesús Úbeda Herrera.

Through the efforts of the cursillistas, the incidence of alcoholism, spousal abuse, and interpersonal violence began to decline in many shantytowns and rural communities. Working-class and peasant women were increasingly enthusiastic about the cursillo movement, as they saw their quality of life improved amid positive consequences for their families and households. The curbing of machista masculinity assured that money once misspent elsewhere would now remain within poor households, and men would not return home under the influence to take their frustrations out on their wives or children. A Maryknoll nun from the United States who worked in the region noted that "the effect of the cursillos had been to unleash a torrent of energy which had previously been dissipated in drinking, womanizing, indulging in material possessions, and gambling."[38] Homicides became less frequent in villages with long-standing family feuds that had often broken out in weekend clashes with machetes or pistols. Guided by "the Word of God," many heavy drinkers gave up alcohol for many years after attending the retreat. "The Church prepared those who later joined the Frente Sandinista," Octavio Cruz explained, "by taking away some of their vices. Drinking guaro and falling down drunk, it just wasn't right . . . or having many women and a bunch of kids who suffer the consequences of a drunk, irresponsible father with so many vices."[39] Indeed, the Cursillos de Cristiandad began with an individual transformation, posing a strong challenge to the forms of masculine sociability and machismo that the Somoza regime had embraced.

In his preaching, Padre Julio subtly identified the family breakdown, vice, and violence that plagued rural and city folk as the product of larger social injustices. As Lilia Ramona Moncada, a campesina from Santa Cruz remembered, "Padre Julio told us about 'justice' but, I mean, he couldn't just come out and say things because it was dangerous, but we started understanding."[40] Over time, he and other diocesan priests came to agree that the Church, "as a free space," should offer "a clear political discourse that—basing itself on faith—would help Christians face the national reality."[41] For their part, campesinos almost universally reported that the cursillos constituted a jarring rupture—a "before" and "after"—in their conceptions of the world. In retrospect, they often described themselves before the cursillos as having been "asleep," "blind," "in darkness," or "blindfolded."

Consider the following accounts from campesinos who attended cursillos in the 1970s:

Celso Lazo (Santa Cruz): We learned about injustice (*la injusticia*). . . . Everyone should get the salary that they deserve for their work, and no one should be exploited with a miserable salary. That was the worst thing that went on in those days: the injustice. The capitalists had no shame in making their workers labor all day and night for a tiny wage, with no social services, and, if they got sick, they were fired.[42]

Don Santos (Las Labranzas): We learned about the amount of money Somoza had . . . the amount of land . . . and the many of us who had nothing. That's when I started to think about the great injustices. That's when I learned about the injustice that Somoza was doing. I didn't even know what "injustice" was before! We lived in darkness! Back then, we were so happy (*contentos*), so used to having the yoke around our necks that we didn't even complain.[43]

Esteban Matute (La Montañita): Padre Julio asked us how we felt; if we were happy (*tranquilos*). We answered that yes, we were happy. But he told us, "You don't understand who is oppressing you! You don't know what this man is doing to you." They presented some skits, and we started waking up. We started realizing that we were ignorant: we had lined up to vote for a man so he could be there forever exploiting us, bleeding us dry. But in our ignorance, that's what we were doing.[44]

María Briones (Sabana Redonda): We campesinos never had the chance to learn to read. We thought Somoza was a god on earth. . . . We first started to learn when Padre Julio López took us to a retreat for three days. They made us see that we were enslaved and who was doing wrong in the country. One of the men who helped Padre Julio in the cursillo said Somoza was enslaving us and that we should only humble ourselves before God on earth. And that if we had to die, our bodies would die, but our souls would live on; that we should not be scared of anyone.[45]

This critique of a status quo once considered the product of divine writ, marked a paradigm shift for many, helping to shape a new worldview. Campesinos now saw their lives juxtaposed with that of Somoza, a man many of them had previously regarded as a "god on earth." These new ideas put into question not only Somoza's legitimacy as a ruler but also the social order the regime reinforced.

Unlike other accounts of liberation theology as emerging out of a millenarian, popular Christianity with deep links in Catholic utopianism, in the Segovias it functioned as a demystifying force with an emphasis on practical, everyday concerns.[46] A mechanical technician who participated in the Diocese of Estelí's cursillos in the 1970s explained that they helped

the campesinos to realize the exploitation that they were living in, why it was happening, the rights they had, and how to participate as a community to achieve better living standards. It raised their consciousness so they would consider themselves as *people* and not just instruments to be exploited. It was the definitive awakening of the campesinos. . . . People threw themselves into the struggle because they wanted to see Nicaragua freed from corruption. We had no future, no hope except that everyone's lives would get harder every day, with more ignorance and more vice. That was how Somoza maintained himself in power: he kept the population stupid and ignorant by providing them with vices, drugs, and alcohol.[47]

This rejection of vice and embrace of the concept of justice were central to participants' new understanding, as were the efforts to eradicate the quotidian violence that had given Nicaragua one of the highest homicide rates in the world.

The cursillos bore their first political fruits when the next election rolled around. In La Montañita, campesinos refused to cast their votes on behalf of Somoza, as they had always done in the past. The local juez de mesta became infuriated and threatened them: "If you don't go vote, they're going to throw you all in jail or kill you." Still, the campesinos remained determined, Esteban Matute recalled: "If they kill us, they kill us. We're not going to give our vote for a man on earth: we only give our vote for God."[48] In Santa Cruz, Padre Julio and José del Carmen Araúz, a local peasant youth, founded the Christian Youth Movement (Movimiento Cristiano Juvenil). Araúz, later known as "El Segoviano," a neighbor remembered, had a reputation as something of a hard drinker before attending the cursillos, but he became a changed man through his participation. The Christian Youth Movement he led soon gained even greater enmity from the National Guard and the landowners as it moved from the question of vice to that of rural wages. By mid-1975, Araúz remarked, the group began to feel worried for their safety: "We didn't have any links with anyone in the FSLN to tell us what to do. We knew that arms would be necessary, but we didn't know where to get weapons and how to confront the Guardia, how to defend ourselves from repression."[49]

### "We Are Humble but Conscious": Radio Schools and the Challenge to Authority

In the neighboring department of Madriz, the Church employed different tactics in evangelizing the far-flung peasant homesteads along the

Honduran border. Padre José del Carmen Suazo, a priest from Sutiaba in León of indigenous background, arrived in Somoto in the 1960s and began hosting weekend seminars similar to those in Estelí.[50] Local campesinos loved Padre Suazo for his amiable demeanor and easy use of peasant slang and cadence. When villagers in impoverished Madriz faced drought and hunger in 1972 and 1973, Suazo initiated projects establishing wells, irrigation systems, and collective plots planted with drought-resistant crops.[51] With the help of agronomists and veterinarians, the Church in Somoto also founded Community Boards (Juntas Comunales), 4-H Youth Clubs, wives' clubs, and cooperatives.[52] In his sermons, Suazo subtly implored the campesinos of Madriz not to enlist in the National Guard as hundreds did during times of unemployment and hunger.[53] Though he could not speak openly, he reminded them of the First Commandment ("Thou shalt have no other gods before me"), a sly reference to Somoza, purported by some campesinos to be a "god on earth."[54] Importantly, Suazo also welcomed the arrival of a new educational service into the region: the Radio Schools of Nicaragua (Escuelas Radiofónicas de Nicaragua, ERN).

Led by a Spanish priest, Bonifacio Echarri, the ERN had been inspired by a Colombian model of literacy education for peasant adults in isolated communities without access to schools. As part of Radio Católica, the ERN provided radios, batteries, chalkboards, and books to peasant communities. Each evening, campesinos huddled around a shared radio for lessons in reading, writing, and basic mathematics. Scattered among the broadcasts were messages promoting public health and moral and civic community development. The ERN's aim, Echarri declared, was "to eradicate from our land our greatest enemy: ignorance."[55] The radio schools spread far and wide, even in areas dominated by Somoza supporters and National Guard families.[56]

The ERN's daily broadcast opened with the song "Campesino" by Nicaraguan folk singer Jorge Isaac Carvallo, which contained a strong message of peasant empowerment. Its lyrics were remembered even decades later by many of the former students:

*Campesino, aprende a leer,*
*campesino, aprende a estudiar,*
*campesino, si lees y estudias,*
*será tuyo el suelo donde has de sembrar.*

*Por tu sudor nace el cultivo,*
*por tu sudor sale el pan,*
*y otros comen la tortilla y ni gracias te dan.*

*Campesino, levanta tu frente,*
*también eres gente,*
*no te humilles más.*
*Con tus manos izquierda y derecha,*
*hacés la cosecha para los demás.*

Campesino, learn to read,
campesino, learn to study,
campesino, if you read and study,
the land where you work will be yours.

From your sweat come the crops,
from your sweat comes the bread,
and others eat the tortilla and do not even give you thanks.

Campesino, raise your head,
you too are a person,
don't belittle yourself.
With your left and right hands,
you bring in the harvest for everyone else.[57]

With its denunciation of injustice and exploitation, the song alone put fear into the hearts of the Somocista political bosses who lorded over Madriz as their personal fiefdom. Jefe político Tula Baca was so worried about the ERN that it was reported she traveled "around the valleys telling humble campesinos that this educational campaign was completely 'communist.'"[58]

In the remote indigenous community of San José de Cusmapa, close to Honduras, the ERN became an authentic mass movement. Religious groups in Cusmapa had long aimed to provide the order and structure that the state did not by generating an orderly civic life. An Italian priest, Rafael María Fabretto, had helped organize the town over the previous decade, leading numerous social development projects. Cusmapa residents gained experience in community activities and voluntary labor, with the campesinos coming together to build roads, schools, and health clinics.[59] Augusto César Salinas Pinell, a young schoolteacher, spearheaded the radio schools in Cusmapa. The government had sent him to the distant village as retribution for joining the 1970 teachers' strike.[60] Though he came from a poor family in Somoto, even he was shocked by the widespread poverty, disease, hunger, and malnutrition that he found in Cusmapa.[61] Having been recruited to the FSLN by trade unionists in Estelí, Salinas worked as an auxiliary teacher for the ERN during the evenings and commuted on horseback on the weekends to remote communities along the Honduran border. "He entered into the radio schools to organize people, the campesinos," his wife, Esmeralda Marín, explained. "He had more access to the groups and could talk to the people. Or at the night schools, which he promoted here in the town; that's where he got the best elements that later went underground."[62]

Over time, the ERN helped to forge unity among locals to challenge the power of corrupt caciques. Cusmapa was ruled during these years by two ladino Somocistas from Estelí, Rafael Irías and his wife, Guisela Garamendia, who took over many of the town's political posts, such as mayor, municipal treasurer, judge, and bailiff. The couple, abusing their power, trucked lumber out of the town on a daily basis without paying into the Indigenous Community coffers.[63] Such was the family's fearsome grip on the village that, when a previous PLN mayor attempted to charge them for the trees cut down, Irías's sister had threatened that Rafael "would shoot him" (*recibirlo a balazos*) if "he kept insisting."[64] That same ex-mayor was shot dead at his dinner table little more than a year later under mysterious circumstances.[65] Even the Somocista jefe político of Madriz admitted privately in a telegram to Managua that the couple used "any pretext to apply fines, particularly against humble campesinos whom they jail without justification."[66] Timid peasants had long endured their abuses, but the mobilization facilitated by the Church and the ERN gave them the fortitude to denounce the pair. The Indigenous Community wrote a lengthy missive to the minister of the interior signed by its president, Julián Vásquez Alvarado:

Our community of San José de Cusmapa has for many years been suffering a series of arbitrary acts, threats, and hostility to its dignity by Rafael Irías González and Guisela Garamendia de Irías, a couple who has monopolized politics in our community for their personal interest. . . .

This man and woman, protected in their roles as authorities and violating all principles of the law, have carried out a series of threats against our humble Indigenous Community members whose land they try to take, using all manner of subterfuge, from simple trickery to threats of jailing, while applying a series of fines with the goal of obtaining money due to the humility and fear of our campesinos, who, threatened by these authorities, give in to their demands. . . .

Our town of Cusmapa, humble but tenacious, has for ten years struggled without rest to achieve greater socioeconomic development, carrying out a series of community-development projects, including schools, medical dispensaries, community centers, country roads, nutrition centers, soup kitchens, artesian wells, phone lines, electrification, etc., works that speak for themselves and of the desire for improvement that we want to achieve. With the help of our parish priests, Padre Fabretto and Monseñor José Suazo, we have been able to obtain them for our well-being. Caritas, FAO and AID, the Ministry of Health, the Ministry of Public Works, and other national and international organizations are the friends that have helped us in our struggle against misery. They know the nobility of our race and the healthy desire we have, not for personal gain but to share well-being with all of the dispossessed.

. . . We are humble but conscious that the authorities are to serve and improve the town, but our authorities in Cusmapa are currently doing the exact opposite: they threaten and exploit our village and look for ways to destroy it.

By appealing before your honorable person, we ask for your understanding and help. What we describe here are not lies or exag-

gerations, they are the faithful testimony of the sad situation that
we are living here in Cusmapa: the law of the powerful, an archaic
and feudal law, that does not square with our Christian and democratic principles.[67]

Posing their challenge to the village powerbrokers by highlighting
"the nobility of our race" and "our Christian and democratic principles," the indigenous peasants reiterated their loyalty to the state
while harshly questioning its local functionaries. In the letter, the community juxtaposed the graft and abuse meted out by the political authorities to the projects for social and moral uplift fostered by the
Church. With the assistance of Christian and schoolteacher allies, indigenous peasants now proved capable of raising their demands for
change. Rather than the meek, fearful campesinos of yesteryear, they
were now ready to speak out and denounce the regime's corruption
and quotidian violence. Soon, many members of the community went
much farther to contest the system.

Perhaps the Christian movement's most confrontational challenge
to the political authorities came in the town of Condega, to the north
of Estelí, where Nicaraguan priest Westher López had organized
Christian Base Communities (Comunidades Eclesiales de Base, CEBs)
from his arrival in 1973. Catholic nuns and priests had been active in
Condega in recent years, establishing a high school and promoting AA
chapters.[68] Following the election in September 1974, which included
municipal elections and the presidential election, the community
sprang into action. Condega's mayor, Magdaleno Cerrato, was declared
"reelected" by official results, despite widespread claims that he had
stolen and sold aid intended for earthquake victims at his corner store
(*pulpería*). To his opponents, it was the ultimate act of moral depravity.
Members of opposition parties and Christian activists cried foul and
launched a protest movement calling for Cerrato's resignation. Youths
soon covered the town with graffiti messages of moral indignation,
such as "Magdaleno get out, the people hate you" and "the voice of
the people is the voice of God."[69] Stepping up their protest against the
mayor, more than two dozen young people peacefully took over Condega's Catholic church in the name of "the people," promising to hold
it until Cerrato left office.

Those occupying the church chose Aura Velia González—the daughter of former Somocista mayor Romeo González—as president of the Protest Board (la Directiva de Protesta). Upon accepting her new charge, she proudly declared that the "struggle will continue" until a new mayor was named.[70] (A number of the protesters suggested that Aura Velia herself was the right person for the job.) The church occupiers issued a collective statement explaining their aims that was signed by more than 1,000 residents:

> A general assembly was held in the Catholic church of this city, with the goal of electing from the participants—all of them townspeople from the city of Condega and delegates of the neighboring valleys—a Committee of Protest against Municipal Mayor Magdaleno Cerrato Torres. The reason for the election of this committee is the poor municipal administration and the anomalies that we consider to be hurting the management of our beloved city. The committee elected this morning has the obligation of making the pertinent efforts before the president of the Supreme Electoral Tribunal. . . and the honorable minister of the interior . . . so that our demand, efforts, and force remain within civic bounds without ever breaking with the principles of our political constitution and our representative democracy, and will not accept within it elements that are motivated by personal interests and hope to use our movement to subvert public order or to attack our constituted authorities, as we are inspired to make this serious decision to petition the competent authorities by the ideals of our Nationalist Liberal Party, perfectly represented in the worthy person of General Anastasio Somoza Debayle.[71]

Given the militant nature of their protest action and the likelihood of state repression, the committee strategically used language flattering of the regime and issued a pointed statement distancing themselves from the political opposition ("elements . . . that hope to use our political movement to subvert public order or attack our constituted authorities"). Despite their claims to the contrary, however, Cerrato's alleged abuses—corruption, diversion of foreign aid, and fraudulent reelection—closely paralleled allegations against "the worthy person

of General Anastasio Somoza Debayle" himself. The occupation of
the church fizzled out and did not successfully oust the mayor, but it
contributed to a political awakening in Condega with long-term consequences.

## Constructing Guerrilla Support Networks in the Segovias

Three months later, on December 27, 1974, the Sandinistas returned to
the headlines with a dramatic assault on the Managua mansion of Somocista Jose María "Chema" Castillo, taking numerous regime loyalists hostage during a Christmas party. The FSLN killed Castillo—a
former minister of agriculture and member of a powerful Estelian
family—during the attack. After a tense stand-off, the Sandinistas
traded the hostages for eighteen Sandinista prisoners held by the regime, the publication of an FSLN communiqué, and a million dollars
in cash. Somoza responded to the brazen operation by declaring a state
of siege that imposed martial law and censorship of the media.[72] This
high-profile action restored the public standing of the FSLN, an organization many Nicaraguans believed to have been defunct. It was in the
wake of this event that the FSLN would begin to forge its links to the
Christian mobilization occurring in the rural north.

During the early 1970s, the Sandinistas' perception of religion
had also shifted in a new direction. Whereas the founders of the FSLN
had been predominantly anticlerical Marxists who saw Catholicism
as "false consciousness" and an "opiate of the masses," many of the
younger cadres had initially been drawn into political activism from a
Christian perspective gained at parochial schools. Through his conversations with priests influenced by liberation theology, Carlos Fonseca
concluded that Christians could and should play an integral role in the
revolutionary movement in an overwhelmingly Catholic country such
as Nicaragua.[73] Accusations that the guerrillas were atheists and communists scared away many in the Segovias. At the same time, the FSLN
also began to dramatically revise their strategy for guerrilla warfare.
The Sandinistas, Fonseca argued, had fallen into what he called a
"mountain–city paralysis," in which only the capital Managua and the

remote northeast were privileged as sites for guerrilla activity. Such a strategy had effectively excluded many of Nicaragua's rural areas and its provincial cities. Fonseca called on the FSLN to now focus on those areas adjacent to cities, towns, and haciendas.[74] He argued that remote jungles were not the only locales that offered protection and that "zones with more limited cover might be more advantageous if the actual inhabitants of the place are the ones involved."[75] The rising tide of the Christian movement of the Segovias would provide just such a natural entry point for the FSLN.

Employing the new approach set out by Fonseca, guerrilla cadres were dispersed throughout the country with plans to establish supply chains and networks of civilian supporters. In the Segovias, their main project was to organize the clandestine "Augusto César Sandino Trail," a supply route to connect León and Chinandega in western Nicaragua to the northeastern mountain redoubts where a permanent guerrilla squadron was operating. The network of civilian supporters and safe houses was to link Cusmapa, Las Sabanas, San Lucas, Macuelizo, and Limay in the west to Pueblo Nuevo, Estelí, and Condega, and, from there, eastward through Buena Vista, La Montañita, Los Planes, and Yalí. After crossing into the department of Jinotega, goods and combatants could travel secretly toward FSLN bases in Cerro Kilambé, El Cuá, and Jalapa.[76] The goal was to incorporate so many supporters, guerrilla Manuel Morales recalled, "that we would be able to travel across the country without having to set foot on the highways, just through the people."[77] In addition to Morales, Sandinista cadres, such as Bayardo Arce, Omar Cabezas, and Augusto Salinas Pinell, were sent by the FSLN to organize civilian cells and recruit guerrillas from among the peasant population. The 1970s saw the growing participation of female Sandinistas in the Segovias, such as Mónica Baltodano, a former student activist from León.

Often, the families most open to the guerrillas were those already exposed to the work of the cursillos, the ERN, and other Christian organizations. The Sandinistas considered the recently formed Christian networks as veritable "quarries" for their organizing and tapped into the movement by way of personal contacts with laypeople and clergymen.[78] With guerrillas Bayardo Arce ("Oscar") and Julio Maldonado ("Arturo") based along the Honduran border, the Sandinistas recruited followers in each of Cusmapa's outlying valleys, building upon the infrastructure established by the ERN. Padre Bonifacio Echarri, the ERN's national coordinator, joked years later to FSLN organizers that "all of the work we did in the radio schools, you guys took them away!"[79] In Condega, the guerrillas contacted the Centeno sisters, who had recently helped organize the church occupation demanding the mayor's resignation. The eldest sister, Amanda, who later took up arms herself, explained: "All of our political reflection took place in the space of the Christian Base Community, not in the FSLN. What the Frente did later was to win these people over, to locate the centers of analysis and mobilization."[80] The Centenos were active in organizing these efforts, and their brother Antonio ("Toñito") guided guerrilla Omar Cabezas to the rural communities to the east of the town beyond the coffee estates of Darailí, San Jerónimo, and Venecia, where rural trade unions had once been active in the 1960s.[81]

Notably, many of the first campesinos recruited by the Sandinistas in the Segovias had previously been supporters of the Conservative Party, the anticommunist, traditionalist faction led by the anti-Somoza landowners. Marginalized by Somoza clientelism, grassroots Conservatives were open to any efforts to eject the ruling Liberals from power at the community and national level. The Conservative slogan of "God, Order, and Justice" seemed to dovetail with the FSLN's moralizing discourse critiquing the spread of vice. As we saw in chapter 1, many Segovian Conservatives had strongly backed 1967 presidential candidate Fernando Agüero, risking attack by the GN and members of AM-ROCS. Agüero's openly patriarchal election platform described the "man as the head of the family as the starting point of our program" and called for fathers to be "embedded in the family, which is the base of society."[82] Their platform included a range of Alliance for Progress–style economic reforms, but the Conservative program emphasized "the restoration of civic and spiritual values" as the first priority, given that "spiritual improvements must take precedence over the material improvement of the nation. Civil society is based on tranquility, order, and justice. The Catholic religion is the religion of almost all Nicaraguans and our Christian morality is at the foundation of the customs and tradition of the Nicaraguan people."[83]

The Sandinistas would take up this line of critique but insist that "tranquility, order, and justice" required transformations in material conditions. Despite embracing Agüero's campaign, many Conservative campesinos had lost faith in the party following the GN massacre in Managua in February of that year (which some of them had witnessed firsthand and felt "used" as cannon fodder by party bosses) and Agüero's subsequent power-sharing pact with Somoza Debayle in 1971.[84] Interestingly, among some of these families, the name Sandinista was likely to stir up negative family memories. As a Liberal general, Augusto César Sandino and his troops had been the scourge of the Conservatives in the Segovias, whom he considered little more than puppets of the United States. FSLN leader Carlos Fonseca complained that after a decade of organizing, some Segovian peasant supporters still saw the guerrillas as "some kind of leftist Conservatives and mix their sympathy for the combatants with illusions in the traditional bourgeois opposition politicians."[85]

The FSLN's most fruitful link to the Christian movement came in 1975, when a group of Sandinistas escaped to Estelí, fleeing GN repression farther to the north. They found refuge in the rectory residence of Padre Julio López, with whom they established a close working relationship. With his help, the guerrillas found shelter in the homes of trusted middle-class cursillistas, such as the Barredas and doña Dolores Arróliga. From their urban base, the FSLN also spread into the rural areas where the cursillo movement had found adherents in recent years. In Santa Cruz, the FSLN formed a new guerrilla squadron named after Sandino's Gen. Pedro Altamirano. They received the assistance of Christian community members, many of them previously staunch Conservative Party families.[86]

The most effective organizing tool for the guerrillas in rural areas was the *Cartilla Campesina*, an FSLN manual that explained in straightforward language how the peasantry had been exploited and marginalized by the landowning elite, which it called *los grandes ricos*. The document—a primer read aloud in hushed tones at night—followed the message of liberation theology heard in the cursillos, Christian Base Communities, and radio school broadcasts. Linking inequalities of wealth and exploitation in the countryside to the nation's external dependence, the *Cartilla* explained:

> From the calloused hands of thousands and thousands of campesinos in Nicaragua come the coffee, cotton, corn, beans, plantains, and other agricultural products, and cattle. But the money that

comes from the campesinos' work only benefits a small group of *grandes ricos millonarios*. The Yankee imperialists form a part of this evil gang (*pandilla*) . . . paying low prices for the coffee and cotton, they buy from us . . . [while selling] us tractors, machetes, medicine, etc. at very high prices. The other members of this mafia that devours the campesinos are the grandes ricos millonarios led by the Somoza family. When this handful of grandes ricos takes the fruit of the hard work of the campesinos, something terrible happens. The grandes ricos and their lazy families enjoy all sorts of luxuries and pleasure while the campesinos suffer from everything: hunger, sickness, ignorance, and lack of clothing.[87]

The text had strong resonance with the language of the labor unions of the 1960s and the lyrics of the ERN's theme song, which reminded the campesinos, "From your sweat comes the crops / from your sweat comes the bread / and others eat the tortilla and do not even give you thanks."

The *Cartilla*'s text also focused on the role of the government, reiterating the confluence of interests between the regime and the hacendados: "The heads of the government and the Guardia are not poor campesinos but grandes ricos. The Somoza family is not a family of poor campesinos but grandes ricos. The colonels and ministers are not poor campesinos but grandes ricos. It is as clear as the summer sun that the calamities that the campesinos suffer are not from the curse of some strange unknown spirit. These calamities are caused by the grandes ricos and their government and their Guardia."[88] With its simple phrasing and use of repetition, the Sandinistas were able to communicate a powerful, populist discourse of moral condemnation. They asked campesinos to put aside traditional, supernatural explanations for their misfortune, which blamed "the curse of some strange unknown spirit." The *Cartilla* concluded by calling on all campesinos to unite and stand up for their rights, all while never explicitly mentioning the FSLN or armed struggle.

The itinerant guerrillas also carried with them the "Historic Program of the Sandinista National Liberation Front," a 1969 document that spelled out the basic plans of a future revolutionary government. It called for an end to the Somoza dictatorship, the National Guard, and U.S. domination of the country. The program set the framework for a mixed economy, with large sectors of industry, utilities, and banking to be nationalized and confiscated from their current Somocista owners. Regarding social policy, the "Historic Program" demanded a dramatic expansion in access to health care and education—starting with a "massive campaign" to eliminate illiteracy—for all Nicaraguans, particularly the campesinos. The text also called for an agrarian reform to break the grip of the "grandes ricos" and provide land, credit, and employment to campesinos. In its section on "Administrative Honesty," the FSLN also promised to end "governmental corruption" and to "abolish the criminal vice industry (prostitution, gambling, and drug dealing)," and to severely punish persons who engage in crimes such as "embezzlement, smuggling, trafficking in vices, etc."[89] However, the "Historic Program" did not merely emphasize the effects of moral degeneration, but included a plan for "The Emancipation of Women." This section pledged to promote full equality between men and women by, among other proposals, assuring women access to education, maternity leave, and day care centers, and to "eliminate prostitution and other social vices, which will raise women's dignity."[90]

In oral histories, campesinos from across the Segovias revealed strikingly similar reasons for their initial decision to back the guerrillas. Many were attracted by the promise of access to social services and by the possibility of achieving human dignity and moral regeneration.

Participants in the Christian movement recalled the pitch made by their guerrilla contacts in the following ways:

> Juan Antonio Espinoza (Cusmapa): He told us that if the FSLN won, we were going to have schools and any campesino would be able to study at the university or at a high school. He told us Somoza never cared about the campesinos, but if the Sandinistas won, everyone would learn to read and write. I really liked that because I thought: I'm going to learn to read and write. And maybe go to university or high school. This really inspired me. The other thing that inspired me was he told us that the campesinos weren't going to be exploited but were going to be treated as human beings.[91]

> Juan Alvarado Sánchez (Cusmapa): He told us that we should fight for the Frente Sandinista because over time our children would be

able to enjoy benefits: the children would get access to medicine, shoes, and clothes. These would be free. The campesinos would have more jobs, and they would be better paid, and we'd get better prices for our crops. And the adults would have schools, too.[92]

María Briones (Sabana Redonda): He told us that the campesinos would be able to read, that the campesinos were all going to be equal and we would have medical treatment whether we had money (*riales*) or not. And that we were all going to be treated the same: both the haves and the have-nots. The Somoza dictatorship never told us that! There were the rich, and then there were the poor; those that knew how to read and those that couldn't read. He never cared about those that couldn't.[93]

Octavio Cruz (Santa Cruz): He also said that we were going to get rid of the massive number of cantinas and vice . . . guaro is a social ill for Nicaragua; we are not educated enough to drink guaro. And also prostitution; we fought so that it would be abolished; so that women would be respected. That was the struggle we took up due to our Christian beliefs. We supported the Frente Sandinista so that these things would be eliminated.[94]

Though the specifics varied, both men and women saw revolution as providing a pathway "to be treated as human beings" in a more just, moral system in which they could achieve personal renewal through access to education, health care, and an end to state-sanctioned vice. It is also highly noteworthy how rarely grassroots participants spoke of anti-Yankee nationalism or the call for land reform, both of which are often considered underlying causes of the Sandinista Revolution.

For those who accepted FSLN appeals, there were numerous roles that they could play in the clandestine support structure. Sebastián Zavala, from rural Condega, later testified that Omar Cabezas had told him "one could work with the guerrillas not just with a gun in their hand, but also in other ways, like giving them food, planting crops for them to harvest, carrying packages, or lending them tools."[95] Others worked as *correos* (messengers or couriers) or as *chanes/baquedanos* (expert guides through the woods and mountains). Perhaps most risky of all was offering one's home as a safe house where guerrillas secretly hid out for long periods of time. Some campesinos even began training in military maneuvers and the use of arms. Moisés Córdoba, a campesino from Canta Gallo worked with Cabezas in choosing those to recruit, particularly focusing on Conservative families. His father, Leandro Córdoba, had given aid to Augusto César Sandino in his youth, and now called on his entire extended family to wholeheartedly support the FSLN.[96]

Late-night conversations with the guerrillas deepened their hosts' understanding of the cause for which the young militants were fighting. Likewise, some FSLN fighters developed an appreciation for the consciousness that had taken root through the Christian faith. "There was such harmony, it was like a family atmosphere between the guerrillas and the Christians," Padre Julio remembers fondly. "We had the same goal of a revolutionary change, but it was challenging and dangerous. The Christian families listened to them, talked to them, and they listened to us. There was great reciprocity. Although each of us had our part to play, they served as a stimulus for us. But as Christians, our job was to do it without any political aspect. But we thought it through, and we all agreed that we needed a revolutionary change. So our task was to 'wake the sleeping' and [the guerrillas'] was to 'organize the awake.'"[97] The presence of the armed insurgents also fostered a profound sense of community and indeed nascent kinship ties because of the commitment to the project of social change and their shared risk. In some cases, host families even came to treat the young rebels (los muchachos) as surrogate sons and daughters. This experience, however, was soon truncated by a bloody wave of National Guard repression throughout the Segovias. Campesinos had become invested in the morality of their cause; the repression unleashed by the state would in some cases further strengthen that sentiment.

### "Sealed with Their Actions": Arrests, Torture, and Killings, 1975–1976

In July 1975, following the detection of two FSLN rural guerrilla training camps in northwestern Nicaragua, the National Guard carried out a rolling crackdown against all those suspected of collaborating with the guerrillas. The GN informed the U.S. ambassador that they had successfully killed seven men and two women in a pair of attacks in El Copetudo in Nueva Segovia and in El Sauce in the department of León.[98] The GN began to uncover the Sandinistas' clandestine web of civilian supporters, capturing six men in San José de Cusmapa alone.[99] Many individuals who confessed under torture provided the names and locations of others who were then captured and interrogated. The secret police tracked the fleeing guerrillas into the mountains of rural Condega and arrested the Córdobas and nearly the entire male population of the community of Los Planes the following June. The wave of repression continued with the arrest of numerous high school teachers and students who had earlier participated in the church occupation. Sandinista organizer and onetime Cusmapa schoolteacher Augusto Salinas Pinell was gunned down in June by a National Guard patrol.[100] In late November, the GN discovered the FSLN squadron hidden in Santa Cruz and shot two guerrillas dead, including Santiago Baldovinos from Condega, whose father was a Somocista municipal magistrate. This skirmish was followed by another sweep against the local population, with thirteen more rounded up in a single day.[101]

Through interrogation and torture, the GN continued unearthing the secret network established by the guerrillas. The Sandinistas, just like their supporters, were largely caught off guard by the sudden clampdown. Bayardo Arce wrote to Omar Cabezas, complaining of the "lack of preparation of our support base to withstand the investigation so that many of those captured were surprised and vomited all they knew, incriminating themselves and others and the repression expanded."[102] He ordered Cabezas to "politically and psychologically prepare" the campesinos of Condega in case of further arrests, "insisting that FOR NO REASON should they reveal our presence in the zone, MUCH LESS that they helped us in any way."[103] Cabezas had little time to prepare his peasant contacts, as the GN swept into the area and captured vast numbers of campesinos.[104]

The GN subjected the prisoners to brutal forms of torture that served both to extract information and inflict punishment. The U.S. embassy in Managua admitted to the State Department that the Somoza regime was involved in a highly repressive campaign against the civilian population of the north. Ambassador James Theberge wrote that "torture techniques have been used assiduously in investigations" in the Segovias, particularly through the use of electric shocks. He fallaciously claimed that there was no "consistent pattern of gross human rights violations," but admitted that the GN "probably questioned several thousand people and detained many for various periods of up to eight weeks. . . . There have been many well-documented charges of serious mistreatment such as methodical beatings and other physical abuses."[105]

One campesino in Condega was dragged from his bed and driven to the National Guard base in Estelí. Once there, he was blindfolded and led to another room by an obese soldier with a reputation as a torturer of great sadism. Several years later, he described the abuse in detail:

> They tied my feet with electric wires. One of them sat on my hands, another on my feet, and another one on my stomach. . . . They told me that I must be well paid by the Frente [for refusing to give them information]. They told me, "You're going to tell us the truth," and immediately gave me an electric shock. But because I didn't tell them anything, they gave me so many shocks that I lost consciousness. They broke my nose. They broke my teeth and forced me to eat them. I didn't say anything; I preferred that they kill me and not the muchachos that I knew were from the Frente. They took me to the shower and then again to that room, where they connected [the wires] to my little toe and my ear. . . . They asked over and over again. Because I didn't say anything, they beat me with their rifle butts, connected the wires, and kicked me. They also kicked my testicles. To this day, they get inflamed when I walk too much.[106]

This brutal experience was similar to that of the campesinos from other communities, such as the man from Santa Cruz arrested with his wife and three small children (ages one month to four years) after a shootout near their home. "They treated us in a disgusting way," he described, "hitting us, blindfolding us, and giving us electric shocks. The infants weren't tortured, but my wife was. They hit her, and they tortured one of my children."[107] In both cases, the peasant families' bravery and silence in the face of such brutality stood as a marker of their commitment and sense of sacrifice for the revolutionary cause.

The GN even murdered some campesinos for refusing to provide information on the whereabouts of the guerrillas. Christian activists Luciano and Ricardo Sánchez Alvarado from Cusmapa apparently died at the hands of the Guardia in custody at the Ocotal military garrison. Their corpses were never found.[108] Their cousin claimed that soldiers forced the two onto their stomachs and stood on their backs. "They pulled back their heads," he asserted, "and used their bayonets to slit their throats. . . . They were brave men. They didn't surrender."[109] Another campesino from Santa Cruz was blindfolded and beaten to death in the Estelí base.[110] A female Christian community member from Santa Cruz, pregnant at the time of her arrest, miscarried as a result of GN abuse.[111] Though no women were killed in this wave of repression, the government now knew that women were also actively involved in the guerrilla support structures.

The long-term effects of the state repression of 1975 and 1976 varied widely. The Guardia increasingly came to see all Christian activism as synonymous with insurgency and harassed many innocent members of Catholic lay organizations. Among the cursillistas, Padre Julio noted, "some lost hope and got scared. For others, it strengthened their belief in the revolution."[112] José Carmen Araúz recalled that after the arrests, only six of his Christian Youth Movement's eighteen members decided to continue, but "others were too terrified to participate in the fight for justice. They said, 'What's it even matter how we live on earth? In heaven, we're going to have eternal life!'"[113] Some even blamed the priests for getting them involved in activities that had provoked such repression. A woman in Santa Cruz later complained that Padre Julio had induced them to participate for vague goals, telling him, "You made us into Sandinistas." Another female resident of the village later lamented, "In this community, all that is good and all that is bad is the work of Padre Julio."[114] In the Segovias, the GN subjected ERN teachers to constant surveillance and burned workbooks as subversive propaganda. Often, neighbors turned their backs on the men arrested in the raids, fearing for their safety. Prisoners from Cusmapa recalled returning home from jail to find the village's houses plastered with

Anastasio Somoza Debayle's campaign posters in a show of loyalty to the regime.

For others, however, the wave of torture and extrajudicial killings only strengthened their resolve. In Condega, the arrests prompted repudiation of the GN's harsh treatment of friends and family members. "It was hard when they got free," one campesino prisoner's father recalled of watching them return home after months behind bars: "I was in the park and it made me want to cry. Two of them could have fit into one pair of pants. They didn't know where they were; they were disoriented. But there was so much admiration for them. Everyone that saw them became compañeros."[115] The term "compañero" here clearly took on a political meaning, referring to those who supported the revolutionary movement.

This moment marked a clear shift from widespread discontent with the Guardia Nacional's vice-filled, disorderly methods to a growing hatred of the GN as the embodiment of the violence and corruption that defined the Somoza regime. The prisoners' tales of anguish bore witness to the regime's brutality. Condega activist Moisés Calero noted that in the Christian seminars they often spoke of the power of love and the inherent violence of the dictatorship in abstract terms. "But then came the repression," he said, "and the more repression the Guard carried out, the more they sealed with their actions what we said with words."[116] Carmen Araúz, for his part, officially joined the FSLN and went on to gain renown as a guerrillero under the nom de guerre "El Segoviano." Teenage Christian activist Amanda Centeno also directly joined the Sandinistas after she was arrested and taken to the GN base at Ocotal. Behind bars, Centeno was able to deceive the Guard by playing on gender and class stereotypes, "pretending to be a humble campesina who didn't know anything," she said. Aware that FSLN members were currently hiding out in her sister's house, she refused to give them information. "I was protecting my sister," she explained. "I told them what they already knew, that the guerrillas had shown up at the high school, but I described them by giving a completely fabricated description."[117] Once released, she soon learned that many of her close friends and family members had gone into exile after her arrest, a fact the GN was sure to find highly incriminating. Thus, she too immediately fled the country and only returned to Nicaragua several years later as an armed and trained guerrillera.[118]

State terror against campesinos was so disproportionate that it prompted outrage and lent legitimacy to the Sandinistas' call for armed struggle. As also happened in El Salvador during these same years, the question of state terror and "martyrdom" was soon folded into the new Christian worldview of liberation theology, justifying popular resistance.[119] In 1976, the FSLN Regional Command wrote an open letter to the cursillos of Estelí, calling on participants to take a clear stand against the regime's violence, "given that in the Church's action, HUMAN BEINGS are fundamental and the essence of Christianity is to LOVE THY NEIGHBOR."[120] Writing of the campesinos taken prisoner by the GN, they asked cursillistas to protest before the authorities for the physical safety of those still in custody. "We conceive the duty of the Christian in Nicaragua today to be one of reflection . . . AND ACTION," they wrote in their statement. "What is important is that you do not remain with your arms crossed and your mouth closed," because of the fear provoked by the "presence of the military uniform and the ear of the informant (oreja)."[121] In this letter, the cursillos' goals of "justice, freedom, and social equality" became inextricably connected with the end of the Somoza dictatorship and its atrocities.[122] In Estelí, the blueprint for a deepening alliance between the Christian communities and the FSLN had been further articulated, partly as a result of GN violence.

Even Conservative Party leaders in Managua were forced to speak out against the wave of arrests and torture that targeted many of their voters. The Conservatives, the U.S. embassy noted, admitted that "many of their cadres in the Segovias, despite strict party orders to the contrary, are cooperating with the FSLN, which has an undeniable mystique and popularity in the region," while others "who are not cooperating are being rounded up, detained, and physically mistreated anyway."[123] In response to the events taking place, President Somoza called a press conference at the height of the state of siege to condemn "international communism," "Marxist entities," and "terrorists" that he claimed were carrying out a "systematic campaign against Nicaragua."[124] In addition to his denunciation of FSLN activities, however, he made an important announcement that he was calling on all GN comandantes across the country to carry out "the immediate and indefinite closure of all of the illegal gambling centers that have been functioning in the country to the detriment of the Nicaraguan home and public morality."[125] The ban on illegal gaming proved to be a short-lived public relations gesture; GN officers soon allowed them to re-open. However, the very fact that Somoza brought up the issues of the family household, vice, and "public morality" at this exact moment suggests that he knew full well that "international communism" was not solely to blame for the unrest that his regime was facing. Indeed, he seemed to understand that the regime's system of vice was a fundamental cause of the righteous indignation bubbling up from below in an alliance between Christian conservatives and leftists. In response, the FSLN alleged that Somoza's U.S. advisors in the CIA were behind this effort to "dress the dictator up as a moralist" by "recommending he say that he is going to close down the brothels and illegal gambling halls."[126] What Somoza did not comprehend was that the GN's persecution of the peasants had not silenced the movement, but rather that victims' suffering was seen as assuring the future promise of moral regeneration.

CONCLUSION

The consciousness-raising that liberation theology provided in the Segovias upended the outlook of men and women from various social classes. The message of empowerment embodied in the cursillos, radio schools, and Christian base communities became a powerful tool of political mobilization that breathed new life into the FSLN. In these Church-led activities, grassroots Christians came to understand new concepts such as "justice," "injustice," and "slavery," and to see personal moral renewal as part and parcel of a wider social and political revolution. Most activists experienced their conversion or rebirth as a rapid shift and cognitive break in their lives and worldview. It was a moment, both men and women consistently recalled, that removed "the blindfold" from their eyes. Liberation theology laid the groundwork for new protest movements against GN-backed brothels and cantinas, exploitative "grandes ricos," and corrupt and abusive political bosses.

During the early 1970s, the FSLN tapped into this rising tide of religious organizing as their cadres spread throughout the Segovias, appealing to the more traditionally conservative social sectors. A vast number of Christian families soon came to provide a backbone for the handful of armed guerrillas active in the rural north. Promising a better future of health care and education for all and an end to the injustice and depravity of Somoza's Nicaragua, the Sandinistas found many willing backers within the Christian movement. Armed struggle emerged as a potentially viable way to bring about societal transformation, as Christian activists of all backgrounds projected their vision of moral regeneration onto Sandinismo. Indeed, the language found in Sandinista documents such as the *Cartilla Campesina* closely mirrored and mutually shaped the language of liberation theology at the grassroots level. Liberation theology certainly awoke rural Nicaraguans to their reality, but it was their tremendous commitment and sacrifice that would see the regime decisively challenged from below.

Before these diverse movements could coalesce into a formidable political challenge, however, the regime was able to derail the Sandinistas' network of civilian supporters. With the arrest and inhumane torture of large numbers of campesinos throughout the Segovias, the Somoza government revealed its willingness to violate basic moral codes and to countenance state terror against unarmed civilians. For many of the victims, their families, and their neighbors, the grotesque treatment of the prisoners laid bare the amoral nature of the regime and the GN. Torture and the disappearance of family members profoundly affected survivors, and many lived silently with the trauma for years to come. However, seen through the emerging prism of moral regeneration, some victims gained further strength in their belief in future vindication. Nicaragua's campesinos had, in their eyes, indeed become the "Living Christ" persecuted by the regime. As one participant recalled learning at the cursillos, "if we had to die, our bodies would die, but our souls would live on; that we should not be scared of anyone."

To better understand the role that these acts of political violence played in the history of the Sandinista Revolution, however, we must also interrogate the mind-set behind those perpetrators of mass violence and those low-level agents who were complicit in buttressing the regime. In chapter 4, we will turn to the other side of this story to examine the very institutions responsible for these human rights abuses and atrocities: Somoza's GN and secret police.

# CHAPTER FOUR

# "THEY PLANTED CORN AND HARVESTED GUARDIAS"

Somoza's National Guard and Secret Police at the Grassroots

On leave to his rural town in the Segovias, the typical National Guard recruit returned home with an air of invincibility. One evening in early 1979, emboldened by a few rounds of guaro, one such soldier from San Juan de Limay stumbled out of the village's billiard hall shouting that he had recently killed two local youths "for being Sandinistas and communists."[1] A witness claimed to have heard him boast in a threatening tone: "'These kids think they can beat us, but we'll roll over them'. . . He said he knew who the others were that were with the Sandinistas and that General Somoza was possibly going to give him a scholarship to study in Chile."[2] Just two years earlier, he had been just another desperately poor campesino from a hamlet on the outskirts of Limay. Now, as a rank-and-file member of Somoza's army, he possessed empowerment and impunity. Many remember peasants from the Segovias who had similarly left their village in *caites* (traditional artisanal sandals) returning just months later as part of the GN, well-fed, with shiny black leather boots, a khaki uniform, a crew cut, and a pocketful of córdobas.

In this way, the National Guard cunningly converted men from Nicaragua's most dispossessed social groups into its own violently loyal enforcers. This particular young man from Limay had been recruited to the army in 1976 at twenty-two and received training at the GN's infamous EEBI training facility. Peasants in the Segovias later

accused him of committing vicious acts of torture against alleged guerrillas, peeling off their skin, ripping out fingernails, castrating them,
and slitting their throats. All this less than two years after his recruitment. The story of this individual soldier brings together the essential
elements of the National Guard's internal culture: an exaggerated personal loyalty to the Somozas and the promise of social mobility, an aggressive masculine sociability patterned around hard drinking, vice,
and interpersonal violence, and a visceral anticommunist ideology. The
situation was similar to that described by Steve Stern for colonial
Mexico: the "violent masculinity"—given free range by the Guardia—
reflected "interior hypersensitivity and rage, a bursting forth in exaggerated swaggers of manhood and inexplicable ventings that bear little
specific or rational connection to the target."[3] For many who were vic-
timized by the GN, the helmeted, uniformed Guardia became the ultimate symbol of unleashed violent masculinity: the Somoza regime
incarnate.

Although many in the rural north were joining the Sandinista
movement, the National Guard continued to hold sway in the Segovias' most impoverished corners as the single largest employer. Ironically, the same poverty-stricken conditions that had given rise to
the FSLN—such as a lack of access to education and high levels of
unemployment—also undergirded the GN's ability to find willing recruits from among the rural population. The arid town of Somoto,
in the department of Madriz, for instance, was famed as a recruiting
ground for the military.[4] So many indigenous peasants from the barren,
isolated region had enlisted in the GN that a famous adage claimed, "In
Somoto, they plant corn and harvest Guardias" (*En Somoto, siembran
maíz y cosechan Guardias*).[5] A resident later testified that GN recruit-
ers "made flattering proposals . . . They took unwary youths to fill the
ranks of the army, telling them that they would rise economically and
educationally, and many times I saw them convince these young people
to enter the National Guard."[6] Somoto local and Sandinista Manuel
Maldonado—whose own brother and nephew were killed by the GN—
later wrote, "The previous system caused great problems in this department and took advantage of all of these factors so that a majority of the
campesinado would serve to perpetuate the regime in power: primitive agriculture, a lack of factories, almost no commerce, and a very

backward culture. With this panorama, there was no other path but to turn into an oreja [secret police informant] or a Guardia."[7] His explanation offers an entry point for understanding how and why so many came to participate in the state's repressive apparatus. Maldonado also identifies the vital role of orejas, or "ears," local civilians who served as paid informants for the secret police. The denunciations made by these civilian collaborators—both male and female—broadened the radius of repression in the Segovias. Without these agents, the Guardia violence would have been neither as effective nor as deadly.

A relatively small army, the National Guard played a central role in bolstering the Somoza regime throughout its history. Some observers have even described the GN as "an armed political party" or "a separate military caste, loyal only to their own leader, not to the nation as a whole."[8] Formed by the U.S. military occupation of the 1920s and 30s, the Guardia received its arms, funding, and military training from the U.S. government. From the early 1930s, the GN was under the personal control of the Somoza family. The first Nicaraguan director of the Guardia was Gen. Anastasio Somoza García, and he was succeeded in power by West Point–educated Gen. Anastasio Somoza Debayle, and then later by Gen. José Somoza, Somoza García's son outside of marriage. By the late 1970s, Anastasio Somoza Portocarrero, General Somoza Debayle's son and an army major himself, appeared set to become the third generation of Somozas to lead the GN. Following the rise of the Sandinistas, the dictatorship and its U.S. backers sought to modernize the antiquated military and intelligence apparatus for the needs of Cold War counterinsurgency. Failing to professionalize the GN or to win the hearts and minds of the population, these transformations led to an increasing tempo of torture, killings, and other acts of brutality.

In earlier chapters we considered the Guardia's role in promulgating vice and carrying out political repression, but the only way to truly understand this organization is from the vantage point of its rank-and-file recruits. In this chapter I seek to understand how some of society's most marginalized became tethered to the regime's structures of oppression and counterinsurgency against peasants and the working class. Somoza's National Guard provided material, symbolic, and ideological incentives that led large numbers of Nicaraguan men to join the secu-

*Figure 4.1.* Soldiers of the Guardia Nacional parade in Managua, 1978. Courtesy of Instituto de Historia de Nicaragua y Centroamérica.

rity forces. Once inside the institution, the GN converted many "ordinary men" and youths into accomplices or agents of state terror who followed the corrupt orders given to them from above[9] (see fig. 4.1).

As has been true throughout Latin America, the military was an important site for the formation of personal identities and national discourses related to race, ethnicity, gender, and social class. Much of the literature, however, has emphasized elitist, top-down attempts to control "destructive" masculinity through conscription as part of nineteenth- and twentieth-century nation-building processes.[10] Nicaragua's National Guard fostered neither law nor order, as the country's crime and murder rate rose ever higher. For the impoverished (often rural and indigenous) men from the Segovias who enlisted in the GN rank-and-file, the military held out the possibility of achieving masculine honor as "real men" through access to limited material rewards, a celebration of disorderly machista behavior, and impunity for sub rosa criminal activities.[11] Of course, this sense of manhood required total submission to the figure of the caudillo and his continuing rule. The environment within the GN increasingly corrupted enlisted men:

first through access to vice and bribery, and then via an initiation to quotidian forms of violence and brutalization. By the time the regime faced an existential challenge, they had been well primed to carry out unfettered repression against Somoza's opponents with scant reference to morality. These developments form the other side of the story of the Sandinista Revolution and help explain the dynamics that pushed the nation to the point of civil war and revolution.

## From Peasants into Somocistas: Recruitment and Social Mobility

From the time of the U.S. marines' war against Sandino, the National Guard of Nicaragua had disproportionately recruited its privates (*soldados rasos*) from among the peasantry of the Segovias. The GN quickly became, Michael Schroeder argues, "an integral part of Segovian (and Nicaraguan) society, deeply embedded in the social fabric of the region (and country)—its families, communities, towns, farms, ranches, haciendas, indigenous communities, and patronage networks."[12] Military recruitment within the Segovias began as an effort by U.S. policymakers to impose their vision of order and stability on Nicaragua in the 1920s and 30s, but it developed into a veritable regional tradition over the following decades. In some parts of the rural north, a Sandinista organizer noted in the 1970s, most "families were in some way or another involved with the National Guard," whether that be a father, brother, or son who was in Somoza's army or the civilian militia.[13] In particular, the economically depressed department of Madriz gained an early and long-lasting reputation as a "breeding ground" and "nursery" (*vivero*) for the "harvesting" of National Guard soldiers. Many recruits came from the valleys around Somoto, such as Santa Isabel, Sonís, and Santa Rosa, and also the indigenous communities of San Lucas and Cusmapa to the southwest.

Many of those who joined the GN followed in the footsteps of fathers who had enlisted during the U.S. occupation, but a surprisingly large number had parents or grandparents who had once supported Sandino's nationalist insurgency. An indigenous campesino from Totogalpa who became a Guardia in 1947 (and rose to become a personal bodyguard and telegrapher for the Somozas) recalled that his grand-father had once backed Sandino and hosted meetings between the rebel leader and Liberal campesinos.[14] One former Guardia from San Fran-cisco in Somoto noted that his father had fought in Sandino's EDSN, under the orders of Gen. Carlos Salgado.[15] Another ex-Guardia from San Lucas similarly described how the Marines had punished his father and three uncles for backing the nationalist insurgency. "The *gringos* imprisoned all those that participated with Sandino," he explained. "My father was a prisoner in Ocotal for a year, building a runway. An uncle of mine was imprisoned there just because he helped both sides."[16] Despite their direct suffering at the hands of the GN, he said that his family supported his decision to enlist in Somoza's military. Given the poverty and lack of employment opportunities in the rural north, for many, becoming a Guardia was not a decision of political ideology so much as a survival strategy.

Political loyalties sharply divided some Liberal families during the Somoza era. The Flores Obregón brothers from Somoto, whose fa-ther had fought alongside Sandino in the country's 1926 civil war, took very different lessons from that history. The eldest son, Emilio, at-tended the National University and became a medical doctor in Pueblo Nuevo, Estelí. He was an outspoken anti-Somocista, a defender of San-dino's legacy, a leader of the Independent Liberal Party in his town, and an early clandestine backer of Carlos Fonseca's FSLN.[17] Access to a university education, however, was a rare opportunity in those years. Emilio's younger brother, Guillermo, instead entered the Na-tional Guard's Military Academy upon graduating high school in 1944 to continue his studies. He later explained, "I entered the Military Academy, not with the intention of committing any crimes, but to serve *la Patria* (the country). . . . By then, there were no marines. The government of that time gave the opportunity to enter the Military Academy where you could study any career, and, seeing the sacrifices of my parents, I decided to fill out an application and pass the physical and intellectual exams."[18] Guillermo gained the nickname "Piplaca" in the army, which refers to the sound of hitting something. Following a path diametrically opposed to that of his brother, he became a stead-fast Somocista military officer. He rose to the rank of brigadier gen-eral and was implicated in the repression of student protests in León in the 1970s. Clearly, family legacy alone did not determine one's political allegiance.

Instead, poverty, limited access to land, and unemployment were key factors that pushed many Segovian campesinos into the arms of the GN. Although the Pan-American Highway contributed to commerce and economic growth in Estelí, its construction left the department of Madriz wholly isolated. The international highway formerly passed through Somoto on its northward path to the Honduran border at El Espino, but when the Pan-American Highway shifted the crossing to Las Manos near Ocotal in Nueva Segovia, Somoto once again became a backwater. As we saw in chapter 1, even other municipalities in the department of Madriz, such as the flourishing, coffee-growing areas of San Juan del Río Coco and Telpaneca, now funneled their goods through Estelí instead of their departmental capital of Somoto.[19] During the 1940s and 50s, a journalist wrote, Somoteños regularly found work in road construction. However, by the end of the 1960s, the economy in Somoto had declined dramatically. It was moving in the opposite direction of the economically booming "Estelian miracle" down the road: "The jobs have slowly disappeared. . . . The lives of the workers and peasants are shameful, and artisans have left the city to head to Managua in search of a better market for their products. The little capital that is here is stagnant, while loan sharks have multiplied. The city continues to be attractive in its façade and nothing more. Misery and hunger abound below the surface."[20] These were the sorts of social conditions that the National Guard and the Somoza regime relied on to maintain a steady stream of recruits.

In explaining their reasons for joining the GN, many former soldiers emphasized the pressing material necessities of their families: mothers, wives, sisters, children. "A son of a bitch who had a handful of land wouldn't join the Guardia if he had a place to work," remembered one ex-Guardia from Estanzuela, outside of Estelí. "The only ones who went into the Guardia were the campesinos, day laborers (jornaleros) who worked on other people's haciendas. Because of poverty."[21] Throughout the twentieth century, access to land in the Segovias was limited by demographic pressures, the expanding holdings of commercial landowners, dispossession of ejido and indigenous lands, and clear-cutting by lumber companies. A campesino from San

Lucas who enlisted in the GN recalled that the plot of land his father owned within the Indigenous Community holdings had been stolen by a wealthy ladino landowner ("*un rico*") who "left them lying in the street. We had to look for a way to make a living."[22] Finding work during coffee and cotton harvests proved insufficient—it offered employment for a few months a year, but it left at least nine months without any income.

Recurrent droughts (*sequías*) visited the western Segovias every few years, leaving dry, dusty fields, shriveled *milpas* (corn patches), and hunger in its wake.[23] Some peasants fled to the agrarian frontier in eastern Nicaragua to find unclaimed lands in better climes, but many descended from their scattered homesteads to the nearby military base in Somoto in search of a job. A soldier from Santa Isabel, Somoto, claimed that he signed up in 1959 only after "three years in which it didn't rain. The rich didn't give work to the poor, so I lost all of my money. Poverty made me enter the army."[24] Family responsibilities also drove men to enlist to provide for children, siblings, and parents.[25] "I knew the Guardia was bad, but necessity made me join," a GN from Somoto claimed. "They gave you food, shoes, and clothing. My wife helped by making tortillas and ironing clothes, and my sons [worked] as shoe shiners."[26] Family needs often motivated men to join the GN, but their dispersal across the republic fostered absentee fatherhood by design and left behind thousands of female-headed households throughout the rural north.

Wages in the military were low, but the pay still exceeded what campesinos could earn on the haciendas.[27] In addition to their pay, the GN gave soldiers three meals a day, clothing, shoes, housing, and medical services. "We may have earned sixty pesos there," recalled a Guardia from Sonís, who joined in the 1940s, "but out of that salary, we had everything left over for spending. They didn't take us by force! We went on our own free will!"[28] Signing a three-year contract with the National Guard offered what one writer called a "local version of the American dream" of social mobility.[29] Young men who had never traveled beyond the nearest market town were whisked away in military vehicles to bustling Managua and on to the far corners of the country. The soldados rasos also gained symbolic and arbitrary power granted by their uniform and their U.S.-made Garand rifle. A peasant from

Totogalpa who worked on a coffee plantation witnessed a Guardia from his village come home, "and every time I saw him dressed in his uniform, it made me jealous. I joined the GN because I wanted to be a soldier."[30]

Once in the armed forces, the young men from the Segovias were trained for a wide range of jobs and gained numerous skills. Their tasks went well beyond combat missions, patrolling the borders, and protecting banks and government facilities. Within the GN, peasants served as masons, carpenters, electricians, gunsmiths, secretaries, radio operators, telegraphers, drivers, tailors, gardeners, bodyguards, tractor operators, cooks, barbers, and musicians. Campesinos from the Segovias gained a reputation as soldiers with a fierce loyalty to the caudillo and subservience to the ruling family. The dynasty's founder, Anastasio Somoza García, his son Anastasio Somoza Debayle, and the rest of the family surrounded themselves with the indigenous peasants-turned-soldiers from the Segovias, including their chefs, drivers, and bodyguard corps (known as the Green Berets or Pumas).[31] A German journalist who interviewed General Somoza Debayle in 1961 commented that his entire security detail came "from the most remote villages where there are no schools. Men who don't know how to read are more trustworthy and less susceptible to communist propaganda."[32] The infamous Somoza Battalion (*Batallón Blindado "General Somoza"*) was also largely staffed with soldiers from Madriz. "*El soldado somoteño*," bragged a former GN infantryman, earned a reputation as, "a humble and hard-working soldier, with discipline. The sweetness of a Somoteño as a soldier is his 'Sí, señor!' This 'yes, sir!' was not only how they answered but they actually did what they were told. The soldiers from other departments were always more disobedient."[33] He remembered with great pride the evenings on which General Somoza Debayle would swing by the barracks in Managua to take the soldiers from Somoto to one of his many haciendas for a night of hard drinking, engaging in the culture of masculine vice with the dictator himself.

Some ladino (nonindigenous) town dwellers claimed the indigenous campesinos' deep commitment to the regime was a product of their ethnicity, an extension of their traditional loyalty to their tribal chiefs or caciques. This ethnic essentialism was interestingly embraced by the campesino soldiers themselves as a positive marker of distinction — the once marginalized now possessed a direct link to the most powerful men in the land.[34] Under the traditional racist paradigm, Jeffrey Gould has explained, indigenous people or *indios* (in derogatory terms) had been viewed by Nicaraguan ladinos "as objects of pity, a degraded race."[35] Their ethnicity now empowered them through a symbolic inversion of racial and gendered hierarchies.[36] At the same time, a stark sense of hierarchy and dependence imbued the relationship. "When one enters into battle for a cause, it doesn't matter if you die," said a former Guardia from Yalagüina, Madriz, who fought against the Sandinistas. Asked the cause for which he fought, he paused and smiled. "We were . . . [pause] . . . We loved Somoza very much. He was our leader . . . [pause] . . . And we loved Nicaragua."[37] An indigenous campesino who worked as a bodyguard and telegrapher for both Anastasio Somoza García ("Tacho Viejo") and Anastasio Somoza Debayle ("Tachito" ) said that "they were very good to me. Why should I lie? We received everything we needed: clothes, shoes, slippers, and a tie to go out. They gave us more money for expenses."[38] Another soldier and Evangelical pastor in Somoto proudly declared that in his fifteen years of service, he did not miss a single day of work: "Those that were well-behaved got scholarships to study other things. We always dreamt of a better future. They helped me become what I am today. They helped me."[39] The National Guard was "apolitical" by statute and soldiers were not permitted to campaign or vote, but every single soldiers' GN ID recorded their political party by default as "Liberal." It was clear, once they joined the National Guard, where their loyalties lay.

The celebration of subservience within the GN is highly evident in the account of an indigenous soldier from the valley of Sonís trained by the U.S. embassy in Managua to protect the dictator from assassination. He recalled with great pride that other participants in the course refused to take the final exam, which required drinking an alleged poison, but he simply swallowed down the liquid. As he tells the story, the U.S. instructor was surprised and somewhat taken aback:

"Look, did you know that was poison?" "Yes, sir." "Then why did you drink it?" "Because I am taking a course and the instructions were clear." "But why would you die for this person?" "You know why?" I told him. "Because there are tons of people of my quality (*porque la calidad mía somos todos los que habemos*) but a person of the quality of a president or a first lady, there is only one. There are tons of us — thousands — but the quality of these people, only a few. It is worth dying for that sort of person." The gringo [instructor] hugged me and lifted me up in the air. "That's it! Give your life for theirs!" He jumped up and hugged me. The gringo really liked that.[40]

By responding correctly, he later found himself promoted to serve as a personal cook and food-taster for the Somoza family. This anecdote suggests a highly disparaging view of the self vis-à-vis both the dictator and his U.S. benefactors. At the same time, the soldier's behavior reflects a keen awareness of the deference that the powerful both cherished and materially rewarded. He was, it could be said, the perfect client.

Advancement within the ranks of the GN opened up lucrative opportunities for personal enrichment. Much of this wealth went into the hands of higher-ranking officers (*oficiales*) from middle- and upper-middle-class backgrounds who had graduated from the Military Academy and become large landowners and business associates of the Somozas. The fault lines were incredibly clear when it came to the GN's bifurcated internal class structure. The vast majority of the officer corps were lighter skinned and far more likely to come from cities than the masses of lower-level "indio" privates with darker skin and a more indigenous appearance. Treatment of rasos by the oficiales was often harsh, disrespectful, and even violent toward their subordinates. Some enlisted men from poorer backgrounds, however, rose through the system to become *oficiales de corbata negra* (black tie officers) and owners of illegal brothels and gambling dens. These Guardias went from campesinos with little more than an adobe hut in their rural village to the owners of small businesses in various Managua neighborhoods. The Somozas' private cook reflected on his success: "In Reparto Schick, I built a house. I had a little store in San Judas, I had a bar in Las Mesitas, a beer hall in Reparto Schick. It was a very sinful place (*muy zángano*). God punishes you for these businesses; they're bad news (*tungos*). A bar with pretty girls . . . the Bible says that we should not eat the flesh of a poor woman, or sell it. Or even worse: I sold liquor and cigarettes. I owned all these kind of businesses."[41] Despite stated regrets about profiting from women's exploitation, he nonetheless remained proud of the social mobility he had achieved thanks to his employment in the military. For the lowest-level Guardias who were also of poor backgrounds but did not rise through the ranks, the primary form of illicit enrichment was extortion through small-time bribes (*mordidas*) for traffic violations and the like.[42]

Being a National Guard gave the men a sense of impunity, which fostered a rowdy, masculine culture of vice within the organization. The machista behavior present in everyday life was celebrated and taken to extremes within the GN. Acts of reckless violence that left people injured or killed rarely led to a dishonorable discharge, let alone criminal prosecution. Indeed, one government opponent remarked, it was "absolutely impossible to get a member of the National Guard tried for anything he did against civilians. They were little gods."[43] Campesinos from the hamlet of Santa Isabel complained that a local soldier mistreated the population, telling them "that he was the law in Somoto" and that "if he heard that anyone in the town was working with the Sandinistas, he would grab them and kill them no matter who they were."[44] Another Guardia from Somoto fired his gun at some high school students in Matagalpa who had thrown urine, rotten eggs, and tomatoes at his vehicle as a prank. When it turned out their parents were prominent Somocistas, he apparently faced reprimand. He later laughed off the claim that the GN expelled him for shooting the youths: "If I had actually killed students, they wouldn't have fired me but rather promoted me because that's what the Guardia was like."[45]

Often, high levels of alcohol consumption fueled violent altercations between soldiers, especially in the cantinas where they spent much of their free time. The desire for and objectification of women were also central to this machista culture. Fights over women led to many barroom brawls, such as the one in which a soldier from Somoto was stabbed multiple times by the bodyguard of Col. Fermín Meneses.[46] In another case, neighbors accused a Guardia from Yalagüina of "a crime he committed in a cantina in Somoto in which he killed a child aged seven to ten, sinking his knife into his stomach."[47] They later claimed that the Guardia had not faced any legal repercussions for this heinous act. In August 1977, another army private shot two people, including a sixty-year-old woman, in a cantina in Somoto, and *La Prensa* merely reported that, as usual, "liquor was believed to be the cause of the tragedy."[48] Accusations like these give us a sense of the culture of masculine brutality and impunity fostered within the GN. Though punishment was sparse, senior officers occasionally violently reprimanded soldiers who arrived to work under the influence. In 1975, one sergeant slammed an inebriated private from Somoto against the wall face-first, smashing his cheek and lip. "Seeing the blood on my face, I lost faith in the Guardia," the private later lamented, his male honor tarnished.[49]

Vice plagued the internal culture of the GN, but outrageous actions perpetrated while intoxicated on occasion surpassed even the GN's limits and led to repercussions. For example, one Guardia from Santa Isabel was court-martialed for getting drunk, disarming a fellow soldier, firing four cartridges at him, and threatening the life of a cantina owner.[50] Another soldier from Yalagüina shot and killed a fellow Guardia in a conflict over money in a cantina in the Campo Bruce neighborhood of Managua. His prior record included demerits for attacking a GN patrol with his bayonet "in a drunken state" and crashing a Toyota vehicle, causing 800 córdobas of damage. After procuring a lawyer with money made by selling the family's ox, he was able to obtain his release and only serve one year behind bars for homicide.[51] Given the centrality of the cantina to military life, at times the GN even used bars and brothels as a place to find recruits. In one case, a campesino arrested for drunken disorderliness at a popular cantina in Estelí spent two days behind bars before being offered a job as a soldier. He immediately accepted and was released from jail directly into military service.[52]

The abuse and licentiousness engendered within the institution, however, was not necessarily to the liking of all recruits. Some neither thrived nor adapted to the military nor wanted a career as a Guardia. City life far from family was trying, and many quickly tired of the harsh treatment meted out by senior officers.[53] Often, campesinos joined the GN in tough times to supplement household income, with plans to return to their villages when the weather improved. For these men, Somoza's Guardia was a temporary escape hatch from rural unemployment and drought. Some men cycled in and out of the GN every few years over their lifetime. Take, for instance, the soldier from Somoto who joined in 1957 and returned home after completing his three-year contract, only to rejoin in 1963. In 1968, he again successfully solicited his discharge but was called up to reenlist in 1972 following the devastating earthquake in Managua. This time, he would remain in the GN until the fall of Somoza seven years later.[54]

Sometimes, dissatisfied recruits simply fled back home without permission in order to tend to their milpa or find work in the coffee harvest. These illegal desertions ironically helped to assure a captive labor supply for the armed forces. Considered criminal fugitives for violating their contracts, they were given a choice when caught: a lengthy prison term or extended military service. GN records reveal countless cases of desertions, arrests, courts-martial, and forced reenlistments for longer terms. One man from San Lucas served eight months before deserting and heading back to the countryside, where he lived on the lam for a year and worked in agriculture. When a neighbor denounced him to the authorities, he was captured and sent to prison in Managua to serve a two-year sentence. "I was there seven months," he remembered, "and the comandante asked me when they took me out of jail if I wanted to return to the army."[55] After his time behind bars, he jumped at the chance to reenlist, remaining in the military for many years to come. The GN sentenced another Guardia from Yalagüina who had deserted to two years in prison. He hoped to do his jail time behind bars and return home, but after twenty-three months in prison, he said, the GN pressured him into signing yet another three-year contract.[56] These cases suggest the diverse motivations that led men to enlist in the GN. For those who assimilated into their roles within of the Guardia, however, their everyday lives soon became structured by an environment of corruption, vice, and violent impunity.

## COLD WAR MODERNIZATION, GUERRILLA WARFARE, AND ANTICOMMUNISM

From its roots in the U.S. occupation, the National Guard maintained an identification with the U.S. military. Although its dependence on the Americans may have limited its nationalist legitimacy, affiliation with the superpower provided a certain degree of pride, even among the institution's most subordinate members. "All of the military tactics were from the United States," reminisced a beaming ex-Guardia from Totogalpa. "Everything that we used was American: the clothes, the hat, and the boots. It was all from the United States."[57] Another former soldier from San Lucas spoke in even more blunt terms: "The Guardia was *norteamericano*. The Somozas were *norteamericanistas*. It was a government helped by the United States in cash (*billetes*) and arms. . . . To have an army, you need cash."[58] Some of those millions of dollars of support given to Somoza, in turn, found their way down to the Guardias. This vision of gifting as the patron's benevolence bolstered the promise of social mobility that drew many campesinos to join the GN.

The fact that so many soldados continued to conceptualize the Guardia in patron–client terms suggests the failure of later efforts to reform the GN along Cold War lines. Particularly after the 1959 Cuban Revolution, the United States and the Somoza regime tried to modernize and ready the National Guard to confront the rising threat of guerrilla warfare. Officers and privates alike were regularly sent for training at the infamous School of the Americas (SOA), located on Fort Gulick in the Panama Canal Zone.[59] Between 1950 and 1965, a total of 808 officers were trained in the United States or at the Canal Zone, making Nicaragua the country in Latin America with the highest ratio of U.S.-trained officers.[60] The GN sent an additional fifty-two officers to U.S. military academies and 303 to the SOA between 1970 and 1975.[61] For rank-and-file soldiers, these experiences generated a feeling of accomplishment. "I studied in Panama in the School of the Americas in Fort Gulick and Fort Sherman," a campesino in Yalagüina recalled with great pride. The courses he passed included "jungles, parachuting, tank mechanics, and armory. I was there three times for training courses that lasted for three months each. The instructors were all gringos."[62]

As with military forces throughout Latin America, both the police and military branches of the National Guard were refashioned during the 1960s and 70s to combat "internal enemies."[63] Antiguerrilla training courses on "Urban Counterinsurgency" and "Guerrilla Warfare" held at the SOA during these years called on officers to "adjust their doctrine to how the revolutionaries use their guerrilla combatants, increasing—if necessary—to the same level of criminality (juridical repression)."[64] These blunt references to "criminality" and "juridical repression" suggest a new willingness by both the GN and its U.S. backers to approve the application of violence, including torture and summary execution. Such repression was necessary, they claimed, to meet the threat of irregular forces who were often indistinguishable from the civilian population.

In addition to shifts in military strategy, the modernization process sought to transform the worldview of the GN. Rather than loyalty to the caudillo and his patronage, U.S. officers attempted to instill an anticommunist ideology that would trump devotion to any one individual. In these classes, the U.S. trainers emphasized the need to defend the country against the threat of "international communism." To appeal to nationalist sentiments, GN ideologue Emilio Padilla presented the FSLN as a mere "façade organization dependent on Moscow whose comandante is Fidel Castro, who has the responsibility of developing subversion in Latin America."[65] The GN increasingly cast guerrilla combatants as Cubans, Russians, or other foreigners, rather than fellow Nicaraguans. In the same article, Padilla challenged the FSLN's claim to the nationalist legacy of Sandinismo, writing that "Sandino was a confused man. He did much damage to la Patria. He killed, mutilated, and burned alive thousands of his fellow citizens who did not agree with his politics. He was a confused man, we repeat, but his ideas were saturated with undeniable nationalism. Sandino was depraved but not a communist."[66]

While repeating official claims that Sandino had been "depraved," he emphasized his "undeniable nationalism" to draw a sharp contrast with the "communist" FSLN. Padilla also attempted to undercut the Sandinistas' appeals to moral regeneration and family harmony: "Statistically, it has been shown that 95 percent of the members of the group known as the Sandinista National Liberation Front are bad students, drug addicts, and young people with family problems. Where they have shown a certain ability to whip up support is by offering unwary campesinos lands that already have legitimate owners."[67] Inverting Sandinista discourse, students and young people were here cast as morally corrupted outsiders "with family problems" responsible for tricking hapless campesinos. In Argentina and Brazil, right-wing, anticommunist military regimes effectively used such language linking moral panic about youth, sexual liberation, and gender norms to "communist subversion."[68] However, given the unique circumstances in Somoza's Nicaragua, such right-wing moralism found almost no resonance among the population, falling flat against their lived experience. More successful was the GN's subtler efforts to foster class resentment among the rank-and-file: not against the grandes ricos and the politically powerful, but instead against the upwardly mobile high school and university students of the cities who were seeking to overthrow their personal benefactor, General Somoza.

Ideology and political commitment were almost never a motivating factor for military enlistment. Once inside the institution, however, Guardia recruits were bombarded with anticommunist ideology. Few of them claimed to have completely grasped the language, but most had some sense of a looming threat on the horizon if the Sandinistas were to triumph. "They taught us that Nicaragua was an underdeveloped country and those who were fighting, like the FSLN, didn't come for the interests of the people but to implant communism in the country," an infantryman from Palacagüina explained. "That's what they taught us in the classes and that we had the duty to make sure that the GN would not fall because if the GN fell, thousands of Nicaraguans would die."[69] A soldier from San Lucas described his officers' insistence that the Sandinistas wanted to impose communism, which they described as a dictatorship in which "they gave you all your food." "They told us, even though you don't have a place to live, you have freedom," he said. "At least you can go out and take a stroll. With communism, you won't have the right to do anything."[70] Another stated that trainers taught them that the FSLN were enemies "because they were people who came aided by Cuba and Cuba is communist, so the same thing that happened in Cuba was going to happen here. Our family members were all going to be killed."[71]

The May 1965 U.S. invasion of the Dominican Republic proved an important testing ground for the new counterinsurgent strategy. The National Guard joined an Organization of American States (OAS) "peacekeeping force" directed by the U.S. Marine Corps, alongside troops from the fellow military dictatorships of Paraguay, Honduras, and Brazil. Though often overlooked, the invasion and occupation of Santo Domingo saw hundreds of Nicaraguans sent into battle against "communism" for the first time. They were essentially sent to prevent the fall of a U.S.-backed regime threatened by a popular uprising. However, a Guardia recalled, "they told us that we went to prevent communism. . . . I didn't want to go, and almost no one else wanted to go, but we had to because those were the president's orders."[72] Another Guardia remembered being told that it was a battle against "the troops that Fidel Castro had there. I went for two and a half years. We saw little combat ourselves because the U.S. Army had things under control, but there was always some combat."[73] Although the soldiers were told so at the time, Cuba did not, in fact, have troops operating in the Dominican Republic.

Back home in Nicaragua, the fight against "communism" took two very different forms. The U.S. Alliance for Progress program, launched by President Kennedy in response to the Cuban Revolution, called on Latin American militaries to play a central role in economic development, the construction of infrastructure, and social services. Known as *Acción Cívica* (Civic Action), these initiatives included building roads, houses for the poor, modernizing agriculture, and distributing social aid. These U.S.-designed programs aimed to "win the hearts and minds" of the rural population to undercut support for the guerrillas.[74] Many GN soldiers were sent to a special Acción Cívica battalion and began operating tractors, building houses, installing electricity, giving injections to the sick, treating children with gastroenteritis, inseminating cattle, and drilling artesian wells in drought-prone areas. Because of corruption, however, much of the battalion's work was done not in poor villages but on the haciendas of well-connected Somocista landowners, such as those of Alfonso Lovo Cordero in Madriz and Estelí.[75] These efforts to reform public perceptions of the GN thus failed as the institution fell back into its familiar patterns of graft and corruption.

In tandem with these programs, the GN also launched a violent counterinsurgency campaign against those isolated villages accused of supporting the Sandinistas. Dating from the late 1960s, the GN concentrated its repressive operations in the remote mountainous regions of the departments of Matagalpa and Zelaya, where the FSLN had been operating. In this fight, GN recruits developed a firm notion of the "communist" enemy, with soldiers receiving official commendation for "good behavior and participation in armed encounters with subversive groups."[76] In Waslala, a soldier from Pueblo Nuevo noted, "during the two months that I patrolled, we marched through the area. The captain told us to keep our eyes peeled to avoid an ambush by the guerrillas. They called them *yeicos* and, of course, we were happy when we captured a yeico."[77] Another Guardia from Somoto who served in the mountainous north admitted that arresting and threatening campesinos formed an integral part of their military strategy.[78] Given that most of these abuses took place in distant, sparsely populated regions, most Nicaraguans remained utterly unaware of the scale of the atrocities the GN was committing until the mid- to late 1970s. In just a few years, though, the GN's gross human rights violations became too glaring to hide.

## La EEBI: Forging a Counterinsurgent Youth

In the wake of the much-publicized 1974 Sandinista assault on the home of Chema Castillo, the National Guard aimed to construct a new, more battle-ready force able to meet the guerrilla challenge. Anastasio Somoza Portocarrero, the dictator's son, led efforts to improve the GN with a new counterinsurgent infantry brigade that was to be better trained and better armed.[79] The plan was to double the size of the GN from 8,000 to 15,000 soldiers over a period of three years, with most of the recruits undergoing intense preparation for warfare. Mockingly referred to as "el Chigüin" (the little kid), Somoza Portocarrero had studied at Harvard University and received military training at Fort Bragg in North Carolina. Rather than retrain the GN's aging and often obese "old guard" who had by and large never seen a day of combat, his father gave Somoza Portocarrero control of the Basic Infantry Training School (la Escuela de Entrenamiento Básico de Infantería, EEBI). He expanded the institution's budget and made major investments in armaments, uniforms, foreign trainers, and facilities starting in 1976–77. The appointment of the twenty-five-year-old "kid" (rather than any of the GN's top officers) shocked many Nicaraguans, both inside and outside of the GN.

With its new officer class, the EEBI aimed to modernize the GN to prepare for combat against armed threats. By improving the training program, Somoza Portocarrero claimed, they would convert the caudillo-style constabulary force into a genuinely national, professional military, with a clear anticommunist mission. El Chigüin explained to the U.S. embassy that past criminal behavior had occurred because the GN was "primarily comprised of people coming from the poorest of the poor in Nicaragua. They are uneducated and are sadly lacking in the ability to deal properly with the general populace. . . . In the past, the Guardia was content to sit in their sleepy guard post and rake in graft, but those times are gone forever."[80] Instead of dependence on the Somoza family and the Liberal Party, the GN was supposedly going to be trained to be loyal to the nation and the government. A former EEBI trainee recalls el Chigüin told the recruits "that every soldier had the duty to win over the people . . . not with words but with actions . . . [and] to be conscious that we lived for the people and needed the people because they paid taxes and that was where our salaries came from."[81] However, the very fact that the dictator's son personally headed the institution negated these pronouncements, revealing exactly where power continued to reside. The EEBI's official magazine heralded its efforts to create "*a new type of Soldier . . .* an authentic citizen. . . . A Spartan warrior trained for war because it is necessary in order to live in peace."[82] Though intended as a training facility for the wider GN, the EEBI gained significant autonomy and began functioning almost as an independent, elite counterinsurgent unit. As enrollment grew, many worried it was developing into a second "army-within-an-army" that could be used to assure political power remain within the family.

The exact role of the United States in the gestation of this new brigade remains unclear. A 1975 CIA report fretted that Somoza's plans to bring in American trainers to the EEBI would "provide both the FSLN and conventional opposition groups a new, potentially damaging issue. [Somoza's] opponents are certain to condemn the instructors as foreign mercenaries and play on fears of foreign intervention. If the reported Guardia unit should adopt aggressive tactics, there is a good chance of excesses that would outrage civilian sensibilities and enhance the FSLN's prospects for new recruits and further successful operations."[83] Such preoccupations proved startlingly prescient. Despite this apparent hesitancy, the U.S. officials later vociferously praised Somoza

Portocarrero's "motivation, leadership, and professionalism" and received EEBI recruits at the SOA while the GN sent others for preparation in Brazil, Chile, Guatemala, and El Salvador.[84] A small number of mercenaries, including Vietnam War veteran and martial arts expert Mike Echanis, arrived in Managua from the United States to directly lead the training. Among the group was a Vietnamese man who had fought in the South Vietnamese army, whom the recruits referred to as "el Chino." Whether these men were sent by the CIA or privately contracted by el Chigüin has never been definitively ascertained.[85] In addition, two anti-Castro Cubans who had previously served in Batista's military were brought in to teach the Nicaraguan soldiers how to avoid the mistakes made in Cuba two decades earlier.[86]

While the Segovias continued to serve as the GN's recruiting grounds, the EEBI now only accepted teenagers at the height of their physical prowess into the rigorous training program. Incorporating many young men not only improved battle readiness but created a mirror image of the FSLN's young guerrilla fighters; a number of those who joined the EEBI were young teens and even some adolescents. They were drilled in marching for hours on end, did continuous aerobic exercise, learned both judo and karate, and were taught to cross rivers and navigate mountain passes.[87] An eighteen-year-old from Yalagüina described the daily schedule at the EEBI: "From four to six in the morning, we did two hours of running. From six to eight, we rested while we ate breakfast. From eight to ten, we lined up for marching and military formation. From ten to twelve, we received classes on the assembly and disassembly of arms. At noon, we had lunch, and they gave us an hour for cleanup. From one to three, we did push-ups, rowing; just exercise. At three, we did chores. On Fridays, they showed us movies—cowboys, shoot-outs, and all of that. They also taught those who didn't know how to swim."[88]

The day-to-day drills and hazing included beatings and harassment serving to break the young men down mentally. One soldier from Somoto explained proudly that "the training was hard. Passing through the famous EEBI made one into a man (*tener cara de hombre uno*) because they spit on us, they kicked us. They basically tortured us in order to make a soldier."[89] Sand was thrown in their faces, testified a recruit from Santa Isabel, and they were forced to eat painfully large numbers of chilies.[90] Surviving the degrading training indeed gave one a sense of masculine supremacy, personal honor, and loyalty to the higher commands, but without any serious constraint or attempt to reshape male violence. Whereas the traditional GN pushed "popular, civilian manhood" to its ultimate extremes, the EEBI barracks and training went well beyond typical machismo and fostered a harsh and violent "military masculinity" that emphasized a willingness to kill.[91] A team of Canadian psychologists studying EEBI adolescent soldiers captured after the revolution concluded that the boys' military "training was characterized by extreme discipline very often including physical violence to the recruits, that it was conducted in a moral climate which had the most basic disregard for the right of civilians, and that the children themselves showed evidence of limited moral understanding and development."[92]

The EEBI at times seemed to be training not to maintain firm social control, but to unleash disorderly and unreserved violence against the civilian population. For instance, opposition reports claimed that recruits were taught to chant "*¡Arriba la Guardia! ¡Abajo el pueblo!*" (Up with the Guardia! Down with the people!), and a military cadence calling on them to "drink the blood of the people."[93] An EEBI soldier from San Juan de Limay in Estelí later testified that during his rotation at the Cibalsa military base they were told "they were training us to take us to the mountains to kill . . . the guerrillas." While they were marching, they were called "tigers" and forced to chant "'You want the blood of the people!' We had to say it because if you didn't, they beat us and said, 'Don't be cowards (*no se ahueven*). One day, you're going to be good little soldiers.'"[94] These forms of brutalization and indoctrination served to convert campesino recruits from average Nicaraguan peasant youths into counterinsurgent soldiers capable of great cruelty when following orders.

Despite these attempts at ideological indoctrination, the reforms unintentionally enhanced the army's clientelistic and personalistic nature. Not only did the GN's membership grow rapidly along with the range of material benefits offered, but Somoza's own son had a hands-on role within every aspect of the new project. In the EEBI itself, a massive portrait of the dictator Somoza Debayle hung on the wall, watching over the mess hall. A soldier from Santa Rosa, Somoto, noted that when they crossed paths with Somoza Portocarrero, they were told to shout, "For you, Sir, I will give my life for yours!"[95] Compared to the GN as a whole, the new recruits gained numerous perks and privileges: superior housing, better medical assistance, food, clothes, and a monthly salary of more than 550 córdobas.[96] At an exclusive store on the base, EEBI soldiers bought televisions, stereos, radios, whiskey, clothes, perfume, and other imported goods duty-free.[97] All of these perquisites led to tensions with older Guardias who felt passed over by the youth. The EEBI also gave soldiers the chance to receive training abroad and return as instructors at the school. Somoza Portocarrero, one recruit said, "was attuned to everything you needed as a soldier. [He told us,] 'You have to advance, not remain as a simple soldier.' He called us into his office. 'You're going to Fort Sherman to a pilot's course.' 'You're going to Chile to study jungle combat. It's for your own good to advance as a soldier.'"[98] Guardias such as this recruit or the one mentioned in this chapter's introduction were among those Segovian peasants who remained unstintingly loyal to the GN because of these promises of professionalization, moving up in rank, and social mobility. As we will see in the next section, it was the combination of this new infantry brigade and the rapid expansion of the GN's intelligence apparatus that would produce an unprecedented level of bloodshed during these final years of the Somoza dictatorship.

## OREJAS: SURVEILLANCE, TORTURE, AND COLLABORATION

In tandem with the development of the new counterinsurgent infantry battalions, the Somoza regime amped up its intelligence-gathering apparatus to carry out repression through extralegal means. To stamp out the opposition, the GN's secret police, the Office of National Security (OSN), covertly recruited a vast network of paid informants throughout the cities, towns, and villages of the Segovias. During the 1960s, the United States began encouraging technological advancement in intelligence gathering in Central America, giving the GN ample aid.[99] By 1969, Estelí became the first city outside of Managua with a permanent OSN office.[100] Officers were sent to the SOA in the Panama Canal Zone to complete U.S. military courses in both intelligence and counterintelligence, many of them gaining renown as ruthless torturers.[101] The OSN soon established the Anticommunist Service (Servicio Anticomunista, SAC), a highly selective branch tasked with capturing or killing top Sandinista leaders.[102]

GN interrogation methods emphasized sheer physical brutality rather than sophisticated psychological manipulation. Electric shocks, fists, boots, and gun butts were the main tools of the trade and, in many cases, served as much as a form of punishment as a technique for extracting information. The disorienting *capucha* (hood), a black sack tied over prisoners' heads for weeks or months at a time, became a trademark of the secret police in its treatment of political prisoners.[103] Some of those tasked with carrying out the torture were highly trained professionals. Consider, for example, the case of an intelligence agent from Somoto who entered the Military Academy in Managua after earning excellent grades at his public high school. Upon graduation from the Academy, the OSN placed him in an undercover post monitoring opposition politicians serving in Somoza's government. For his effective performance, he was transferred to the SAC and given advanced courses in fingerprinting and photography, which he used to trace participants in anti-Somoza protests.[104] A woman captured by the GN later testified that he had personally tortured her and, though he wore "blue jeans, the Guardias called him 'boss.'"[105] Some of the soldiers took pity on her and begged the SAC agent, "She's a woman, don't treat her so bad." However, the victim later testified that he simply responded, "'She's not a woman, she's a yeica,' and opened something that I suppose was a box or something metallic, and he applied the tip of a cable to my ears."[106] According to her testimony, after passing out from the electric shocks, she regained consciousness and discovered that the two guerrillas restrained alongside her were now dead. With the torture (and soon, killing) of women accused of being Sandinistas, GN repression reached new extremes.

The OSN received information to target activists from paid local informants, drawn from among the civilian population. These orejas—termed "paramilitaries" by some—listened in on neighbors and kept their eyes open for any antiregime activity. A single informer could derail the best-laid, secret plans of dozens of activists and produce numerous deaths. As a popular saying went, "the tongue doesn't have

bones, but it breaks bones." All of those benefiting from the state's patronage structure, such as public employees, schoolteachers, AMROCS
members, and reservists, were widely viewed as likely orejas.[107] The
publicly identified orejas in Estelí included people from all walks of
life, including taxi drivers, popsicle sellers, radio technicians, and
leather workers. Referred to by the GN as "collaborators" or "honorary agents," these agents received "significant economic benefits" for
their denunciations.[108] In Somoto, a resident recalled, many townspeople were quick to enlist in the secret police and denounce their
neighbors as alleged subversives. "Being an oreja was the only job anyone had here for the Somoteños," he said, with shame. "As there are no
factories or jobs, it was not to get rich. It was just to meet their needs
that the people sold the youth. Just by denouncing one person, they
had enough to eat. They sold humanity like you would sell a horse."[109]

Former GN officers have complained in retrospect of the incom-
petence of these informants and their utter lack of efficacy.[110] "I give
most of the blame to those people we called the orejas," an Academy-
trained EEBI commander from Somoto said of the repression. "Eight
out of ten times that they informed to us, it was just because they didn't
like someone. If the Guardia is here on their base, they don't know
what's going on in that community. So someone comes and says 'so-
and-so is doing this,' and you had to respond. Maybe you went there,
and there was actually nothing, but in the process, someone died, and
that's where the accusations against us came from."[111] Even though this
claim is patently self-serving in aiming to absolve the GN for their
crimes and presenting extrajudicial killings in passive terms ("in the
process, someone died"), it indicates the role that civilian informants
played in prompting military violence. The crude nature of intelligence
gathering and GN response only further heightened the sense of disorder and lawlessness that undergirded the regime.

In addition to direct cash payments, the OSN membership card
given to "honorary agents" greatly empowered the orejas, opening
doors for government employment or impunity before the law, much
like the infamous Magnífica distributed during elections.[112] Some orejas
openly flaunted their OSN links and hoped to inspire fear among their
neighbors, at times even threatening GN officers. One prominent oreja
who ran a travel agency in Estelí felt powerful enough to publicly in-

sult the National Guard. The local comandante wrote to Somoza, complaining, "He pretends to be a friend of the government and the National Guard, but it's not true," and that the oreja had called the GN "a bunch of thieves and killers."[113] His status as an OSN agent, he seemed to believe, placed him above the comandante in the military hierarchy.

In addition to government employees, many orejas were the very same underworld figures and cantina caciques who engaged in illicit activities with the collusion of the GN. Owners of bars and gambling dens often provided a bevy of gossip and rumors gleaned from conversations overheard in their establishments. For instance, an OSN agent and onetime Somoza bodyguard from Estelí ran "Los Ángeles," a cantina and brothel in Managua frequented by OSN officers. The aunt of a twelve-year-old girl claimed that he and the brothel's madam had entrapped teenage campesinas trafficked from the north, such as her niece, whipping them, forcing them to drink alcohol, and even branding them like cattle. He denied the accusations but admitted paying 100 córdobas a week to the GN to keep the business open.[114] In another case, a particularly menacing oreja was said to have murdered a bartender in an Estelí cantina (in a dispute over an unpaid two peso drink) at the very time that he was supposed to have been in jail for stabbing his first wife to death in Pueblo Nuevo. "With the chronic corruption of the dictatorship," an accuser claimed, "this individual was given his freedom and appeared in Jalapa working as a member of the Investigation Police."[115] The lurid details of the cases are difficult to confirm, but these stories give a sense of the OSN's immersion in the Somocista system of violence, criminality, and impunity.

Many orejas also shared in the culture of masculine sociability and vice of the National Guard, and they were often spotted drinking and gambling with the soldiers. An elderly informant in Condega spent his days lounging in the town's park, observing all that went on, and his nights at the GN base playing rounds of *desmoche*, the quintessentially masculine Nicaraguan card game.[116] According to the town's former mayor, Romeo González, "He pretended to be very humble and dumb to carry out his work, but he received a monthly salary of 400 córdobas."[117] In Estelí, a gun salesman known for drinking, shooting dice, and playing cards with GN officers was among those honorary agents provided with photos of suspected Sandinistas. If he saw any of them, he was to "denounce them immediately and help capture them . . . he'd go around with [the GN] and point out which houses were identified with the Sandinista struggle."[118] Neighbors claimed he was often seen "with members of the Seguridad Somocista, hosting meetings of all the paramilitaries in the city. Everyone here was afraid of him."[119]

At times, orejas themselves constructed expansive chains of informants throughout the rural north. "Gustavo," an auto mechanic in his fifties based in Condega, for instance, worked in close association with a traveling medicine and clothing salesman who regularly passed through the towns and villages of the rural north plying his wares.[120] "We discovered bit by bit and with some work that this network existed," a Sandinista intelligence officer later testified, "but it was much larger and, with its interconnections, it encompassed practically all five departments of the Segovias."[121] In Condega alone, he estimated that there were forty-five members of this secret organization, including both prominent and influential Somocistas (such as former mayors, hacendados with histories of stealing land, and the local judge), as well as others further under the radar (jueces de mesta, public employees, cantina owners, and convicted thieves).[122]

Gustavo submitted comprehensive reports every fifteen days, including the names and addresses of families accused of supporting the FSLN. To closely monitor the opposition González family, Gustavo even moved his auto shop to the patio directly adjacent to the family's home, even though its small driveway had little room for repairing vehicles. On his property, he grew a small plot of illegal marijuana plants in plain sight, which was unsurprisingly ignored by visiting GN officers. Jaime González recalled that one evening, "I saw something strange in a *mamón* tree in the property where Gustavo lived. This strange form was Gustavo himself who had climbed the tree after hearing the sound of cars pulling into our garage, and was spying inside, probably trying to see who was entering the house. He had probably been doing this for a long time."[123] Having lived in the community for decades, Gustavo formed ties of friendship, business, and even family with both the National Guard sponsors and the targets of his surveillance.[124]

With the help of civilian informants, the GN was able to track down and kill top Sandinista leaders throughout the 1970s. Most informants were male, but there were some notorious cases of women who were implicated in the oreja networks. One of the most infamous and feared orejas in Estelí was "la Porra Azul," a middle-aged ambulant saleswoman, known for her flashy outfits and addiction to gambling. She gained access to "all of the houses because she sold cigars as a subterfuge to find out everything," recalled one local.[125] The FSLN believed that she was responsible for the 1970 arrest of Denis Zamorán, a Sandinista guerrilla who had studied in the Soviet Union and trained at Palestinian camps in Jordan. In their official communiqué after his capture and death in Estelí, the GN declared that Zamorán had "thrown himself from the vehicle while it was moving at eighty kilometers an hour and crashed against the pavement."[126] Locals greeted this version of the events with universal skepticism, and the population learned to fear la Porra Azul.

In July 1976, the GN tracked down Augusto Salinas Pinell, the idealistic former schoolteacher who led guerrilla organizing in the Segovias with the *Cartilla Campesina* in hand.[127] When Salinas arrived in San Juan del Río Coco and met with "Chispero," a townsman he had known from his teacher days, the latter promptly relayed his presence to the OSN.[128] A GN patrol soon murdered the guerrilla under suspicious and unclear circumstances. The government claimed that Salinas (whom they described as "the leader of the group that indoctrinated campesinos in the northeastern zone of the country") was gunned down while resisting arrest, others insisted that the GN summarily executed or even tortured him before his death.[129] For his role in facilitating Salinas Pinell's death, Chispero was rewarded with induction into the OSN, as he later described: "The officer congratulated me and said that he was going to assign me personally. This same man gave me the OSN card and asked for a photo."[130] Soon thereafter, Chispero went into the vice business with the local GN comandante, jointly opening illegal gambling dens in the village homes of two women. This collaboration proved highly profitable, with the comandante receiving thousands of córdobas in kickbacks.[131]

Itinerant salesmen, market women, and local cantina owners offered a steady supply of information, but the OSN's greatest intelligence coups came from its direct infiltration of the FSLN itself. Captured Sandinista activists came to collaborate with the secret police due to torture, threats, monetary inducements, or ideological appeals. In Condega, for instance, the OSN recruited a high school student who

had previously served as a correo, transporting packages between guerrilla safe houses for the FSLN. Because he was of Chinese ancestry, the
OSN codenamed him "Mao Gómez."[132] With the onslaught of repression in the mid-1970s, the GN captured Mao. Before his torture, however, Capt. Ricardo Lau, a GN prominent intelligence officer also of
Chinese descent, secured the student's release and asked him to join in
their efforts to destroy the FSLN. Over a meal at the family's restaurant, Mao claimed that Lau told him "that the guerrilla movement was
causing damage with its Marxist theories among high school students
and in some sectors of the people . . . that the student leaders were
wielding Marxist theory to trick the average students at the schools.
He invited me to collaborate and said that, as we were supposedly 'fellow countrymen,' I should cooperate and help him in his work."[133] For
a salary of 300 córdobas per month, Mao reported on student activism
in Condega and later at the National University, and also provided the
location of guerrilla encampments.[134] Whether it was ideology, fear, or
financial compensation that drove his decision to cooperate with the
OSN is unclear from the available documentation. Despite his years of
collaboration, the information provided by Mao Gómez apparently did
not directly result in the arrest or murder of Sandinistas.

The OSN's most effective infiltration of the FSLN, however, took
place in Somoto, the Segovias' most pro-Somoza town. From 1975, the
secret police archives reveal a stream of detailed reports on internal
Sandinista activities in Madriz. The man later accused of providing the
information, "Jaime," was a schoolteacher and refrigeration technician
who had been active in leftist groups alongside Dr. Dávila Bolaños
since the 1960s.[135] In Somoto, Jaime explained, given locals' total identification with the National Guard, "the Frente Sandinista was never
able to gain a social base, it could not penetrate. You could count those
of us who supported them on one hand. It was terrifying to work here.
The ideology just didn't enter."[136] Indeed, Jaime's brother—as with
many Somoteños—was a member of the National Guard.

His collaboration with the OSN seems to have begun following his
1975 arrest during the repression in Condega. Unlike others arrested at
the time, Jaime was quietly released and not sent to face charges before
the military court, raising eyebrows among some of the guerrillas.
FSLN organizer Mónica Baltodano wrote that Jaime had long lacked

"Sandinista attitudes," was arrogant, a gossip ("*cuechero*"), and too "interested in money."[137] Asking to be remunerated monetarily for his contribution to the movement contrasted sharply with the ethos of self-sacrifice that guided other FSLN supporters. At another point, he explained that he had personally recruited a new person to work with the Sandinistas: the female owner of a drive-in motel (with rooms rented out by the hour for couples) along the Pan-American Highway in Estelí with an attached restaurant known for its loud jukebox, flowing liquor, and prostitutes. Baltodano was furious at him, not only for acting outside the chain of command but for bringing in someone involved in the underworld of vice. She angrily asked him, "How could we accept the help of someone so immoral?"[138] To make things worse, FSLN contacts strongly suspected that the woman was an oreja.[139] At the same time, however, the Frente felt dependent on Jaime because he was "the only person in Somoto that responded to us and so we could not stop working with him."[140] During this period, the FSLN gave Jaime the important task of establishing a clandestine route between Honduras and Nicaragua to transport people and weapons.[141]

Though seemingly coerced into collaboration through torture, in some of the secret police reports Jaime seemed to have fully embraced his role as a double agent.[142] For instance, while meeting with Sandinista organizer Bayardo Arce in Estelí, he reported spotting a secret police agent nearby. In his OSN report, he told his secret police handler that he "stepped aside to give the young man a chance to carry out his operation," presumably either the capture or assassination of the FSLN leader.[143] Though the agent continued walking, Jaime sent word before his next meeting with Arce that "if the OSN believes it to be convenient to get him (*quebrarlo*), do it and don't worry about me."[144]

Thanks to the detailed information the OSN received regarding FSLN movements between Nicaragua and Honduras, the National Guard was able to carry out numerous attacks. In 1977, Mónica Baltodano's car was fired upon before her arrest by the GN. "In jail," she wrote, "I came to the conclusion that only [Jaime] . . . could have been involved in this attempted murder. He was the only person I had met with on this occasion."[145] The next month, two FSLN members— Raúl González and Juan de Dios Muñoz—were killed by the National Guard shortly after dropping Jaime off at his home in Somoto. The GN claimed that there had been a shootout, but González's brother and cousin—both doctors—participated in his autopsy and alleged that his cadaver showed no bullet holes. The signs of intense beating led the González family to believe that Raúl had been captured and tortured to death by the OSN.[146]

Given difficult communication between clandestine Sandinistas, the suspicions about Jaime did not reach the guerrilla leadership. On April 13, 1978, Jaime was again entrusted with a vital task: bringing the FSLN's most-prominent female guerrilla leader, Doris Tijerino, and others across the Honduran border. Upon reaching Nicaraguan territory, the group walked into an ambush, in which the GN shot down a worker from Somoto and captured Tijerino.[147] The regime cast the capture of Doris as a significant blow against the Sandinistas, parading her before the media. In custody, she began "to deduce that, from the information the OSN had . . . there was a possible infiltration as few people that had passed through that location had reached their destination, as the majority had been killed or imprisoned."[148] Back in Somoto, an apparently dissimulating Jaime went door-to-door collecting money for the family of the murdered man.[149]

Just three months later, on July 15, GN agents gunned down José Benito Escobar in Estelí, shooting the senior FSLN leader in the back in broad daylight. The murder occurred just moments after Escobar had left a clandestine meeting arranged and attended by Jaime. In fact, the meeting was at the very drive-in motel and restaurant along the Pan-American Highway owned by the "immoral" woman he had personally recruited to help the guerrillas. In the wake of the shooting, Tijerino (who had been in a relationship with Escobar) wrote a letter from prison to the FSLN leadership detailing her misgivings and calling on them to cease all work in Somoto. "There were so many coincidences," Baltodano later wrote, "we were sure that this man was the one who handed over all of these compañeros."[150] It was a painful revelation for Baltodano, who had spent time hiding in Jaime's home, played with his young children, and had seen firsthand the poverty in which the family lived.[151] Jaime's case illustrates the important role that informants played in obstructing the course of FSLN mobilization in the Segovias and directing the GN toward its targets. Again, the state continued to draw on the country's most desperate to aid them in their counterinsurgency, the very sector of society that the FSLN simultaneously sought to empower and activate against the regime.

CONCLUSION

The paradox of the GN was that the vast majority of its grassroots members came from what Somoza Portocarrero called "the poorest of the poor." These men, who suffered under Nicaragua's status quo, came to commit acts of tremendous violence to assure that the regime remained in power. To landless and desperate campesinos, the GN provided employment and the possibility to advance from their lowly social station. In addition to these material benefits, serving as a Guardia also gave an intoxicating sense of male power, fearlessness, and impunity to some of the most marginalized members of Nicaraguan society. Importantly, the primary locus of GN socialization and interpersonal violence was the cantina, that masculine space so fundamental in Somoza's Nicaragua. In light of these material and psychosocial benefits, it is little surprise that the campesino recruits developed a profound sense of dependency and willingness to engage in political repression.

As a direct product of the U.S. military, the GN underwent profound transformations during the Cold War era, particularly following the 1959 Cuban Revolution. Sensing that the obsolete and corrupted GN was militarily unprepared for the hovering guerrilla threat of the 1970s, the Somozas established the EEBI to begin preparation for counterinsurgency. Through its training of Guardias, the United States attempted to inject a potent anticommunist discourse and practice into the Nicaraguan military, casting the Sandinistas as symbolically outside of the nation. Unsuccessful though they were in their attempt to politicize and professionalize the GN by breaking with the paternalism and caudillismo of the institution, the reforms nevertheless increased battle-readiness and enhanced the GN's orientation toward brute violence.

The GN's intelligence branches were also expanded during this era to spy on, capture, torture, and infiltrate opposition groups. In such activities, the GN relied on the same corrupt networks of public employees, "cantina caciques," and jueces de mesta, who were granted cash payments and personal power in exchange for information. Using these new and expanded structures, the OSN was remarkably successful in targeting, arresting, and killing top Sandinista leaders in the

Segovias. This transformation was one of both scale and character. Over a relatively short number of years, the GN's core shifted from one centered on vice, quotidian violence, and criminal impunity to one in which political violence and gross human rights violations would become its primary, daily function. However, rather than squelching the opposition, the GN's ever-greater recurrence to state terror became instead a fundamental factor galvanizing mass upheaval and moral indignation against the regime.

# CHAPTER FIVE

# "A CRIME TO BE YOUNG"

Families in Insurrection, September 1976–September 1978

On the fourth day, high on marijuana and hate,
they boarded their airplanes with two crisscrossed triangles
and from the sky
—oh, our pure northern sky—
spinning in black orbit
with satanic precision and calculation, they let fall on us
the shriek of bombs, machine guns, napalm, and rockets
opening deep ditches with cries of destruction and fear
    without limits
in what was once our city of life, song, and peace.
For seven days it rained flaming lightning bolts of fire.
We buried our dead children in the same patios where they
    grew up
next to our dead siblings
next to our dead grandparents.
Below the rose patch, we buried them all,
and we couldn't even spill tears because the terror had left
    our eyes dry,
and we couldn't shout because the pain had taken our voices.

—Alejandro Dávila Bolaños, poem following
the 1978 insurrection

In September 1977, the GN comandante of Estelí, Col. Carlos Edmundo Vergara, published an article in the official GN magazine *Acción Cívica* heaping praise on the city. He championed the town's economic dynamism, noting that it was Nicaragua's fastest growing municipality outside of the capital. He concluded his profile: "The young people of Estelí are healthy, studious, and responsible. In this, one has to admire the open collaboration given to us by their parents. We have not had any problems with the youth, as they don't fall for the siren songs of the professional agitators who show up in these parts from time to time."[1] Though this statement betrays his trepidation about FSLN activities among young people, it speaks volumes as to how quickly the situation would devolve over the coming months.

Just a year later, the majority of Estelí's teenagers, children, and many of their parents had become firmly united against the Somoza regime and the National Guard. The FSLN insurrection, launched in early September 1978, and its bloody suppression by the GN, the EEBI, and the Nicaraguan Air Force (Fuerza Aérea de Nicaragua, FAN) left the city utterly decimated. "Estelí is practically abandoned," a Sandinista communiqué announced. "The majority of the population and especially the youth of Estelí form part of the FSLN guerrillas or, better put, the Sandinista army that we are forming. No young person can safely stay in the city."[2] Many of the same young people that Vergara had celebrated as "healthy, studious, and responsible" had now escaped the GN and were heading to the mountains to train for future combat.

The security forces' blanket persecution of young males as potential Sandinistas led to the common saying that it was now "a crime to be young." Nowhere in Nicaragua was this more palpable than in the streets of Estelí, where the arrests, beatings, and even murders of students galvanized an entire city behind the FSLN's revolutionary efforts. Increasingly, participation by young people in the uprising became less a question of political commitment than one of mere survival. Teenagers and even younger children became not only targets of political violence but soon participants in the armed struggle.[3] Even the most impartial observer concluded that the GN had now violated all moral norms, attacking the sanctity of the family, the home, and the innocence of children's lives. As Dávila Bolaños wrote in the poem in the epigraph to this chapter, Estelianos "buried our dead children in the same patios where they grew up / next to our dead siblings / next to our dead grandparents." This destruction, visited from above upon the city by "satanic" forces "high on marijuana," destroyed the interior universe of the family home. Many adults—mothers in particular—likewise threw themselves wholeheartedly into the struggle against Somocista violence.

I shall demonstrate that the 1978 insurrection was not merely a military conflict between two armies but that it derived directly from the hidden actions of thousands of unarmed revolutionaries. In the process, they contributed to the fashioning of their practical vision of insurgent morality. In response to the state terror, a steadfast alliance emerged between young, often male, guerrilla combatants (los muchachos, "the boys" or "the kids") and mothers (las madres), which coalesced the city into what was often described by participants as "a single family." These middle-aged and older women—the most unlikely of revolutionaries—provided food, water, medicine, and protection, becoming what one guerrilla commander called "the vanguard" of the battle against the GN in Estelí.[4] As Lorraine Bayard de Volo argues for the decade of the 1980s, images of maternal suffering became a powerful force of moral legitimacy for the FSLN.[5] This potent image emerged during the insurrection, with women mobilizing as revolutionaries in their own right, drawing on their traditional gender roles and maternal identity to support the military efforts of the guerrillas.[6] According to some estimates, by 1978, between one-third and one-half of all households in Nicaragua were headed by a single parent, while close to half of those killed in the insurrection were born out of wedlock and raised by a single parent (their mother in most cases).[7] As we'll see in this chapter, the participation of women and youth within the Sandinista insurrection cannot be understood in isolation. It was instead the dynamic interactions between both "the kids" and "the mothers" as part of the nascent emerging family-oriented vision of revolution that made the Sandinista insurrection possible.

Though the September insurrection proved unsuccessful in the short term, the battle would last longer in Estelí than anywhere else in the country. In its aftermath, much of the city's youth retreated to the mountains with the guerrillas, becoming *combatientes populares* of the FSLN as a direct result of state terror. Previously, the locus of denunciation had been the system of corruption, inequality, and vice and its role in familial dissolution. With the GN's direct physical attacks against teenagers and children, its violence against Nicaraguan families came to symbolize the moral depravity of the dictatorship. The Sandinistas offered the fleeing youths not only protection but also a viable method (taking up arms) to fight back, a route that was previously only sought out by a small number of the city's population. In response to GN's ever-more chaotic violence and disorder, the revolutionaries now promised a new order. Novel familial values of solidarity and social leveling—between poor and rich, rural and urban, educated and uneducated, female and male, young and old—were nurtured in the neighborhood committees and guerrilla encampments alike. For those in the insurgent mass movement, such a shift in social and familial relations was not utopianism, but the practical experiences of egalitarianism and a life uncorrupted by vice.

## In Search of a New Direction: FSLN Factions and Youth Militancy

Between 1975 and 1977, the dictatorship had been effective in tracking down and nearly eradicating the FSLN leadership in the Segovias. With the torture and killing of many Sandinista supporters, guerrilla cadres withdrew from the rural areas to safe houses in the cities. The repression during the state of siege also shattered the solidity of the FSLN as a cohesive unit, as some within the organization began to clash over the causes of their apparent failure. Compounding the problem of disunity was the death of FSLN founder Carlos Fonseca, who was killed by the GN in Zinica in the mountains of Matagalpa in November 1976. He had returned to Nicaragua to convene a meeting of the FSLN leadership precisely to promote unity within the splintering guerrilla ranks. Fonseca had been the leader most responsible for the Sandinistas' formation and ideological evolution. Many perceived his death to be a decisive blow to the organization, and by the end of 1977 only eleven FSLN members were still operating in the mountains of the north.[8] The organization had reached a crossroads marked by intense internal debates over revolutionary strategy and tactics. Soon, the Sandinistas fractured into three separate "tendencies" (*tendencias*) or factions, each of which claimed to be the true representative of the Sandinista legacy.

The tendency known as the Prolonged Popular War (Guerra Popular Prolongada, GPP) basically endorsed a continuation of the strategy that the FSLN had been following since the early 1970s. The GPP called for the construction of a mass movement of various social sectors—particularly students and campesinos—that would fight a lengthy war of attrition in the rural areas against the dictatorship. "In the mountains, we will bury the heart of the enemy," their slogan claimed. Many of the guerrillas active in the Segovias region mentioned in previous chapters—such as Bayardo Arce, Mónica Baltodano, and Omar Cabezas—were affiliated with this faction. The second and smallest faction was known as the Proletarian Tendency (Tendencia Proletaria, TP), which called for a significant shift from a rural guerrilla front to a more classic Marxist-Leninist party of the working class. This tendency had almost no presence in the region.

The third faction, known as the Terceristas, or the Insurrectional Tendency, differed from both the GPP and the TP in several ways. It called for neither a lengthy period of preparation in the distant jungles nor clandestine party-building; instead, they aimed to launch an immediate armed uprising against the GN in the country's largest cities. Because of their emphasis on violent action over clandestine organizing, some Sandinistas from other tendencies criticized the Terceristas as militarists and reckless adventurists. The Terceristas also proposed postponing the class struggle against the "grandes ricos" (as the *Cartilla Campesina* had called them), in order to construct a broad national alliance of all those who opposed Somoza, including wealthy opposition businessmen.[9] And because of its contacts abroad, the Tercerista faction gained unprecedented access to considerable sums of money and arms from sympathetic governments, such as Costa Rica, Venezuela, and Panama. In Estelí, the Terceristas' leader was Francisco Rivera, the younger brother of trade unionist Filemón Rivera, who, a member of the FSLN's National Directorate, had himself been gunned down by the Guardia in rural Matagalpa in 1975.[10]

In the region of Estelí, organizing had long been carried out by those Sandinistas who joined the GPP, and this tendency continued to predominate in the region. Chased from rural areas where repression had targeted members of the Catholic movement, GPP strategy now focused on high school students as a large social group that they could recruit for the armed guerrilla struggle. The activism of Leonel Rugama, Igor Úbeda, and others in the 1960s had revealed the potential of high schools in generating committed revolutionaries. In recent years, university students affiliated with the GPP had backed younger student groups, such as the Movement of High School Students (Movimiento de Estudiantes de Secundaria, MES). In 1976 and 1977, the GPP dispatched guerrilla organizers Monica Baltodano and Socorro Sirias to Estelí to resuscitate the process of mobilization truncated by state violence. The two young women, it seems, were considered less likely to be recognized and targeted by the city's intelligence services as Sandinistas. They organized three assemblies held in El Calvario in which locals gathered to air their grievances against the government, inviting participants with "*moscas* [tiny pieces of paper with messages], posters, and by word-of-mouth."[11] Efforts to promote student activism, however, were soon stifled by the National Guard, as Colonel Vergara "called in many parents and made them sign a document taking responsibility to stop their children from going around 'doing these things.'"[12] The GN commander thus proved temporarily able to manipulate family relations and garner the cooperation of parents fearful for their kids' safety.

In response, the organizers focused their efforts on less outwardly political activism. Sirias wrote to Bayardo Arce recommending "city improvement activities, planting trees in parks, establishing medical dispensaries in the different neighborhoods, cultural activities such as recitals, panels, and student theater."[13] By way of these organizations, Arce explained, they could slowly raise consciousness by starting from "student issues, then moving onto the concrete social problems of the students and, if possible, onto national politics."[14] These diverse student activities were to be fostered by the clandestine organizers, Sirias explained, "without ever losing sight of the main goal, which is to lay a solid base of support and strengthen the Sandinista army."[15] Those students who demonstrated an interest in political issues within these activities were then invited to join the Revolutionary Student Front (FER), the Sandinista group active at the National University in León. Arce suggested groups of five or fewer to meet weekly to study "historical documents, sociology, Marxist philosophy, political strategy, and tactical publications . . . security methods and the principles of the organization, etc."[16] Finally, outstanding FER members were to be recruited to *pre-militancia* (pre-membership) within FSLN urban guerrilla cells. "We have to make it clear that MES, FER, and FSLN membership are all A MEANS and not an end," Arce detailed in the letter. "The MES is a means to draw in students, the FER to draw in MES members, the FSLN to draw in FER members, so that 'the people' are drawn into the FSLN through popular revolutionary armed combat."[17] Pace and process varied, but ultimately there was no question as to the Sandinistas' aim: they needed all those willing to join the armed struggle.

Despite these sophisticated plans for recruitment, often young people proved indifferent and apathetic toward the movement. At the other extreme, however, were the small number of recruits who wanted to proceed immediately to armed actions against the GN and considered the slow work of organizing too ineffective and tedious given the risk of repression.[18] Some GPP members even began to migrate toward the Tercerista position, believing that stepped-up urban warfare was the most effective way to challenge the regime, and they started recruiting members for that purpose. On May 4, 1977, for instance, FSLN-GPP members targeted the security detail protecting the home of diputado René Molina, killing two Guardias and seriously injuring two others.[19] A shocked U.S. embassy official wrote that the blast was "the first evidence of urban terrorism" and perhaps a harbinger of things to come.[20] At this stage, neither the dramatic and bloody attack nor the new recruitment efforts underway resulted in rapid growth in youth participation, as the FSLN cadres had hoped.

FROM BONFIRES AND BURIALS TO POPULAR FURY

This moment coincided with emerging difficulties in Somoza's long-standing relations with the regime's primary international backer, the U.S. government. In 1976, for instance, the U.S. Congress began withholding financial support from the Nicaraguan government following Catholic Church reports of mass killings of campesinos. In January

1977, President Jimmy Carter, a Democrat, entered the White House and began putting pressure on Somoza, singling out Nicaragua as an example of his new human rights policy. When Congress restored some of the withdrawn aid, the Carter administration blocked it. Somoza, for his part, was infuriated that the U.S. government would dare criticize a loyal ally facing a "communist" insurgency. In July, he suffered a heart attack and headed to the United States for treatment, vanishing from the political scene for many weeks and placing the question of succession squarely on the table.[21] Partly because of the Americans' insistence, Somoza lifted the three-year-old state of siege in September. Rather than lowering tensions, the situation continued to devolve shortly after Somoza's announcement, as the Terceristas launched a series of armed attacks against the GN throughout the country the following month.[22]

Further mayhem was to follow early the next year. On January 10, 1978, Pedro Joaquín Chamorro, editor and publisher of *La Prensa* and a longtime Somoza critic, was assassinated in broad daylight in downtown Managua. From a prominent Conservative dynasty, Chamorro had also been the leader of the Democratic Liberation Union (Unión Democrática de Liberación, UDEL), an anti-Somoza alliance that included opposition parties, professionals, and business groups.[23] Chamorro's murder provoked a sensation of fury against the Somoza regime, which was widely believed to be behind his death. Soon, mass riots rocked Managua, a popular uprising broke out in Masaya, and smaller protests took place in provincial cities, such as Estelí.[24] Though the Sandinistas would later lionize Chamorro as a martyr of the revolution, at the time, they had a more nuanced interpretation given that he had long opposed the Left. The FSLN was, however, willing to fan the flames the popular outrage for their own purposes. One Estelian activist recalled their feelings upon learning of the assassination: "For us as members of the student movement and pre-militants, we considered the death of Pedro Joaquín Chamorro one of the biggest mistakes of the dictatorship and an instrument we could use to consolidate the work of the movement. Now, when it came to the people in general, they were in a frenzy! He was a public figure that had created an image of himself as a defender of the poor, which was not a real image because of his class status. But the lack of clarity of the people made them rise up in fury. We used this moment to consolidate the movement."[25] Another Sandinista activist, though not personally a Chamorro follower, noted that "many people saw a liberator in him. But people are like that. If they say Señor X is a great leader, they become rather *caudillista*. So the death of Dr. Chamorro deeply pained them."[26]

Following the Chamorro assassination, the private sector and traditional opposition parties openly joined in the anti-Somoza fight, with the Chamber of Commerce declaring a general strike against the government. In April, high school students led a nationwide campaign demanding better conditions for Sandinista prisoners held in solitary confinement. With encouragement from FSLN organizers behind the scenes, students in Estelí seized the cathedral, the Agricultural School, and four other high schools.[27] News reports from Estelí noted that "though protesters were monitored by the GN, they were not bothered at any time."[28] In the face of this challenge, GN Colonel Vergara was for a time extremely cautious in his use of force, fearful of provoking an even more explosive public uproar. Vergara had been caught off guard by the "healthy, studious, and responsible" students that he had recently lauded.

In a remarkable protest on April 23, a group of young school kids, including many under the age of ten, carried out a "children's protest," mimicking the actions of their older siblings. They banged pots, lit fireworks, and burned tires and a dummy (*muñeco*) representing the dictator, all while shouting "Somoza, get out" and "down with repression." As the children carried out their miniature protest, a blue truck without a license plate drove by and suddenly fired a series of shots in the direction of the kids. The bullets struck and killed twelve-year-old protester Wilfredo Valenzuela. Two other young boys, aged four and six, were also left wounded on the ground nearby. The town was in shock and rumors quickly spread as to who was responsible. The shooter was alleged to have been the son of Gen. Fermín Meneses, the very GN officer and local landowner previously implicated in the 1969 shooting deaths of two students in Estelí. The population referred to the killer as a "paramilitary" and "oreja," while the GN claimed that he had been high on marijuana at the time of the attack.[29] Whether they intended this as an excuse for his crime or to explain the killing as the action of a deranged individual is unclear. However, the detail only further reminded the population of the unrestrained indulgence in illegal vices by Somoza's supporters.

A crowd of all ages quickly assembled and stormed toward the mansion of René Molina, the all-powerful diputado, smashing the windows of the Somocista-owned movie theaters along the way. All those in the crowd knew the deep connection between Molina and Somoza and their many business dealings. From the balcony of the Molina residence, so-called paramilitaries fired live rounds of ammunition against the marchers, wounding six people. That evening, Estelí glowed with bonfires and the GN jeeps patrolled in fear of an imminent insurrection.[30] The murder of Wilfredo, declared one young man, had "provoked the fury of the people, it lit the fuse . . . the streets were overflowing. Everyone had to help . . . it was a great help in waking the spirits of the people."[31] Because of the combination of factors, including the earlier work of the cursillos and the guerrilla organizers, the population responded to the atrocities through mass action. The results that the Sandinistas had hoped for finally materialized.

Life as usual seemingly came to a halt in Estelí. When the sun rose the following morning, no one went to work, and bonfires smoldered across the city. Following the burial of young Wilfredo, a procession of thousands marched from the cemetery back to the center of town along the main boulevard, which they now anointed "Sandino Avenue." They headed again toward the Molina house, where paramilitaries had fired at the crowd the previous day. GN comandante Vergara pleaded with the crowd to desist, but he was unable to stop them from looting and burning the diputado's house. An estimated group of "3,000 young people, adults, women, of all social strata" then proceeded to set the Liberal Party headquarters on fire.[32] Unlike the earlier blazes of 1965 in which Somocista properties were also set aflame, this attack was not the work of unknown individuals operating under cover of night but of the population at large and in clear view. Molina was infuriated by the lack of a response by Vergara, who seemed scared of further provoking the rioters. Playing his role as intermediary, Colonel Vergara achieved an armistice between the movement and the authorities. In a tripartite agreement with Dávila Bolaños and Somocista leader José María Briones, the GN officer agreed to stop using tear gas and preventing food from reaching the cathedral, which was still occupied by the high school students.[33]

This tenuous ceasefire did not last very long. Weeks later, on May 24, another group of young children occupied the teachers' college, demanding justice for the death of their friend, Wilfredo. In response, the National Guard stormed the building with guns blazing, wounding five people, including an eight-year-old child, and arresting thirty others. Once again in response to violence directed at children, Estelí rose up in indignation and rioting enveloped the city. Popular anger was not randomly directed: rioters burned the El Padrón cigar factory (belonging to Somoza's Cuban associates) and the property of the Meneses family. In a single day, anti-Somocistas burned eighteen buildings to the ground, leaving property damage estimated at a whopping 12 million córdobas. As with the arson of previous decades, protesters selected the buildings because of their association with the regime. For instance, *La Prensa* notes that "the wicks were not sparked" at a department store whose owner pleaded that he was not a Somocista.[34]

Some within the regime believed Comandante Vergara's initial attempts at conciliation were the cause of the spiraling unrest in Estelí and pressured for a harsher crackdown. The U.S. embassy claimed that Vergara had earned "a reputation of being friendly and understanding among the opposition," but the growing resistance in Estelí raised the question "as to whether a soft response to demonstrators encourages violence that could be prevented by a tougher preventative or reactive policy."[35] Following the riots, Estelí's Somocista mayor, Francisco Moreno, tendered his resignation, publicly criticizing the GN's failure to end the protests and writing that the city had been "for the past several weeks entirely in the hands of subversive groups . . . without the most minimum of protection by those who have an obligation to impose order."[36] Vergara was soon removed from his position by Somoza and replaced by Col. Gonzalo Martínez, known as a hardliner more willing to directly confront the demonstrators.[37] The government perceived repression as a way "to impose order," but the regime's chaotic violence was increasingly seen by the civilian population to be the primary destabilizing force in Nicaragua.

Sure enough, the oppressive atmosphere in the city escalated rapidly following the riots of April and May. Orejas denounced neighbors as Sandinistas, and the GN captured and tortured many young people, particularly those spotted walking alone at night.[38] As repression increased, the number of teenagers that sympathized with the Sandinistas also swelled. Similar protest activities were taking place throughout Nicaragua during these months, but mass participation in Estelí was among the very highest in the country. By July, FSLN organizer José Benito Escobar predicted that Estelí would become a major theater of operations in any future conflict, given the high levels of support for the Sandinistas. In his report, Escobar went as far as to suggest that close to 100 percent of those between sixteen and twenty years old and nearly 75 percent of those between twenty-one and thirty now backed the FSLN.[39] The balance had irrevocably shifted: much of the population now rejected the Somozas, seeing them as the perpetrators of heinous violence against the youth.

## The Insurrection of the Defense Committees: Mothers, Sons, and Neighborhoods

The city's parents had previously discouraged their children from joining in protests and political activities, but in light of the mounting repression, many families now saw them as morally justified. Women, particularly the mothers of youths who had been imprisoned or beaten by the GN, were at the forefront of these efforts. As the state violence spread, many women in the city felt the need to help the anti-Somoza movement in any way possible. They formed a local chapter of the Association of Women Facing the Nation's Problems (Asociación de Mujeres ante la Problemática Nacional, AMPRONAC), which embraced women's maternal gender roles in order to denounce the growing violence. In its very first statement, AMPRONAC in Estelí decried the "barbarously primitive attitude of the Guardia in the use of the force of bayonets against the weak shouts of children. For a while it has been a crime to be young. NOW IT IS A CRIME TO BE A CHILD!"[40]

Women's participation often began as an extension of traditional female gender roles, but they at times directly challenged the sexism of the society in which they lived.[41] Francisca Dormus, for instance, became a founder of AMPRONAC in Estelí, against the wishes of her fearful and machista husband, who insisted she stay out of politics. Given her prominence in the anti-Somoza movement, she was soon recruited by the guerrillas to hide a cache of weapons. Knowing her husband would never approve, she accepted their request without letting him know. When her young daughters spotted her placing large, oblong sacks under her bed, Dormus told them that they were simply bags of corn. Upon her husbands' return home, the girls begged their *papi* to make them *esquite* (toasted corn kernels), as their mother was at a women's group meeting in the city center. When he told them that corn was out of season, they directed him to the sacks where he found the bombs, pistols, and grenades that the Sandinistas had entrusted to his wife. Both terrified and furious, he set out to find and confront his wife. Francisca described their argument vividly: "He told me, 'Get over there (*andáte*) and get those weapons out of the house or I will denounce you to the Guardia.' But I told him, 'You can denounce me but they're going to kill me, they're going to kill the children, they're going to kill your family.'"[42] With that, she returned to her meeting and did not go home until much later in the day. Bravely standing up to her husband and refusing to get rid of the arms proved a foundational moment in Dormus's political trajectory, both as a Sandinista and a feminist. The weapons remained hidden in her home for months, to be handed over to the guerrillas during the insurrection, and her relationship with the girls' father soon ended.

The violence in the city also called into question the masculine honor and paternal duty of the city's adult men, such as doña Francisca's husband, perceived to have failed in their moral obligation as fathers and husbands to stand up to the GN onslaught. The murdered child Wilfredo Valenzuela became "a symbol for those men that had been conformists. It forced them to react," explained the male leader of the Parents' Association of Estelí (Asociación de Padres de Familia de Estelí), which was also formed to support the striking and protesting youth.[43] The Parents' Association denounced "the annihilation of our defenseless children protesting in a civic manner for a free patria with democracy and respect for human rights."[44] Up to this point, the city's middle-aged and older men had been seen by the younger generation as cowards, afraid of the GN, seduced by vice, and absent from both family life and political struggle. Now, a growing number seemed ready to step up and participate in collective action against the dictatorship. Regional branches of new national organizations formed overnight, such as the Nicaraguan Democratic Movement (Movimiento

Democrático Nicaragüense, MDN) and the Broad Opposition Front (Frente Amplio Opositor, FAO). Local professionals and businessmen led both organizations, with the MDN headed by longtime cursillo leader Felipe Barreda. Most men did not engage in the armed struggle alongside the youth, but many came to support the insurrection. As Michelle Chase argues in the case of the Cuban Revolution, middle-aged men mobilized out of their "paternal duty . . . of being an honorable husband or father," casting their "political engagement in familial terms."[45] These latecomers to the movement soon received top billing in the civic organizations and strike committees, but women were clearly the real force behind organizing at the neighborhood level.

The families of young protesters also organized as part of the opposition movement through the Church lay organizations founded by Padre Julio. Additionally, student marches often began at the church in El Calvario, where families and young activists rallied, and then headed out toward the city center. Wealthy families continued to attend Mass in the city's cathedral, but workers and campesinos flocked to El Calvario.[46] The small church overflowed with those anxious to hear the homilies of Padre Julio and sing along to "La Misa Campesina," written by folk singer Carlos Mejía Godoy and inspired by liberation theology. Even some non-Catholics began attending religious services to join in the protest movement. A retired, former schoolteacher recalled the atmosphere. "I'm not religious, but the pulpits were the trenches," she explained. "In Mass, they gave us reports. It was a means of information, a meeting place that was 'respected' to a certain degree by the dictatorship. But if all the people participated, it wasn't a question of religious creed. Among the clergy, there was always a progressive part and another part that blessed the bombs and guns [of the GN]."[47] At the church, students read out newsletters and communiqués from the FSLN and the other opposition organizations, while Padre Julio denounced the crimes of the regime in his sermons.

Cursillo leaders also did their part to help young activists and began establishing Civil Defense Committees (Comités de Defensa Civil, CDCs), neighborhood organizations that grew directly out of the Catholic community groups. The genesis of this effort lay with Padre Julio and some of his closest friends among the laity. Josefa "Chepita" Ruiz recalled a conversation that she and her husband, Rodolfo "Chilo Negro" Rodríguez, had with the priest over breakfast one day: "My husband told him, 'Look, Julio, we have to organize. If not, they are going to finish us all off and kill off all the young people.' Because at the time when the organization began, three or four young people were dying every day. 'We have to do something, Julio,' he told him. 'How can we accept that three young men die every day?' They waited on the corner outside of the school and without saying anything they captured them and sometimes disappeared them."[48]

The CDCs began in El Calvario by agitating for the release of imprisoned youngsters but quickly spread to other neighborhoods and the nearby countryside with the help of cursillistas. Padre Julio described how the CDCs developed a complex structure to protect local families and young people: "They got lawyers, doctors, and started to teach first aid. The women with a little bit more income formed an organization called AMPRONAC to help those in jail. At this time, the cathedral was taken over, and we all tried to participate in different ways. There was a sociologist who helped us carry out surveys of the population. El Calvario was very united, very family-oriented. All of the kids were out protesting. There was such a beautiful environment. I think it is very difficult to imagine it without having lived through it."[49] A manual explained that CDCs were to incorporate the "natural leaders from the sector," men and women who were elected to form a community directorate.[50] Rather than partisan groups, the CDCs were open to "all of the neighbors, men and women, independently of their ideology . . . the only requirement is to be anti-Somocista."[51]

In the face of the disorderly and chaotic violence of the National Guard, the CDCs sought to impose a sense of order and control upon the urban space of the city, constituting a germ of the new society to come, one based on a familial ethic of care, mutual aid, and solidarity. The committees were structured in an inclusive and highly democratic manner, beginning at the household level and incorporating all family members. Many men, such as Chilo Negro, took on leadership roles, but women made up a very high percentage of the active membership. From each manzana (lot), a leader was chosen to form a committee with the rest of the cuadra (city block). The leaders of three neighboring city blocks then elected a representative to the citywide Executive Committee that met regularly at the parish church in El Calvario. At each level, the CDCs established a system of commissions: health, supplies, propaganda, self-defense, and security.[52] Magdalena Derruti, an early participant in the cursillos, described the CDC:

> A perfect organization born in the Church, made up of the religious and the nonreligious. There were sixty-two Christian communities. It was formed by getting together men and women and picking a secretary, a treasurer, and [someone responsible for] defense. We looked for a lawyer and formed a committee of supplies and organized a bodega between all of us. . . . We elected our representatives very democratically and distributed thousands of flyers with simple and clear instructions. We also had a commission for water that cleaned the wells. The meetings were constant; the activity was permanent. And it functioned very well.[53]

Common crime and vice practically vanished from some neighborhoods thanks to the vigilance of the neighbors in the CDCs.[54] Organizers applied the same defense committee model in rural areas where the cursillo movement had been successful, such as San Roque, La Montañita, Santa Cruz, and El Regadío. However, in the villages, the structure was based on hamlets (*comarcas*) and valleys (*valles*) rather than blocks and neighborhoods.

The Terceristas soon incorporated the CDCs into their preparations for an all-out urban insurrection against the dictatorship. In June 1978, Tercerista leader Francisco "Chico" Rivera was dispatched back to his hometown of Estelí to lay the groundwork for a future uprising. He was surprised to find many of the city's families already organized for self-defense. Committee members began secretly breaking passageways between the walls dividing neighbors' patios, creating hidden corridors that would allow guerrillas to transit directly across a city block. They also started stockpiling medicine, bandages, basic grains, and—in some cases—weapons and ammunition. Gun ownership was widespread, and farmers and ranchers donated numerous hunting rifles, shotguns, and pistols to the FSLN. The Terceristas' intricate planning pleasantly surprised GPP leader Bayardo Arce, who wrote, "It seems that they have understood that a spontaneous uprising of the people is not a sure thing."[55] The CDC model was so successful that the United People's Movement (Movimiento Pueblo Unido, MPU), a civil society umbrella organization secretly allied with the Terceristas, adopted Estelí's committees as a model promoted throughout Nicaragua. Forming CDCs across the country, they claimed, would allow "the masses to participate in their locales in the total confrontation that we are heading toward with the dictatorship."[56] Though spearheaded by his Tercerista rivals, even Bayardo Arce saw the CDCs as vital to the revolutionary effort. He ordered GPP members in Estelí to begin "organizing CDCs and leading them because they are the embryo of a significant mass movement in the process of formation and our future influence depends on what we do right now."[57] The CDCs, many believed, were not merely a mechanism of resistance but the blueprint for a future order of moral regeneration that was to supplant the violent disorder of Somocismo.

Many of the city's teenaged boys looked to the bearded guerrilla fighters (*barbudos*) who clandestinely descended from the mountains as "real men," models of masculine duty who were—unlike many of the city's adult males—willing to physically confront the dictatorship by taking up arms.[58] During the night, the youth were schooled in military tactics by guerrillas on the outskirts of town, within the confines of safe houses, or in the workshop of the Drivers' Union (Sindicato de Transportistas Unidos).[59] The death of FSLN-GPP leader José Benito Escobar at the hands of the GN on July 15 put the whole town on edge.[60] Coincidentally, the following day, the Twelve (*los Doce*), a group of prominent opposition writers, businessmen, professionals, and clergymen arrived in the city as part of their national tour across the country.[61] To herald their visit, activists decorated the city in red-and-black Sandinista flags. In their procession, the Twelve visited various key points around town, leaving flowers where Wilfredo Valenzuela had been shot down and presenting a wreath to the families of the two students killed by the GN in 1969. Jesuit priest Fernando Cardenal, one of the Twelve, spoke directly to the older people in the crowd, calling on men of his generation to step up and support the youth. "The problem of Nicaragua," he said, "is that we adult men never got involved in politics and because of this, the kids and young people are dying. And because the earlier generations didn't get involved in politics, the gangsters or the mafia have taken over politics to the disgrace of Nicaragua."[62] Even on that day the state violence continued unabated. Following a wake and Mass held for Escobar in El Calvario, protesters demanded the GN hand his remains over to his widow. Instead, the GN reacted once again by opening fire on the marchers, killing twenty-three-year-old student Vladimir Hidalgo. A thirteen-year-old boy who came to his aid was also shot and wounded after shouting at the soldiers, "Kill me too, you coward."[63] That night, activists dug ditches across the Pan-American Highway, knocked over light posts, and robbed an armaments store in Estelí of twenty guns and thousands of rounds of munitions.[64] Estelí had become a city under military occupation with sudden eruptions of protest and confrontation.

The raging conflict led even the top echelons of the Catholic Church hierarchy to take an increasingly oppositional stand against the regime. In early August, Nicaragua's bishops issued a surprisingly radical pastoral letter that called for "a new sociopolitical order making possible humane conditions for the majority of the people in the areas of nutrition, health, education, housing, employment, land, wages, and human rights."[65] Partly in response to the Church's new orientation, the GN and secret police now targeted the clergy itself. The U.S. embassy reported in mid-August that numerous attacks against the Church had taken place in the Diocese of Estelí. Following GN threats against Padre Julio, the embassy noted that "persons unknown fired shots in front of the church during Mass and threw bombs at the priests' residence."[66] The homes of priests in Jalapa and Ocotal in Nueva Segovia were also attacked by armed orejas, while in Somoto, Monseñor José del Carmen Suazo "was taken prisoner by elements of the GN with some campesinos and, reportedly, was present while two of the campesinos were beaten in the command post."[67] The U.S. ambassador claimed that "all of these alleged incidents took place in the northern area of the country where, traditionally, a more 'frontier-type' approach to law and order exists," and that similar "incidents . . . can be expected as the Church takes an increasingly strong stand on current events."[68] For people in the Segovias, however, this "Wild West" "frontier-type" violence against the Catholic clergymen only served to further expose the complete lack of both "law and order" under the Somoza regime.

On August 22, a squad of Terceristas disguised as EEBI soldiers captured the National Palace in Managua, taking many prominent

Somocista congressmen and government officials hostage in one fell swoop. The FSLN traded their captives for a large sum of money, safe passage out of the country, and the release of dozens of imprisoned Sandinistas. The buses carrying the Sandinistas to the international airport provoked loud cheers from crowds of onlookers.[69] When a new national general strike was declared several days later, the GN immediately detained hundreds of its organizers across the country. In Estelí, the GN captured the leadership of the local civic organizations, such as the Chamber of Commerce, the Red Cross, the Bar Association, the Medical Society, and the Dental Association. These were the respected, male professionals of the city who had stood up at significant personal risk to embrace the national strike against the regime. Among this group were Iván Kauffman and Luis Irías Barreda, members of the Red Cross and Chamber of Commerce; cursillista Dr. Saturnino Mejía of the Dental Association; and socialist Dávila Bolaños, representing the Medical Society. The men were imprisoned in the GN base and violently interrogated over the coming weeks while in custody. With airplanes flying overhead, Col. Gonzalo Martínez donned camouflaged fatigues, preparing for an imminent attack by the FSLN.[70] After the sun went down on September 9, the city of Estelí rose up in arms under the leadership of the Terceristas, as the Sandinistas launched coordinated insurrections in the country's other major cities, such as Masaya, León, Matagalpa, and Chinandega.

## "All One Family": Insurrection and the Operación Limpieza of September 1978

The September insurrection represented a parting of waters in the history of the insurgency, as open warfare finally broke out between the FSLN and the Somoza government. Particularly in the case of Estelí, civilians were at the very center of the upheaval. By the wee morning hours of September 10, a small group of guerrillas led by Francisco Rivera laid siege to the GN base. Armed with only four FAL machine guns and a collection of rifles and pistols, the insurgents rallied the population, who came together to set up barricades and gather more weapons. Upon seizing the city, they set ablaze the seat of local government, the Palacio Departamental, and the facilities of Nicaragua

Cigar, a tobacco company owned by Somoza and financed with state resources.[71] As the battle raged, the local hospital began to fill with the wounded and dying. At the same time, troops commanded by Facundo Picado held off GN reinforcements arriving from Condega to the north.[72]

The population at large, primed by months of repression, threw themselves into action as guns were distributed. The logic of the insurrection flowed directly from the previous five months of protest and reprisal, and from the legacies of the movements of earlier years. Working-class neighborhoods, such as El Calvario and El Zapote, that had been bedrocks of protest since the 1960s now served as strongholds of the insurrection, backed at the local level by fearless mothers and student activists. The FSLN converted Padre Julio's El Calvario church into a command post from where the guerrilla commanders would direct the insurrection.[73] Likewise, campesinos from the villages active in the cursillos, such as San Roque, La Montañita, and Santa Cruz, streamed into town armed with their hunting rifles and joined in the battle. Teenage boys were at the forefront of the uprising, with many taking up arms for the first time, manning the barricades, and hurling homemade bombs (*bombas de contacto*).[74] Younger children also helped assemble barricades, recover guns from fallen Guardias, and deliver messages and food to the guerrillas. Adult men joined in the support network, and some even joined in the firefights and became Sandinistas. Divisions between factions of the Frente faded as the GPP joined in the insurrection and coordinated with the Terceristas.[75]

Military resistance to the National Guard became a citywide effort, as nearly each family member contributed his or her own "grain of sand" (*granito de arena*) toward the war effort. The insurrection was carried out through the unity of the young combatants and the middle-aged women of the neighborhoods that supported them. The women of Estelí, guerrilla leader José del Carmen Aráuz ("El Segoviano") recalled, were "messengers, ran safe houses and meeting points, got food, medicine, and information, organized their sector, cooked, attended to the wounded. . . . In the sector where the war happened, almost all of the women helped. Including in El Calvario, it was the women and not the men! The men wear the skirts here, the participation of the women as a support network was incredible (*salvaje*)."[76]

Though he celebrated women's participation in the uprising, El Segoviano notably still relied on gendered stereotypes in his criticism of males who did not lead the efforts. In many cases, the women were the mothers, aunts, and grandmothers of the very youths joining in the fight, or sometimes neighbors without children who also became "mothers" to the muchachos through a sort of political fictive kinship.[77] "We were all one family," CDC activist and Social Christian Party member Magdalena Derruti recalled. "There was great solidarity, we were a single family against a single adversary. There were no class distinctions. The Frente could never have done it alone. It was the work of all of us."[78] These civilian supporters gave rise to the saying that "the revolution is not just a gun, but also a tortilla," while another cursillista claimed that "the war imposed a socialist type of organization that consolidated the communitarian spirit deeply rooted in our city."[79] El Calvario leader Chepita Ruiz claimed that in the face of the violence, Estelí lived a moment of unity. Both the rich and poor came together during the insurrection, making it "the only time that we all truly felt like sisters and brothers."[80] In her diary written during the upheaval, another "mother" to the muchachos, Magdalena de Rodríguez, wrote in verse:

Magic of the Revolution
How you humanize, this is a common-union
of spirits and things. For the first time,
there exists a single family in Nicaragua.[81]

Such experiences during wartime served as the basis for an alternative vision of community and egalitarianism, counterpoised to the hierarchy, selfishness, and moral degradation of the Somoza regime. Despite the devastating violence of the insurrection, these moments of unfettered solidarity also had an unforgettable effect, as participants gained firsthand experiences of the ideals of insurgent morality and the revolutionary vision of familial harmony.

The violence visited upon the city reached extremes not witnessed elsewhere in Nicaragua. Bearing in mind its position along the Pan-American Highway to the northern border, control of Estelí became a strategic objective for the guerrillas and the GN alike. Despite the risk of massive civilian casualties, Somoza ordered the GN to use heavy artillery and aerial bombardment before sending infantry forces to recapture the cities. By Friday, FAN airplanes began strafing and bombing the city to break the will of the guerrillas and their civilian backers. Hundreds were killed and wounded, with entire families incinerated in their homes. The National Guard's indiscriminate bombardment left the city decimated, as the flames leaped from building to building. An FSLN-GPP report stated that as "the planes began sporadic attacks and shootings, the population began its exodus from the city."[82] For Romelia Almendárez, a fifty-two-year-old housewife who participated in the struggle against her husband's wishes, "Those incredible days of bombing. It was horrible: the sound of the aircraft; the destruction of much of the neighborhood. Our homes were considered the safest places until this happened"[83] (see fig. 5.1). From an aerial view, there was no way to draw distinctions between those who supported Somoza and those who provided support to the muchachos. In the violence from above, victims were denied their political identities, as the FAN hoped to flatten the city if necessary. By behaving as though the entire city was allied with the rebels, the government inadvertently helped to turn that perception into a reality.

*Figure 5.1.* Estelí residents observe damage left by a rocket fired by the National Guard at the Pensión Juárez following the insurrection, September 26, 1978. Photograph by F. Escobar. Courtesy of Instituto de Historia de Nicaragua y Centroamérica.

Throughout Nicaragua, the GN had proved unable to quell the upheaval and quickly retreated behind their garrison walls. The military bases under siege in each city were rescued only through the arrival of elite infantry brigades stationed in Managua. The EEBI, as we saw in chapter 4, was made up of young GN recruits who had recently undergone intense training in counterinsurgency. Through the intervention of these troops, the government was able to successively recapture each of the cities, until Estelí alone remained in the hands of the insurgents. On September 17, the EEBI began an assault focused on the northern part of town near the cemetery utilizing heavy artillery and tank fire, allegedly leaving hundreds dead and wounded.[84] Essential goods such as food, medicine, and water began to run out. As they seized parts of Estelí, the GN allegedly used gasoline fires to smoke out the insurgents and punish those civilians who had given them aid.[85]

As an extension of the earlier violence, the GN killed unarmed civilians on a massive scale during the insurrection. Revealed as far from invincible, the GN responded by combatting the challenge with indiscriminate force. "In my experience, the repression before the insurrection was more of an orderly repression," said guerrilla Leonel Raudez. "But from September, it wasn't just against the leftists and the students; it was against the people in general, it became about eliminating everyone. That was their idea. As a consequence of this repression—this disorderly repression—they even bombed the houses of Somocistas!"[86] After a week of combat in the city, the FSLN ordered a withdrawal on Sunday, exiting as a much-inflated guerrilla force flush with *combatientes populares*, often teenage boys, who had joined the Sandinistas in the heat of the battle. Fewer than two dozen Sandinistas had launched the uprising, but there were now hundreds of young men (and some women) under Francisco Rivera's command. These guerrillas had captured much their new weaponry from the GN during the insurrection.

As occurred in other cities, once Estelí fell back under the control of the regime, the GN began carrying out what they termed an *Operación Limpieza* (Cleanup Operation). In these actions, the GN went from house to house summarily executing those they suspected of having joined in battle, many of them young males aged fourteen to twenty-one.[87] Because Estelí had been the city with the most popular participation in the insurrection and had resisted the longest, its population faced extreme vindictiveness from the GN. If it had been "a crime to be young" before the uprising, it was now a capital offense. A former EEBI soldier who participated in the Cleanup Operation in Estelí later defended their actions: "Many say that the battle ended and we grabbed every civilian who was there. As members of the army, we went into each house, searched it, and if we didn't find any arms, the family was fine. . . . But if we found weapons, or guerrilla pamphlets, or red-and-black-flags, we knew that these people . . . [*pause*] . . . I mean, we didn't kill the whole family like they later said, we just grabbed the targets and killed them. Those were the orders we had."[88]

However, such evidence was not necessary for "the targets" (young men and boys) to be shot dead on sight. The summary executions that followed the insurrection were among the most serious war crimes and atrocities that the GN had committed up to that point. Another Guardia that fought against the FSLN during the September insurrection described the Cleanup Operation: "Even when we were in combat, they were dressed as civilians. So if we caught them alive, they were killed (*iban de viaje*). And if we caught them surrendering, they were also killed . . . because they were from the Frente. All of those that were their informants and civilian backers, they were killed too."[89]

Padre Julio López himself barely escaped death at the hands of the GN, leaving Estelí on Sandinista orders as the insurrection came to an end.[90] His fellow Catholic priest "Chico" Luis Espinoza was shot dead by the GN on September 13 as he drove into the town of Condega. At the time of his death, he had been rushing a pregnant woman to the hospital, alongside José Norberto Briones, who was the head of Estelí's fire department, a cursillista, and the brother of Somocista senator José María Briones. GN bullets killed all three. Their corpses were left abandoned as the GN tore apart the vehicle, and stole their money and the car's radio. According to some reports, the National Guard had mistaken Chico Luis for Padre Julio, the man they considered the primary "instigator" of the insurrection.[91] These acts of reckless violence were not isolated episodes but part of the concerted, albeit disorderly and brutal, efforts to destroy opposition at all costs.

The National Guard was responsible for the vast majority of civilian deaths during the insurrection, but the Sandinistas also killed numerous civilians and Guardias while in control of the city. This aspect of the insurrection is, however, often left out of the heroic memories of the upheaval. Most infamous among their victims were the dozens of executions, or *ajusticiamientos* (literally, "bringing to justice"), of those accused of serving as orejas in the OSN's surveillance networks.[92] These orejas, as we saw in chapter 4, were widely blamed for facilitating the arrests, torture, and murder of opposition members. Shortly after seizing the town, the FSLN conducted "people's trials," dragging captured Guardias and "paramilitary" informants before residents, who loudly denounced their abuses in a scene of popular indignation. Many of the city's most infamous orejas—those nicknamed Porra Azul, Zanate, and Hueso Fino—were "tried" in this way. Those found "guilty" were apparently tied to posts and shot down by the guerrillas. The GPP later reported that when the moment came to retreat, the guerrillas' makeshift headquarters was "full of oreja prisoners, in total about twenty-five or thirty. A selection of them was made, and we proceeded with the firing squad."[93] The guerrillas rationalized the killing of civilians by claiming that to retreat with so many prisoners was impossible and to leave them behind meant putting the community at risk of denunciation. The crowds released some orejas following teary-eyed apologies to their neighbors and pledges to stop serving as government informants. When the GN returned, however, many of these men and women resumed their previous roles. As we will see in chapter 6, the September insurrection was not the only time that Sandinistas carried out large-scale executions of alleged orejas.

The warfare of the September insurrection reduced the once-thriving regional hub to a disaster scene. "Estelí is no longer a city but just a geographical speculation," wrote the shocked correspondent for *La Prensa* upon his arrival. "The sign is still in the same place, but the city does not exist. It was wiped off the map"[94] (see fig. 5.2). The newspaper referred to the repression as "Dantesque," and "northern refugees with reddened eyes and bitter faces . . . described the blood-curdling way in which the people of Estelí were massacred."[95] Many now repudiated the National Guard with the epithet of *"los genocidas"* for the mass killings they carried out through their tank attacks, aerial bombardments, and the summary executions of the Cleanup Operation.

Despite their collaborative efforts during the uprising, FSLN factions disagreed in their assessments of the September insurrection. The

*Figure 5.2.* Aerial view of the physical destruction of several blocks in Estelí following the September 1978 insurrection. Photograph by Berríos. Courtesy of Instituto de Historia de Nicaragua y Centroamérica.

Terceristas celebrated the successes, but the GPP leadership remained hesitant. Bayardo Arce, for instance, wrote to a fellow guerrilla complaining of the "consequences of the Tercerista insurrection. . . . The repression practically made Estelí disappear, decimated our infrastructure, hundreds of our civilian supporters have fled, [and] the enemy is now raiding and killing."[96] However, a GPP guerrilla who had fought in the city disagreed with Arce, writing with pride that the uprising "left a mark of strength and bravery on our Estelian brothers; it was in those moments of combat that I realized that the FSLN flag waves with most force and brilliance in the streets of Estelí."[97] Indeed, the city of Estelí now represented a bastion of opposition to the regime; though weakened, the memory of its sacrifice was indelible.

### "Only in the Mountains": Consciousness and Egalitarianism after the Insurrection

Throughout Nicaragua, FSLN membership exploded overnight as a consequence of the September insurrection. Estelí saw FSLN numbers balloon from a handful of guerrilla fighters to hundreds of fresh recruits. The once small Carlos Fonseca Northern Front now included teenage combatants who had retreated to the mountains to escape the National Guard's sweep of Estelí. A Sandinista supporter from Pueblo Nuevo referred to the terror imposed by the GN in the recently recaptured cities:

> That is what made Somoza fall. The way he treated the people; the repression. To be more specific: the Cleanup [Operation] against the young people. If he had found another approach and not this repression, it would've been much harder to defeat him. Because the kids (*la muchachada*) would never have gone to the mountains. Those kids who went because of their ideals, had already gone. But the rest of them all went afterward because of the repression. From my perspective, they were forced to go. So many kids didn't want to get involved in real guerrilla activities but, at that moment, they simply had to go.[98]

Unlike earlier years in which joining the Sandinistas was practically a death sentence, in the new context, *not* to become a revolutionary was a much greater risk. Many of those who joined the struggle, as a result, remained unclear about the guerrillas' political aims. A young guerrilla from Estelí explained that very few joined out of ideological commitment: "The mothers decided that rather than get killed, the young people should grab a gun and fight. That's to say, it was only in the mountains that they got consciousness and began to see the reason for the struggle."[99] The madres saw the FSLN as a source of protection—one that they as mothers could no longer provide—for their children who faced possible death if they remained unprotected against the bloody retribution of the GN.

The new guerrilla combatants had a wide spectrum of motivations for heading to the mountains, and the FSLN rarely turned away those who sought to join. Although some did, in fact, seek out the Sandinistas because of revolutionary consciousness, others simply understood that staying at home was now impossible given the risks of torture or death. In addition, a "minimal" number of those who headed to the guerrilla encampments were common criminals—drug dealers, thieves, cattle rustlers—hoping to escape justice.[100] Comandante Rivera

reported to his superiors that there were "many people whose discipli-
nary behavior in combat was not very correct," a problem he hoped to
rectify through intensive training.[101] Among the new combatants, Rivera found some that did not even like the organization's namesake;
Augusto César Sandino, their families had taught them, had been nothing but a bandit![102] For these unlikely revolutionaries, a new vision of
insurgent morality would only emerge in the thick of the struggle and
their exposure to guerrilla sociability in the montaña.

The strenuous life in the rural camps—sleeping on the ground,
marching through the forest for hours on end, a lack of food or water—
helped forge new identities among the untested insurgents. "It was
there that they showed who had consciousness," the student athlete-
turned-guerrilla Martha Úbeda recalled, "because some of them went
along just because they were scared of getting killed in the city. It was
very tough; we had to walk from five in the morning to five in the
evening. From six to eight, we had criticism and self-criticism ses-
sions. Political and military preparation was fundamental.[103] During
political training, the guerrillas explained that the FSLN was not fighting merely to defeat the GN and topple Somoza but also to achieve a
social revolution.

"Politically, we tried to clarify our ideas and the basic principles of
our struggles to the new compañeros: the right to housing, health care,
education, the right to have land," said guerrillero Feliciano López.
"We explained what the dictatorship, imperialism, and the revolutionary movement were. They also learned war ballistics, firing positions, assaults against bases, artillery assaults, explosives, sabotage,
antitank strategy, mortar weapons like the FAL, the RPG-2, and machine guns like the M-42 and M-30."[104] Because military training took
up most of the time, few combatants developed an intensely ideological
understanding of the conflict in which they were fighting. Indeed, former guerrillas recalled praying, singing, playing games, and socializing
in the encampments far more than the comandantes' political speeches.
Their direct experience of revolutionary camaraderie proved more central in the shaping of their Sandinista consciousness than ideology.

Many traditional hierarchies and social barriers in Nicaraguan
society—between rich and poor, educated and unschooled, urban and
rural, male and female, young and old—began to come crumbling
down in the context of guerrilla warfare.[105] It was not some sort of

radical utopianism of the "world turned upside down" but moral regeneration as a practical, day-to-day experience that was most appealing to the young guerrilleros. As we saw among the CDCs during the insurrection, the war produced camaraderie, social leveling, and mutual dependence on one another for survival as *one family*. "It was a life of *compañerismo*," Leonel Raudez fondly remembered of his time with campesino fighters in the encampments. "These were friendships you can never forget. No one distinguished between one person and another."[106] Peasant teens had long lived in a separate world from city boys, particularly when compared to the sons of well-off doctors and lawyers, but they now converged in a single fighting unit and had much to learn from one another. With their experience in rough living and the rural environment, campesinos proved irreplaceable teachers for the inexperienced teens from the city. In the camps, this feeling of shared sacrifice was reflected in the oft-repeated trope, "if we had one tortilla, we all shared it." Statements such as this reflected not only temporary sacrifice but a model of the very social relations and values they hoped would take hold in postrevolutionary Nicaragua (see fig. 5.3).

*Figure 5.3.* FSLN Comandante Francisco Rivera in the mountains above Estelí with children in a guerrilla encampment. Courtesy of Instituto de Historia de Nicaragua y Centroamérica.

Joining the guerrilla army and heading to the mountains forced many young people to undergo a rapid maturation process and abandonment of previous vices, such as alcohol and drugs, which were off-limits in the encampments. One young guerrilla, who had been in high school before joining the FSLN, recalled that, in retrospect, his life and that of his friends in Estelí had too often been one of partying (*bacanal*): "Somoza must have been thrilled with us. The youth lived totally blinded by vices and marijuana. It isolated us from seeing the exploitation. We felt so privileged simply because we got to attend high school."[107] Interestingly, this political "awakening" represented similar personal transformations to those experienced by those who participated in the cursillos. Another seventeen-year-old rebel from Condega who had been into drugs and alcohol before heading to the guerrilla encampments commented: "The revolution was a total change of my life. Before, everyone around me was corrupted, I was corrupted too. Before I began my contact with the Sandinista Front, I was destroying myself and also 'the people,' because I am part of 'the people,' too."[108] Teenagers who had once been known for their addiction to vices, Christian activist Moisés Calero recalled, were "transformed when they went to the mountains, they came back capable men with great ability. The people began to trust them. They came back to struggle and to ask for our help with a great spirit."[109] Masculinity had long manifested itself through machismo, hard drinking, and interpersonal violence. This had been many of their fathers' reality, but it did not have to be theirs, and the revolution provided them new avenues for their youthful male assertiveness. By breaking with the moral corruption of Nicaraguan society, some young fighters began to define themselves as "New Men" who had undergone a moral renewal that paralleled the struggle against what they saw as the depravity of the Somoza dictatorship.

As the FSLN fostered a new sense of masculinity, social leveling even began to expand into the relations between men and women. The middle-aged *madres* in the city played a central role in the insurrection's civilian support structure, as did campesina women in the countryside. Some young women and teenaged girls also took up arms and fought in guerrilla brigades, challenging machista stereotypes and patriarchal gender norms in the process. The best known include Fátima

Pavón, daughter of a GN officer from La Trinidad, and Martha Úbeda, a gold-medalist sharpshooter as a student-athlete and the sister of several FSLN combatants.[110] Nearly all of the young women who joined in the guerrilla army in Estelí were young high school and university students, rather than adult women or campesinas.[111] As Luisa María Dietrich Ortega argues regarding the cases of Peru, El Salvador, and Colombia, the participation of young men and women in the armed struggle led to a shift in gender relations. Life in the encampments caused what she described as "the temporary construction of particular guerrilla femininities, which allow male–female bonding and comradely complicity, and unveil expressions of guerrilla masculinities beyond the predominant association of men with violence."[112]

One should be careful not to exaggerate the extent of women's incorporation into the FSLN, as was common in the aftermath of Somoza's defeat. Karen Kampwirth in her comparative study of female guerrillas notes that even though widely repeated estimates of women in the Sandinistas were as high as 30 percent, only 6.6 percent of the casualties in the insurrection were female.[113] Former guerrilleras noted that there were proportionally very few women among the FSLN columns fighting in the Segovias during much of the war. In Martha Úbeda's column, she estimated, only 6 women fought alongside 250 men. "There were lots of male high school students and lots of campesinos. Many women didn't go because the conditions were very rough," she explained. Once past these barriers to entry, however, in the ranks of the guerrilla army, "one didn't look at whether you were a man or a woman, we were all the equals. The treatment was the same, mutual respect. The same rights and responsibilities. But don't think that there were a ton of women there."[114] Despite the relatively low numbers of female combatants in Estelí, this does not mean that new gender relations did not begin to emerge.[115] Aura Estela Talavera, a young woman from Condega who joined during the September insurrection, concurred with Úbeda's interpretation. She recalled that "even sleeping in tents surrounded by hundreds of men—including many criminals— there was total respect for the women. No one would've dared lay a finger on a woman against her will."[116] Such an abuse would have run directly counter to the insurgent morality and egalitarian vision the Sandinistas claimed to be establishing.

Some adult men came to shift their perceptions as they witnessed the crucial role of young women in combat throughout the nine months of insurrection. Justo Úbeda Altamirano, the uncle of Martha and her sister Luz (who also took up arms), described this revelation: "Although we thought that women were slightly weaker than men; well, that turned out to be a lie. It was proven in the war that there are women who are more valiant than we men."[117] Overly romanticized accounts often gloss over the perpetuation of subtler forms of sexism and inequalities between male and female members in the FSLN ranks. For many men, ridding themselves of vices such as drinking and drug use proved easier than abandoning their ingrained male chauvinism. Sandinista comandantes, in particular, were not immune to this behavior. With young men greatly outnumbering the female guerrillas, it is undeniable that a large number of the female guerrillas soon became the girlfriends of high-ranking Sandinista comandantes. This situation was suggestive of a machista power dynamic that continued to function even in the fabled montaña. Compared to what came before, however, young women's participation in direct combat against the regime marked a stunning turn of events.[118] Despite the continuing obstacles, these women earned great respect from their fellow combatants for their abilities and leadership in the battle against Somoza.

## Conclusion

The insurrection of September 1978 showcased both the possibility of mass participation in the insurgency and the price that many Nicaraguans were willing to pay to oust Somoza and the GN. In the months before the uprising, the Sandinistas built on both old and new networks of discontent in population centers such as Estelí. The assassination of prominent men such as Pedro Joaquín Chamorro and José Benito Escobar provoked fury, but the deaths and injuries to young children and youth proved far more unforgivable in the eyes of Estelí's families. The Catholic movement played an important role in channeling this moral indignation, principally through the formation of CDCs, which laid the infrastructure for the popular upheaval. The most striking accomplishment of the insurrection in the eyes of participants, though, was the way in which it forged a "single family" out of a diverse population. Survivors emphasize that almost all contributed to the fight by setting up safe houses, building barricades, and/or providing logistical support to the rebels.

Though the guerrillas gained considerable popular backing in their siege of the GN in Estelí, the overwhelming firepower of Somoza's military soon decimated their hopes for rapid victory. In the aftermath, the regime unleashed the worst of its repressive capabilities, targeting the youth whose very role in the struggle was only further legitimated by each death at the hands of the reckless GN. As the GN ratcheted up violence, it was increasingly visualized as a force of disorder and chaos, and the insurgents cast their struggle as a pathway to stability, order, and tranquility. Mothers now urged their young sons and daughters to join the guerrillas, who could offer their children the protection that their husbands or they themselves could no longer guarantee. Though a large number of adult men joined in the struggle, leading opposition organizations, it was the mothers who mobilized in whichever way they could. Many who joined the Sandinistas during the insurrection gained a new sense of moral regeneration and social leveling in the guerrilla encampments in the montaña. The new social relationships they constructed helped to concretize the patterns they hoped would replace the degradation of Somoza's Nicaragua. Over the coming months, however, the regime's security forces would continue to reach new depths of brutality as they expanded their radius of repression, seeking to maintain the dictator in power at all costs.

# CHAPTER SIX

# "HOW COSTLY IS FREEDOM!"

Massacres, Community, and Sacrifice, October 1978–July 1979

In the ten months that followed the September 1978 insurrection, Nicaragua lived through a watershed moment of violent upheaval and state terror. The rapid escalation of the military confrontation was palpable, especially for campesinos in the Segovias, whose communities now bore the brunt of the regime's fury. One peasant woman from La Montañita noted that the Guardias that came in search of the guerrillas in late 1978 "were wearing camouflaged face paint, all exactly alike. But they didn't mistreat anyone and just came through asking if we had seen any unknown people." Those Guardias who invaded their homes in January of the following year—young troops from the EEBI—she recalled, were far different: "They wore masks and were very serious; they had very serious expressions. They didn't ask questions; they just aimed rifles at us."[1] By early 1979, word had reached the GN that the region's villagers had been secretly spiriting food to nearby FSLN camps. Anyone suspected of supporting the guerrillas—as minute as their aid may have been—now risked being brutally murdered along with all members of their family.

During these months, the U.S. embassy reported "a high level of armed insurgency and repressive action . . . [with] reports of beatings, torture, and death appearing daily."[2] Throughout 1979, the GN carried out numerous full-scale massacres of unarmed men, women, and children in rural Estelí with the apparent aim of draining the proverbial sea in which the guerrillas swam. Unable to best the FSLN on the field of battle, the soldiers turned toward "soft targets" among the civilian population, burning peasants alive in their homes after raping and torturing family members.[3] Rather than focusing on specific targets, the GN attacked entire families, killing elderly men and women, children and babies, and subjecting young mothers to sexual violence in front of their husbands. The stark contrast between the modes of violence inflicted by the two sides of the conflict was apparent to most of the population.[4] According to the available data, Estelí was among the most viciously targeted departments, with campesinos making up the single largest group of victims, a pattern not repeated elsewhere in Nicaragua.[5]

The struggle over vice and corruption had served to launch the revolutionary movement, but the GN's extreme violence had clearly become the fundamental moral question by 1979. The increasingly isolated and weakened regime proved incapable of staving off the guerrilla threat; its efforts at counterinsurgency precipitated further bloodshed and political polarization. In the aftermath of each atrocity, the staggering death toll and bone-chilling accounts of survivors led to a clear surge in Sandinista support in much of the countryside. Survival and the promise of moral regeneration would continue to breathe life into the struggle and provide hope for the reconstruction to follow such widespread destruction.

Although they were defining events in the lives of many Nicaraguans, the massacres detailed in this chapter go unaddressed in the many publications dealing with the Sandinista Revolution. Such extreme levels of brutality and suffering are also absent in romanticized and heroic accounts of the insurrection proffered by Sandinista leaders. At the grassroots level, however, such tragic events form the very essence of what it meant to become a revolutionary. Geoffrey Robinson has argued that "mass violence must be understood not only as an *outcome* to be explained," but also "as a vital part of the process through which identities, loyalties, and enmities . . . are formed, solidified or broken."[6] It was precisely the horror inflicted upon the towns and villages encircling Estelí that fostered a robust Sandinista identity, linking together resistance and sacrifice as part of the emerging insurgent morality. Even decades later, the state terror inflicted upon noncombatants helps to explain the Sandinista identity of many families, communities, and towns. Participants grafted their experiences onto the moralizing narrative of the revolution itself, in which each life lost was seen as a necessary contribution to the defeat of Somoza. Rarely were the tragic events recounted as mere victimization, but the survivors instead emphasize the agency of those killed. The insurgents' victory, they believed, would redeem their loved ones' sacrifices. Elsewhere in Latin America, peasant accounts of counterinsurgency and state terror have been narrated in quite different registers. Striking in its absence from popular accounts of state violence in rural Estelí is the classic trope that the civilian population was trapped "between two fires" (guerrillas on the one side, the military on the other) or that the military "killed the just for the sinners," as was claimed in the aftermath of state massacres in Guatemala and El Salvador.[7] Unlike those cases, in which campesinos denied supporting the rebellion after the insurgents' defeat, those targeted by the state in Nicaragua instead identified themselves and their murdered family members as the very catalysts of the victorious revolution.[8] They linked their efforts on behalf of the guerrillas to the earlier consciousness-raising in the cursillos and the hopes that their children would be able to attend school, have access to medical care, and experience the moral renewal of Nicaraguan society.

Community and individual accounts, however, often silence the more complex reality of political violence in the Segovias during 1979. The FSLN also carried out extrajudicial killings of their opponents, though on a far lesser scale than the GN. Sandinista comandante Humberto Ortega argued that the rising upheaval in the Segovias was precisely because most of the population "had a dead relative or friend; there was a thirst for revenge. Popular vengeance is what the people wanted, and we weren't going to oppose it."[9] Thus, in the eyes of Sandinista supporters, killings—even against prisoners and unarmed men and women—were cast as highly targeted and "defensive" in nature, counterpoised to the indiscriminate collective punishment meted out by the government. However, witnessing mass killing at the hands of the government did not always produce pro-Sandinistas identities. In fact, in those rural towns deeply loyal to Somoza on the eve of the insurrection, exactly the opposite dynamic took place. Those massacres committed by the GN were virtually forgotten, while episodes of killing at the hands of the Sandinistas became dramatically amplified in community narratives. These unresolved tensions hung in the air even decades after the downfall of the regime and the triumph of the revolutionary movement.

## The Northern Front and the Massacre of El Tular

With the GN's recapturing of the country's major cities following the September 1978 insurrection, some outside of Nicaragua believed that the guerrilla challenge had failed. Within the mountains of the Segovias, the opposite was clear. The leaders of the Carlos Fonseca Northern Front were enthused about their prospects, as their rural encampments swelled with newly recruited muchachos from the urban barrios. According to Comandante Francisco Rivera, while "the city of Estelí was swarming with Guardias, the countryside and the villages were swarming with guerrillas."[10] As Rivera reported, he instructed seasoned Sandinistas and recruits to begin "a revolutionary campaign directed toward the masses. We have found support among the campesino population to explore zones and find routes to attack the enemy, and thus we have greater and larger control of the zone."[11] The FSLN also began militarily training peasant youths to "create Sandinista campesino militias to channel September's revolutionary potential."[12] Amid the chaos of the war, the guerrillas set about imposing some sense of organization and order in their areas of control.

During late 1978 and early 1979, Somoza was being pressed by the Carter administration to leave power through ongoing OAS-mediated negotiations with the opposition. Such efforts came to naught. To the Sandinistas, however, it seemed that the U.S. State Department aimed to bring about "Somocismo without Somoza," through which the Liberal Party and a "reformed" National Guard would continue to wield power during a pro-U.S. transitional regime.[13] What the U.S. government did not understand was that, following the large-scale violence during September, the elimination of the National Guard as an institution had become a nonnegotiable demand. Given the GN's penchant for extreme violence, the guerrillas were able to maintain the moral high ground and, with it, the people on their side. Over the coming months of civil war, the guerrillas continued to launch military strikes against the GN garrisons in Estelí and other regional towns in the Segovias.[14] In lightning raids between January and March, the guerrilla forces laid siege to Estelí's command base, ambushed GN jeeps, and held up banks. In the process, they also burned down one remaining cigar factory and a number of cantinas, brothels, and gambling dens. Attacks such as these, which again targeted Somocista-owned businesses and centers of vice, were less publicized compared to those that had taken place before the war. Nonetheless, such actions showcased the direct continuities between the earlier upheaval and this phase of open insurgency.[15]

With more than 800 combatants, clandestine camps were established in various rural locales, including San Roque to the west of Estelí, near La Montañita, Santa Cruz to the southeast, El Regadío to the northwest, and Canta Gallo and Cerro Cuba in Condega to the northeast. Peasants living in the rural hamlets adjacent to guerrilla camps provided rice and beans, water, coffee, ears of corn (*elotes*), tortillas, cheese (*cuajada*), and bread. Campesinos also slaughtered large numbers of cattle in Estelí to feed the guerrillas.[16] The vast majority of this support appears to have been voluntary rather than coerced.[17] The willingness of the rural population to help the "muchachos" was partly a product of their earlier participation in the Catholic movement. Not surprisingly, those communities who had encountered the discourse of liberation theology during Padre Julio's cursillos proved most receptive to the guerrillas' message of armed resistance.[18]

National Guard search-and-destroy missions in rural Estelí during these months increasingly turned their wrath against peasant communities. In operations carried out in the wake of pitched battles against the insurgents, the GN unleashed their vengeance against the nearby population they believed had provided supplies to the Sandinistas. Many observers claim that Somoza's soldiers were often drunk or high while heading into battle. In late 1978 and early 1979, the GN sent several large battalions into the hills of Estelí to annihilate the numerous Sandinista encampments in El Guaylo and El Tular, but they proved unsuccessful.[19] The battle at El Tular began on New Year's Day and, according to the FSLN, saw 150 guerrillas escape from 500 Guardias from the EEBI and troops of Central American Defense Council (Consejo de Defensa Centroamericana, CONDECA), apparently sent by Honduras, El Salvador, and Guatemala.[20] Vastly outnumbered and pounded with intense aerial bombardment by the National Air Force, the FSLN reported only six guerrillas lost and fifty GN casualties.[21] The GN communiqués inverted these figures, claiming thirty-three guerrillas killed to just three Guardia deaths.[22]

Following the clash in El Tular, the GN trained their firepower against the homes of humble campesinos who lived near the site of the battle, slaughtering entire families. The twenty-one victims of the GN massacre included infants less than a year old, young children "still wearing their little rubber boots," and an elderly woman of seventy-six.[23] The GN burned their homes to the ground along with all of the coffee, corn, beans, and sorghum in the hamlet.[24] One teenage female guerrilla fighter from Estelí remembered finding marijuana, alcohol, and "trophies" from the women that they had raped and killed in the backpacks left behind in El Tular.[25] Following the massacre, Salomé García (a local campesino) recalled trying to convince his brother Plácido to flee with him before the GN arrived, but Plácido chose to stay behind to support the guerrillas. Several family members had participated in the cursillos and saw it as their Christian responsibility not to abandon los muchachos. "He helped them with what he could, but he did very little," Salomé described. "They told him about loyalty. He said to me, 'No one will die because of my mouth. I'd rather die than let them kill someone else.' Including him, sixteen members of our family were killed."[26] The silence of Plácido helped to safeguard the location of the muchachos in the mountains, but the GN targeted not only him as the patriarch but his entire family. Amid such bewildering violence, many Sandinista sympathizers understood their victimhood at the hands of the military as a sacrifice for the community and the wider cause. As the National Guard ran up against such devotion and commitment to the insurgency over the coming months, they would perpetrate a series of similar massacres throughout the department of Estelí.

## The Massacre of La Montañita

The massacre in El Tular was not to remain an isolated incident but was instead indicative of the counterinsurgency strategy that the EEBI would take against the region. By the end of the month, the GN turned its destructive force against the campesinos of La Montañita, murdering seven local farmhands in the most extreme of ways. This village had lived through an extended period of moral renewal and political engagement under the guidance of Padre Julio and the laypeople of the cursillo movement. From September 1978, villagers had been providing grains and other provisions to the passing guerrilla columns from the hacienda of Alejandro Briones, where many of them worked.[27] The GN arrived in La Montañita on January 21, demanding the location of the guerrilla camps while looting the peasants' shacks of their few possessions. Seven villagers were dragged away by the soldiers, and their family members headed down to the city's GN base the following day to petition for their release.[28] What they did not know was that the soldiers had not taken the campesinos to the town, but rather to a nearby farmhouse where the soldiers continued to torture them through the night. The men were electrocuted and their heads beaten until their eyes came out, and multiple soldiers raped a young woman. The seven corpses—blindfolded with their hands tied behind their backs—were dumped at a river embankment with their throats slit. The killers toppled a stone fence on top of their bodies. By the time neighbors found them, vultures and dogs had already picked at their remains.[29]

Those villagers in La Montañita who survived the ordeal sought to understand the nightmare visited upon the community. Some emphasized the personal greed that allegedly led the juez de mesta to denounce them in the first place. To them, long-standing struggles over land ownership led this particular family to side with the GN. One neighbor noted: "They promised to finish all of us off so that all of the land would belong to them. . . . So the Guardia protected them and didn't protect us. And they protected the Guardia. They all had their rifles and pistols and went around armed, carrying a poster of Somoza."[30] Given his social proximity to the community, the juez's role was foregrounded in survivors' accounts. Unlike the distant figure of Somoza or the masked troops that committed the atrocities, the juez's family had longtime connections to those he was said to have denounced. The split between this family and the village population as a whole provided a clear dividing line of culpability in accounts of the violence. Neighbors perceived the juez's action as a betrayal, which some survivors depicted as an avaricious act of opportunism to steal land.

Narratives of these times of terror do not foreground victimization but rather present their sacrifice as an extension of their resistance and dignity. Peasant women in La Montañita who lost family members in the massacre emphasized the rebellious statements that they made to the GN. Venancia Olles recalled telling the troops, if they were going to kill her brother, "that they should take me and kill me too. So they told me, 'Woman, I would love to take your life. You better get out of here,' and they threatened me with their rifles. I asked them, 'What's his crime?' They said, 'We'll arrest you too, woman.' I told them, 'You are supposed to be the authorities, but you go around kidnapping people.' That's what I told them."[31] Such words of defiance feature prominently in campesina accounts of repression. Here, she also zeroes in on the fact that the GN's claims to authority had been hollowed out and wholly delegitimized by their criminal actions. At the same time, the survivors also highlighted their ability to remain silent or dissimulate when threatened with violence. The husband of Petrona Cruz Briones was among those captured that day. He was tortured in front of her and her children to provide information about the guerrillas. She explained, "We didn't say anything, so they told me that they were going to kill him. I said that they could take my life instead, but I couldn't tell them anything. 'Of course, you can,' they said. '[The guerrillas] eat here.' I knew that I gave them food and my husband did too, but to save myself and out of fear, I had to lie to them."[32]

The GN also carried out acts of extreme sexual violence and humiliation against locals during their attack. Even in the face of such transgressions, many residents of La Montañita were not cowed but rather proved willing to risk their own lives for others. "One of the women they killed," a villager recalled, describing a particularly traumatic event, "was raped in front of her husband. The husband said, 'I'd rather you kill me than do this to my *señora*.' They put her on the floor naked in front of children and the elderly."[33] In seeking to explain how the female victim could have endured such horrendous abuse without revealing the location of the FSLN camp, another local woman widowed by the GN speculated: "She said, 'It's better I die and don't tell them where they are,' because if she died, it would be just her. But if she told them, many more would die."[34] By not revealing the rebels' location, the victims helped to ensure that guerrilla fighters and other

community members would survive and that the struggle against Somoza could go on.

## "The Massacre of the Well" in Santa Cruz

Following the events in La Montañita, one of the most brutal GN
atrocities in the Segovias took place on March 9, when a large contingent of infantry forces arrived in the valley of Buena Vista in Santa
Cruz in search of a reputed FSLN encampment. With no guerrillas in
sight, the GN convoy instead captured thirteen villagers, whom they
tortured, killed, and threw down a nearby well. A cement wash basin
was dumped on top of them and explosives detonated so as to destroy
the well. Those killed included eleven members of the Girón and
Lanuza families and two other campesinos who happened to be chopping firewood in the forest nearby when the troops arrived. Julio
Girón, a local campesino, spotted the Guardias and tried to alert his
family, but he found his house already empty.[35] His wife and four children were among those murdered. The National Guard later falsely
claimed that there had been a battle with a "nest of insurgents" that left
eleven "irregular combatants" dead but no GN casualties.[36]

As elsewhere, the National Guard demanded the whereabouts of
the guerrillas, but none of those murdered were believed to have given
any information. Tree branches were later found riddled with teeth and
pieces of scalp suggesting that soldiers had used them to beat the victims during the interrogation. As in La Montañita, sexual violence was
among the most shocking transgressions attributed to the GN forces
by some survivors. A local woman claimed that the soldiers "captured
them at six in the morning and did what they wanted with them. They
took earrings from the girls—little girls, four and six years old. They
raped them and did horrendous things. I know this because a Guardia
who was captured in Matagalpa after this happened told someone here
from Buena Vista. 'I was there,' he said, 'in the patrol and the chief ordered me to rape these two girls, but I didn't want to.' They did horrible things and then they killed them."[37] The veracity of this specific
claim, the thirdhand account of an alleged personal confession, cannot
be definitively confirmed. In this period of rampant state terror, however, such dramatic accounts spread far and wide.

Though the broader region of Santa Cruz was a bastion of support for the guerrillas, the hamlet of Buena Vista did not have a reputation for political activism. Given the lack of clarity as to who was working with the guerrillas, locals became divided as to why the GN had attacked their village. Many residents were adamant that there "never was, never has been, and never will be a guerrilla camp in Buena Vista" because of the limited tree cover and its easily accessible location near the highway. Others replied that the alleged "guerrilla camp" targeted by the GN had been merely an isolated handful of wounded muchachos without arms, munitions, food, or medicine. Their presence, it was said, had been inadvertently revealed to the regime when one of the villagers working in Managua invited a man—claiming to be a revolutionary from El Salvador—to meet with the guerrillas. The decision to trust this individual, apparently an OSN informant, remained a painful memory for Valentín Girón Lanuza, whose family members died despite their limited political allegiance. Though he personally was a Sandinista sympathizer, he emphasized that those killed were not active in the Christian movement or in supporting the local FSLN encampments:

> As the saying goes, "where Vicente goes, the others follow" (*adonde va Vicente, va la gente*). They didn't have the experience we'd acquired from our work with the priests. We would never have let a man like that visit here and leave; we would've handed him over to the guerrillas. And not only did they let him leave; they even gave him the tiny amount of money they had so he could buy arms and medicine for the guerrillas. Instead, the massacre came. The guerrillas hid and fled, running away. There was no one here who could fight. I tell this story because I lived it and all of my people ended up in that well.[38]

Despite mutual recriminations and ambiguity over the extent of the victims' participation, the utter brutality of the GN action placed the Buena Vista massacre into the wider story of moral indignation and revolutionary upheaval. Padre Agustín Toranzo, a young Spanish Jesuit who had helped lead the cursillo movement in Estelí, was among those who arrived three days later to excavate the bodies and witness evidence of the GN's crimes. He was shocked at what he discovered. In his service for the deceased, Toranzo allegedly stunned funeral goers, publicly identifying the GN as the guilty party and calling on the men to defend their families and the wider community. "Those *huevos* you have are not just to get women pregnant!" Toranzo is said to have scolded the adult men, using vulgar language. "But to stand up for yourself and not let them kill us all like they killed these people."[39] Toranzo echoed the by-now common critique of the failure of many adult men to step up and support the cause: The youth were already involved, the women were making incredible sacrifices, but where were the men?[40] Some were shocked by the language he used, but his critique of the campesinos on the grounds of their masculine obligation as fathers and husbands struck a chord. Though the GN attempted to present the massacre as a mere skirmish with the guerrillas, the news of the atrocities revealed by the excavation spread like wildfire. As narratives about the massacre ricocheted around Estelí and the Segovias, the FSLN was also forced to respond. It became clear that they could not abandon rural communities that were imperiled and in the line of fire.

### The Second Insurrection and the Massacres of April

By March 1979, the three FSLN tendencies (GPP, TP, and Terceristas) agreed to reunify under a single national command structure and to begin planning for a "final" military campaign against the regime. In Estelí, campesinos pressed the Sandinistas' Northern Front to carry out a decisive attack against the GN to protect civilians from the widening reign of terror. Sandinista Filemón Moncada recalled how the Guardias in control of the city showed no clemency toward those campesinos suspected of buying supplies in bulk for the FSLN: "They ripped out their eyes, ripped out their tongues, and dumped them at the entrance of the city. This was to scare the campesinos that the same thing would happen to them if they helped the guerrillas."[41] The recently formed Permanent Human Rights Commission (Comisión Permanente de Derechos Humanos, CPDH) reported that many captured by the GN in the Estelí area had become *desaparecidos* (disappeared), vanishing after their arrest, much like the victims of the Southern Cone military dictatorships in Argentina and Chile.[42]

Guiding the GN in their campaign of violence against the rural communities was an informant known as "Cherry," a former GN soldier from Santa Cruz who lived in the neighborhood of El Calvario in Estelí. During the September insurrection, he joined his neighbors and fought alongside the Sandinistas, retreating with them to the countryside. Some claim that he infiltrated the FSLN on orders of the GN, others insist that he fled from the Sandinistas only after attempting to rape a female combatant—fearing severe punishment by the FSLN. The son of an American highway contractor and a campesina from Santa Cruz, Cherry, in the words of one former guerrilla, stood out as "light-skinned with green eyes and blonde hair, a big man . . . a real North American."[43] Amid the battalions of helmeted, uniformed, and masked GN troops, Cherry struck a uniquely fearsome figure whose name crops up in many of the survivor accounts of the period. As an oreja, he was uniquely dangerous because of his intimate knowledge of FSLN operations in rural Estelí. He could provide the GN with the identities of many of the guerrillas and the campesinos that helped them, and also the locations of the guerrilla encampments.[44]

In response to the continuing atrocities, Comandante Francisco Rivera headed from Honduras to Estelí to personally lead a massive strike against the GN in the Segovias. Approximately one hundred armed guerrillas dressed in olive green carried out a military incursion into the city on April 8 (Palm Sunday) and would remain there throughout Holy Week. Though the guerrillas had not planned a popular uprising, the FSLN attack quickly developed into another full-scale insurrection largely because of the desire of the city's population to strike back.[45] Many locals—especially those personally affected by GN violence—threw up barricades and joined in the fight, following the script they had learned in September.[46] While the Sandinistas were laying siege to the command post, simultaneous raids sought to divide GN forces, hitting various military bases throughout the Segovias.[47]

The residents of the poor and working-class barrios long sympathetic to the Sandinistas once again aided the Terceristas under Francisco Rivera (using the pseudonym "Rubén") and Juan Alberto Blandón ("Froylán"), and the GPP forces under Julio Ramos ("13").[48] Unlike September, however, the GN held the highest points in the city, including the cathedral, the girls' parochial school El Rosario, the National

Bank, and the telephone company TELCOR installations. From these strategic positions, they could easily pick off the guerrillas manning the barricades. Additionally, the National Guard flooded the city with an estimated 2,000 EEBI reinforcements. When the guerrillas attempted to halt the arrival of these troops, the GN once again responded with aerial strafing and heavy artillery bombardment. During the week of combat, guerrilla firepower successfully "neutralized" a Sherman tank, and rebel forces in nearby Condega shot down a Cessna airplane on its way to bomb Estelí. However, as the battle dragged on, the insurgents were increasingly overwhelmed by Somoza's army.[49]

In the recaptured parts of the city under GN control, the EEBI forces proceeded to again carry out a brutal Cleanup Operation against the civilian population, beginning on April 12.[50] Mercedes Mendoza witnessed a large squad of Guardias arrest her husband, her teenage nephew, and ten other young men who lived nearby. "We found them seven months and twelve days later with all the others," she said, "their bodies destroyed and riddled with bullets . . . . on the Estelí airstrip."[51] One of the Operation's primary targets was the San Juan de Dios Hospital, where wounded civilians and guerrillas were treated throughout the insurrection. Once the GN seized the building, they carried out a massacre that violated the most basic laws of war. According to numerous witnesses, the now-infamous Cherry accompanied EEBI troops commanded by Maj. Franklin Montenegro ("Sagitario") to the hospital and proceeded to identify the wounded as guerrillas. One of the young victims, suffering from appendicitis, was dragged from his hospital bed never to be seen alive again, despite his father's desperate pleas to the authorities for information.[52] In addition to the young men targeted as Sandinistas—some of whom were found later with their throats slit— the soldiers also turned against the medical staff attending to the patients. They forced doctors Alejandro Dávila Bolaños and Eduardo Selva and the nurse Cleotilde Moreno from the operating room and executed them outside.[53] Rosa Celinda Bellorín, whose seventeen-year-old son was also among those killed in the hospital, described those tense moments as they were relayed to her by witnesses. "They took off his clothes," she recounted. "Then they took Dr. Selva and Dávila Bolaños, who were on the floor, and told them to get up, along with my son. The witnesses saw them take them alive outside of the hospital, as they didn't kill them inside. They heard the machine gun blasts, and it seems like it took place somewhere nearby because that's where the wife of Dr. Dávila Bolaños found his glasses and pen."[54]

Alejandro Dávila Bolaños had been practically the founding father of the revolutionary movement in Estelí. However, even though many of his students had joined the FSLN since the 1960s, the doctor had personally long opposed the Sandinista strategy of armed struggle as a loyal cadre of the Socialist Party. In his final diary entry, written on April 8, he described the arrival of the guerrilla columns into the city and his plans to head to the hospital to help with the wounded. "How costly is freedom!" he wrote. "All this young blood sacrificed! Let us never forget this. This price should remain in everyone's conscience."[55] Freedom meant not merely the removal of Somoza but the freedom to remake Nicaraguan society on a new basis, without the vice, violence, and inequality in which they lived. Such sacrifices were not based on some utopian promise but emerged directly out of the population's practical experiences lived over the intensity of the previous year. When the time came to retreat, FSLN fighter Feliciano López tried to convince the doctor to leave with the guerrilla columns: "He told me, 'I'm not going to put my hands down until the revolution triumphs. I'm going to the hospital because there are many people to save. If they kill me, fine. If not, I'll find some way to catch up with you.' The important thing I heard him say was that he was conscious of the fact that they could kill him. But he knew that many more patients would die without his help. That tells us that he risked his life for his patients and, for this, I consider him a real hero."[56] In a guerrilla communiqué, the FSLN denounced the "cowardly" manner in which the GN killed the unarmed medical professionals carrying out their "sacred duty."[57] Somoza, for his part, merely responded to the claims of GN culpability in a press conference by referring to the allegedly "missing" Dávila Bolaños as "the greatest Communist agitator in Estelí."[58]

During the tumultuous Holy Week in Estelí, the GN again fanned out to the rural areas in search of the guerrilla forces and their non-combatant sympathizers. When the son of the juez de mesta in La Montañita—a GN reservist and paramilitary—was killed in a shootout with the FSLN, the GN stormed the village with a list of houses accused of furnishing support to the guerrillas. According to several accounts, the soldiers set about torturing and killing campesinos, before dousing their homes with gasoline and setting them ablaze. Dogs trapped in one of the houses let out howls of panic as the buildings burned down around them. Many of the approximately twenty-nine people killed that day were women, children, and the elderly. A local survivor noted that the Guardias first "burned the house of Lorena Cruz and burned her with two unmarried daughters and her son, her nephew, and my husband's nephew," while in another home they killed the family of Francisco Cruz, "a humble man who didn't bother anyone and lived with his mother-in-law and two other elderly people."[59] Unlike their earlier targeting of those families fingered directly for providing food to the guerrillas, Silveria Cruz noted, the GN now killed many "innocent people who knew nothing about the muchachos or where they were. They also killed two kids who didn't know anything; they just ran into them on the path and killed them."[60] It was no longer a question of political ideology: in this orgy of violence, the village as such had been targeted and only the juez de mesta's immediate family was exempt from retribution. Survivor accounts emphasized that the juez was regularly spotted with the GN in the days following the massacres. The soldiers camped at his home and feasted on the livestock of the murdered families. A neighbor, María González, described how the juez's family "took care of them as though it were a party: with meat from slaughtered cows and pigs."[61]

During the previous uprising, the Sandinistas had planned simultaneous insurrections in other cities, such as León, Matagalpa, Masaya, and Chinandega, which had dispersed the GN's forces. Now, government forces were able to focus almost all of their energy against the Segovias. In the bloody combat, Juan Alberto Blandón, commanding the operation, was among those gunned down.[62] Some families who had lived through the previous uprising in September begged the Sandinistas to keep fighting and not withdraw, knowing well the fate that awaited them at the hands of the GN. Other city residents, however, insisted that they were willing to die if it meant that the FSLN could escape to fight and win another day. When the order was given to depart, the guerrillas gathered up many of their civilian backers before dawn—estimated at 2,500 men, women, and children—and led them on a mass exodus to Tomabú hill, the site of a large guerrilla camp.[63] In their retreat, the group broke through three GN rings, leading to numerous guerrilla casualties as they departed on April 14.[64] It was a moment that would long live in the memories of the town's revolutionaries. Essentially, all those civilians remaining in the city had to leave their homes toward an uncertain future, but with a deep awareness that it would not be in vain. They had definitively cast their lot with the Sandinistas, who provided cover and protection during the retreat. In the montaña, families joined their sons and daughters, whom they had previously entrusted to the guerrilla army.

### "White Hand" Massacres in Condega and La Trinidad

Unable to stem the revolutionary tide, the regime now began using clandestine death squads to eliminate their opposition. Rather than campesinos, those targeted were rural middle-class families suspected of abetting the insurgency. To maintain a modicum of plausible deniability, the GN was said to rely on a secretive group known as the *Mano Blanca* (White Hand), who largely operated under cover of night.[65] As early as May 1978, the U.S. embassy had received reports of "clandestine pro-Somoza terrorists described as a White Hand type organization," similar to paramilitary death squads that operated in El Salvador and Guatemala.[66] An EEBI soldier stationed in Estelí during 1979 claimed to know the membership of this group:

> The infamous White Hand were Guardias from Managua, from the OSN. If someone said that in a house there were Sandinistas, they came at night and boom. These White Hands were people that were in jail for killings, rapes, robberies. . . . They were members of street gangs like *los Hienas, los Tigres, los Vengadores* [the Hyenas, the Tigers, the Avengers] . . . all of the scum that the Guardia had in La Modelo prison. They let them out to fight, organized them in this way so they could come and do this kind of thing. . . . They knew that by giving weapons to this type of men and letting them loose, that they would do terrible things.[67]

Members of the so-called White Hand were said to wear GN uniforms at times, and on other occasions they dressed as civilians or even wore the olive green fatigues and red-and-black bandanas of the FSLN to pin their actions onto the insurgents. Such "false flag" massacres were terrifying for survivors but had varying effects on different communities.

In the town of Condega, the well-regarded González family was the primary target of this new form of death squad activity. Though a traditional, landowning Liberal lineage, many in the González family had come to oppose the regime over the previous decade. The patriarch Romeo González had been the town's Somocista mayor in the 1960s, but his daughter Aura Velia led the protest movement in 1974, and his son Raúl had been brutally murdered by the GN in 1977. In the lead-up to the insurrection, while her male siblings joined the guerrillas, Aura Velia and her sister Wilma had formed a local chapter of the opposition women's organization AMPRONAC. A family friend, Rosa Zeledón, recalled Aura Velia's passionate pleas explaining to them what they needed to do: "She told us that not only the men could fight. She told us . . . that we had to have consciousness and join in the struggle. And that we women have to defend ourselves even if all we had were rocks.[68] Along with their husbands—storeowner Juan Francisco Guillén and schoolteacher Julio Castillo Ubau—the sisters also helped lead the town's branch of the protest umbrella group, the MPU. Through the committees, they coordinated first-aid training and the stockpiling of supplies. For these activities, they had been denounced on numerous occasions by the town's network of orejas (described in chapter 4). After arresting, torturing, and releasing Juan following the April insurrection, GN troops returned to ransack both sisters' homes on May 2, apparently finding nothing incriminating.[69] The GN patrols returned to their base before the nightly curfew, which began at sundown.

Late that night, armed men arrived at the home of Aura Velia and Juan. While the attackers were beating Juan, the men extorted jewels and money from the couple and threatened their eleven-year-old daughter. Unbeknownst to the assailants, the couple's teenage sons had been able to hide in their nearby bedroom. "I heard her say, 'Don't kill them, don't kill them,' with cries of despair," one son later testified.[70] His brother remembered hearing his mother "tell them to kill her but not to do anything to anyone else. The Guardias told her to lie down on the floor. I heard a shout. It wasn't like a scream, but as though she was being drowned."[71] Once the men departed, the sons emerged to find their mother and their younger sister face down in puddles of their own blood with their throats slit. The boys' father, however, was nowhere to be found, having been dragged from the house at gunpoint by the attackers. Taking with them their infant niece who was staying at the family's house that night, the two boys rushed to Venecia, their grand-parents' hacienda, to warn them of the ongoing attack.

From Aura Velia's house, the death squad headed to the nearby home of her sister, Vilma, and killed her along with her husband, Julio Castillo. Their four-year-old toddler was shot in the cheekbone (and, amazingly, survived), but the assassins' bullets missed the couple's two other young children.[72] By the time the attackers arrived at Venecia, all five had escaped. Nonetheless, the assailants looted the farmhouse and set it on fire.[73] A family friend who observed the remains of Aura Velia and her daughter the following morning wrote, "It was a horrible image. We all started crying; I had never felt such great sadness."[74] Hours later, the cadaver of Juan Guillén was discovered several kilo-meters from the town, dumped alongside the road to Yalí, apparently stabbed to death with bayonets.[75] In a single night, the attackers had targeted three generations of a single family for death, a fact that reveals both the extent of the FSLN's civilian support and the GN's obscene reaction.

For its part, the GN denied the following day that any patrol had been in the area of the two houses the night before and blamed the mas-sacre on an armed band of criminals masquerading as members of the National Guard.[76] Family members noted that the shells left on the floor by a Garand, the National Guard's standard issue weapon, clearly told a different story.[77] La Prensa was also incredulous, asking how the massacre could have possibly happened without official collusion: "How could the Guardia not hear the shots given how close they were? How was the vehicle of the murderers able to drive around with such liberty at such late hours?"[78] Attempts to place blame on others were unsuccessful, as Condega residents were well aware of the family's public political activism. The massacre definitively wedded much of the population of Condega to the Sandinista cause, with many becoming concerned that they too risked being killed by the White Hand or the EEBI. After the burial of the victims, the town's terrified and infuriated residents began packing up and leaving. Within no time, Condega was, a resident later testified, "completely empty because the murdered were held in high esteem by the population."[79] A flood of 5,000 residents from Condega and neighboring areas streamed across the border into Honduras. Many young people, however, instead took to the hills to join the guerrillas and help overthrow a regime capable of committing such a deplorable act.[80] The GN left them with few options: either flee or risk being targeted for complicity with the Sandinistas. At the same time, the mass flight from the town demonstrated a great deal of unity among the community.

Just weeks later in La Trinidad, to the south of Estelí, a quite similar massacre of unarmed civilians took place. Many blamed the White Hand, but the political consequences were far different in that town. Unlike other rural communities in the department of Estelí seen as pro-FSLN, La Trinidad remained staunchly Somocista and quiescent even through the recent years of social mobilization and military conflict. When the White Hand struck in this town, its primary target was the family of Padre José del Carmen Suazo. Monseñor Suazo, originally from León, had brought his mother and sisters to live in La Trinidad where he served as the parish priest. His family continued to live in the town after the Church transferred him to Madriz in the 1960s. In a village where most families had roots going back generations, the Suazos were still considered relative newcomers even after living there for years. During the late 1970s, both Suazo and some members in his family were rumored to be anti-Somocistas. Suazo himself was arrested in Somoto in 1978 and only released following a spontaneous protest by the townsfolk. In La Trinidad, his nephew Oscar had recently been denounced by the orejas for spray-painting FSLN graffiti.[81]

The massacre of the Suazo family in La Trinidad took place the night of June 8, 1979, just four days after the Sandinistas declared a nationwide general strike, as part of their strategy to bring down the regime. That evening, the Suazos were celebrating the birthday of a classmate of seventeen-year-old Oscar. Unbeknownst to them, after evening curfew, a van had arrived and dropped off a group of White Hand members in the town square outside. They allegedly sat in the park, drinking guaro, and waiting for an opportune moment to strike. It was around eight o'clock when "the Guardia came in and killed everyone they found," explained Blanca Rosa Castillo Díaz, the priest's sister-in-law and mother to several of the victims. "They were looking for Padre Suazo. When they couldn't find him, they killed the others. We didn't even know the padre was with the Sandinistas."[82] The paramilitaries pummeled the boy celebrating his birthday before shooting him and killing six others, including Padre Suazo's seventy-year-old mother, doña Rosita. After leaving the Suazos' home, the assailants moved on to other households in La Trinidad, killing at least three other people.

One of two survivors of the massacre, thirteen-year-old Javier Suazo, recalled the events, emphasizing the final words of resistance his older brother offered to him:

> My brother told me, "They've killed me." He'd been shot, but he was still alive. He told me that if I survived, I had to become a [guerrilla] combatant; that I had to fulfill that promise. Then they shot my little brother. That was the most painful for me because he was only five years old. They shot him with a .45 with something like thirty bullets. In total, seven people died there. I saved myself by climbing into the bed. I don't know why, but I saw my salvation under the bed, and while hiding there, four bullets came close to me. I hid myself between the bed and the wall. When they turned the lights out, I covered my arms with blood and lay on the floor, so they thought that I was dead. And they kicked my little sister. After that, they killed my aunt. She told them they could steal whatever they wanted, but to not kill the kids. They killed my mother and my little grandma (*mi abuelita*). And then my other aunt. And then they left. After that, I grabbed my little sister, who was pouring blood, and took her to my uncle's house.[83]

Javier's testimony of the events parallels the descriptions of dignity and sacrifice embedded in many other survivor narratives. Whether an actual exchange or not, his oath to his dying brother to join the FSLN directly linked the massacre with future participation in the insurgency. As we saw in other cases, martyrdom thus inverted the potentially debilitating effect of political violence at the hands of the state into a compelling call to insurrection.

As elsewhere, the White Hand attempted to muddy the waters, implying that the Sandinistas had been responsible for the killing, apparently painting FSLN graffiti on the house. Progovernment media promptly declared that guerrillas had attempted to murder Padre Suazo but instead executed his family. A small number of town residents did not believe the official story and were so appalled by the GN's shocking violence that they decided to take up arms against the dictatorship. In a case perhaps unique in all of Nicaragua, the town's sitting Somocista mayor, Alcides Molina, resigned his post and headed off to join the Sandinista guerrillas.[84] In contrast to the other massacres, however, the killing of the Suazo family was not congruent with the town's overall political identity. By and large, the local population did not know how to process the massacre given their cognitive dissonance in light of their Liberal political identity. Given the confusion, Padre Suazo himself seemed unable initially to understand which side of the conflict was responsible for his family's murder.[85]

Despite witness descriptions blaming the slaughter on the GN, many in the town chose instead to embrace some variation of the "false flag" interpretation, laying blame at the feet of the hated Sandinistas. In fact, some claimed that the FSLN had killed the family in a Machiavellian plot to create victims and spark unrest. Unlike the case with death squad assassinations in opposition-heavy Condega, few among the Somocista majority in La Trinidad feared that they or their children could be the next to die at the hands of the government. It is telling, though, that none of the former Guardias queried—including those from La Trinidad—denied GN culpability for the Suazo massacre. In contrast to locals with a personal stake in embracing the "false flag" story, former Guardias widely acknowledged the OSN and the White Hand as the perpetrators. A former soldier from San Lucas who knew Monseñor Suazo, for instance, when asked about the responsible party, answered matter-of-factly: "The Guardia and the Seguridad, of course."[86] Another National Guard soldier from La Trinidad stationed in Estelí even reported overhearing an oreja denounce the Suazo family and regretted that he had been unable to get word to "doña Rosita" of the imminent attack.[87] The psychological effect of the Suazo family massacre in the town was supplanted by another act of mass killing committed the following month. On that occasion, however, the deaths were clearly at the hands of Sandinistas and fit far more comfortably within the town's sense of political affinity.

## "Popular Vengeance": Revolutionary Violence in Estelí and La Trinidad

Whereas the overwhelming majority of mass killings were the work of government forces, Sandinista executions of Guardias or "ajusticiamientos" of orejas at times matched the brutality of the regime. The extreme actions that the FSLN took against captured soldiers or civilian opponents complicate romantic narratives that only emphasize GN violence. Still, Sandinista sympathizers emphasize that insurgent violence was instrumental rather than indiscriminate, the product of voluntary restraint in the face of outright repression. The guerrillas, unlike the government, were not accused of killing children, the elderly, massacring entire families, systematically using torture and sexual violence against opponents, or carrying out bombings against civilians. Sandinista atrocities, rather, were limited to the execution of orejas and captured GN soldiers, described as too dangerous to release. The FSLN executed many of Estelí's most notorious orejas in September 1978, in some cases following "people's tribunals" in which neighbors participated as the "jury." Some informers begged for forgiveness and gained clemency, but many of these same individuals later returned to their roles after the guerrillas departed. In April, informants and soldiers were again captured and held by the FSLN in a makeshift prison. This time, however, when they withdrew from the town, the guerrillas executed the entire group. "It was not possible to take them with us," Francisco Rivera (now known as "El Zorro") explained years later, "and letting them go would have been an injustice."[88] The Sandinistas killed thirty prisoners—mostly Guardias and orejas—during the April insurrection, including Dr. Eliseo Yllescas, a magistrate of the Appeals Court and a prominent Somocista.[89] In those areas where the regime's cruelty had alienated the vast majority of the population, Sandinista war crimes were, however, cast by many locals as morally justifiable.

In La Trinidad, a mass killing of alleged secret police informants by the Sandinistas left an open wound. In that village, however, residents experienced the "popular vengeance" of the armed insurgents as political terror directed against the community's kinship networks.

After the fall of the local GN barracks, orders came from the FSLN command to round up a list of men identified as orejas in the area of La Trinidad and neighboring San Isidro. The guerrillas took the Somocista prisoners to El Guasimal—the large hacienda once owned by Liberal cacique Hector Mairena—and executed them in retribution for the earlier massacre of the Suazo family, in which local residents insist the victims had played no part. Among those killed were a former Liberal mayor of La Trinidad, the owner of a gambling den, and six other PLN supporters with deep connections to local society. "They were all Somocistas, but they weren't involved in anything," insisted one furious town resident. "They grabbed them from their homes, took them to El Guasimal and then killed them in the most sadistic of ways."[90] The guerrilla combatant accused of killing the unarmed orejas was one of the very few young people from La Trinidad who joined the armed struggle against the dictatorship. For his role in the deaths of these men, he remained ostracized by townspeople for decades. "They still blame me for executing the orejas," he explained. "I was the one who captured them, but I didn't know they were going to shoot them. . . . And they shot all eight. That's why these people hate me here. I did go and bring them there, but I swear I didn't know they were going to kill them (*que los iban a palmar*)."[91] The executions of the orejas fit into the dominant community narrative as a clear-cut example of Sandinista brutality. Much like the killings by the GN in countless other villages, residents could not forgive FSLN's arbitrary actions. From the perspective of many residents of La Trinidad, the massacre of the orejas perpetrated by Sandinistas loomed far larger as an injustice than that of the Suazos.

Following the state violence inflicted on families and communities, some young FSLN recruits even came to rationalize brutality as a way to forcibly counter the abuses of their adversaries. A young guerrilla combatant left orphaned by the massacre in La Montañita reflected that when the GN had captured his family, they had "burned them alive, to laugh about it. So it got to the point where when we grabbed one of them, we had to do the same. We had to do what they did. They grabbed our families and hurt them. So we had to do the same thing that they did. . . . [*pause*] To burn them alive."[92] Imitative violence was not the standard response of the FSLN to GN barbarities, but this was certainly not the only guerrilla atrocity carried out in the Segovias. Such actions ran directly counter to FSLN founder Carlos Fonseca's early vision of "revolutionary morality," in which he called on the guerrillas to respect the lives of the GN and only execute those guilty of horrendous crimes.[93]

Largely silenced in traditional accounts, episodes of mass killings perpetrated by the insurgency remain a difficult memory for many participants to assimilate into their stories of sacrifice and triumph. "It's painful to say it," one Sandinista combatant reflected, "but all sorts of things happen in war. For the safety of the families of those of us who were in the guerrilla army, we had to silence these people because they were a great danger to us."[94] As we see in his statement, he continued to frame their actions as a way to prevent further bloodshed. Another former guerrilla, reflecting back on these events, offered a more critical account of the oreja killings: "In my personal opinion, we shot people that we shouldn't have. Because I think the ones who gave the orders were much guiltier than the little guy [the orejas]. I don't know why it happens that the poor always defend the powerful. In April alone, many of those people were killed and in September too. In each of these actions, there were some injustices. Unfortunately, arms corrupt a person. Maybe some of those people had nothing to do with the war and were killed out of personal vengeance. It was not all rose-colored or the fairest thing to do."[95] Such thorny and contradictory memories, however, are often obfuscated in triumphalist accounts in search of simplistic histories of state violence and popular resistance. Indeed, given the ambiguous and problematic nature of the ajusticiamientos, these actions were minimized in the dominant historical narratives, if mentioned at all. As the war came to an end and prisoners could be safely held, the FSLN increasingly sought to prevent the killing of Guardias and orejas. These men, Sandinista commanders explained, would be sent before tribunals after the revolution triumphed.[96]

## THE FALL OF ESTELÍ AND THE MASSACRE OF EL COLORADO

In efforts to finally dislodge the Somozas from power, the Sandinistas in June 1979 launched renewed uprisings in the country's major cities and an all-out war across the southern border. The guerrilla forces now launched insurrections in the capital Managua for the first time. The government successfully beat back an FSLN invasion from Costa Rica, but accounts of spiraling violence against civilians had turned international public opinion against Somoza. As reports of GN atrocities came to light, one country after another broke diplomatic ties with the regime during early-to-mid 1979. The United States' last-ditch attempt to secure an OAS resolution to send "peacekeeping forces" to Nicaragua and forestall a Sandinista victory was voted down by the other Latin American governments. The Somoza regime's days appeared numbered.[97]

With weapons and ammunition pouring in from the Tercerista high command, Francisco Rivera and the Northern Front continued to launch major military assaults in the Segovias. On May 23, they set up an ambush on the highway between Estelí and Condega, firing on GN reinforcements, allegedly killing sixteen and injuring twenty others.[98] Two nights after the massacre of the Suazos, the GN's White Hand struck again, killing Dr. Orlando Ochoa, the local Red Cross director, his wife, Miriam, and a young girl who lived with them. Ochoa, the third doctor murdered in Estelí, was rumored to have sent medical supplies to the Sandinistas in the mountains.[99] By this point in the civil war, Estelí had become a virtual ghost town, with very few civilians still camped out in the ruins. Though often described as "the third insurrection" (*la tercera insurrección*), the battle that began with attacks on June 9, in fact, took the form of a thirty-seven-day military siege of the GN base and various smaller GN command posts. Importantly, the 120 Sandinista troops who marched into the town under the orders of Elías Noguera ("René") in mid-1979 were not the untested youths of September who had rallied spontaneously to the exhortations of the FSLN. Their columns were now significantly better trained and armed. Many even wore olive green uniforms with insignias identifying their battalions and units. Starting from their strongholds in El Calvario and El Zapote, the Sandinistas pressed onwards toward the GN command post in a grinding house-by-house struggle. GN comandante Vicente Zúñiga ("Sombra") concentrated his forces inside of the base, as tanks and FAN planes began once again to pound the city.[100]

The final assault against the National Guard in Estelí took place on July 16 and has become a thing of legend among Sandinistas. In a clever strategy devised by local workers, a single-motor crop duster airplane was painted red and black and converted into an improvised bomber. And even though bombing the base did not immediately force the GN from their garrison, the psychological effect was immense. The insurgents now sent an unmanned tractor careening toward the military garrison, forcing a breach in its outer walls. Those soldiers inside now attempted to flee through a hail of Sandinista bullets. Comandante Sombra, dozens of his troops, and numerous jueces de mesta and orejas were gunned down in the ensuing firefights. Hundreds of Guardias more—including the bases' most infamous torturer—were captured alive.[101] Soon after that, Sandinistas also captured and imprisoned the infamous Cherry.[102] He died shortly following his arrest in suspicious circumstances while purportedly attempting to escape custody. As someone widely reviled by peasants for his role in mass killings throughout the villages, it seems likely that his death was an act of "popular vengeance" by FSLN members or sympathizers.

Before the Sandinistas could claim official victory over the Somoza regime as a whole, however, the fleeing GN carried out a final wave of mass killings in the mountains to the northeast of the city. Even when their cause appeared lost, the troops showcased no remorse in attacking unarmed peasants. At the eleventh hour of the battle, a stream of Guardias had abandoned the fight and headed toward the Honduran border.[103] Having hunkered down inside the base during a month of combat, they fled with a visceral hatred of the civilian population. En route to the border, the escaping convoy marched through the coffee-growing region between Pueblo Nuevo and San Juan de Limay, an area that had remained relatively quiet during the previous months of the civil war. However, even in this remote border area, the FSLN had apparently won the backing of at least some local campesinos.

When young soldiers from the EEBI, disguised as guerrilleros in red-and-black bandanas, marched through the communities adjacent to the coffee plantations shouting revolutionary slogans, they received cheers. Peasants in the area had heard over the radio that Estelí had fallen to the guerrillas and believed the convoy to be the victorious Sandinistas. One of those who rushed to offer support was a schoolteacher who owned a small store in Laguna Negra. "Undoubtedly," her uncle noted, "she was using the store to supply the guerrillas."[104] Upon the arrival of the "muchachos," locals offered them food to celebrate their victory. For her generosity, she was raped and murdered by the marauding group. A growing contingent of soldiers arrived—older men wearing GN uniforms and not disguised as guerrillas—and along with the EEBI infantrymen proceeded to massacre the campesinos.

The escaping Guardias continued their bloody march toward the coffee plantations of La Máquina and La Fraternidad. "My wife's uncle was captured," a man from Pueblo Nuevo recalled. "They took him prisoner and killed him in La Máquina. There was a massacre of so many people. The Guardias just started killing; they killed just for fun."[105] The EEBI soldiers, still posing as guerrillas, mendaciously called on all males from the next village to join them in an attack against the GN base in Somoto. A man, who was fifteen years old at the time, explained that on that fateful day, "We campesinos couldn't tell that we had been tricked because they put all the young Guardias up front and the old men stayed behind. They came along tricking people and taking them with them . . . all those they found in their path that day, whether they were little boys or old men. They also grabbed a bunch of the shoeless kids who were walking around here that day. From La Fraternidad, they grabbed all of those who were coming home from work."[106] By the time they realized that these men were from the GN, the peasants were unable to escape. The survivor continued his account:

The Guardia said, "Walk straight, don't look around" . . . because the area was filled with the blood of those they were slaying. As we were walking, we saw them with their bayonets dripping blood; they seemed to love slitting throats. We were walking and couldn't make any quick movements or say anything. And they went on happily shooting their guns. When they got bored and left, my father stood up. "You survived, my son?" "I did. And you?" "I'm fine." We walked to another ditch and saw that it was the hole into which my grandfather had fallen [upon his death]. . . . They captured more people farther ahead, including my uncle and a little thirteen-year-old boy. And they just kept going and going. People have asked me how many of them there were. Well, you could look down the entire trail in both directions and see only guns. Just for fun, they killed all those they got their hands on.[107]

The death march of El Colorado is unlike the stories of the campesinos burned in their homes in La Montañita or even those dumped in the well in Buena Vista. In these narratives, peasants immediately recognized victimhood as a noble sacrifice or a form of resistance through silence. For survivors of the massacre at El Colorado, coming as it did after the GN's defeat, constructing meaning out of the state violence proved more challenging.

Rather than a moment of tragedy in a history of community and family activism, the Colorado events provoked horror in their lack of justification. Campesinos consistently narrate the massacre as coming totally out of the blue and shattering their lives. In secondhand accounts, the GN's actions take on a genuinely demonic form, with one man claiming that the murdered campesinos had "their throats slit, and the Guardias took their blood in bags to drink."[108] Others insist that the defeated GN killed the peasants to cannibalize their corpses, given their hunger after the long weeks of siege in Estelí. "The Guardias that were fleeing ate the campesinos," one man asserted. "They ate them. They took off their flesh with knives and ate them after roasting it."[109] Another guerrillero recalled hearing that they had removed a man's heart and eaten it.[110] Such descriptions of GN actions are impossible to confirm, but such widespread oral accounts are powerful in that they elevate the metaphor of the "bloodthirsty Guardias" into a reality. Despite locals' very limited prior interactions with the guerrillas and the fact that the battle in Estelí was over, the utter depravity of the GN in its final hours forever solidified an understanding of the GN as a diabolical force that killed "just for fun."

Juxtaposed with the "popular vengeance" that the FSLN inflicted on captured orejas and Guardias, GN violence in El Colorado surpassed all previous levels of lawlessness. The community's experience of the massacre led many campesinos to see the Sandinista victory as their own, despite having little contact with the guerrillas over the months of armed insurgency. Their sacrifices and those of their family members were now intimately linked to the mass upheaval that sent General Somoza into exile the day after the fall of the GN base in Estelí (July 17, 1979). The FSLN came to power and declared the Sandinista Revolution just two days later.

CONCLUSION

This chapter has explored the culmination of the civil war with a focus on the experience of several episodes of mass killings carried out by the two sides of the war. As the Somoza regime lashed out against an amorphous civilian population accused of providing succor to the FSLN, entire communities were subjected to staggering terror on a scale previously unseen under Somoza rule. These included urban and rural massacres perpetrated by infantry brigades, death squad assassinations in the towns by the White Hand, and the final spasms of retribution as the defeated GN fled the country. These gruesome acts experienced in quick succession by a terrified population assured a depth of support for the insurgency it did not find elsewhere in rural Nicaragua. The Sandinistas were themselves also responsible for a lesser quota of the atrocities carried out during the insurrection.

In many locations, narratives of massacre thus proved vital to the formation of new revolutionary political identities. Occurring over a brief period of several months, these stories—recounted over and over again and now passed down across generations—form the bedrock of political affinity and community solidarity that has persisted for decades. Given the specific events and diverse previous histories in each locale, narratives of state terror took the form of discourses of resistance, bewilderment, and sometimes even outright collective amnesia. Though often glossed over in official celebrations of the revolution— with their emphasis on guerrilla heroics and prominent leaders—these painful episodes of mass killing and political violence were the paramount events of the insurrectionary era. The history of this violence also allows us to witness the human cost that many communities bore, with entire families decimated in the tumult. This view also helps us reveal how the locus of the Sandinista Revolution was at the grassroots level and the product of profound sacrifices by many families and communities. This "high price of freedom" was paid not only by the guerrilla combatants often given the credit but also by the thousands of unarmed and mostly anonymous civilians killed at the hands of the GN throughout Nicaragua. In the aftermath of such seemingly boundless violence, many survivors became more deeply wedded to the overall project of social transformation and moral renewal for which they believed their loved ones had given their lives.

# WHITHER THE REVOLUTION?

Nicaragua and the Sandinistas since 1979

Shortly after learning of the fall of the GN garrison in Estelí on July 16, 1979, Gen. Anastasio Somoza Debayle resigned from the presidency and left for the United States in the early hours of the following morning. A young guerrilla fighter remembered, "We had a meeting in the city where they were telling us that Somoza was going to leave, but we still had to finish off the Guardia and create a new army of campesinos, workers, students, and honest intellectuals." As they were speaking, word came over the radio that the dictator had departed the country on a flight to Miami. "Somoza left. . . . Somoza left! He left! He left! He had left. I looked around, and everyone was crying."[1] For many in Estelí, the news brought an intense mix of joy and pain. "Some cheered and shouted from great happiness," another guerrillero recalled. "Others cried in sadness for all of the innocent people who had died. . . . There were a lot of different emotions."[2] Somoza's handpicked successor would not last forty-eight hours in power, as the popular insurgency continued to thrash the disoriented and rapidly disintegrating GN. Estelí again broke into celebration on July 19 as word arrived that the FSLN had seized the seat of power in Managua.

Following years of activism, armed struggle, and sacrifice, Estelí's families in the city and the countryside saw their contributions as key to the process that had culminated in the dictator's ouster. The unrestrained state terror against the population was over, but after so many months of warfare, the city had been reduced to rubble. "Estelí has nothing now," said Luis Irías Barreda, the new director of the city's Red Cross, as he surveyed the scene with a visiting *New York Times* reporter a few days later. "All the businesses are gone, all the hospitals, schools, and banks have been burned down, and even our headquarters has been destroyed."[3] Memories of the experiences its people endured, however, remained indelible. In the ruins left behind by the war, the Nicaraguan people would begin constructing their new future, always in the shadow of those whose lives were lost in the fight for freedom. Rather than chaos, the Sandinistas set about imposing law and order, a guerrilla fighter recalled: "Once the Frente had control of Estelí, people began to return to the city. From that very moment, mechanisms of order and safety were established. . . . Stealing was forbidden. . . . There was no looting; there was also no vengeance against personal enemies. . . . There were no executions after the city was under the control of the Frente. There was a sense of order in the city. Even though the Guardia—supposedly the authority—was gone, mechanisms of control were already functioning, and the city returned to normality."[4]

The Sandinistas made efforts to eliminate vice, violence, and criminality during the early period of revolutionary transformation. Within days of coming to power, the new junta proclaimed a series of decrees: immediately dissolving the Constitution, Congress, and the GN, confiscating the property "of the Somoza family, military officers, and all government collaborators who have left the country," and removing all images, statues, and insignia of the former regime.[5] The governing junta's fifth decree, emitted on July 20, imposed prison sentences for "vagrancy, public drunkenness, drug addiction, and prostitution," and for "gambling, sex trafficking, drug trafficking, or any other activity that violates human dignity."[6]

Rather than executions of former regime agents, as occurred in Cuba following that country's revolution two decades earlier, the FSLN abolished the death penalty. There would be no open "reign of terror" against the remnants of the *ancien régime.* "Relentless in combat and generous in victory" became a Sandinista slogan. The new government held trials for those accused of having formed a part of Somoza's army or having served as orejas for the OSN. Though a legally questionable process, the maximum punishment for ex-Guardas was limited to thirty years in jail, and those not implicated in serious crimes were later granted amnesty. The GN was replaced by the Sandinista People's Army (Ejército Popular Sandinista, EPS) and Sandinista Police (Policía Sandinista, PS), both of which were made up of former guerrillas and incorporated vast numbers of women into their ranks. No longer would a single institution be responsible for both military and domestic security, as during the long decades of Somocismo. The police force, in particular, promised a very different treatment of the civilian population based on human rights and an end to the toxic masculinity, petty corruption, and quotidian violence of the Somoza years. Unlike other police forces throughout Latin America, the PS did not gain a reputation for violent repression, torture, or abuse. Following a brief spike in 1980–81, the indices of crime, homicide, and vice of the Somoza period dropped precipitously over the years following the revolution. The authorities closed hundreds of cantinas, and some brothels and gambling dens were publicly razed to the ground and replaced by schools. They also placed restrictions on guaro sales and launched official campaigns to bring about an end to alcoholism, drug abuse, and gang activity. Though the police enforced the ban on prostitution, they did not target sex workers, but instead considered them victims of injustice and inequality. Though it had its limitations, the government established rehabilitation centers, sewing cooperatives, and restaurants to provide the women aid in finding new trades and employment.

Through their social programs and mass mobilization, the FSLN sought to uproot the pervasive ignorance, inequality, and poverty that had allowed Somocismo to thrive. The National Literacy Crusade (Cruzada Nacional de Alfabetización, CNA) was modeled on the Cuban example and built on the work of the radio schools, sending tens of thousands of idealistic high school students to live in the countryside for several months to teach campesinos to read and write. In less than a year, the illiteracy rate in Nicaragua was reduced from approximately half of the population to less than 13 percent, according to government statistics. The department of Estelí took the lead in the CNA, contributing the country's largest number of teenaged literacy teachers and the most campesinos taught to read. Under the FSLN, the government built schools on a previously unseen scale. Additionally, child and infant care centers were established to provide free day care for working mothers. The revolutionaries dramatically expanded access to health care, with an emphasis on preventative medicine and a series of successful vaccination campaigns against common diseases carried out through mass mobilization. These initiatives rapidly lowered the infant mortality rate, and Nicaragua under the FSLN was considered by some international organizations to be a model for what developing countries could do with very few resources. Young women and men were at the very forefront of all of these national projects.

The revolutionary government enacted reconstruction plans for economic development, with the vast wealth of the Somoza family (aside from the millions ferreted abroad before the revolution) brought into state ownership as part of the new mixed economy. Land reform was also carried out, returning property ownership to the dispossessed and reducing the inequality in landholding that had widened over the previous decades. Beginning with Somocista landowners, the new government also confiscated large, idle haciendas, converting them into either state-owned farms or campesino cooperatives supported with cheap state credit. As with the Literacy Crusade, the Segovias was again the region of the country most affected by land reform, with vast arable lands in departments of Estelí, Madriz, and Nueva Segovia expropriated. Furthermore, the mansion of René Molina, which had been looted and burned by protesters in 1978, was confiscated and converted into the Leonel Rugama Cultural Center, offering free poetry, painting, dance, and theater classes, and other activities. The Frente erected another cultural center in the region on the grounds of the former GN base in Condega, where the regime had once tortured political opponents. The new labor movement established a worker-run zapatería workshop cooperative in Estelí with the backing of Adrián Gutiérrez. The Sandinistas linked all of these projects together as part of its call for moral regeneration and its discourse of the New Man and New Woman. Emerging out of the popular upheaval and insurgency, many activists possessed *una mística*, or political mystique, which called for sacrifice, solidarity, and reciprocity for the good of the country. Indeed, many Nicaraguans finally felt that they were "treated as human beings." These psychological benefits of freedom amplified the strength of the newly achieved social rights (schools, health clinics, land).

Even as the economic situation declined throughout the 1980s, many remained drawn to the Sandinista cause and its vision of moral renewal. In the Segovias, the most fervent revolutionaries were those who had lived through the Somocista state terror and massacres at the hands of the GN during the regime's final year in power. Over the years of the revolution, Estelí was celebrated for its insurrectionary history and emerged as one of the most passionately pro-Sandinista cities, with much of the town engaged in the various tasks of building the revolutionary government. Every July 16, the population poured into the streets to celebrate the triumph of the insurrection in the city and to mourn the countless young people lost in the struggle. Ceremonies and programs were held regularly throughout the 1980s to honor and support the Mothers of the Heroes and Martyrs, those women whose children had been killed fighting in the revolution. In every election held in Nicaragua since 1979 up through 2017, the city—and often the entire department—of Estelí voted overwhelmingly for FSLN candidates.

Thanks to the Sandinista mística, even government opponents admitted, the new administration was the cleanest and least corrupt ever seen in Nicaragua. Francisco Rivera, "El Zorro," the man who had led the guerrillas to victory in Estelí, often caught rides to Managua on the back of a pickup truck to attend high-level meetings. The CDCs, which had played such an integral role in the revolution, were now renamed the Sandinista Defense Committees (Comités de Defensa Sandinista, CDS), responsible for promoting neighborhood improvement and keeping crime and vice-related activities under control. Having played an important role as "madres" to the "muchachos" during the insurrection and as female guerrilleras, women from working-class neighborhoods continued to be active in the CDSs after the Sandinistas came to power. Many women served in high-ranking government positions, while AMPRONAC converted into the Luisa Amanda Espinoza Association of Nicaraguan Women (Asociación de Mujeres Nicaragüenses Luisa Amanda Espinoza, AMNLAE), an official Sandinista organization. AMNLAE at times supported the fight for further rights and equality for women, access to contraception, and the prevention of domestic abuse and machismo. Influential Catholics—including many women—assured that the "pro-life" FSLN never passed a law giving women reproductive rights, but the Somoza-era law banning abortion was never applied during the 1980s. In addition to the CDS

and AMNLAE, numerous other mass organizations, which represented campesinos, workers, farmers, and young people, were formed
and given representation within the revolutionary state that the Sandinistas began building. Despite these accomplishments, there were those
who were isolated by the FSLN regime, which—flush with widespread
support—felt no need to accommodate its critics. Rather than finding
a place in this new order, the private sector and local elites—even those
that had supported the uprising against Somoza—were increasingly
alienated from the new government because of its socialist orientation
and redistribution of wealth. Many would later join in efforts to overthrow the Sandinistas.

After the FSLN triumph, the revolutionary junta was not given
much of a respite and soon found itself under attack by the United
States. The Carter administration proved wavering in its backing for
the Somoza dictatorship and was eventually forced to acquiesce to the
regime's fall from power. In 1980, however, Republican Ronald Reagan
defeated Carter for the U.S. presidency and promised a return to a
muscular Cold War foreign policy. The tiny Central American republic
of Nicaragua, Reagan claimed, stretching credulity, somehow now represented a threat to the United States. Under his presidency, the United
States imposed a trade embargo against Nicaragua, much like the one
that Cuba had long endured, and blocked the country from receiving
funding from international financial institutions in which the United
States held the deciding vote. Most importantly, Reagan directed the
CIA to organize armed attacks against Nicaragua by former GN officers and other Nicaraguans trained at U.S. military bases across the
border in Honduras. Known as the "Contras," or counterrevolution-
aries (*contrarevolucionarios*), these forces began carrying out cross-
border raids that soon spiraled into yet another civil war. Unlike the
FSLN insurgency, which had once destroyed brothels, cantinas, and
gambling halls, the highly armed Contras instead burned down newly
built schools, health clinics, cooperative farms, and water purification
facilities, focusing their ire against the most visible accomplishments of
the revolution. The Contras, similar to the GN and EEBI out of which
they emerged, were accused of terror attacks, widespread rape, torture,
and the murder of peasants and Christian activists. Among the Contras' widely mourned victims were Estelí's prominent cursillo leaders,

Felipe and Mary Barreda, whom they kidnapped, tortured, and killed in early 1983. At the time, they had been participating in voluntary work in a coffee-picking brigade during the harvest in an area near the war zone to prevent the Contras from sabotaging one of the most fundamental cornerstones of the national economy.

Despite these gratuitous abuses and human rights violations, Reagan infamously referred to the Contras as "the moral equal of our Founding Fathers and the brave men and women of the French Resistance" in their fight against "Cuba-backed," "totalitarian," and "Communist" Nicaragua.[7] Even when the U.S. Congress attempted to block military aid to the Contras because of their glaring and systematic abuses, the White House assured millions in aid through clandestine channels, leading to the infamous Iran-Contra scandal that rocked the Reagan administration. Allegations arose that the CIA and the Contra army had worked with drug traffickers to finance their operations. In a landmark 1986 decision, the International Court of Justice found that the United States had violated international law by supporting the Contras' war crimes and using the CIA to mine Nicaragua's harbors.

During the early years, Sandinista militias mobilized to beat back this "imperialist" military threat with thousands of volunteers ready to stave off U.S. efforts to restore Somocismo to power. Again, the FSLN militia expanded early and rapidly in Estelí, incorporating much of the civilian population into its training program. Patriotism and national pride now played a galvanizing force as Nicaraguans fought against the Contras, drawing on the historical memory of nationalist resistance to U.S. invasions throughout Nicaraguan history.

Years of foreign aggression and economic embargo, aggravated by Sandinista economic plans, however, served to grind down the revolution. Nicaragua went from a growing economy with deep inequality to one of the poorest countries in the hemisphere, with social protections in place for the most destitute. The Sandinista government was forced to dedicate more than six-tenths of its national budget to military defense. As the conflict dragged on and thousands were killed on both sides, the economy crumbled, hyperinflation ran into thousands of percent, and the government instituted rationing. The Segovias once again became a war zone, and large-scale farming came to a standstill in many areas of the north. Most damaging to public opinion, however, was the compulsory military draft, known as Patriotic Military Service (Servicio Militar Patriótico), which the Sandinista government implemented to defeat the well-armed and well-financed Contras. Because of superpower intervention, the war of the 1980s proved to be much more of a genuinely nationalist struggle than the uprising against Somoza had been. Still, as the combatants on both sides of the conflict were Nicaraguans, the draft infuriated many families who saw their sons sent off to die at the front. Though the Nicaraguan army grew into the largest in Central America to meet the Contra challenge, the revolutionary mystique was damaged.

The war, imposed on the country from outside, only further aggravated divisions that existed within Nicaraguan society. In those areas of the country that had not lived through the repression of the Somoza years, campesinos often experienced the revolution and, in particular, its program of land reform as an outside imposition. In distant locales in the Segovias along the agrarian frontier and the Honduran border—exactly where Sandino had once battled the U.S. occupation—the Contras now recruited many disgruntled campesinos through both coercion and material incentives. On the country's Atlantic coast, the Contras took advantage of ethnic divisions between the Miskito Indians and the Nicaraguan state to help catalyze another front in their counterrevolutionary war. Through its counterinsurgency campaigns, the Sandinistas at times forced some peasants into the hands of the U.S.-backed Contras, much as Somoza had done during the insurrection. At the same time, the FSLN's clumsy economic plans privileged the interests of the cities over those of rural areas. Many rural Nicaraguans were appalled to see the government seizing sacks of food from poor peasants who hoped to sell their produce at market prices. With little input from smallholders, the Sandinistas' early land reform plans aimed initially at building large state farms and cooperatives, neither of which squared with campesino aspirations for land ownership and private property.

Likewise, the insurrection-era alliance between the guerrilla movement and the Catholic Church now proved to be a double-edged sword as many within the Vatican-aligned hierarchy strongly opposed what they called the "communist" government. The decision of the FSLN to merge their cause with that of liberation theology had been a true boon to the revolutionary movement during the period leading up to the insurrection. In many ways, this blending of religion and political commitment continued well into the 1980s. Following the fall of Somoza, several Catholic priests even took on prominent positions and served as ministers within the Sandinista government. "Between Christianity and revolution, there is no contradiction," went an official Sandinista slogan, and Catholic laypeople participated fervently in all of the revolutionary programs. When the new government attempted to carry out radical social change, however, some of the Church leadership quickly returned to its traditional role in favor of the status quo. These developments led to a fracture within Nicaraguan Catholicism between the so-called popular Church, loyal to the revolution, and those factions increasingly opposed to the FSLN. Some members of the hierarchy also came to openly back the counterrevolution, which contributed to the climate of violent polarization, given their continuing influence over the Nicaraguan public. In light of the military conflict and the ideological shifts within the Church itself, the radical liberation theology of the 1970s gradually lost its powerful hold over the course of the decade. Even some of the priests who had supported the revolution, such as Padre Julio López, criticized the growing state domination of civil society and the imposition of a military draft that would send thousands to their deaths.

The social leveling of the period of insurrection and guerrilla warfare in which all were "one family" and all tortillas were shared began to break down. The Contra war further accentuated some of the most authoritarian characteristics of the FSLN, born out of a guerrilla army and accustomed to a vertical military chain of command. This top-down vision of rule in which the nine male guerrilla comandantes made all decisions supplanted the grassroots energy unleashed in the social movements and the insurrection. Women contributed actively to the revolution at the local level and even took on prominent roles in the national government, but men continued to dominate top leadership positions. Despite projecting an image of selflessness and abnegation, some of the new leaders increasingly behaved like a new elite whose lives were far removed from the daily suffering of their compatriots. The government also became heavy-handed in silencing dissent, at times violating freedom of the press by closing La Prensa or even jailing nonviolent political opponents. At the neighborhood and village

level, the CDSs, which proved effective at foiling counterrevolution-
aries, were likewise accused of behaving autocratically, threatening to
denounce neighbors to the authorities. Many began whispering that
some of the pro-Sandinista activists in the CDSs ("the eyes and ears of
the revolution") had once been orejas under Somoza. Rumors spread
that leading comandantes were even permitting Colombian cartels to
use Nicaragua as a drug transshipment point to raise funds.

A democratic election was convincingly won by the FSLN in 1984,
installing one of the nine Sandinista comandantes, Daniel Ortega, as
president. The Reagan administration denied the election's legitimacy,
and its backing for the Contras continued unabated. By the time presidential elections were held again in February 1990, the economy had
largely collapsed, and the population was ready to end the economic
embargo and the Contra war (as the United States promised if the Sandinistas were voted out). Violeta Chamorro, the widow of assassinated
*La Prensa* publisher Pedro Joaquín Chamorro, became the sympathetic
candidate of a united opposition alliance of fourteen parties brought together under the aegis of U.S. advisors. In such adverse circumstances,
Ortega lost this reelection bid. Though he won a convincing victory in
the Sandinista heartland of Estelí, at the national level, he received only
41 percent of the vote to Chamorro's 55 percent. He handed over the
presidential sash to the new head of state, effectively bringing the Sandinista Revolution to an end in the first peaceful, democratic change of
power in Nicaragua's history.

Respecting the election results and surrendering power to the opposition gave Ortega credibility as a statesman, but the events that followed proved far less auspicious. Indeed, revolutionaries celebrated a
commitment to high moral standing and personal sacrifice during the
early days of the revolution, but these ethics were now jettisoned by
top FSLN party members. Following the electoral defeat, a number
of these officials quickly privatized public companies, lands, vehicles,
and mansions into their own names. This seized property, mocked as
*la Piñata*, laid the groundwork for the emergence of a new class of Sandinista capitalists who continue to hold significant economic power
in Nicaragua today. Ortega, who became the FSLN standard-bearer
throughout the 1990s and 2000s, was seen as an increasingly problematic figure, both authoritarian and self-interested. In 1998, Ortega's

stepdaughter came forward to publicly accuse the ex-president of years of sexual abuse and rape, shaking the movement to its core and calling into question the leadership's remaining claims to moral regeneration. In July of that year, Francisco Rivera, hero of the insurrections in Estelí, passed away, unemployed and suffering from liver damage caused by years of alcohol abuse that had followed the revolution's denouement. Perhaps remembering the insurgent morality of the "shared tortilla," he had long handed out his salary as an FSLN diputado to campesino families who had given him aid during the fight against the Somoza regime. Unlike his millionaire former comrades in arms, Rivera had not enriched himself and instead died in debt.

From 1990 to 2006, parties linked to the country's traditional Conservative and Liberal family factions ruled the country, carrying out neoliberal economic reforms demanded by the International Monetary Fund (IMF) and the World Bank. Although they restored a modicum of normality to the war-torn country, these parties systematically undid the few remaining social accomplishments from the years of revolution. The new government quickly privatized the public sector, and peasant cooperatives began to fall apart. René Molina and other onetime Somocistas returned to the country, now as U.S. citizens, to receive reimbursement from the Nicaraguan government for property confiscated during the revolution, including land redistributed to the campesinos (Molina even came to serve in the government as minister of tourism under Liberal president Arnoldo Alemán). Moreover, to repay IMF loans, steep cuts were made to nearly all public services.

Social indicators from infant mortality, literacy rates, years of education, and life expectancy continued their precipitous decline. A Danish photojournalist who had visited Nicaragua regularly during the revolutionary years of the 1980s recalled that "despite widespread poverty and the tensions of warfare present . . . basic standards of decency and family unity prevailed."[8] When he returned in the 1990s, however, he found a torn family fabric, with cities overflowing with homeless street children and child prostitutes selling their bodies to adult men in order to survive amidst the waves of free-market capitalism. The only silver lining was the ability of Nicaraguan National Police (formerly the Sandinista Police) to successfully control criminal violence and gang warfare. When it came to questions of crime, Nicaragua continued to be a true exception within the region ("the safest country in Central America"), an enduring legacy of the revolution. The Nicaraguan Police prevented the scourge of drug cartels, criminal gangs, and high murder rates that caused such disastrous results in nearby Honduras, Guatemala, and El Salvador. This marked a striking shift from the Somoza decades when Nicaragua was regularly one of the most violent countries in the world. The model of community policing inherited from the revolutionary era gained renown for its efficacy in helping young people escape the vice and violence in their communities.

During these difficult years, many who had participated in the revolution attempted to pass onto their children the vision of social justice, moral regeneration, and the equality of the shared tortilla. Forged through labor unions, student activism, Catholic cursillos, Civil Defense Committees, guerrilla encampments, and—later—the mass mobilizations of the 1980s, insurgent morality and its vernacular expressions continued to shape the experiences of Nicaraguans, whether they considered themselves Sandinistas or not.

## Toward 2018: The Revolution's End or Its Rebirth?

When Daniel Ortega returned to the presidency in 2007, he ran on a wholly different platform than that of the revolutionary FSLN of the 1980s, let alone the social and moral renewal the Sandinistas had promised as guerrilla fighters. His electoral coalition included business elites, former Contras and Somocistas, and reactionary members of the Catholic hierarchy who had once aligned with the United States against the revolution. Though the government used the slogan "Christian, Socialist, and in Solidarity" (*Cristiana, Socialista y Solidaria*) and denounced "savage capitalism," radical change was now off the table. As he had previously done within the Sandinista party, Ortega concentrated power, packing courts, manipulating the electoral system, and shutting down opposition parties. Revisions to the law placed supreme power over the National Police directly into the hands of Ortega, hampering the professionalization that had occurred during the years of non-Sandinista rule.

Ortega's government converted the FSLN from a vanguard party into an electoral machine: its membership card was now distributed en masse and sometimes required for state employment or access to government programs, much like la Magnífica in the time of Somoza. Press reports documented business contracts and foreign aid being siphoned out to loyal allies and the increasingly wealthy Ortega family. Many within Nicaragua, including former guerrillas and Sandinistas, denounced how the revolution had been betrayed by those who claimed to rule in its memory. It was common to hear the phrase "I'm a Sandinista but not a Danielista." Ortega drew particular scorn from the international Left for supporting a draconian antiabortion law that banned the procedure even in cases in which the mother's life was at risk.

Although it was a deadly, antifeminist law, this vote was not a complete betrayal of the Sandinista past, given the blending of conservative, Catholic, and radical discourses of family and gender at the party's grassroots. Indeed, the population of the Segovias continued to vote time after time for Ortega's neo-Sandinismo in increasing numbers from 2006. In 2011, after using the Supreme Court to overrule the constitutional provision barring reelection, Ortega was overwhelmingly returned to power for a second term. Though opponents cried foul, public opinion polls still suggested strong popular support for Ortega's party, particularly among the poor. Newly implemented FSLN policies, such as tuition-free public education, college scholarships, access to health clinics, the distribution of livestock to peasant women ("Zero Hunger"), microcredit to small businesses ("Zero Usury"), and zinc roofing for the poor, were mocked as insignificant populist handouts by Ortega's well-off opponents. To his urban and rural base of support, however, these small-scale welfare programs were perceived as signs of a government finally looking out for the poor after the years of neoliberal austerity.

Grassroots FSLN party activists—mostly female-headed families—recognized that the government was not above reproach, but they saw it provide concrete resources and a social safety net for their families. Indeed, such poverty-alleviation programs and the expansion of social services did not offer a horizon of wide-scale social transformation, but they undoubtedly provided some measure of economic opportunity for many poor Nicaraguans. In the department of Estelí, the FSLN became hegemonic in every municipality, even winning power in the Liberal stronghold of La Trinidad in 2012. Interestingly, every single municipality in the department of Madriz, once the bastion of the GN and Somocismo, was now governed by an FSLN mayor. Some took this as a sign of the success of Sandinismo to permeate once-hostile areas, but Ortega's government increasingly mirrored Somoza's effective patron–client network and one-party regime.

Ortega's pragmatism (his critics would say opportunism) also evinced a rather cunning willingness to learn from the failures of his earlier stint in power. Unlike the 1980s, when embargo and war had sent the economy into a tailspin, the new Sandinista government— working hand in glove with the private sector and foreign investors— now assured macroeconomic stability, a rising rate of investment, and declining poverty and unemployment rates. The FSLN government improved infrastructure throughout the country, such as highways and roads that had long remained unpaved. Under Ortega, Nicaragua became the fastest growing economy in Central America, while Estelí, with its resurgent tobacco industry producing high-quality cigars for the foreign market, surged ahead as the second center of national commerce after Managua. The city's first American-style mall—an air-conditioned, ultramodern structure with a food court, escalators, department stores, a multiscreen movie theater, and even a hotel— was inaugurated during Ortega's second administration. Unlike the revolutionary years marked by shortages and deprivations, the 2010s witnessed ever-increasing levels of consumerism, including personal computers, smartphones, household appliances, and automobiles. Though he still postured against "Yankee imperialism" in international forums, repeating the script from the 1980s, Ortega now cooperated with U.S. drug-interdiction efforts and invited North American corporations into the country.

Nicaragua, of course, continued to deal with high levels of poverty and more than its share of social injustice. Despite economic growth and populist policies, the country experienced widening social inequality. Poor Nicaraguans became less impoverished, but the elite— now including many Sandinista families among their ranks—gained wealth on a scale never before imagined. Many of the grievances that once drove the insurgent morality of the 1970s still remained: rates of alcoholism remained incredibly high, cantinas and brothels continued to operate, and miniature "casinos" crammed with noisy one-armed bandits were found throughout the country. Rumors again implicated government and police officials in protection rackets that permitted Sandinista loyalists to engage in criminal and vice-related activities, such as drug trafficking and prostitution, with impunity. Ortega's government delivered stellar economic growth, low crime rates, and declining poverty, but the revolution's aim of moral regeneration was long forgotten. Political corruption and economic inequality remained the order of the day. The addition of open state violence to this mix would lead to eerily familiar results.

The apparent stability and political apathy in Nicaragua was suddenly shattered in April 2018. Just a year and a half earlier, Ortega had won more than 70 percent of the vote, which gave him his fourth (and third consecutive) term in office. In a sign of the personalistic and family-oriented regime, his vice president was now his wife, Rosario Murillo. His monopoly of power and manipulation of the democratic process, however, led to mass abstention. Many Nicaraguans felt they now lacked any political channel to air their grievances. When Ortega attempted to cut social security benefits for the elderly while raising employee and employer contributions, small-scale protests denounced government corruption on April 18. In response, protesters faced brutal violence at the hands of the National Police and Sandinista party members. Thanks to the widespread presence of smartphones, these violent attacks were captured on video and spread rapidly on social media. Practically overnight, the decade-long stasis came to an end. Many of the country's young people rose up against the Ortega government, drawing on the repertoires of resistance bequeathed by the revolution. They built roadblocks across the country's streets and highways and used rocks, slingshots, and *morteros* (homemade fireworks-launchers) to defend themselves from attack by the authorities.

In response to this mostly peaceful civic rebellion, Ortega's regime unleashed a wave of repression on a scale unseen in decades. The National Police, accompanied by armed and masked government supporters (referred to as "paramilitaries"), made an all-out assault on students and youthful opposition members, carrying weapons of war and shooting to kill. "Ortega and Somoza are the same thing" (*Ortega y Somoza son la misma cosa*) went a common chant heard in the streets. The death toll rose rapidly, from dozens in the first weeks to hundreds as the months of tension went by, and state violence took on increasingly chaotic forms. Peaceful mass demonstrations with hundreds of thousands of participants were fired upon by progovernment agents. Masked men stormed student-occupied universities and even unloaded their weapons against a Catholic church where student protesters had found refuge. Just as during the insurrectionary years of 1978–79, the police and paramilitary forces stood accused of murdering adolescents, children, and babies, as they fired upon the youthful protesters and unarmed civilians. In a nightmarish incident that echoed the worst crimes of Somocismo, an entire Managua family of six was burned alive in their home in broad daylight by masked men. Progovernment TV stations denied the very existence of irregular armed forces and slandered protesters as "terrorists," but hundreds of videos circulated on social media and exposed what was actually happening in the streets.

It was as though Nicaragua was reliving the era of the insurrections against the Somoza regime in reverse, with the erstwhile revolutionaries now the agents of repression against the younger generation. Having participated in the struggle against Somoza in their own youth, the FSLN leadership now countenanced many of the very same crimes that once led to the fall of the dictatorship. Moral indignation surged to unprecedented levels and the primary demand became the departure of Ortega, his wife, and the Sandinista party from power. Similar to the revolutionary struggle of the 1970s, an end to state terror soon became the most significant rallying cry that superseded all other demands. The government's calls for "law and order" and "tranquility" and blame upon foreign actors rang as hollow as those of Somoza nearly four decades earlier, given state responsibility for the overwhelming majority of the violence.

Born long after the Sandinista Revolution, Nicaragua's youth were raised in a society that celebrated the defeat of a dictatorship through a popular uprising while watching a new authoritarian regime consolidating in front of their very eyes. Ortega and his wife denounced the protesters as "right-wing vandals," but many of those in the barricades were from Sandinista families, the children and grandchildren of the women and men who had once participated in the insurrection against Somoza. As protesters began firing back at the police and paramilitaries in unequal combat, the specter of yet another civil war seemed to be hanging over the country. It remains an open question as to how this crisis will be resolved, but the Nicaraguan people have a rich reservoir of experiences and successes to draw on in their search for a peaceful end to the injustice and division in which they once again find themselves immersed. Though pro-Ortega forces still laid claim to the imagery and slogans of the revolution, the youth raising the blue-and-white Nicaraguan flag in the face of police gunfire perhaps embodied its essence of moral regeneration to a far greater extent than those who now wave the red-and-black banner. Indeed, as we have seen throughout this study, the revolution's insurgent morality was never the property of the leadership but rather the hard-fought achievement of the Nicaraguan people as a whole.

# NOTES

## Introduction

1. Comandante Francisco Rivera, March 1979, Centro de Historia Militar (hereafter CHM), Fondo Sonoteca 103.

2. "Contingentes a Jinotega; Frente Sandinista de Liberación Nacional habla de 'zona liberada,'" *La Prensa* (hereafter *LP*), May 21, 1979.

3. "¿Por qué lucha el FSLN junto al pueblo?" *Lucha Sandinista*, June 1978.

4. Michael J. Schroeder, "Horse Thieves to Rebels to Dogs: Political Gang Violence and the State in the Western Segovias, Nicaragua, in the Time of Sandino, 1926–1934," *Journal of Latin American Studies* 28, no. 2 (1996): 392.

5. Humberto Ortega Saavedra, "La insurrección nacional victoriosa (Entrevista por Marta Harnecker)," *Nicaráuac* 1 (May–June 1980): 30.

6. Timothy P. Wickham-Crowley, *Guerrillas and Revolution in Latin America: A Comparative Study of Insurgents and Regimes since 1956* (Princeton, NJ: Princeton University Press, 1992), 131–38, 246–47.

7. Towns such as Jinotega and Ocotal, where Sandino and his men had been active, largely refused to support the FSLN during the upheaval of 1978–79; see Francis Pisani, *Los muchachos* (Managua: Editorial Vanguardia, 1989), 27. George Black notes: "Old sympathies for Sandino did not prevent a percentage of peasants from being convinced Somocistas, while many were at least superficially under the sway of the dictatorship's ideological control"; Black, *Triumph of the People: The Sandinista Revolution in Nicaragua* (London: Zed, 1981), 79.

8. Walter Raymond Duncan, *Latin American Politics: A Developmental Approach* (New York: Praeger, 1976), 49.

9. Similar terms that are used to describe the Somoza regime are "neopatrimonial" and "kleptocratic"; see Richard Millett, *Guardians of the Dynasty* (Maryknoll, NY: Orbis, 1977); Wickham-Crowley, *Guerrillas and Revolution in Latin America*, 269; John A. Booth, "The Somoza Regime in Nicaragua," in *Sultanistic Regimes*, ed. H. E. Chehabi and Juan José Linz (Baltimore: Johns Hopkins University Press, 1998), 131–52; Jeff Goodwin, *No Other Way Out:*

*States and Revolutionary Movements, 1945–1991* (Cambridge: Cambridge University Press, 2001), 182. Many of these "state-centric" accounts implicitly argue that regime type and divisions between the state and national elites permitted the revolutionaries' success. This scholarly tradition follows the work of Theda Skocpol, *States and Social Revolutions: A Comparative Analysis of France, Russia, and China* (Cambridge: Cambridge University Press, 1979).

10. Jeffrey L. Gould, "'For an Organized Nicaragua': Somoza and the Labour Movement, 1944–1948," *Journal of Latin American Studies* 19, no. 2 (1987): 353–87; Gould, *To Lead as Equals: Rural Protest and Political Consciousness in Chinandega, Nicaragua, 1912–1979* (Chapel Hill: University of North Carolina Press, 1990); Knut Walter, *The Regime of Anastasio Somoza, 1936–1956* (Chapel Hill: University of North Carolina Press, 1993); Victoria González-Rivera, *Before the Revolution: Women's Rights and Right-Wing Politics in Nicaragua, 1821–1979* (University Park: Pennsylvania State University Press, 2011).

11. Millett, *Guardians of the Dynasty*; Richard Grossman, "'The Blood of the People': The Guardia Nacional's Fifty-Year War against the People of Nicaragua, 1927–1979," in *When States Kill: Latin America, the U.S., and Technologies of Terror*, ed. Cecilia Menjívar and Néstor Rodríguez (Austin: University of Texas Press, 2005), 59–84.

12. Militaries have played the role of providing manhood to subaltern peoples throughout Latin American history. However, the notion of "proper manhood" varies widely, and the GN's pattern differed greatly from the masculine "Prussian" soldier of the Brazilian military; see Peter M. Beattie, *The Tribute of Blood: Army, Honor, Race, and Nation in Brazil, 1864–1945* (Durham, NC: Duke University Press, 2001), 69. The Mexican army during the late nineteenth and early twentieth centuries was similarly identified with vice and violent masculinity. However, in response, middle-class reformers and military officers attempted to uproot "traditional behaviors" and impose "'morality,' a concept deemed essential to the progress and modernity of the nation," an emphasis missing in Somocista Nicaragua; see Stephen B. Neufeld, *The Blood Contingent: The Military and the Making of Modern Mexico, 1876–1911* (Albuquerque: University of New Mexico Press, 2017), 22.

13. Between 1961 and 1967, the years for which statistics are available, there were between 23.1 and 30.9 homicides per 100,000 people each year; United Nations Statistical Office, *Demographic Yearbook 1960* (New York: UN, 1960), table 19; United Nations Statistical Office, *Demographic Yearbook 1966* (New York: UN, 1967), table 20; United Nations Statistical Office, *Demographic Yearbook 1967* (New York: UN, 1968), table 24; Stuart Hunter Palmer, *The Violent Society* (New Haven, CT: College & University Press, 1972), 28–29; "Atribuyen a Nicaragua primer lugar violento," *LP*, May 11, 1968.

14. Patrick Nicholas Theros, interview by Robert J. Alexander, Managua, June 26, 1967, Papers of Robert J. Alexander, reel 10, frame 841.

15. David R. Powell and Kevin B. Youngs, *Report of the Public Safety Program and the Nicaragua National Guard, June 1970* (Washington, DC: Agency for International Development, 1971), 20–21.

16. Rodolfo Gutiérrez Pimentel, *Alcohol y alcoholismo en Centroamérica: Informe de un estudio* (San Salvador: Secretaría General de la Organización de Estados Centroamericanos, 1970).

17. As Elizabeth Dore and John Weeks put it, "The Sandinistas themselves, as well as most writers sympathetic with their cause, contextualised their struggle almost exclusively within a narrative of US imperialism"; Dore and Weeks, *The Red and Black: The Sandinistas and the Nicaraguan Revolution* (London: Institute of Latin American Studies, 1992), 2, 25–28. Michel Gobat argues from a very different angle in that upper-class support for the revolution came from anti-imperialist sentiment and "anti-bourgeois spirit" dating to the time of U.S. military intervention; Gobat, *Confronting the American Dream: Nicaragua under U.S. Imperial Rule* (Durham, NC: Duke University Press, 2005), 267–80. For more critical readings of the FSLN that center Marxism-Leninism rather than nationalism, see David Nolan, *The Ideology of the Sandinistas and the Nicaraguan Revolution* (Coral Gables, FL: Institute of Interamerican Studies, Graduate School of International Studies, University of Miami, 1984); Dennis Gilbert, *Sandinistas: The Party and the Revolution* (New York: Basil Blackwell, 1988).

18. The extent of nationalism in the revolutionary upsurge—as compared to the postrevolutionary period—has similarities to the classic debate between Alan Knight and John M. Hart over the nature of the Mexican Revolution. For instance, Hart casts the revolution as a "war of national liberation against the United States," but Knight argues that (at least during the period of armed conflict) "the idea of a virulently nationalist popular revolution was largely a myth"; Hart, *Revolutionary Mexico: The Coming and Process of the Mexican Revolution* (Berkeley: University of California Press, 1987), 320; Knight, "The United States and the Mexican Peasantry, circa 1880–1940," in *Rural Revolt in Mexico: U.S. Intervention and the Domain of Subaltern Politics*, ed. Daniel Nugent (Durham, NC: Duke University Press, 1998), 27.

19. Steven Palmer, "Carlos Fonseca and the Construction of Sandinismo in Nicaragua," *Latin American Research Review* 23, no. 1 (1988): 91–109. See also Donald Hodges, *Intellectual Foundations of the Nicaraguan Revolution* (Austin: University of Texas Press, 1986).

20. Matilde Zimmermann, *Sandinista: Carlos Fonseca and the Nicaraguan Revolution* (Durham, NC: Duke University Press, 2000), 9.

21. Gould, *To Lead as Equals*, 294–95.

22. Ibid., 296.

23. Jeffrey L. Gould, *To Die in This Way: Nicaraguan Indians and the Myth of Mestizaje, 1880–1965* (Durham, NC: Duke University Press, 1998), 228–72.

24. Brown downplays the U.S. influence and counterrevolutionary atrocities to a fault, but Horton proves far more attune to foreign intervention and Contra terror in inflaming tensions; Lynn Horton, *Peasants in Arms: War and Peace in the Mountains of Nicaragua, 1979–1994* (Athens: Ohio University Press, 1998); Timothy Charles Brown, *The Real Contra War: Highlander Peasant Resistance in Nicaragua* (Norman: University of Oklahoma Press, 2001).

25. Carlos M. Vilas, "Family Affairs: Class, Lineage and Politics in Contemporary Nicaragua," *Journal of Latin American Studies* 24, no. 2 (1992): 309–41. Another title that embraces an emphasis on the "great families" of the country is the journalistic and anti-Sandinista account by Shirley Christian, *Nicaragua, Revolution in the Family* (New York: Random House, 1985).

26. Nara Milanich, "Whither Family History? A Road Map from Latin America," *American Historical Review* 112, no. 2 (2007): 449.

27. For an analysis of how both the political Right and Left in Chile have used metaphors and images of nuclear family in electoral campaigns and political struggle since the 1970s, see Gwynn Thomas, *Contesting Legitimacy in Chile: Familial Ideals, Citizenship, and Political Struggle, 1970–1990* (University Park: Pennsylvania State University Press, 2011).

28. Estimates of single-parent female households range approximately from one-third to one-half of all households by 1978; see Karen Kampwirth, *Women and Guerrilla Movements: Nicaragua, El Salvador, Chiapas, Cuba* (University Park: Pennsylvania State University Press, 2002), 25.

29. Elizabeth Dore, "The 'Holy Family': Imagined Households in Latin American History," in *Gender Politics in Latin America: Debates in Theory and Practice*, ed. Elizabeth Dore (New York: Monthly Review Press, 1997), 101–17.

30. Margaret Randall, *Sandino's Daughters: Testimonies of Nicaraguan Women in Struggle* (New Brunswick, NJ: Rutgers University Press, 1981); Kampwirth, *Women and Guerrilla Movements*.

31. Lorraine Bayard de Volo, *Mothers of Heroes and Martyrs: Gender Identity Politics in Nicaragua, 1979–1999* (Baltimore: Johns Hopkins University Press, 2001).

32. Maxine Molyneux, "Mobilization without Emancipation? Women's Interests, the State, and Revolution in Nicaragua," *Feminist Studies* 11, no. 2 (1985): 227–54; Roger N. Lancaster, *Life Is Hard: Machismo, Danger, and the Intimacy of Power in Nicaragua* (Berkeley: University of California Press, 1994); Margaret Randall, *Sandino's Daughters Revisited: Feminism in Nicaragua* (New Brunswick, NJ: Rutgers University Press, 1994); Ilja A. Luciak, *After the Revolution: Gender and Democracy in El Salvador, Nicaragua, and Guatemala* (Baltimore: Johns Hopkins University Press, 2003); Karen Kampwirth, *Feminism and the Legacy Of Revolution: Nicaragua, El Salvador, Chiapas* (Athens: Ohio University Press, 2004).

33. Rosario Montoya, *Gendered Scenarios of Revolution: Making New Men and New Women in Nicaragua, 1975–2000* (Tucson: University of Arizona Press, 2012), 121.

34. Donna J. Guy, *Sex and Danger in Buenos Aires: Prostitution, Family, and Nation in Argentina* (Lincoln: University of Nebraska Press, 1991); Eileen Findlay, *Imposing Decency: The Politics of Sexuality and Race in Puerto Rico, 1870–1920* (Durham, NC: Duke University Press, 1999); James Alex Garza, *The Imagined Underworld: Sex, Crime, and Vice in Porfirian Mexico City* (Lincoln: University of Nebraska Press, 2007); William French, "Moralizing the Masses," in *Latin America's Middle Class: Unsettled Debates and New Histories*, ed.

David Stuart Parker and Louise E. Walker (Lanham, MD: Lexington Books, 2012), 79–104; Tiffany A. Sippial, *Prostitution, Modernity, and the Making of the Cuban Republic, 1840–1920* (Chapel Hill: University of North Carolina Press, 2013).

35. Mona Ozouf, "Regeneration," in *A Critical Dictionary of the French Revolution*, ed. François Furet and Mona Ozouf (Cambridge, MA: Harvard University Press, 1989), 778–91; Kate Transchel, *Under the Influence: Working-Class Drinking, Temperance, and Cultural Revolution in Russia, 1895–1932* (Pittsburgh: University of Pittsburgh Press, 2006); Zhou Yongming, "Nationalism, Identity, and State-Building: The Antidrug Crusade in the People's Republic, 1949–1952," in *Opium Regimes: China, Britain, and Japan, 1839–1952*, ed. Timothy Brook and Bob Tadashi Wakabayashi (Berkeley: University of California Press, 2000), 380–403; Katherine Elaine Bliss, *Compromised Positions: Prostitution, Public Health, and Gender Politics in Revolutionary Mexico City* (University Park: Pennsylvania State University Press, 2010); Gretchen Pierce, "Fighting Bacteria, the Bible, and the Bottle: Projects to Create New Men, Women, and Children, 1910–1940," in *A Companion to Mexican History and Culture*, ed. William H. Beezley (Malden, MA: John Wiley & Sons, 2011), 505–17; Gretchen Pierce, "Pulqueros, Cerveceros, and Mezcaleros: Small Alcohol Producers and Popular Resistance to Mexico's Anti-Alcohol Campaigns, 1910–1940," in *Alcohol in Latin America: A Social and Cultural History*, ed. Gretchen Pierce and Áurea Toxqui (Tucson: University of Arizona Press, 2014), 161–84; Rachel Hynson, "'Count, Capture, and Reeducate': The Campaign to Rehabilitate Cuba's Female Sex Workers, 1959–1966," *Journal of the History of Sexuality* 24, no. 1 (2015): 125–53.

36. Sean Quinlan, "Physical and Moral Regeneration after the Terror: Medical Culture, Sensibility and Family Politics in France, 1794–1804," *Social History* 29, no. 2 (2004): 139.

37. Liberation theology in Nicaragua led to a significant body of literature during the 1980s. For some of the best-known titles, see Roger Lancaster, *Thanks to God and the Revolution: Popular Religion and Class Consciousness in the New Nicaragua* (New York: Columbia University Press, 1988); Philip Williams, *The Catholic Church and Politics in Nicaragua and Costa Rica* (Pittsburgh: University of Pittsburgh Press, 1989); Michael Dodson and Laura Nuzzi O'Shaughnessy, *Nicaragua's Other Revolution: Religious Faith and Political Struggle* (Chapel Hill: University of North Carolina Press, 1990). Most texts on liberation theology emphasize intellectual, symbolic, or institutional analysis rather than how these ideas were taken up by local actors prior to the 1979 revolution.

38. Gilbert M. Joseph, "What We Now Know and Should Know: Bringing Latin America More Meaningfully into Cold War Studies," in *In from the Cold: Latin America's New Encounter with the Cold War*, ed. Gilbert M. Joseph and Daniela Spenser (Durham, NC: Duke University Press, 2008), 400.

39. Jonathan Glover, *Humanity: A Moral History of the Twentieth Century*, 2nd ed. (New Haven, CT: Yale University Press, 2012), 48.

40. The FSLN planned to publish multiple volumes from the oral history accounts of the insurrection. However, perhaps due to the exigencies of the Con-

tra war of the 1980s, only a single book was ever released: Instituto de Estudio del Sandinismo, *Y se armó la runga . . .! Testimonios de la insurrección popular sandinista en Masaya* (Managua: Editorial Nueva Nicaragua, 1982). These published testimonies from the Masaya oral histories were later analyzed from a sociological and anthropological perspective in two articles: Jean-Pierre Reed, "Emotions in Context: Revolutionary Accelerators, Hope, Moral Outrage, and Other Emotions in the Making of Nicaragua's Revolution," *Theory and Society* 33, no. 6 (2004): 653–703; and Bradley Tatar, "Emergence of Nationalist Identity in Armed Insurrections: A Comparison of Iraq and Nicaragua," *Anthropological Quarterly* 78, no. 1 (2005): 179–95. Reed focuses on the role of mobilizing emotions among combatants amidst the upheaval; Tatar emphasizes "nationalist identity" as a fundamental factor spurring participation.

ONE.    *State of Disorder*

1. Mariano Buitrago to Cmte. Uruiel Fuentes, forwarding communication from Pedro Cardoza, Juez de Policía, February 25, 1970, Archivo General de la Nación (hereafter AGN), Fondo Gobernación, Sección Alcaldías Municipales, box 16, folder "La Trinidad."

2. Petition to Ministerio de Gobernación, October 17, 1970, in ibid.

3. Lt. Col. Álvaro Valle Salinas to Mariano Buitrago, n.d., in ibid.

4. M. G. and L. G. to Mariano Buitrago, October 14, 1970, in ibid.

5. Mariano Buitrago to Pedro Cardoza, October 19, 1970, in ibid.

6. Lancaster, *Life Is Hard*, 39. For the use of popular idioms of masculinity by the Trujillo dictatorship in the Dominican Republic to bolster political legitimacy among working-class men, see Lauren H. Derby, *The Dictator's Seduction: Politics and the Popular Imagination in the Era of Trujillo* (Durham, NC: Duke University Press, 2009).

7. Katherine E. Bliss discusses the multiple roles of madams in Mexico City: former sex workers, exploiters of young women, and intermediaries with the state; see Bliss, "'Guided by an Imperious, Moral Need': Prostitutes, Motherhood, and Nationalism in Revolutionary Mexico," in *Reconstructing Criminality in Latin America*, ed. Carlos Aguirre and Robert Buffington (Lanham, MD: Rowman and Littlefield, 2000), 176–77, 180–81. For reference to the "precarious and perhaps hard-won" honor of madams/former prostitutes who operated brothels owned by their male partners in the Costa Rican banana enclave, see Lara Putnam, "Sex and Standing on the Streets of Port Limón, Costa Rica, 1890–1910," in *Honor, Status, and Law in Modern Latin America*, ed. Sueann Caulfield, Sarah C. Chambers, and Lara Putnam (Durham, NC: Duke University Press Books, 2005), 163.

8. Manuel Paiz F., "Augusto Calderón Sandino," *La Información* (Bluefields), April 17, 1934. Somoza García even went as far as to commission a ghost-written book based on Sandino's documents in order to cast the nationalist insurgency as bloody and cruel; see Anastasio Somoza García, *El verdadero Sandino: o, El calvario de las Segovias* (Managua: Tipografía Robelo, 1936).

9. "El pueblo espera con ansia el proceso que se ofreció seguir los sucesos del 21 de febrero," *LP*, May 31, 1934.

10. "Declara General Somoza," *LP*, September 10, 1934. The Liberal Party leaders from the departments of Estelí, Nueva Segovia, Jinotega, and Matagalpa even requested Somoza García name a vice president from the Segovias ("Piden la Vicepresidencia para Las Segovias," *LP*, June 25, 1936).

11. Oscar-René Vargas, *Floreció al filo de la espada: El movimiento de Sandino, 1926–1939. Once ensayos de interpretación* (Managua: Centro de Estudios de la Realidad Nacional, 1995), 491.

12. Anastasio Somoza Debayle, *Primer mensaje al Congreso Nacional* (Managua: Imprenta Nacional, 1968), 20.

13. "Nicaragua: The Champ Is Dead," *Time*, October 10, 1956; William Krehm, *Democracia y tiranías en el Caribe* (Buenos Aires: Editorial Parnaso, 1957), 173–78; Peter H. Smith, "Development and Dictatorship in Nicaragua: 1950–1960," *The American Economist* 7, no. 1 (1963): 31; Marshall Smith, "One More Somoza in Nicaragua," *Life*, April 28, 1967; Jaime Wheelock, *Imperialismo y dictadura: Crisis de una formación social* (Mexico City: Siglo Veintiuno Editores, 1976), 171–75.

14. Gustavo Alemán Bolaños, *Los pobres diablos: Segunda parte de un lombrosiano: Somoza: 1939–1944* (Guatemala City: Editorial Hispañia, 1947), 53; Krehm, *Democracia y tiranías en el Caribe*, 176; Luis Gonzaga Cardenal, *Mi rebelión: La dictadura de los Somoza* (Mexico City: Ediciones Patria y Libertad, 1961), 191.

15. Smith, "Development and Dictatorship in Nicaragua," 27.

16. René Molina Valenzuela, interview with author, Ometepe, Rivas, 2010; Julián N. Guerrero Castillo and Lola Soriano de Guerrero, *Estelí (Monografía)* (Managua: Artes Gráficas, 1967), 99–100; Orient Bolívar Juárez, *La catedral de Estelí: Historia y arquitectura* (Managua: Editorial Hispamer, 1993), 131–32. According to *La Prensa*, Molina's father, Antonio Molina, and jefe político José María Briones also profited by selling their land for the company's landing strip, camp, housing, etc. ("Bajos salarios y mal trato a trabajadores nicas en el norte," *LP*, November 7, 1957).

17. "Nuevo miembro de la Junta Consultativa del Banco Nicaragüense," *LP*, February 11, 1971; "Proyectarse para fundar banco en Estelí," *LP*, January 5, 1972.

18. José Simón Delgado, "La ciudad de Estelí, desde 1823 hasta 1976," *La Nación*, December 18, 1976.

19. These included the following families: Valdivia, López, Reyes, Lanuza, Castillo, Aráuz, Molina, Briones, and Moreno. For more information, see José Simón Delgado, "La ciudad de Estelí, desde 1823 hasta 1976," *La Nación*, December 18, 1976. Political developments in the Segovias strongly contradict Michel Gobat's assertion that "the rural base of the region's lengthiest dictatorship consisted of medium scale farmers rather than large landlords" (Gobat, *Confronting the American Dream*, 273).

20. Isolda Rodríguez Rosales, *Anécdotas nicaragüenses: Estelí, Matagalpa, Chontales, Managua, Granada, Rivas* (Managua: Fondo Editorial CIRA, 2004), 10.

21. This was also true in the wider bureaucracy. Given the lack of a professional civil service, government employment was considered party patronage; see Mariano Fiallos Oyanguren, "The Nicaraguan Political System: The Flow of Demands and the Reactions of the Regime" (PhD diss., University of Kansas, 1968), 45.

22. María Dolores Álvarez Arzate, "Relaciones sociales y de parentesco en dos familias de Estelí, Nicaragua," in *Familia y diversidad en América Latina: Estudios de casos*, ed. David Robichaux (Buenos Aires: CLACSO, 2007), 359–60.

23. Antonio Molina had married into the prominent Valenzuela family, founding a political dynasty that would remain dominant throughout the decades of Somoza rule; see Ciriaco Rodríguez y Palacios, *Cuando el ayer es hoy: ¡Viva Estelí, que es mi pueblo!* (Hollywood, CA: Orbe, 1973), 135; José Floripe Fajardo, *Estelí en retazos* (Estelí: Editorial Letras, 2004), 84; and Juárez, *La Catedral de Estelí*, 153.

24. Guerrero Castillo and Soriano de Guerrero, *Estelí (Monografía)*, 180.

25. Centro de Investigación y Estudios de la Reforma Agraria (CIERA), *Nicaragua, y por eso defendemos la frontera* (Managua: CIERA-MIDINRA, 1984), 213–16, 221.

26. CIERA, *Diagnóstico Socioeconómico de PRONORTE* (Managua: CIERA-MIDINRA, 1980), 85; CIERA, *Nicaragua, y por eso defendemos la frontera*, 226–27.

27. Marcial López L. to Ministro de Gobernación, June 21, 1939, AGN, Fondo Gobernación, Sección Jefatura Política, box 46, folder 5.0.

28. "Presos por robar café y eran los propios dueños," *LP*, February 13, 1957.

29. Francisco Salgado to Ministro de Gobernación, April 28, 1952, AGN; Francisco Salgado to Ministro de Gobernación, May 4, 1952, AGN; Cástulo Ramírez, Presidente Comunidad Indígena de San Lucas, etc. to Ministro de Gobernación, June 3, 1952, AGN; Junta de la Comunidad Indígena to Ministro de Gobernación, June 21, 1952, AGN, Fondo Comunidades Indígenas, box 104, folder 39. Indeed, the village of Santa Isabel had earlier been split off from San Lucas and annexed to Somoto, its indigenous lands converted in municipal holdings and snapped up by Somoteño planters (Gould, *To Die in This Way*, 186–87).

30. Testimony, Jaime González Almendárez, AGN, Fondo Procuraduría General de la República, Tribunales Especiales de Justicia, (hereafter AGN-PGR), trib. 6, caso 31, April 12, 1980, 31.

31. Mauricio Portillo, interview with author, Somoto, Madriz, 2010; Justo García Aguilar, Viceministro de Gobernación, to Tula Baca de López Núñez, Jefe Político, October 18, 1973, AGN, Fondo Gobernación, Sección Jefatura Política, box 50, folder 9.0. Like Dr. Ríos in San Lucas, the indigenous community later accused Portillo of seizing their centuries-old royal titles in order to negate their legal claims; see Mario Rizo, *Historia del pueblo indígena de Telpaneca* (Managua: UNICEF, 2009), 107.

32. Gould, *To Die in This Way*, 10–18.

33. René Molina, interview with author, Ometepe, Rivas, 2010.

34. Banco Central de Nicaragua-Ministerio de Economía, Industria y Comercio, *Compendio estadístico, 1965–1974* (Managua: Editorial y Litografía San José, 1976), 418.

35. Carlos Maturana, interview by Robert J. Alexander, INFONAC, June 28, 1967, Papers of Robert J. Alexander, reel 10, frame 826; "Cubanos despierten malestar en Estelí," *LP*, January 28, 1967; "Difícil situación de cosecheros de tabaco," *LP*, May 14, 1968; "Fábrica de tabaco cierra en Estelí," *LP*, September 29, 1969; "Para los tabacaleros, las duras, para el intermediario, el oro," *LP*, October 13, 1969; "Cosecheros de Tabaco del norte se organizan," *LP*, April 27, 1970; "45 millones están en peligro: Otro mal programa de INFONAC," *LP*, July 12, 1971; "Aumentó producción de Tabaco en fin de enero," *LP*, February 9, 1972; "Inicia operaciones una gran fábrica de puros tipo habano," *Novedades*, July 10, 1965; "Trabajo para 300 personas dará la fábrica de puros de Estelí," *Novedades*, July 18, 1965.

36. "Atacan maltarato de cubanos en tabacales," *LP*, March 13, 1969; "Con metralletas cuidan cubanos los tabacales," *LP*, March 24, 1969; "Tabacaleros del norte no cumplen con el mínimo," *LP*, May 28, 1975; Alejandro Dávila Bolaños, *El interrogatorio: Escrito en la cuarta semana de diciembre de 1978* (Estelí: Loaisiga, 1979), 13.

37. John Morris Ryan et al., *Area Handbook for Nicaragua* (Washington, DC: U.S. Government Printing Office, 1970), 86.

38. Álvarez Arzate, "Relaciones sociales y de parentesco en dos familias de Estelí, Nicaragua," 360.

39. Ibid., 368.

40. Smith, "Development and Dictatorship in Nicaragua," 27.

41. Jaime Wheelock's classic argument that rural Nicaraguan had been largely proletarianized over the period of Somoza rule (and, in particular, with the introduction of coffee) is not substantiated in the departments of Estelí and Madriz (Wheelock, *Imperialismo y dictadura*, 21–24). Critiques of his interpretation, based on the nineteenth- and early twentieth-century agrarian history are found in Julie A. Charlip, *Cultivating Coffee: The Farmers of Carazo, Nicaragua, 1880–1930* (Athens: Ohio University Press, 2003); Elizabeth Dore, *Myths of Modernity: Peonage and Patriarchy in Nicaragua* (Durham, NC: Duke University Press, 2006).

42. Ministerio de Economía, Dirección General de Estadística y Censo, *Censos nacionales, 1963*, Vol. 5, *Población* (Managua: DGEC, 1964), 363.

43. Antonio Centeno, interview with author, Condega, Estelí, 2008.

44. As early as the 1940s, there is evidence of strikes on the coffee estate of Darailí; see Mario A. Trujillo Bolio, *Historia de los trabajadores en el capitalismo nicaragüense (1850–1950)* (Mexico City: Centro de Estudios Latinoamericanos-UNAM, 1992), 185.

45. Encuesta de Trabajadores del Campo, 1980, cited in CIERA, *Nicaragua, y por eso defendemos la frontera*, 63. This evidence contradicts Timothy Wickham-Crawley's claim that "sharecropping forms of tenancy are unimport-

ant throughout Nicaragua," (Wickham-Crawley, *Guerrillas and Revolution in Latin America*, 234).

46. Salvador Loza and Mario Rizo, *Mística y coraje: Testimonio del guerrillero Salvador Loza* (Managua: Amerrisque, 2009), 31.

47. William Kennedy Upham, "A Sociological Analysis of Man–Land Relations in Central America" (PhD diss., University of Florida, 1969), 276–77.

48. Marco Orozco Espinoza, interview by Y. C., Tres Esquinas, Santa Cruz, Estelí, 1980, Instituto de Historia de Nicaragua y Centroamérica, Archivo Oral de la Cruzada Nacional de Alfabetización (hereafter IHNCA-CNA), 1A-691.688.

49. Anastasio Rivas Cruz, interview with author, El Regadío, Estelí, 2008.

50. "Bajos salarios y mal trato a trabajadores nicas en el norte," *LP*, November 7, 1957.

51. See chapter 4 for more about the social origins of the National Guard privates.

52. Ministerio de Economía, Dirección General de Estadística y Censo, *Censo 1963, Cifras provisionales, Boletín 1* (Managua: DGEC, 1963), 3–9; Banco Central de Nicaragua-Ministerio de Economía, Industria y Comercio, *Compendio estadístico, 1965–1974*, 87; Guerrero Castillo and Soriano de Guerrero, *Estelí (Monografía)*, 87, 92.

53. Guerrero Castillo and Soriano de Guerrero, *Estelí (Monografía)*, 101; Colonel Carlos Edmundo Vergara, "Estelí, la ciudad de mayor progreso del Norte," *Acción Cívica*, September 1977.

54. "Un ambicioso plan para dar servicio de aguas negras a Estelí," *LP*, November 15, 1957; "Alcalde contradice: Dejó un superávit," *LP*, June 4, 1963; "Alcalde preocupase por adelantos de la ciudad," *LP*, October 12, 1963; "Serios problemas afronta a Estelí," *LP*, October 11, 1967; "Medio millón de córdobas para municipio de Estelí," *Novedades*, July 13, 1965; José Simón Delgado, "La ciudad de Estelí, desde 1823 hasta 1976," *La Nación*, December 18, 1976; Guerrero Castillo and Soriano de Guerrero, 131–32; Estelí (Nicaragua), *Alcaldía Municipal de Estelí: Censo general año 1971*(Estelí, 1972).

55. Francisco Rivera Quintero and Sergio Ramírez, *La marca del Zorro: Hazañas del comandante Francisco Rivera Quintero* (Managua: Editorial Nueva Nicaragua, 1989), 25.

56. Loza and Rizo, *Mística y coraje*, 36; see also *LP*, "Ciudadanía pide al gobierno mejoras para los estelianos," *LP*, October 17, 1967.

57. For some of the many denunciations of conditions, lack of medication, safety, and quality of the public hospitals in Estelí and Somoto, see: "Hospital de Estelí en completo abandono," *LP*, July 6, 1957; "Nuevo directivo en Hospital de Estelí," *LP*, July 11, 1957, "Construcción del Hospital de Somoto en un lugar prejudicial," *LP*, March 17, 1959; "Problema médico en el Hospital de Estelí," *LP*, May 15, 1959, "Medicinas son un lujo en Hospital de Estelí," August 20, 1963; "Gran problema del hospital de Estelí," *LP*, April 24, 1964; "Comité de Salud trata de mejorar el Hospital de Somoto," *LP*, October 13, 1964.

58. Curanderos were active in Estelí, Santa Cruz, San Roque, Palacagüina, and Condega; "Arrestado por haber ejercido en Estelí la curandería," *LP*, May 23, 1956; "El curanderismo activo," *LP*, July 6, 1957.

59. By 1954, however, Somoza could brag that the country had more schoolteachers than Guardias (Ryan et al., *Area Handbook for Nicaragua*, 335). The building of schools also increased with U.S. funding via the Alliance for Progress in the wake of the Cuban Revolution ("Estelí contará con moderno Centro Escolar que tendrá capacidad para 900 alumnos," *Novedades*, October 10, 1963; "Veinte y dos nuevas escuelas terminó de construir la Alianza en distintos lugares del país," *Novedades*, January 1, 1964).

60. "Instituto Nacional para ciudad de Estelí," *LP*, February 24, 1965; "Se abre nuevo Centro Universitario en Estelí," *LP*, May 16, 1969.

61. Ministerio de Economía, Dirección General de Estadística y Censo, *Censos nacionales, 1963* (Managua: DGEC, 1964), 2:6.

62. For an examination of authoritarianism and electoral politics in a similar Central American context, see Erik Ching, *Authoritarian El Salvador: Politics and the Origins of the Military Regimes, 1880–1940* (Notre Dame, IN: University of Notre Dame Press, 2014).

63. Despite the fact that executive power had consistently changed hands only through violence, Mariano Fiallos Oyanguren says that elections had "extraordinary importance as the only means of legitimization. There has been no period in Nicaraguan history in which elections have not been scheduled every two, four or six years" (Fiallos Oyanguren, "The Nicaraguan Political System," 49).

64. González-Rivera concludes that voting for the Liberal Party permitted an "expression of citizenship in a country without an electoral tradition or a tradition of popular democracy" (González-Rivera, *Before the Revolution*, 60; see also 62–68, 83).

65. Rafael Gutiérrez, "El alcoholismo," *Revista Conservadora* 4, no. 21 (1962): 26.

66. Róger Mendieta Alfaro, *El último marine: 1980, año de la alfabetización* (Managua: Editorial Unión Cardoza, 1980), 101.

67. Fiallos Oyanguren, "The Nicaraguan Political System," 50; Beverly Castillo Herrera, *La tradición oral en la conformación de la identidad histórica-cultural del municipio de Condega: Historia, tradiciones y costumbres* (Estelí: Centro de Investigación y Comunicación Social SINSLANI, 2006), 77.

68. Walter, *The Regime of Anastasio Somoza, 1936–1956*, 176; Fiallos Oyanguren, "The Nicaraguan Political System," 94–95.

69. González-Rivera, *Before the Revolution*, 57–58. As González-Rivera shows, this was the product of a long struggle by women for the right to vote that was silenced by the Somozas taking credit. In February 1946, the wives and daughters of prominent opposition families (PLI and the Conservative Party) in Estelí held a foundational meeting of the local committee of the Women's National United Front (Frente Unido Nacional Femenino) calling for women's suffrage ("Organízase Frente Unido Femenino en Estelí," *La Nueva Prensa*, February 13, 1946).

70. "AMROCS in Somoto," *Novedades*, March 26, 1966. U.S. ambassador Shelton described these groupings as "separate entities independent of the regular PLN structure but on a direct line to General Somoza. They provide a substantial supplement to the political power of the regular PLN machine"; see "The

Governing Liberals," U.S. Embassy Cable 296, January 24, 1974. Wikileaks, Public Library of U.S. Diplomacy (hereafter PlusD).

71. "Denuncian un delito contra el sufragio; el Jefe Político de Estelí coacciona a los Jueces de Mesta," *LP*, July 26, 1946.

72. Kennedy Crockett, "Role of the Military in Latin America: Nicaragua," U.S. Embassy Cable A-172, September 11, 1969, included in David R. Powell and Kenneth B. Youngs, *Report of the Public Safety Program and the Nicaragua National Guard, June 1970* (Washington, DC: Agency for International Development, 1971), 96.

73. Anonymous, interview with author, San Lucas, Madriz, 2010.

74. A dissident Liberal diputado for Estelí admitted as much in 1934 ("En el plebiscito pasado, se gastó . . .," *LP*, July 20, 1934). In the 1936 elections, which handed the presidency to Somoza García, so much tax-free guaro was distributed that the minister of finance even suggested switching to a lower-quality grade. For the 1945 elections, the PLN assured that each town in the department of Estelí received C$200 and 150 liters of liquor (Walter, *The Regime of Anastasio Somoza, 1936–1956*, 59, 145).

75. Somoza García's perennial Conservative "opponent" and occasional partner Emiliano Chamorro complained of such practices in his autobiography *El último caudillo: Autobiografía* (Managua: Ediciones del Partido Conservador Demócrata, 1983), 381. Even the U.S. embassy concurred that la Magnífica was a form of "not so subtle coercion," which "did violence to the legally established secret ballot" (Leland Warner, "The Week after Election Day," U.S. Embassy Cable 3530, September 10, 1974, PlusD).

76. René Molina Valenzuela, interview with author, Ometepe, Rivas, 2010.

77. Walter, *The Regime of Anastasio Somoza, 1936–1956*, 151–52; Fiallos Oyanguren, "The Nicaraguan Political System," 47.

78. Nicaragua, *Constitución política y leyes constitutivas de Nicaragua* (Managua: Talleres Nacionales, 1939), art. 31; Nicaragua, *Constitución política de Nicaragua y leyes constitutivas de Nicaragua* (Managua: Talleres Nacionales, 1948), art. 31; Nicaragua, *Constitución política, ley de amparo y ley marcial de Nicaragua* (Managua: Talleres Nacionales, 1951), art. 34. Officially, sale of aguardiente was banned around election time ("Medidas tendientes a garantizar el orden durante las elecciones de febrero ordena el Presidente," *Novedades*, January 19, 1963).

79. For a consideration of the link between alcohol consumption, masculine sociability, and violence in modern Mexico, see Stanley Brandes, "Drink, Abstinence, and Male Identity in Mexico City," in *Changing Men and Masculinities in Latin America*, ed. Matthew C. Gutmann (Durham, NC: Duke University Press, 2003), 153–56.

80. "Hechos de sangre por pleitos y por el licor," *LP*, February 4, 1963.

81. "Balacera y tres muertos en Estelí durante manifestación somocista," *LP*, October 21, 1971.

82. "Decenas golpeados e instrumentos destruidos (Estelí)," *LP*, November 6, 1971.

83. José Eulogio Hernández Alvarado, interview with author, Las Sabanas, Madriz, 2010.

84. "Gran mitín opositor UNO en Estelí," *LP*, November 27, 1963; "Enorme concentración opositora en Estelí," *LP*, December 13, 1966.

85. "Otro signo de fraude electoral: Maniobran con cantones," *LP*, August 26, 1966.

86. González-Rivera, *Before the Revolution*, 113–26.

87. For an overview of AMROCS violence nationally during the lead up to the election, see Fiallos Oyanguren, "The Nicaraguan Political System," 126. Unique about AMROCS was its presence in many rural communities. Large groups were found in nearly all of the rural Madriz communities outside of Somoto known for large numbers of National Guards. For their declarations of allegiance to Somoza from Santa Isabel, Santa Teresa, Tamarindo, Cacaulí, and El Espino, see *Novedades*, May 16, 19, 27, 1966. When General Somoza visited Somoto in October on a campaign stop, large numbers of campesinos mobilized by AMROCS formed "long caravans on horseback" to wait his landing on the airstrip ("Madriz volcó su entusiasmo para aclamar al General Somoza," *Novedades*, October 12, 1966).

88. "Magnífica actitud de la GN ante AMROCS provocadores," *LP*, November 26–28, 1966; "Culatean a joven opositor en Estelí," *LP*, December 8, 1966; "Amrocs inscribiendo," *LP*, December 19, 1966.

89. "Grave tensión hay en Estelí," *LP*, November 19, 1966.

90. Oyanguren, "The Nicaraguan Political System," 133; Black, *Triumph of the People*, 43–44; John A. Booth, *The End and the Beginning: The Nicaraguan Revolution* (Boulder, CO: Westview, 1985), 89; James Dunkerley, *Power in the Isthmus: A Political History of Modern Central America* (London: Verso, 1988), 233.

91. Turner Shelton, "The Governing Liberals," U.S. Embassy Cable 296, January 24, 1974, PlusD.

92. "No ha hecho nada el Alcalde de Somoto?" *LP*, September 5, 1956.

93. "Un pueblito de Nicaragua, y una triste historia," *LP*, July 11, 1956. A decade later, while serving as diputado, he was accused of participating in the trafficking of contraband across the Honduran border. Not surprisingly, no criminal charges were brought against him ("Capturan contrabando a Diputado Héctor Mairena en la aduana del Espino," *LP*, April 7, 1965). Authorities throughout the Segovias stood accused of similar methods of rule. The mayor of Palacagüina was accused of using his position to "throw people in jail, demand arbitrary fines, registration fees, service fees, emoluments that are not required by law, provoking conflicts with grave consequences [and] violating constitutional guarantees" (Letter, Alcaldía de Condega to Ministro de Gobernación, April 24, 1939, AGN, Fondo Gobernación, Sección Alcaldías, box 15, folder 5.0).

94. "Acusa irregularidad en elección de jurado," *LP*, February 15, 1967; "Desmienten al Juez de Estelí," *LP*, February 19, 1957; "Confirma el Juez de Estelí irregularidades al elegir los jurados," *LP*, February 21, 1957.

95. Jueces de Mesta from Caucalí, El Rodeo and El Limón to Ministro de Gobernación, July 31, 1971, AGN, Fondo Gobernación, Sección Jefatura Política, box 50, folder 9.0.

96. Walter, *The Regime of Anastasio Somoza, 1936–1956*, 82. In 1962, further autonomy was restored but "municipal officeholders were invariably wealthy landowners or businessmen who received power and illicit income in

exchange for mobilizing political support for the Somoza regime at the local level"; R. Andrew Nickson, *Local Government in Latin America* (Boulder, CO: Lynne Rienner, 1995), 211–12.

97. "Liberalismo de Estelí, abandonado por el gobierno," *LP*, February 21, 1956.

98. Instituto Centroamericano de Administración de Empresas, Centro de Asesoramiento, *Estudio de las municipalidades en Nicaragua* (Managua: INCAE, 1973), 4.

99. A. Sánchez to Ministro de Gobernación, May 25, 1973, AGN, Fondo Gobernación, Sección Alcaldías Municipales, box 14, folder 5.4.

100. Romeo González Espinoza, Alcalde of Condega, to Antonio Coronado Torres, Viceministro de Gobernación, July 15, 1967, AGN, Fondo Gobernación, Sección Alcaldías, box 16, folder 5.1. Permitting political and family allies to usurp ejido lands without charging the proper fees was an issue that dated back decades. A local official in Pueblo Nuevo alleged in 1940, for instance, that "family connections between the users of ejido lands and the people in the local government [and] considerations of friendship have caused the municipality to not charge the taxes, leading a passive resistance to not fill out the legal forms, thus damaging the municipal budget" (Ulises Piñeda to Ministro de Gobernación, June 6, 1940, AGN, Fondo Gobernación, Sección Alcaldías, box 16, folder 5.4, folder 22).

101. José Indalecio Rodríguez, Jefe Político of Estelí, to Vicente Navas, Ministro de Gobernación, August 31, 1967, AGN, Fondo Gobernación, Sección Alcaldías, box 16, folder 5.1.

102. Romeo González Espinoza, Alcalde of Condega, to Antonio Coronado Torres, Viceministro de Gobernación, September 8, 1967, AGN, Fondo Gobernación, Sección Alcaldías, box 16, folder 5.1.

103. Lilliam Vílchez de Benavides to Antonio Coronado Torres, Viceministro de Gobernación, May 3, 1967, AGN, Fondo Gobernación, Sección Alcaldías, box 15, folder 5.0.

104. Lilliam Vílchez de Benavides, "Carta abierta a la ciudadanía esteliana," June 4, 1968, AGN, Fondo Gobernación, Sección Alcaldías, box 15, folder 5.0.

105. "Intriga política contra Alcaldesa (Estelí): Siempre los negocios," *LP*, April 9, 1968.

106. "Recibí alcaldía con 3 millones de deuda, dice Alcaldesa Vílchez Ruiz," *LP*, January 1, 1968.

107. "Intriga política contra Alcaldesa (Estelí): Siempre los negocios," *LP*, April 9, 1968.

108. Lilliam Vílchez de Benavides, "Carta abierta a la ciudadanía esteliana," June 4, 1968, AGN, Fondo Gobernación, Sección Alcaldías, box 15, folder 5.0.

109. "Alcaldesa escapa cerco de la GN," *LP*, April 14, 1969.

110. Turner Shelton, "The Governing Liberals," U.S. Embassy Cable 296, January 24, 1974, PlusD. According to Salvador Loza Talavera, it was from the cantinas that regime agents organized the distribution of guaro and nacatamales for the Liberal Party rallies and elections (Loza and Rizo, *Mística y coraje*, 71). The brothels and cantinas were also regularly visited by GN officials and secret police informants (Rivera Quintero and Ramírez, *La marca del Zorro*, 38).

111. Lyman L. Johnson, "Dangerous Words, Provocative Gestures, and Violent Acts: The Disputed Hierarchies of Plebeian Life in Colonial Buenos Aires," in *The Faces of Honor: Sex, Shame, and Violence in Colonial Latin America*, ed. Lyman L. Johnson and Sonya Lipsett-Rivera (Albuquerque: University of New Mexico Press, 1998), 127–51; Brandes, "Drink, Abstinence, and Male Identity in Mexico City"; David Carey Jr., "Drunks and Dictators: Inebriation's Gendered, Ethnic, and Class Components in Guatemala, 1898–1944," in *Alcohol in Latin America: A Social and Cultural History*, ed. Gretchen Pierce and Áurea Toxqui (Tucson: University of Arizona Press, 2014), 131–58; Robert F. Alegre, *Railroad Radicals in Cold War Mexico: Gender, Class, and Memory* (Lincoln: University of Nebraska Press, 2014), 84–85.

112. Gutiérrez, "El Alcoholismo," 26.

113. Nicaragua, *Reglamento de policia de la República de Nicaragua*, 8th ed. (Managua: Tipografía Nacional, 1951).

114. Booth, *The End and the Beginning*, 55–57; Justiniano Pérez, *Semper fidelis: El secuestro de la Guardia Nacional de Nicaragua* (Miami, FL: Orbis, 2005), 46.

115. Rivera Quintero and Ramírez, *La marca del Zorro*, 38.

116. Ramón Mejía Salcedo, "Organization of the Administrative Phase of a Public Health Department in Nicaragua" (Master's in Public Health, University of Michigan, 1945), 32. Such government stimulation of liquor consumption produced social disorder, not—as occurred a century earlier in the 1840s—popular resistance to government monopoly and taxation of aguardiente; see E. Bradford Burns, *Patriarch and Folk: The Emergence of Nicaragua, 1798–1858* (Cambridge, MA: Harvard University Press, 1991), 147–48.

117. "Como en Oeste norteamericano viven estelianos," *LP*, October 18, 1968.

118. Carlos Cuadra Pasos, *Posibilidades de existencia del comunismo en Nicaragua* (Granada: Tipografía El Centro Americano, 1937).

119. This monopoly dated to the mid-nineteenth century in order to increase taxation from the poor and control alcohol consumption, criminalizing home aguardiente production, a largely female domain. Women moved into running cantinas selling purchased alcohol; see Justin Wolfe, *The Everyday Nation-State: Community and Ethnicity in Nineteenth-Century Nicaragua* (Lincoln: University of Nebraska Press, 2007), 60–64.

120. Romeo González to Ministro de Gobernacion, December 23, 1967, AGN, Fondo Gobernación, Sección Alcaldías Municipales, box 16, folder 5.1.

121. "Leyes son burladas en dpto. de Estelí," *LP*, March 19, 1968.

122. Ministerio de Gobernación y Anexos, *Manual del juez de mesta* (Managua: Talleres Nacionales, 1952); Walter, *The Regime of Anastasio Somoza, 1936–1956*, 113.

123. J. F. Romero to Ministro de Gobernación, January 3, 1943, AGN, Fondo Gobernación, Sección Alcaldías, box 16, folder 5.4.

124. Federico López Rivera to Juan Padilla, October 16, 1954, AGN, Fondo Gobernación, Sección Jefatura Política, box 50, folder 9.0.

125. "Menores de edad en Estelí juegan dados," *LP*, June 29, 1957.

126. Letter from Benito Obregón A. to Señor Director de la Prensa, August 29, 1960, "Inauguran juegos prohibidos con toda garantía en Estelí," *LP*, September 1, 1960 (emphasis in original).
127. González-Rivera, *Before the Revolution*, 143, 146–50; Gould, *To Lead as Equals*, 169.
128. "Cantina cerca de escuela," *LP*, August 3, 1963, "Deprimiente espectáculo en las fiestas de Somoto," November 13, 1963; "Muchos males sufren pueblos de Madriz," *LP*, August 27, 1964, "Males que aquejan al departamento de Madriz," *LP*, September 18, 1964; "Indiferentes ante centros de vicio," *LP*, April 18, 1968.
129. Tula Baca de López to Vicente Navas, Ministro de Gobernación, March 23, 1968, AGN, Fondo Gobernación, Sección Jefatura Política, box 50, folder 9.0.
130. Antonia G. to President Somoza, forwarded to Francisco Franco, National Guard Comandante, May 5, 1968, AGN, Fondo Guardia Nacional, Sección Estado Mayor, box 24, file 326. Around the same time, in neighboring Pueblo Nuevo, a brothel was closed by the National Guard because its permission had been granted by the local mayor, when, in fact, such illegal permits were the exclusive purview of the GN; see Antonio Coronado, Vice-Ministro de Gobernación to Entimo Sevilla, March 28, 1968, AGN, Fondo Gobernación, Sección Alcaldías, box 16, folder 5.1. In Estelí, a self-proclaimed "cantina-brothel" owner wrote to the minister to complain of political opponents using the GN to harass his business (Manuel M. to Ministro de Gobernación, June 29, 1965, AGN, Fondo Gobernación, Sección Jefatura Política, box 46, folder 5.0).
131. Coronel Augustín Bodán, National Guard Comandante to General Somoza, May 13, 1968, AGN, Fondo Guardia Nacional, Sección Estado Mayor, box 24, file 326.
132. Adán Sequeira Arellano, "El Abigeato," *Revista Conservadora* 2, no. 13 (1962): 30. G. Ramírez Brown, Viceministro de Gobernación, to Marcial López L., Jefe Político de Estelí, November 13, 1939, AGN, Fondo Gobernación, Sección Jefatura Política, box 46, folder 5.0; Leonardo Argüello, Ministro de Gobernación, to Alcaldía de Limay, January 1, 1942, AGN, Fondo Gobernación, Sección Alcaldías, box 17, folder 5.4. In 1939, a juez de mesta in San Juan de Limay and his two jueces de canton were arrested for banditry (J. Rigoberto Reyes, Jefe del Estado Mayor de la Guardia Nacional to Marcial López, Jefe Político de Estelí, October 6, 1939, AGN, Fondo Gobernación, Sección Jefatura Política, box 46, folder 5.0).
133. Alejandro Briones to Aníbal Ibarra Rojas, Ministro de Gobernación, July 29, 1944, AGN, Fondo Gobernación, Sección Jefatura Política, box 46, folder 5.0.
134. "Presos en Estelí cuatro acusados de robar reses," *LP*, May 3, 1963, "Batida a cuatreros en el norte: Dos son capturados," *LP*, December 20, 1963; "Banda que asolaba a Estelí presa en Managua," *LP*, September 12, 1964.
135. "Incremento a ganadería dan en el sector del norte," *LP*, April 8, 1964.
136. Álvaro Valle Salinas, Cmte. of Estelí to President Somoza and Inspector General Major José Somoza, Jefe del Estado Mayor, Jefe de Seguridad

Nacional, March 6, 1972, AGN, Fondo Guardia Nacional, Sección Estado Mayor, box 22, folder 314.

137. Anonymous, interview with author, La Trinidad, Estelí, 2010.

138. "GN arbitrario amenaza 'si siguen fregando,'" *LP*, June 25, 1971.

139. Engracia J. to Mariana Buitrago, Ministro de Gobernación, February 8, 1971, AGN, Fondo Gobernación, Sección Alcaldías Muncipales, box 16, folder 5.4.

140. Yolanda L. to President Somoza, July 20, 1971, AGN, Fondo Gobernación, Sección Alcaldías Muncipales, box 16, folder 5.4.

141. Lilliam Vílchez a Vicente Navas, Ministro de Gobernación, to President Somoza, August 9, 1968, AGN, Fondo Gobernación, Sección Alcaldías Muncipales, box 16, folder 5.4.

TWO.  *Burning Down the Brothels*

1. "Cadena de incendios en Estelí," *LP*, April 20, 1965; "GN ignora tarro explosivo," *LP*, April 23, 1965; "Oficialmente se sospecha en los fuegos de Estelí" and "Dirigente obrero acusa a Obispo, pide reunión," *LP*, April 25, 1965; "Nuevo incendio en Estelí: Víctima señaló ayer mismo evidencia de mano criminal," *LP*, April 26, 1965.

2. Nolan, *The Ideology of the Sandinistas and the Nicaraguan Revolution*, 22. Humberto Belli writes: "The social base of the Sandinistas was not in the shanty towns where the urban poor of Managua and other Nicaraguan cities lived. Nor was it among the urban workers, nor, least of all, among the religious traditionalist peasants. The social base for the FSLN was the Nicaraguan college campuses and secondary schools"; Belli, *Breaking Faith: The Sandinista Revolution and Its Impact on Freedom and Christian Faith in Nicaragua* (Westchester, IL: Puebla Institute, 1985), 11. In the Segovias, his sociological explanation does not hold up. Slum dwellers, urban workers, and religious campesinos were, in fact, a crucial social base for the movement's development, as were the high school students that Belli correctly identifies.

3. "Bandera de Castro en Estelí," *LP*, March 25, 1958.

4. "Grupo armado en El Corozo; comunicado oficial informa incursión," *LP*, October 4, 1958; "Raudales muerto, anuncia Guardia Nacional; 5 heridos más de los dos bandos en combate," *LP*, October 17, 1958.

5. Carlos Fonseca Amador was a member of this group (Zimmermann, *Sandinista*, 53–55); José Simón Delgado, interview by C. D., Barrio Milenio Hernández, Estelí, 1980, IHNCA-CNA, 1A-265.

6. "Como murió Manuel Díaz y Sotelo," *Impacto*, February 12, 1960; Julio Ramos, interview by J. R. L., Pueblo Nuevo, Estelí, 1980, IHNCA-CNA, 1D-2; Emilio Flores Obregón, interview by D. V., Pueblo Nuevo, Estelí, 1980, IHNCA-CNA, 1D-5. For detailed information on each of the armed attempts to overthrow the Somoza dictatorship prior to the formation of the FSLN, see Chuno Blandón, *Entre Sandino y Fonseca* (Managua: Segovia Ediciones Latinoamericanas, 2008).

7. Oficina de Seguridad Nacional file, "Coronel Santos López," February 12, 1958, CHM, Fondo Movimiento Revolucionario (hereafter CHM-MR), E-001, C-010, 000262.

8. Ibid.

9. Loza and Rizo, *Mística y coraje*, 57; Salvador Loza Talavera, interview by V. G., Rodeo Grande, Estelí, 1980, IHNCA-CNA, 1A-800.801.802.803.

10. Michelle Chase, *Revolution within the Revolution: Women and Gender Politics in Cuba, 1952–1962* (Chapel Hill: University of North Carolina Press, 2015); Lorraine Bayard de Volo, *Women and the Cuban Insurrection: How Gender Shaped Castro's Victory* (New York: Cambridge University Press, 2018).

11. Comité Anti-Comunista Nicaragüense, "Juventud Patriótica: Juventud Soviética de Nicaragua" *Novedades*, May 22, 1962.

12. Salvador Pérez Arévalo, Secretary-General of the Executive National Committee of the JPN to Armindo Valenzuela, President of the Directive of the JPN, Estelí, July 15, 1960, CHM-MR, E-001, C-005, 000091. Pérez Arévalo also congratulated Valenzuela on the "laudable initiative of the young people of this city to organize the JPN through its own spontaneity." For more on the origins of the JPN, see Booth, *The End and the Beginning*, 109; Zimmermann, *Sandinista*, 70–71.

13. "Recogida de jóvenes de JPN realizan en Estelí," *LP*, June 21, 1960.

14. "Bomba en Estelí," *LP*, August 1, 1960.

15. Comandante of Estelí to President René Schick and General Anastasio Somoza Debayle, August 19, 1965, AGN, Fondo Guardia Nacional, Sección Estado Mayor, box 22, folder 314. The report went on to claim that he and his brother "put bombs in the house of the mayor Don Solón [*sic*; his name was Salomón] Gómez and in the house of Don José Antonio Molina, the father of Don René Molina Valenzuela, who died as a result several days later." The latter claim seems to have been based on false rumors.

16. Ibid.

17. "Bomba en Estelí" and "Siguen las persecuciones," *LP*, August 1, 1960; "Arrestos: Occidente 3 y en Estelí 5," *LP*, August 2, 1960; "Bomba fabricada en taller del líder somocista," *LP*, August 4, 1960; "Jóvenes acusados de terrorismo," *LP*, August 5, 1960.

18. Zimmermann, *Sandinista*, 31–32.

19. Similar processes were underway throughout Latin America; see Thomas C. Wright, *Latin America in the Era of the Cuban Revolution*, 2nd ed. (Westport, CT: Praeger, 2001), 39–56, 73–110.

20. "Declaración de Carlos Fonseca," *LP*, July 10, 1964.

21. "Estatutos del Movimiento Nueva Nicaragua (1961)," in Tomás Borge, *La paciente impaciencia* (Managua: Editorial Vanguardia, 1989), 176–78.

22. "Juan" (Carlos Fonseca), "Notas Experiencias Revoluciarias," n.d., CHM-MR, E-001, C-009, 000239.

23. The decision to draw on this legacy went back several years, and the MNN had, in fact, used the red-and-black flag of Sandino with the words "*Yo quiero patria libre o morir*" (I want a free homeland or death) written across it; "Estatutos del Movimiento Nueva Nicaragua (1961)," in Borge, *La paciente impaciencia*, 176–78.

24. Among the organizations that officially or unofficially fed into the new FLN were the JPN, JSN, MNN, MR, and the FRS; see Rivera Quintero and Ramírez, *La marca del Zorro*, 36; Loza and Rizo, *Mística y coraje*, 238–40.

25. Carlos Fonseca Amador, "Sandino, guerrillero proletario," in *Obras* (Managua: Nueva Nicaragua, 1982), 1:368–84; Borge, *La paciente impaciencia*, 140; Zimmermann, *Sandinista*, 72–74; Mónica Baltodano, *Memorias de la lucha sandinista*, Tomo I, *De la forja de la vanguardia a la montaña* (Managua: Instituto de Historia de Nicaragua y Centroamérica, Universidad Centroamericana, 2010), 187. For an alternative interpretation of Sandino that sees peasant grievances as central to the guerrilla war of the 1920s and 30s, see Richard Grossman, "'Hermanos en La Patria': Natonalism, Honor, and Rebellion: Augusto Sandino and the Army in Defense of the National Sovereignty of Nicaragua, 1927–1934" (PhD diss., University of Chicago, 1996).

26. Steven Palmer, "Carlos Fonseca and the Construction of Sandinismo in Nicaragua," *Latin American Research Review* 23, no. 1 (1988): 91–109; Zimmermann, *Sandinista*, 59–62, 143–61; Augusto César Sandino and Carlos Fonseca Amador, *Ideario político de Augusto César Sandino* (Managua: Departamento de Propaganda y Educación Política del FSLN, 1984), 63–64.

27. Ernesto Guevara, *El socialismo y el hombre nuevo* (Mexico City: Siglo Veintiuno Editores, 1979).

28. Fonseca Amador, "Sandino, guerrillero proletario," 377.

29. Pedro Joaquín Chamorro, "Quieren otra vez matar a Sandino," *LP*, February 25, 1965.

30. Nolan, *The Ideology of the Sandinistas and the Nicaraguan Revolution*, 18; Zimmermann, *Sandinista*, 77–80.

31. Tomás Borge, *Carlos, el amanecer ya no es una tentación* (Managua: Editorial Nueva Nicaragua, 1982), 26.

32. Fonseca reminded his followers of the "the rural character of Nicaragua and the advantages that its topography offers" for guerrilla warfare, and the rural population's "relative homogeneity," "the hacienda character of agriculture," and "the traditional participation of the campesino masses in political struggles, not only in a negative sense but in a positive sense"; "Notas sobre algunos problemas actuales," Abril 20, 1972, CHM-MR, E-001, C-009, 000245.

33. Schroeder, "Horse Thieves to Rebels to Dogs," 428.

34. Ernesto Guevara, "La guerra de guerrillas," in *Obras, 1957–1967* (Havana: Casa de las Américas, 1970), 46.

35. Ibid., 46, 64.

36. Carlos Fonseca Amador, "Notas sobre la montaña y algunos otros temas," October 8, 1976, CHM-MR, E-001, C-010, 000259. Fonseca claimed that "the authority won by Sandino" provided a "fertilized terrain," but "the revolutionary virtues of the campesino . . . are condemned to lethargy without the presence of worker and student guerrillas."

37. This is similar to what Jeffrey Gould found in the case of artisan laborers and early "obrerismo" in the city of Chinandega (Gould, *To Lead as Equals*, 67, 73).

38. Rivera Quintero and Ramírez, *La marca del Zorro*, 33; Myrna Mack, *Organización y movilización: La propuesta nicaragüense de los '80 para Centro-*

*américa* (Guatemala City: AVANCSO, Fundación Myrna Mack, 1995), 55; Loza and Rizo, *Mística y coraje*, 42. An amnesty declared by Luis Somoza had allowed Ramón Altamirano to return to Nicaragua.

39. "Nuevo médico de Masaya," *La Nueva Prensa*, February 1, 1946.

40. "Monseñor Chavarría declara: Temo el incremento de violencia en Estelí," *Novedades*, April 23, 1965.

41. "Esposado trajo Seguridad al secretario del PLI de Estelí," *LP*, October 30, 1960. An open letter from eighteen medical doctors working in northern Nicaragua—including a number of GN officers—called on President Luis Somoza to release their colleague; "Médicos del Norte piden libertad del Dr. Dávila Bolaños," *LP*, November 30, 1960; Carlos Pérez Bermúdez and Onofre Guevara López, *El movimiento obrero en Nicaragua: Apuntes para el conocimiento de su historia* (Managua: Editorial El Amanecer, 1980), 3.

42. Rivera Quintero and Ramírez, *La marca del Zorro*, 34.

43. Consejo de Estado, *Primera legislatura, 1980: 4 mayo, 1927–1980, día de la dignidad nacional, instauración del Consejo de Estado* (Managua: Asesoría Jurídica y Divulgación y Prensa del Consejo de Estado, 1980), 36; Rivera Quintero and Ramírez, *La marca del Zorro*, 34.

44. Dámaso Picado, interview with author, Estelí, 2010.

45. Gorky's novel was mentioned as a key text by numerous former students of Dávila Bolaños; see Teófilo Cabestrero, *Leonel Rugama: El delito de tomar la vida en serio* (Managua: Editorial Nueva Nicaragua, 1990), 210; Mack, *Organización y movilización*, 47; Isaac Fernández de la Villa, *El pequeño gigante: La vida de Manuelito Maldonado Lovo* (Managua: Amerrisque, 2009), 34.

46. Rivera Quintero and Ramírez, *La marca del Zorro*, 36, 40. The MR, unlike the PSN, did not claim to be the "vanguard party of the proletariat." Instead, it declared itself "a party of the students, workers, campesinos, bank tellers and salespeople, small farmers, industrialists and professionals; it is a party of the people"; see Partido Movilización Republicana, "Cursos de educación política: Reforma agraria," August 19, 1961, CHM-MR: E-001, C-002, 000057.

47. "Continúa el conflicto obrero-patronal en zapatería de Estelí," *LP*, August 3, 1964.

48. Karol C. Kleiner, *Labor Law and Practice in Nicaragua* (Washington, DC: U.S. Department of Labor, Bureau of Labor Statistics, 1964), 39.

49. Robert Jackson Alexander and Eldon M. Parker, *A History of Organized Labor in Panama and Central America* (Westport, CT: Praeger, 2008), 93–95.

50. Loza and Rizo, *Mística y coraje*, 61–63; Rivera Quintero and Ramírez, *La marca del Zorro*, 43.

51. Loza and Rizo, *Mística y coraje*, 42, 69; Filemón Moncada, interview with author, Estelí, 2008; Adrián Gutiérrez, interview with author, Estelí, 2010; Dámaso Picado, interview with author, Estelí, 2010; Pedro Pablo Espinoza, interview with author, Estelí, 2010.

52. For an analysis of how the Chilean Left of the 1930s and 40s promoted a similarly gendered "socialist morality" that denounced typically male vices (alcoholism, gambling, philandering) and called on militants to behave as moral paragons, see Karin Alejandra Rosemblatt, *Gendered Compromises: Political*

*Cultures and the State in Chile, 1920–1950* (Chapel Hill: University of North Carolina Press, 2000), 185–230.

53. For a critical rereading of the ways in which Cuban authorities carried out the "rehabilitation" of former sex workers during the 1960s, see Hynson, "'Count, Capture, and Reeducate.'"

54. Luis Suárez, *Entre el fusil y la palabra* (Universidad Nacional Autónoma de México, 1980), 96. On the role of AA groups fostering a "reformation of masculinity" and responding to the "the crisis in the family," see William Dawley, "From Wrestling with Monsters to Wrestling with God: Masculinities, 'Spirituality,' and the Group-Ization of Religious Life in Northern Costa Rica," *Anthropological Quarterly* 91, no. 1 (2018): 79–131.

55. Comité Pro-Defensa de la Moralidad, open letter, *LP*, August 4, 1964.

56. Ibid.

57. Pedro Joaquín Chamorro, *Estirpe sangrienta: Los Somoza* (Managua: Ediciones el Pez y la Serpiente, 1978), quoted in González-Rivera, *Before the Revolution*, 180.

58. For the role of "plebeian" men in an antiprostitution "moral transformation" campaign in Puerto Rico that was similarly stigmatizing and repressive toward women, see Findlay, *Imposing Decency*, 77–109.

59. "Organízase comité pro-defensa del Barrio El Rosario en Estelí," *LP*, June 30, 1964; Comité Pro-Defensa del Barrio El Rosario, to President René Schick, *LP*, October 24, 1964.

60. Dámaso Picado, interview with author, Estelí, 2010.

61. "Señorita se queja del Inspector del Trabajo," *LP*, September 15, 1963.

62. "GN allana casas en Estelí: Dos reos, un golpeado por una hoja suelta," *LP*, November 28, 1964.

63. Dámaso Picado, interview with author, Estelí, 2010.

64. Salvador Loza Talavera (Martín), interview by V. G., Rodeo Grande, Estelí, 1980, IHNCA-CNA, 1A.800.801.802.803.

65. Though Zimmerman argues that the Sandinistas "had little or no influence in the labor movement, and the PSN dominated the important unions," in Estelí, there was in fact substantial overlap between the clandestine FSLN and the PSN (Zimmermann, *Sandinista*, 91). The PSN openly reported in 1965 that the communists were cooperating directly with "the Sandino Party. . . in organizing the peasant movement"; Pablo Segovia, "For a National Democratic Front," *World Marxist Review* 8 (1965): 74.

66. Banco Central de Nicaragua, Ministerio de Economía, Industria y Comercio, *Compendio Estadístico 1965–1974*, 87.

67. Decreto Legislativo No. 765: Reformas Fundamentales al Código del Trabajo, *La Gaceta (Diario Oficial)*, October 13, 1962; Resolución de la Comisión Nacional de Salario Mínimo, *La Gaceta (Diario Oficial)*, January 11, 1964; Fiallos Oyanguren, "The Nicaraguan Political System," 157–58.

68. James Robert Taylor, *Agricultural Settlement and Development in Eastern Nicaragua* (Madison: Land Tenure Center, University of Wisconsin, 1969), 180.

69. Frente Estudiantil Revolucionario/Sindicato Agrario de Estelí, "Informe," n.d., CHM-MR, E-001, C-012, 000337.

70. Ibid.

71. Ibid.

72. *Memorias del V Congreso de la Federación de Trabajadores de Managua* (Managua: Imprenta Democrática, 1962), 12. Per capita beef consumption in Estelí was just 31 pounds per year.

73. Ibid. 36.

74. Demócrito Paz, *Apuntes de viaje* (Buenos Aires: Editorial Prometeo, 1975), 93.

75. Loza and Rizo, *Mística y coraje*, 239–40.

76. Notably, these included Rodeo Grande and El Regadío outside of Estelí, and also Canta Gallo in Condega. Each of these three areas later witnessed campesino participation in the Christian movements and clandestine guerrilla networks; Adrián Gutiérrez, interview with author, Estelí, 2010; Salvador Loza Talavera, interview by V. G., Rodeo Grande, Estelí, 1980, IHNCA-CNA, 1A-800.801.802.803.

77. Adrián Gutiérrez, interview with author, Estelí, 2010.

78. "Un fracaso de castristas," *LP*, May 3, 1964.

79. "Un caso curioso en Estelí," *LP*, September 24, 1964.

80. Romeo González, Alcalde de Condega, to Comandante GN, Condega, October 16, 1967, AGN, Fondo Gobernación, Sección Alcaldías Municipales, box 16, folder 5.1.

81. Romeo González to Ministro de Gobernación, Condega, November 13, 1967, AGN, Fondo Gobernación, Sección Alcaldías Municipales, box 16, folder 5.1

82. "Hacendados mal informan a un inspector del trabajo porque aplica las leyes," *Novedades*, October 27, 1964.

83. "Tierras a campesinos de San Juan de Limay," *Novedades*, December 12, 1964.

84. Cabestrero, *Leonel Rugama*, 208–9, 266. Though previously dependent on León, the Diocese of Estelí was founded in 1962, and with the installation of a bishop, the city's church was elevated to the status of cathedral; see Manuel Ortega Hegg and Marcelina Castillo, *Religión y política: la experiencia de Nicaragua* (Managua: Ruth Casa Editorial, 2006), 96.

85. "Monseñor Chavarría declara: Temo el incremento de la violencia en Estelí," *Novedades*, April 23, 1965; "Señalan infiltración roja en el campesinado de Estelí," *LP*, June 20, 1964.

86. Filemón Moncada, interview with author, Estelí, 2008. The renowned labor leader Domingo Sánchez Salgado (Chagüitillo), organizer of Managua's construction workers, was also arrested in Estelí and Cofradías (Pueblo Nuevo) for "leftist activities" in Estelí; "6 presos por actividades izquierdistas," *LP*, January 6, 1965; Consejo de Estado, *Primera legislatura, 1980*, 40.

87. "Cadena de incendios en Estelí," *LP*, April 20, 1965; "Fuegos aún no aclarados: Investigación y temor en Estelí" and "Libertados en Estelí presuntos incendiarios," *LP*, April 21, 1965; "Testigo vio terrorista, bomba de combustible encontrada," *LP*, April 22, 1965; "Nuevo incendio en Estelí: Víctima señaló ayer mismo evidencia de mano criminal," *LP*, April 26, 1965.

88. "Testigo vio terrorista, bomba de combustible encontrada," *LP*, April 22, 1965; "GN ignora tarro explosivo," *LP*, April 23, 1965.

89. "Dirigente obrero acusa a Obispo, pide reunión," *LP*, April 25, 1965.

90. The mentioned wave of repression in the western department of Chinandega is addressed in Gould, *To Lead as Equals*, 225–44.

91. "Dirigente obrero acusa a Obispo, pide reunión," *LP*, April 25, 1965.

92. "Fuegos aún no aclarados: Investigación y temor en Estelí," *LP*, April 21, 1965; "Testigo vio terrorista, bomba de combustible encontrada," *LP*, April 22, 1965.

93. "Testigo vio terrorista, bomba de combustible encontrada," *LP*, April 22, 1965.

94. "Editorial: Los incendios de Estelí," *LP*, April 27, 1965.

95. Dámaso Picado, interview with author, Estelí, 2010; Adrián Gutiérrez, interview with author, Estelí, 2010.

96. "4 presos en mitin MR," *LP*, July 6, 1965; Pedro Pablo Espinoza, interview with author, Estelí, 2010.

97. "Reo enfermo relata andanzas con FSLN," *LP*, July 15, 1969.

98. "Un mes en manos de la Seguridad," *LP*, December 2, 1966.

99. "Ola de detenciones en Estelí: Presunto guerrillero capturado," *LP*, October 18, 1967; "Otro preso en Estelí," *LP*, October 21, 1967. Salvador Loza Talavera blamed the shootout on trade unionists who had fallen back into "their old vices" of drunkenness and "in this state ran into a Guardia patrol" (Loza and Rizo, *Mística y coraje*, 69).

100. Adrián Gutiérrez, interview with author, Estelí, 2010.

101. Ibid.

102. José Dolores Rayo, Jefe Político de Estelí to Vicente Navas Arana, Ministro de Gobernación, April 20, 1967, AGN, Fondo Gobernación, Sección Jefatura Política, box 46, folder 5.0.

103. Filemón Moncada, interview with author, Estelí, 2008.

104. "Guardia Nacional culatea a manifestantes obreros," *LP*, May 4, 1967.

105. Zimmermann, *Sandinista*, 96–97.

106. Rivera Quintero and Ramírez, *La marca del Zorro*, 39.

107. On the sidelines of the OLAS meeting, Dávila Bolaños met with Fidel Castro and U.S. Black Power leader Stokely Carmichael; "Más presos en Estelí," *LP*, June 6, 1967; "Organizado grupo de agitación OLAS; envían delegación a Cuba," *Novedades*, October 1, 1967; "Dos comunistas nicas en Moscú," *Novedades*, October 25, 1967; "Rehusan comer, reos de OLAS," *LP*, October 3, 1967; "Ingresa a hospital a protestar," *LP*, November 3, 1967.

108. "Estelí alcanza segundo lugar en población estudiantil," *LP*, May 16, 1969.

109. Carlos Fonseca Amador, "Mensaje del FSLN a los estudiantes revolucionarios (April 1968)," in *Bajo la bandera del sandinismo* (Managua: Editorial Nueva Nicaragua, 1982), 60.

110. Carlos Fonseca Amador, "Notas sobre la montaña y algunos otros temas," Octubre 8, 1976, CHM-MR, E-001, C-010, 000259.

111. Leonel Raudez, interview by S. T., Ocotal, Nueva Segovia, 1980, IHNCA-CNA, 2A-54.

112. For more on this event, see Francisco J. Barbosa, "July 23, 1959: Student Protest and State Violence as Myth and Memory in León, Nicaragua," *Hispanic American Historical Review* 85, no. 2 (2005): 187–222.

113. "Misa en Estelí por mártires," *LP*, July 24, 1963; "GN disuelve a estudiantes," *LP*, July 24, 1964.

114. "Paro en el instituto de Estelí," *LP*, May 10, 1968.

115. Clemente Rodríguez, Ramón Parrales, Rolando Benavides, Armindo Valenzuela, and Gloria Sotomayor to Indalecio Rodríguez, July 12, 1968, and J. I. Rodríguez to student leaders, July 22, 1968, AGN, Fondo Gobernacíon, Sección Jefatura Política, box 46, folder 15.0.

116. "Intranquilidad en Estelí," *LP*, September 23, 1968.

117. Leonel Rugama, *The Earth Is a Satellite of the Moon*, trans. Sara Miles, Richard Schaaf, and Nancy Weisberg (Willimantic, CT: Curbstone Press, 1985).

118. Carlos Fonseca, "Conmemorando el 15 de Enero de 1970," 1973, CHM-MR, E-001, C-008, 000212.

119. Cabestrero, *Leonel Rugama*, 146.

120. Ibid., 160.

121. Ibid., 272–76, 309.

122. Ibid., 297.

123. Omar Cabezas, *La montaña es algo más que una inmensa estepa verde* (Mexico City: Siglo Veintiuno Editores, 1986), 21–23. For the parallel experiences of the self-sacrificing and contradictory masculinity of the *barbudo* on the Chilean Left, see Florencia E. Mallon, "Barbudos, Warriors, and Rotos: The MIR, Masculinity, and Power in the Chilean Agrarian Reform, 1965–1974," in *Changing Men and Masculinities in Latin America*, ed. Matthew C. Gutmann (Durham, NC: Duke University Press, 2002), 179–215.

124. Sergio Ramírez, *Adiós muchachos: Una memoria de la revolución sandinista* (Mexico City: Aguilar, 1999), 38–40.

125. Luisa María Dietrich Ortega, "Looking Beyond Violent Militarized Masculinities: Guerrilla Gender Regimes in Latin America," *International Feminist Journal of Politics* 14, no. 4 (December 2012): 490.

126. Montoya, *Gendered Scenarios of Revolution*, 8.

127. Loza and Rizo, *Mística y coraje*, 68.

128. Isidora Herrera de Úbeda, interview by C. P. S., Estelí, 1980, IHNCA-CNA, 1A-270.

129. Leonel Rugama, "El estudiante y la revolución," in Cabestrero, *Leonel Rugama*, 284.

130. Cabestrero, *Leonel Rugama*, 285.

131. Isidora Herrera de Úbeda, interview by C. P. S., Estelí, 1980, IHNCA-CNA, 1A-270.

132. "Cae preso, por vivas a Sandino," *LP*, January 26, 1969.

133. "8 muertos en fuertes combates en Managua," *LP*, July 17, 1969.

134. "Desorden general en las escuelas universitarias," *LP*, July 18, 1969; Cabestrero, *Leonel Rugama*, 321; *Leonel Rugama: Datos biográficos* (Managua: Secretaría Nacional de Propaganda y Educación Política del F.S.L.N., 1980), 10.

135. "Por un entierro simbólico, dos entierros verdaderos," *LP*, July 18, 1969, "Profesores, directiva del Instituto condenan matanza," *LP*, July 27, 1969;

"Capturados en Estelí cabecillas de la manifestación Sandinista," *Novedades*, July 26, 1969. Though Barrantes had regularly written articles for *La Prensa*, two days after the deaths, the paper referred to the murdered men as "two extremists," even while noting that yet another *LP* correspondent, Armindo Valenzuela, a Conservative alderman in Estelí, had been captured by the OSN ("Seguridad captura a munícipe de Estelí," *LP*, July 23, 1969).

136. "Profesores, directiva del Instituto condenan matanza," *LP*, July 27, 1969; "Protesta todo el clero de Estelí," *LP*, August 8, 1969.

137. "'Investigan' la Masacre de Estelí," *LP*, August 8, 1969. "Dos importantes cortes militares," *LP*, August 26, 1969; "Alguién por error disparó a la multitud, Meneses alega en Estelí," *LP*, August 28, 1969.

138. José Indalecio Rodríguez to Ministro de Gobernación and President Somoza, July 18, 1970, AGN, Fondo Gobernacíon, Sección Jefatura Política, box 46, folder 15.0; "Propaganda para misas silenciada" and "Concurrida misa de Luis Barrantes," *LP*, July 20, 1970.

139. Many Estelian youths were recruited by José Benito Escobar and Enrique Lorente, particularly for the 1970 guerrilla campaign in Zinica (Cabestrero, *Leonel Rugama*, 249).

140. "No obtuvo una beca y se metió al Frente," *LP*, January 17, 1970; "Funeral rápido a Rugama en Estelí," *LP*, January 18, 1970; "Eliminada otra célula comunista," *Novedades*, January 16, 1970. Cabestrero, *Leonel Rugama*, 406; Ramírez, *Adiós muchachos*, 40; Zimmermann, *Sandinista*, 119. For more on the changing historical memory of this episode, see Hilary Francis, "¡Que Se Rinda Tu Madre! Leonel Rugama and Nicaragua's Changing Politics of Memory," *Journal of Latin American Cultural Studies* 21, no. 2 (2012): 235–52.

141. "Muerto en asalto al Banco Nacional," *LP*, May 5, 1970. Months later police patrols tore apart five houses in Estelí searching for Rugama's friend and fellow student organizer Enrique Lorente Ruiz. Lorente was himself killed by the GN in León two months later ("Perjudicada por la Seguridad, Estelí," *LP*, May 28, 1970).

142. "Guerrilleros Estelianos muertos: 7," *LP*, May 17, 1970.

143. Adrián Gutiérrez, interview by author, Estelí, 2010; "Muerto a balazos agente de Seguridad en Estelí: Ciudad ocupada militarmente," *LP*, March 16, 1970.

144. "Bodegas de tabaco arden en Estelí," *LP*, March 25, 1970; "Fuego consume medio millón en tabaco," *LP*, April 9, 1970.

145. "Guerrilleros Estelianos muertos: 7," *LP*, May 17, 1970.

THREE.    *Persecuting the Living Christ*

1. María Briones, interview by L. G. T., Sabana Redonda, Estelí, 1980, IHNCA-CNA, 1A-753.

2. Ibid.

3. Daniel Levine puts it this way in his critical review of the literature on liberation theology in Nicaragua: "The issues it raises are not the exclusive prov-

ince of professional intellectuals—ordinary people debate and discuss them all the time, and act according to their rights. The methods of intellectual history are, therefore, not adequate to the task. Analysis has got to move out of the library and start listening to popular voices and asking how movements start, grow, and survive"; Levine, "How Not to Understand Liberation Theology, Nicaragua, or Both," *Journal of Interamerican Studies and World Affairs* 32, no. 3 (1990): 231.

4. Elizabeth E. Brusco, *The Reformation of Machismo: Evangelical Conversion and Gender in Colombia* (Austin: University of Texas Press, 2011). However, similar campaigns against alcoholism and "traditional vices" are mentioned in the context of El Salvador and Chiapas, Mexico; see Jenny Pearce, *Promised Land: Peasant Rebellion in Chalatenango, El Salvador* (London: Latin America Bureau, 1986), 285; Christine Eber, "'Take My Water': Liberation through Prohibition in San Pedro Chenalhó, Chiapas, Mexico," *Social Science & Medicine* 53, no. 2 (2001): 251–62; Aaron Bobrow-Strain, *Intimate Enemies: Landowners, Power, and Violence in Chiapas* (Durham, NC: Duke University Press, 2007), 71.

5. Kampwirth, *Women and Guerrilla Movements*, 18.

6. As Roger Lancaster put it in his ethnographic study of liberation theology, the new Christian worldview was "simultaneously and without contradiction, both 'conservative' and 'revolutionary'" (Lancaster, *Thanks to God and the Revolution*, 98).

7. On the role of such a "providentialist" discourse in Nicaraguan political culture, see Andrés Pérez Baltodano, *Entre el Estado Conquistador y el Estado Nación: providencialismo, pensamiento político y estructuras de poder en el desarrollo histórico de Nicaragua* (Managua: Instituto de Historia de Nicaragua y Centroamérica, Universidad Centroamericana, 2003).

8. Diócesis de Estelí, "Presencia cristiana en el proceso revolucionario," in *Apuntes para una teología nicaragüense: Encuentro de teología: 8–14 de septiembre de 1980* (San José: Departamento Ecuménico de Investigaciones, 1981), 45.

9. Ortega Hegg and Castillo, *Religión y política*, 109.

10. Frutos Valle, "Religiosidad popular en Estelí," cited in Diego Irarrázaval, "Nicaragua: Una sorprendente religiosidad," in *Religión y política en América Central: Hacia una nueva interpretación de la religiosidad popular*, ed. Pablo Richard and Diego Irarrázaval (San José: Departamento Ecuménico de Investigaciones, 1981), 38. Lancaster casts liberation theology as emerging directly out of traditional, popular Christianity (Lancaster, *Thanks to God and the Revolution*, 61, 85). In the Segovias, however, the new spiritual currents were a conscious reaction against the traditional practices of folk religion and clearly arrived from outside of the communities.

11. Christian Smith, *The Emergence of Liberation Theology: Radical Religion and Social Movement Theory* (Chicago: University of Chicago Press, 1991), 122–64.

12. *De cara al futuro de la Iglesia en Nicaragua* (Managua: Ediciones Fichero Pastoral Centroamericano, 1968).

13. Juan Hervas, *Manual de dirigentes de cursillos de cristiandad* (Madrid: Euramérica, 1968); Rosa María Pochet Coronado and Abelino Martínez, *Nicaragua—Iglesia: Manipulación o profecía?* (San José: Departamento Ecuménico de Investigaciones, 1987), 75–76; Williams, *The Catholic Church and Politics in Nicaragua and Costa Rica*, 43.

14. Carlos Mantica, "Ubicación del método de cursillos dentro de la Pastoral de Conjunto," in *De cara al futuro de la Iglesia en Nicaragua*, 191.

15. Debra Sabia, *Contradiction and Conflict: The Popular Church in Nicaragua* (Tuscaloosa: University of Alabama Press, 1997), 64.

16. Mantica, "Ubicación del método de cursillos dentro de la Pastoral de Conjunto," 207.

17. Teófilo Cabestrero, *No los separó la muerte: Felipe y Mary Barreda, esposos cristianos que dieron su vida por Nicaragua* (Santander: Editorial Sal Terrae, 1985), 96.

18. Josefa Ruiz Lorente, interview by author, El Calvario, Estelí, 2010.

19. For more information on this Christian Democratic tendency, which paralleled similar developments in other Latin American countries, such as Chile, see Thomas W. Walker, *The Christian Democratic Movement in Nicaragua* (Tucson: University of Arizona Press, 1970).

20. Lt. Col. Ricardo López to President Somoza, June 17, 1969, AGN, Fondo Guardia Nacional, Sección Estado Mayor, box 15, folder 265. When PSC leaders visited the town of Somoto a few years later "with the intention of activating a cell of this organization," as the jefe político put it, they were immediately "captured by intelligence agents to investigate their actions" (Ramón Fiallos Pinell to Leandro Marín Abaunza, Minister of the Interior, July 3, 1974, AGN, Fondo Gobernación, Sección Jefatura Política, box 50, folder 9.0).

21. Rivera Quintero and Ramírez, *La marca del Zorro*, 166–67.

22. Diócesis de Estelí, "Presencia cristiana en el proceso revolucionario," 46.

23. "Moderna y amplia iglesia," *LP*, May 14, 1968; "Baile a beneficio de barrio El Calvario," *LP*, September 6, 1969; Orlando Benavides ("Pancrasio"), interview with author, El Calvario, Estelí, 2010.

24. Black, *Triumph of the People*, 59; Booth, *The End and the Beginning*, 81. Interestingly, though the earthquake is at the center of most narratives of the Sandinista Revolution, it is rarely identified as the key turning point at the level of regional history.

25. Julio López, interview by A. B., Santa Cruz, Estelí, 1980, IHNCA-CNA, 1A-695; Julio López, interview with author, Estelí, 2010.

26. Equipo Pastoral de Estelí, *Camino de liberación* (Managua: Equipo Pastoral de Estelí, 1980), 35.

27. "No aceptan fin de año escolar," *LP*, October 18, 1970.

28. "Ocupan militarmente casa del Obispo," *LP*, October 20, 1970; "Monseñor Carranza protege a maestros," *LP*, October 21, 1971.

29. For rare considerations of prostitution from the perspective of liberation theology, see Margaret Eletta Guider, *Daughters of Rahab: Prostitution and the Church of Liberation in Brazil* (Minneapolis: Fortress Press, 1995); Rita Na-

kashima Brock and Susan Brooks Thistlethwaite, *Casting Stones: Prostitution and Liberation in Asia and the United States* (Minneapolis: Fortress Press, 1996). Guider argues that Brazilian liberation theology failed to transform understandings of prostitutes from sinners to "marginalized women" because of deep-seated Catholic patriarchal conceptions of female sinfulness in that country.

30. Dávila Bolaños, *El interrogatorio*, 23–24.

31. "Apostolado de los Enfermos funda dos filiales," *LP*, May 15, 1975.

32. Julio López, interview with author, Estelí, 2010.

33. Josefa Ruiz Lorente, interview with author, El Calvario, Estelí, 2010; Reina Arróliga, interview with author, Estelí, 2010.

34. Abelardo Velásquez Laguna, interview with author, Santa Cruz, Estelí, 2010.

35. Filiberto Cruz Casco, interview by A. A., El Regadío, Estelí, 1980, IHNCA-CNA, 1A-770.

36. "Gente brava es la de la Montañita," *LP*, February 11, 1965. See also Jaime Herrera Chavarría, *Estampas de mi tierra* (Estelí: Impresiones ISNAYA, 2009), 110–11.

37. Julio López, interview with author, Estelí, 2010.

38. Geraldine O'Leary-Macias, *Lighting My Fire: Memoirs between Two Worlds: The Passionate Journey of a Young American Woman* (Bloomington, IN: Trafford, 2013), 166.

39. Octavio Cruz, interview by A. B., Santa Cruz, Estelí, 1980, IHNCA-CNA, 1A-694.

40. Lilia Ramona Moncada de Velásquez, interview by A. B., Los Plancitos, Santa Cruz, Estelí, 1980, IHNCA-CNA, 1A- 686.

41. Diócesis de Estelí, "Presencia cristiana en el proceso revolucionario," 46.

42. Celso Lazo Valdivia, interview by A. B., Santa Cruz, Estelí, 1980, IHNCA-CNA, 1A-702.

43. Don Santos, interview by L. G., Las Labranzas, La Montañita, Estelí, 1980, IHNCA-CNA, 1A-677B.

44. Esteban Matute Cruz, interview by D. C., La Montañita, Estelí, 1980, IHNCA-CNA, 1A-650.

45. María Briones, interview by L. G. T., Sabana Redonda, Estelí, 1980, IHNCA-CNA, 1A-753.

46. For alternative views, see Lancaster, *Thanks to God and the Revolution*; Michael Lowy, *The War of Gods: Religion and Politics in Latin America* (London: Verso, 1996).

47. William García Rubio, interview by S. E. T., Barrio Leonardo Matute, Ocotal, Nueva Segovia, 1980, IHNCA-CAN, 2A-73.74.

48. Esteban Matute Cruz, interview by D. C., La Montañita, Estelí, 1980, IHNCA-CNA, 1A-650.

49. José del Carmen Araúz (El Segoviano), interview by A. B., Santa Cruz, Estelí, 1980, IHNCA-CNA, 1A-715.714.703.

50. Julián N. Guerrero and Lola Soriano de Guerrero, *Madriz (Monografía)* (Managua: Artes Gráficas, 1971), 67.

Notes to Pages 107–112

51. CIERA, *Nicaragua, y por eso defendemos la frontera*, 337; Angélica Fauné, *Cooperación y subordinación en las familias campesinas* (Centro para la Promoción, Investigación y el Desarrollo Rural y Social, 1990), 104.

52. Testimony, AGN-PGR, trib. 3, case 103, July 16, 1980, 14–15.

53. For more on peasant recruitment to the GN, see chapter 4.

54. José Eulogio Hernández Alvarado, interview with author, Las Sabanas, Madriz, 2010.

55. "Escuelas Radiofónicas: Gran aporte educacional católico," *LP*, August 1, 1965; "3ro año de escuelas radiofónicas," *LP*, April 17, 1968; "6 mil campesinos alfabetizados por radio, Importantísima labor de Radio Católica," *LP*, September 28, 1969; Dodson and O'Shaughnessy, *Nicaragua's Other Revolution*, 119.

56. Asociación Latinoamericana de Educación Radiofónica, *Siempre estuvimos alerta: Testimonios de las escuelas radiofónicas de Nicaragua* (Quito: Secretaría Ejecutiva ALER, 1984), 146–47.

57. Jorge Isaac Carvallo, "Campesino," sung from memory by José Eulogio Hernández Alvarado, interview with author, Las Sabanas, Madriz, 2010.

58. "Alfabetización por radio," *LP*, May 11, 1970.

59. "Campesinos hacen su propio lago," *LP*, July 18, 1968; "Veinticinco años de labor del Padre Fabretto," *LP*, July 4, 1969; "Inauguran carretera a Cusmapa," *LP*, April 27, 1969; Guerrero and Soriano de Guerrero, *Madriz (Monografía)*, 159.

60. "Más maestros trasladados en Somoto," *LP*, February 17, 1970.

61. In fact, the extremely high levels of disease and hunger in Cusmapa at times became national news; see "Epidemia causa cincuenta muertes en pueblo," *LP*, June 16, 1962; "98 por ciento de enfermos en Cusmapa: El hambre aquí es absoluto," *LP*, June 19, 1962.

62. Esmeralda Hernández Marín, interview by J. C. G., Cusmapa, Madriz, 1980, IHNCA-CNA.3C-16.

63. Ramón Fiallos to Ministerio de Gobernación, April 1, 1974, AGN, Fondo Gobernación, Sección Jefatura Política, box 50, folder 9.0.

64. Tula Baca to Vicente Navas, December 12, 1968, in ibid.

65. Julián Vásquez A. to Ministerio de Gobernación, February 27, 1970, AGN, Fondo Gobernación, Sección Alcaldías, box 26, folder "SJ de Cusmapa."

66. Ramón Fiallos to Ministero de Gobernación, April 5, 1975, AGN, Fondo Gobernación, Sección Jefatura Politica, box 50, folder 9.0.

67. Junta directiva, Comunidad Indígena de Cusmapa to Ramón Fiallos P. Jefe Político, March 20, 1974, AGN, Fondo Gobernación, Sección Jefatura Política, box 50, folder 9.0 "Somoto."

68. "Presidente Somoza Aprueba Donación...," November 5, 1968, AGN, Fondo Gobernación, Sección Alcaldía Municipales, box 16, folder 5.0; Alison Rooper, *Fragile Victory: A Nicaraguan Community at War* (London: Weidenfeld and Nicolson, 1987), 43, 57–59, 106; O'Leary-Macias, *Lighting My Fire*, 67–68.

69. Castillo Herrera, *La tradición oral*, 90.

70. "Pueblo contra Alcalde" *LP*, September 11, 1974. Diputado René Molina arrived to negotiate with the protesters but refused ask Cerrato to step down.

71. Comité Pro-Destitución del Alcalde Municipal de la Ciudad de Condega, "Acta No. Uno," September 6, 1974. AGN, Fondo Gobernación, Sección Alcaldías Municipales, box 16, folder 5.1.

72. Frente Sandinista de Liberación Nacional, Comando Juan José Quezada, *Frente Sandinista: diciembre victorioso* (Mexico City: Editorial Diógenes, 1976).

73. Dirk Kruijt, *Guerrillas: War and Peace in Central America* (London: Zed Books, 2008), 51.

74. Carlos Fonseca Amador, "Notas sobre algunos problemas actuales," April 20, 1972, CHM-MR, E-001, C-009, 000245.

75. Carlos Fonseca Amador, "2nda Charla del Co. Carlos Fonseca," September 11, 1973, CHM-MR, E-001, C-008, 000214.

76. Consejo de Estado, *Primera legislatura, 1980*, 19–20; Omar Cabezas, *Canción de amor para los hombres* (Managua: Editorial Nueva Nicaragua, 1988), 39–175; Humberto Ortega Saavedra, *La epopeya de la insurrección: Nicaragua siglo XX: Pensamiento y acción, análisis histórico, narración inédita* (Managua: Lea Grupo Editorial, 2004), 278; Baltodano, *Memorias de la lucha sandinista*, 1:512–13; Fernández de la Villa, *El pequeño gigante: La vida de Manuelito Maldonado Lovo*, 76–77.

77. Manuel Morales Fonseca, interview with author, Managua, 2010.

78. Phillip Berryman, *Liberation Theology: Essential Facts about the Revolutionary Movement in Latin America — and Beyond* (Philadelphia: Temple University Press, 1987), 74.

79. Asociación Latinoamericana de Educación Radiofónica, *Siempre estuvimos alerta*, 146–47.

80. Amanda Centeno, interview with author, Condega, Estelí, 2008.

81. Cabezas, *La montaña es algo más que una inmensa estepa verde*, 243–45; Rooper, *Fragile Victory*, 57–58. In the town itself, the college-educated children of two of the town's prominent Somocista patriarchs (Romeo González and Santiago Baldovinos) also joined the guerrillas during this period.

82. Partido Conservador de Nicaragua, *Programa de gobierno gel Dr. Fernando Agüero Rocha candidato a la presidencia de la República por el Partido Conservador de Nicaragua y bases de acción para un gobierno de unidad nacional* (Managua: Unión Cardoza, 1966), 23.

83. Ibid.

84. Fermin Zedilla Peralta, interview by J. R. L., Robledalito, Condega, Estelí, 1980, IHNCA-CNA, 1B-242; José del Carmen Araúz, interview by A. B., Santa Cruz, Estelí, 1980, IHNCA-CNA, 1A-715.714.703.

85. "Notas sobre la montaña y algunos otros temas," October 8, 1976, CHM-MR, E-001, C-010, 000259; Zimmermann, *Sandinista*, 192.

86. Cabezas, *Canción de amor para los hombres*, 201; Mónica Baltodano, *Memorias de la lucha sandinista*, Tomo II, *El crisol de las insurrecciones: Las Segovias, Managua y León* (Managua: Instituto de Historia de Nicaragua y Centroamérica, Universidad Centroamericana, 2010), 54.

87. *Cartilla Campesina*, n.d., CHM, Fondo Nuevo, box 15, doc. 80, 3.

88. Ibid., 4.

89. *Programa histórico del FSLN* (Managua: Departamento de Propaganda y Educación Política del FSLN, 1984).

90. Ibid.

91. Juan Antonio Espinoza Hernández, interview by J. C. G., Cusmapa, Madriz, 1980, IHNCA-CNA, 3C-7.

92. Juan Alvarado Sánchez, interview by D. A., La Joya 2, Cusmapa, Madriz, 1980, IHNCA-CNA, 3C-13.

93. María Briones, interview by L. G. T., Sabana Redonda, Estelí, 1980, IHNCA-CNA, 1A-753.

94. Octavio Cruz, interview by A. B., Santa Cruz, Estelí, 1980, IHNCA-CNA, 1A-694.

95. "Clínicas, clases y avengas del FSLN," *LP*, August 4, 1976.

96. Leandro Córdoba, interview by J. L., Los Planes, Condega, Estelí, 1980, IHNCA-CNA, 1B-125; Rooper, *Fragile Victory*, 91; Cabezas, *La montaña es algo más que una inmensa estepa verde*, 284–88.

97. Padre Julio López, interview with author, Estelí, 2010.

98. Turner Shelton, "Anti-Guerrilla Activity Reported," U.S. Embassy Cable 3050, August 6, 1975, PlusD.

99. Letter from Bayardo Arce to René Nuñez, April 17, 1976, CHM-MR, E-002, C-017, 000492.

100. "Muerte alto dirigente del FSLN," *LP*, June 28, 1976. For more information on his death, see chapter 4.

101. Letter from Bayardo Arce to Nelson Velásquez, December 15, 1976; Letter from Bayardo Arce to "Leopoldo," November 26, 1976, CHM-MR, E-002, C-019, 000557; Cabezas, *Canción de amor para los hombres*, 231.

102. Letter from Bayardo Arce to Omar Cabezas, forwarded to Augusto Salinas Pinell, June 11, 1976; found by OSN near the house of Leandro Córdoba in Los Planes, Condega, Estelí, and transcribed in OSN file for Bayardo Arce, CHM-MR, E-002, C-017, 000491.

103. Ibid. Arce also regularly sent instructions on compartmentalization to Mónica Baltodano, insisting that "NO ONE, ABSOLUTELY NO ONE except the houses' residents should know that the house is functioning as a safe house. When repression comes, we'll see that we were right" (Letter from Bayardo Arce to Mónica Baltodano, August 8, 1976, CHM-MR, E-002, C-021, 000611; emphasis in the original).

104. Cabezas, *Canción de amor para los hombres*, 138–39.

105. James Theberge, "Summary of Analysis on Hard Core Human Rights Situation," U.S. Embassy Cable 1231, March 15, 1975, PlusD.

106. Testimony, AGN-PGR, trib. 6, case 147, September 9, 1980, 19–20.

107. Anonymous, interview by A. B., Llano Redondo, Santa Cruz, Estelí, 1980, INHNCA-CNA, 1A-702.

108. Los Exiliados Políticos Nicaragüenses, "Las torturas comprobadas," n.d., 19; Los Prisioneros Sandinistas al Pueblo de Nicaragua, "Las golpizas y 36 días de huelga de hambre no amilanan a los Sandinistas," January 5, 1977, CHM-MR, E-002, C-016, 000474.

109. José Eulogio Hernández, interview with author, Las Sabanas, Madriz, 2010. At the time, the FSLN believed that Eulogio was also among the members of the indigenous community killed (Letter from "Iván" (René Núñez) to "Hermano," April 17, 1976, CHM-MR, E-002, C-017, 000492).

110. José Luis Velásquez Araúz, interview with A. B., Santa Cruz, Estelí, 1980, IHNCA-CNA, 1A-725.

111. Letter, Bayardo Arce to "Leopoldo," November 26, 1976, CHM-MR, E-002, C-019, 000557; Letter, Mónica Baltodano to Bayardo Arce, December 2, 1976, CHM-MR, E-002, C-021, 000611; Letter, Bayardo Arce to Comité Regional, December 18, 1976, CHM-MR, E-002, C-021, 000610.

112. Julio López, interview with author, Estelí, 2010.

113. José del Carmen Araúz (El Segoviano), interview by A. B., Santa Cruz, Estelí, 1980, IHNCA-CNA.1A-715.714.703.

114. Miriam Díaz Rodríguez, Ruth Aguilar Pérez, and María Auxiliadora Chiong Gutiérrez, "La herencia colonial en los minifeudos de Santa Cruz (Estelí)," in *El universo de la tierra: Las culturas campesinas en el Pacífico y centro de Nicaragua: Una investigación socio-antropológica de la Universidad Nacional Autónoma de Nicaragua*, ed. Leo Gabriel (Managua: Editorial Universitaria, 1993).

115. Fermin Zedilla Peralta, interview by J. R. L., Robledalito, Condega, Estelí, 1980, IHNCA-CNA, 1B-242.

116. Moisés Calero, interview by E. G., Condega, Estelí, 1980, IHNCA-CNA, 1B-13.14.

117. Amanda Centeno, interview with author, Condega, Estelí, 2008.

118. A number of the high school students who went into exile, including Santiago Baldovino's brother, also went underground and made preparations to leave the country; see Letter, Bayardo Arce to Mónica Baltodano, December 6, 1976, CHM-MR, E-002, C-021, 000611; Castillo Herrera, *La tradición oral*, 96–97.

119. Anna Lisa Peterson, *Martyrdom and the Politics of Religion: Progressive Catholicism in El Salvador's Civil War* (Albany: State University of New York Press, 1997). On the use of martyrdom in solidifying the religious and political authority of the FSLN government during the 1980s, see Lancaster, *Thanks to God and the Revolution*, chap. 5.

120. Letter, FSLN (destacamento del norte) to the 12th Cursillo de Cristiandad, February 1976, CHM-MR, E-002, C-021, 000609 (emphasis in original).

121. Ibid.

122. Ibid.

123. James Theberge, "Conservatives Denounce Human Rights Violations," U.S. Embassy Cable 40182, October 29, 1975, PlusD.

124. "Regresan los del 27 de diciembre; revela Somoza," *LP*, March 26, 1976.

125. Ibid.

126. "CIA da nuevo ropaje a Somoza," *Gaceta Sandinista*, May 1976, 22.

FOUR.    *"They Planted Corn and Harvested Guardias"*

1. Letter, AGN-PGR, trib. 1, caso 87, September 6, 1980, 31.

2. Testimony, AGN-PGR, trib. 1, caso 87, September 6, 1980, 36.

3. Steve J. Stern, *The Secret History of Gender: Women, Men, and Power in Late Colonial Mexico* (Chapel Hill: University of North Carolina Press, 2000), 159.

4. Pilar Arias, *Nicaragua, revolución: Relatos de combatientes del Frente Sandinista* (Mexico: Siglo Veintiuno Editores, 1988), 95; CIERA, *Nicaragua, y por eso defendemos la frontera*, 358–59; Ramírez, *Adiós muchachos*, 132.

5. The sheer number of recruits from the indigenous communities of Madriz supports Timothy Brown's contention that most former Guardias who participated in the CIA-backed, anti-Sandinista Contra army in the 1980s identified as "indios." He, however, stretches this argument to the point of ethnic essentialism (Brown, *The Real Contra War*, 11, 89).

6. Testimony, Manuel Benavides, AGN-PGR, trib. 2, caso 287, 20.

7. Manuel Maldonado to Tribunal Especial, October 4, 1980, AGN-PGR, trib. 8, caso 176, September 9, 1980, 11.

8. Francisco Fiallos Navarro, "La Guardia Nacional ¿Un ejército de ocupación?," *LP*, August 6, 1978; Millett, *Guardians of the Dynasty*, 198. Michael Gobat claims that with the decline of caudillo rule in rural areas, the GN became "a channel for popular demands and aspirations. As such, the Guardia became the most effective instrument through which the state could not only repress popular sectors but also mobilize and control them politically" (Gobat, *Confronting the American Dream*, 271).

9. For the classic study of how "ordinary" Germans were led to commit mass killings through conformity during the Holocaust, see Christopher R. Browning, *Ordinary Men: Reserve Police Battalion 101 and the Final Solution in Poland* (New York: HarperCollins, 1993).

10. Beattie, *The Tribute of Blood*; Nicola Foote and René Harder Horst, *Military Struggle and Identity Formation in Latin America: Race, Nation, and Community During the Liberal Period* (Gainesville: University Press of Florida, 2010); Neufeld, *The Blood Contingent*; Jonathan D. Ablard, "'The Barracks Receives Spoiled Children and Returns Men': Debating Military Service, Masculinity and Nation-Building in Argentina, 1901–1930," *The Americas* 74, no. 3 (2017): 299–329.

11. Similarly, through their participation in the military, Lesley Gill argues, "subaltern" indigenous men in Bolivia "shape a positive sense of masculine identity that is, nevertheless, linked to collusion with their own subordination and tied to other gendered patterns of social degradation"; Gill, "Creating Citizens, Making Men: The Military and Masculinity in Bolivia," *Cultural Anthropology* 12, no. 4 (1997): 527–50.

12. Michael J. Schroeder, "The Sandino Rebellion Revisited: Civil War, Imperialism, Popular Nationalism, and State Formation Muddied Up Together in the Segovias of Nicaragua, 1926–1934," in *Close Encounters of Empire: Writing the Cultural History of U.S.–Latin American Relations*, ed. Gilbert M. Joseph, Catherine LeGrand, and Ricardo D. Salvatore (Durham, NC: Duke University Press, 1998), 236–37, 248–49.

13. Arias, *Nicaragua, revolución*, 95. See also Zimmermann, *Sandinista*, 96–97.

14. Anonymous 1, interview with author, Totogalpa, Madriz, 2008.

15. AGN-PGR, trib. 7, caso 132, September 27, 1980, 26.
16. Anonymous 2, interview with author, San Lucas, Madriz, 2010.
17. Emilio Flores Obregón, interview by D. V., Pueblo Nuevo, Estelí, 1980, IHNCA-CNA, 1D-5.
18. AGN-PGR, trib. 6, caso 27, March 20, 1980, 5–6.
19. Guerrero and Soriano de Guerrero, *Madriz (Monografía)*, 49.
20. "Somoto marcha hacia atrás," *LP*, April 9, 1970.
21. Anonymous 3, interview with author, Estanzuela, Estelí, 2008.
22. AGN-PGR, trib. 3, caso 63, May 28, 1980, 4.
23. Though a constant problem, some of the worst droughts in living memory occurred in the 1970s. During the extended drought of 1971–72, Nicaragua's National Bank declared a "critical situation," which threatened to "bring ruin to the country"; see "Sequia había ya causado serios daños," *LP*, June 14, 1971; "Sequía comienza a hacer estragos," *LP*, June 23, 1976; "Sequía daña más de 20 mil manzanas," *LP*, June 30, 1975; "Pérdida total de granos en Somoto," *LP*, July 17, 1975; "Emergencia por causa de sequía," *LP*, September 16, 1975.
24. AGN-PGR, trib. 4, caso 137, August 11, 1980, 7. Another peasant from San Antonio, Yalagüina, recalled signing a GN contract because "it was a year-long summer and when I saw all of the dust blowing by (*aquel polvazal*), I decided to reenlist because I'm very poor" (Tribunales Especiales, trib. 2, caso 162, September 20, 1980, 4).
25. AGN-PGR, trib. 1, caso 54, 26; trib. 1, caso. 24, 21; trib. 1., caso 331, 11; trib. 8, caso 176, 6.
26. AGN-PGR, trib. 1, caso 117, August 11, 1980, 2.
27. In 1957, a GN recalled that they could earn five pesos in the GN compared to two on the haciendas (AGN-PGR, trib. 1, caso 151, September 8, 1980, 5).
28. Anonymous 4, interview with author, Sonís, Madriz, 2010.
29. Black, *Triumph of the People*, 51; Booth, *The End and the Beginning*, 93.
30. AGN-PGR, trib. 3, caso 227, October 10, 1980, 1. The uniform as a status marker is a recurrent theme in GN accounts. One campesino from San Lucas signed up because "a friend told me that it was nice, they gave you medicine and clothes. And I liked the Guardia for the uniform and the pay" (AGN-PGR, trib. 6, caso 421, 4).
31. The number of Guardias providing personal protection for the Somoza family was enormous. One bodyguard recalled "surrounding the sector where the dictator was to assure no one entered" (AGN-PGR, trib. 7, caso 166, September 24, 1980, 4). The same was true of the security detail that traveled with Somoza during his elections and protected Julio and Roberto Somoza Portocarrero, two of Tachito's sons, and also his mother, Salvadora Debayle (trib. 2, caso 343, November 24, 1980, 3). Another bodyguard from Somoto specifically noted providing security for Tachito's mistress (Dinorah Sampson) at his Montelimar sugar estate and his vacation home on Corn Island (trib. 3, caso 134, 5). Other Guardias from Somoto were assigned to provide security at Sampson's house and even work as her gardeners (AGN-PGR, trib. 7, caso 128, September 27, 1980, 2; trib. 4, caso 137, August 11, 1980, 6). José Rodríguez Somoza, Somoza

García's illegitimate son and a commanding GN officer, also had Guardias protecting his office, hacienda, and his wife's mansion at all times (trib. 1, caso 442, December 6, 1980, 4).

32. Peter Grubbe, "Nicaragua vista por un alemán," *Revista Conservadora* 1, no. 10 (1962): 23–25.

33. Anonymous 5, interview with author, Somoto, Madriz, 2008.

34. David Carey Jr. suggests that Mayan Guatemalans identified with the dictator Jorge Ubico, the only president who visited them and let them wear indigenous garb on some occasions; Carey, "Mayan Soldier-Citizen: Ethnic Pride in the Guatemala Military, 1925–1945," in *Military Struggle and Identity Formation in Latin America: Race, Nation, and Community During the Liberal Period*, ed. Nicola Foote and René D. Harder Horst (Gainesville: University Press of Florida, 2010), 136–56.

35. Gould, *To Die in This Way*, 50.

36. Norma Fuller argues that indigenous men in Peru, denied masculine honor by the dominant discourse, were able to challenge racial hierarchies by embracing virile behavior and "feminizing" nonindigenous men; Fuller, "The Social Constitution of Gender Identity among Peruvian Men," in *Changing Men and Masculinities in Latin America*, ed. Matthew C. Gutmann (Durham, NC: Duke University Press, 2003), 316–31.

37. Anonymous 6, interview with author, Yalagüina, Madriz, 2010.

38. Anonymous 1, interview with author, Totogalpa, Madriz, 2008.

39. Anonymous 7, interview with author, Somoto, Madriz, 2010.

40. Anonymous 4, interview with author, Sonís, Somoto, Madriz, 2010.

41. Ibid.

42. Justiniano Pérez, *Los mitos de la Guardia Nacional de Nicaragua* (Miami, FL: Orbis, 2007), 59. In Estelí, the lieutenant responsible for traffic violations gave out tickets with 200- to 300- córdoba fines, threatening to jail the bus drivers who did not pay up (Humberto Pérez Rugama, "Testimonio Escrito," December 13, 1979, AGN-PGR, trib. 9, caso 386, November 19, 1980, 45).

43. Silvio Incer, interview by Robert J. Alexander, Rio Piedras, Puerto Rico, June 22, 1964, Robert J. Alexander Papers, reel 10, frame 812.

44. "Written Testimony [Santa Isabel, Somoto, Madriz]," AGN-PGR, trib. 2, caso 70. May 23, 1980, 29.

45. AGN-PGR, trib. 1, caso 69, 7.

46. AGN-PGR, trib. 1, caso 155, September 9, 1980, 4.

47. Sandinista Defense Committee, Salamasi, Yalagüina, Madriz to Tribunal Especial, AGN-PGR, trib. 1, caso 203. November 4, 1980, 18.

48. "Raso mata a dos en una cantina en Somoto," *LP*, August 1, 1977.

49. AGN-PGR, trib. 2, caso 170, September 9, 1980, 3.

50. Document, "Cuartel General de la Guardia Nacional de Nicaragua: Baja," AGN-PGR, trib. 2, caso 159, September 19, 1980, 13. Another soldier from Somoto left the GN "because I didn't follow the orders they gave me . . . because I've been a person who liked liquor very much" (AGN-PGR, trib. 2, caso 365, November 28, 1980, 1).

51. AGN-PGR, trib. 6, caso 238, October 8, 1980, 3; Cuartel General de la Guardia Nacional de Nicaragua, "Record de Servicio," May 11, 1980, 22.

52. AGN-PGR, trib. 8, caso 341, November 6, 1980, 3.

53. AGN-PGR, trib. 1, caso 48, 58.

54. AGN-PGR, trib. 1, caso 95, n.d., 1.

55. AGN-PGR, trib. 1, caso 117, August 11, 1980, 3.

56. AGN-PGR, trib. 3, caso 353, January 4, 1980, 3.

57. Anonymous 8, interview with author, Totogalpa, Madriz, 2008.

58. Anonymous 9, interview with author, San Lucas, Madriz, 2010.

59. For a lengthy spread celebrating the SOA from the perspective of the GN officer class, see *Revista de la GN*, April 1972, 19–27. For a critical, scholarly interpretation, see Lesley Gill, *The School of the Americas: Military Training and Political Violence in the Americas* (Durham, NC: Duke University Press, 2004).

60. See Wickham-Crowley, *Guerrillas and Revolution in Latin America*, 79, table 5-9. Many GN officers later accused of human rights violations took numerous courses in the United States or the Canal Zone, while the Military Academy's graduating cadets were all sent to study at the SOA each year; James Theberge, "Human Rights: Response to the Fraser Committee (Part 2)," U.S. Embassy Cable 3520, July 23, 1976, PlusD.

61. Michael Radu, "The Nature of the Insurgency," in *The Continuing Crisis: U.S. Policy in Central America and the Caribbean*, ed. Mark Falcoff and Robert Royal (Washington, DC: Ethics and Public Policy Center, 1987), 413.

62. Anonymous 6, interview with author, Yalagüina, Madriz, 2010.

63. For concurrent developments in Brazil and Guatemala, see Martha Kinsley Huggins, *Political Policing: The United States and Latin America* (Durham, NC: Duke University Press, 1998); Greg Grandin, *The Last Colonial Massacre: Latin America in the Cold War* (Chicago: University of Chicago Press, 2004).

64. Emilio Padilla, "Consideraciones sobre la subversión y la violencia," *Acción Cívica*, December 1977, 39.

65. Emilio Padilla, "Infiltración y Subversión, pt. 1," *Acción Cívica*, April 1976, 33.

66. Ibid., 34.

67. Emilio Padilla, "Infiltración y Subversión, pt. 2," *Acción Cívica*, May 1976, 29.

68. Valeria Manzano, "Sex, Gender and the Making of the 'Enemy Within' in Cold War Argentina," *Journal of Latin American Studies* 47, no. 1 (2015): 1–29; Benjamin A. Cowan, *Securing Sex: Morality and Repression in the Making of Cold War Brazil* (Chapel Hill: University of North Carolina Press, 2016).

69. AGN-PGR, trib. 6, caso 52, May 8, 1980, 5.

70. AGN-PGR, trib. 3, caso 63, May 28, 1980, 5.

71. AGN-PGR, trib. 6, caso 345. November 4, 1980, 4.

72. AGN-PGR, trib. 1, caso 35.

73. Anonymous 6, interview with author, Yalagüina, Madriz, 2010.

74. On the interplay between Civic Action, military training, and the Alliance for Progress, see Wright, *Latin America in the Era of the Cuban Revolution*, 61–70.

75. AGN-PGR, trib. 1, caso 69, 6; trib. 1, caso 151, September 8, 1980, 5; trib. 1, caso 169, September 16, 1980, 4; trib. 1, caso 442, December 6, 1980, 4; trib. 4, caso 240, October 7, 1980, 4.

76. Franklin Montenegro to Anastasio Somoza Debayle, May 10, 1975, AGN-PGR, trib. 1, caso 442, 24.

77. AGN-PGR, trib. 1, caso 180, September 19, 1980, 4.

78. AGN-PGR, trib. 3, caso 343, 4.

79. Pérez, *Los mitos de la Guardia Nacional de Nicaragua*, 125.

80. Mauricio Solaún, "Meeting with President's Son, Major Somoza," U.S. Embassy Cable 4079, August 30, 1978, PlusD.

81. AGN-PGR, trib. 6, caso 52, May 8, 1980, 5.

82. *El Infante*, September 1978, 1 (emphasis in original).

83. "Hired Guns for Nicaragua," CIA Staff Notes, Latin American Trends, July 2, 1975. Declassified Documents DDRA, 8-9.

84. *Acción Cívica*, May 1978, 58–59.

85. "The Black Berets of Hwa Rong Do," *Black Belt Magazine*, September 1978; "In Memoriam: Tribute to a Professional Warrior—Michael Echanis," *Soldier of Fortune: Journal of Professional Adventurers*, February 1979, 50; Mauricio Solaún, "Reports of Alleged American Mercenaries," U.S. Embassy Cable 2011, May 2, 1978; Solaún, "Further Report of Alleged American Mercenaries in Nicaragua," U.S. Embassy Cable 2085, May 5, 1978; Solaún, "Alleged American Mercenaries," U.S. Embassy Cable 2187, May 10, 1978; Solaún "The U.S. 'Mercenary' Issue," U.S. Embassy Cable 3073, July 6, 1978; Solaún, "Amb Conversation with Somoza: May 8," U.S. Embassy Cable 2163, May 10, 1978, PlusD; Dora Luz Romero, "Máquinas Para Matar," *La Prensa Magazine*, April 18, 2010, 20.

86. AGN-PGR, trib. 6, caso 52, May 8, 1980, 5.

87. AGN-PGR, trib. 8, caso 51, May 19, 1980, 5.

88. AGN-PGR, trib. 9, caso 51, September 23, 1980, 5.

89. Anonymous, interview with author, Somoto, Madriz, 2010. The training program was divided into four climatic sequences: the "mountain phase," the "dry phase" in desert conditions, the "humid phase" in swamplands with frequent rain, and the "coastal phase" on the Atlantic littoral (*Acción Cívica*, December 1977, 49).

90. AGN-PGR, trib. 2, caso 70, May 23, 1980, 4.

91. I borrow these terms from Leith Passmore's gendered analysis of conscripts to the Chilean military during the period of Pinochet's dictatorship. The case differs from Nicaragua in that Chilean conscripts were forced to join the military by law; Passmore, *The Wars inside Chile's Barracks: Remembering Military Service under Pinochet* (Madison: University of Wisconsin Press, 2017), 106–40.

92. Federico Allodi, "Somoza's National Guard: A Study of Human Rights Abuses, Psychological Health and Moral Development," in *The Politics of Pain: Torturers and Their Masters*, ed. Ronald D. Crelinsten and Alex Peter Schmid (Boulder, CO: Westview, 1995), 115.

93. Henry Briceño, *Un ejército dentro de un ejército: Bajo el genocidio somocista* (San José: Imprenta Borrase, 1979), 67; Black, *Triumph of the People*, 53–54; Romero, "Máquinas Para Matar," 20.

94. AGN-PGR, trib. 2, caso 80, June 14, 1980, 4. Other former EEBI soldiers strongly denied the claim of the bestializing chants, with one testifying, "They never said I was a tiger, just that I was a soldier who maintained order" (AGN-PGR, trib. 6, caso 52, May 8, 1980, 4). Former GN/EEBI officer Justiniano Pérez claims that this reputation was a myth perpetuated by the FSLN (Pérez, *Los mitos de la Guardia Nacional de Nicaragua*, 132).

95. AGN-PGR, trib. 8, caso 51, May 21, 1980, 5.

96. *Acción Cívica*, February 1976, 38–39; Justiniano Pérez, *EEBI: Los Quijotes Del Ocaso* (Miami, FL: Orbis, 2008), 16.

97. Briceño, *Un ejército dentro de un ejército*, 24; Pérez, *Los mitos de la Guardia Nacional de Nicaragua*, 129.

98. The same EEBI soldier also recalled that he and peers were sent to West Point, Fort Sherman, Fort Gulick, the Canal Zone, Chile, El Salvador, and Petén in Guatemala (Anonymous, interview with author, Somoto, Madriz, 2010). One Las Sabanas resident entered the GN in 1977 and he was sent to the EEBI, "where he remained under the direction of el Chigüin, who designated him as an instructor of these troops due to his technical capacity . . . acquired in a course he took in 1978 in the Salvadoran armed forces." Of the 15 men who took a parachuting course in El Salvador, he recalled proudly, many did not even finish the training because of broken limbs (AGN-PGR, trib. 1, caso 54, 6).

99. Robert H. Holden, "Securing Central America against Communism: The United States and the Modernization of Surveillance in the Cold War," *Journal of Interamerican Studies and World Affairs* 41, no. 1 (1999): 1–30.

100. "Guerrilleros Estelianos muertos: 7," *LP*, May 17, 1970.

101. Fifteen top officers were sent for training in counterintelligence after 1966. Among those intelligence officers trained by the SOA were Samuel Genie, Gustavo Montiel, Bayardo Jirón, Oscar Morales ("Moralitos"), Iván Alegrett, Ronald Sampson, John Lee Wong, Augustín Torres López ("El Coto"), Ricardo Lau, and Gonzalo Lacayo ("Lacayito"); see School of the Americas Watch, SOA/WHINSEC Graduates 1946–2004 Database.

102. Baltodano, *Memorias de la lucha sandinista*, 1:33; Enrique Peña-Pérez, *Secretos de la revolución sandinista* (New York: Book-Mart Press, 2004), 67.

103. Amnesty International, *The Republic of Nicaragua: An Amnesty International Report Including the Findings of a Mission to Nicaragua, 10–15 May 1976* (London: Amnesty International Publications, 1977), 32. See the interview with Samuel Genie, in *LP*, January 11, 1969.

104. AGN-PGR, trib, 3, February 2, 1980, 4–5.

105. Testimony of GRB, AGN-PGR, trib. 3, February 2, 1980, 35.

106. Ibid.

107. One Christian activist claimed, "Just by hearing that so-and-so worked for the government, you knew immediately that they were a 'Guardia.' Even if they didn't wear a uniform or carry a gun" (Anonymous 12, interview with author, San José de Cusmapa, 2010).

108. Peña-Pérez, *Secretos de la revolución sandinista*, 66–67. For discussions of the role of denunciations in the Nazi dictatorship, Stalinism in the Soviet Union, and the Trujillo regime in the Dominican Republic, see Sheila Fitzpatrick and Robert Gellately, "Introduction to the Practices of Denunciation in Modern

European History," *The Journal of Modern History* 68, no. 4 (1996): 747–67; Lauren Derby, "In the Shadow of the State: The Politics of Denunciation and Panegyric during the Trujillo Regime in the Dominican Republic, 1940–1958," *Hispanic American Historical Review* 83, no. 2 (2003): 295–344.

109.  Anonymous, interview by A. U., Somoto, Madriz, 1980, IHNCA-CNA.3A-53.

110.  Pérez, *Semper fidelis*, 96–97.

111.  Anonymous 11, interview with author, Somoto, Madriz, 2010.

112.  See chapter 1 for more on la Magnífica, the PLN membership card distributed to all Somoza voters. The U.S. embassy later noted that OSN paramilitaries were "given credentials as ad honorem members which may help them if they encounter difficulties with the government or are seeking favors" (Mauricio Solaún, "Analysis of 'White Hand' Existence," U.S. Embassy Cable 753, February 6, 1979, PlusD). Some individuals even purchased OSN cards, such as a van driver who paid 100 córdobas for his ID so that he could carry more passengers between Estelí and Managua than permitted by law (AGN-PGR, trib. 5, caso 29, April 30, 1980, 4–5).

113.  Comandante of Estelí to President Schick and Anastasio Somoza, August 19, 1965, AGN, Fondo Guardia Nacional, Sección Estado Mayor, box 22, folder 314.

114.  AGN-PGR, trib. 1, caso 122, August 15, 1980, 5.

115.  Testimony, trib. 6, caso 31, April 12, 1980, 29.

116.  Anthropologist Roger Lancaster writes that desmoche provides Nicaraguan men with "a forum for male socializing and camaraderie as well as an arena for male competition. The game's importance in masculine culture would be difficult to overstate" (Lancaster, *Life Is Hard*, 192).

117.  MININT Declaration, Romeo González Espinoza, AGN-PGR, trib. 2, caso 330, November 20, 1980, 18.

118.  MININT Declaration, AGN-PGR, trib. 4, caso 11, February 4, 1980, 46; MININT declaration of ECC, trib. 4, caso 11, February 4, 1980, 56.

119.  MININT Declaration of J. C. A., AGN-PGR, trib. 4, caso 11, February 4, 1980, 49.

120.  "Gustavo" was also related to Gen. Gustavo Montiel of the GN.

121.  Testimony, Jaime González Almendárez, in AGN-PGR, trib. 6, caso 31, April 12, 1980, 29. Like other orejas, at times Gustavo felt more powerful and important than GN officials, denouncing even the staff of the National Guard base in Estelí as being infiltrated by the FSLN; see Testimony of Guillermo Sovalbarro Rodríguez, trib. 6, caso 31, April 12, 1980, 25; "OSN, Reporte de Información," June 14, 1977 in trib. 6, caso 31, April 12, 1980, 60.

122.  A number of these men were later accused of dumping the body of an unknown young man into a well alongside the road to Yalí (Testimony, Jaime González Almendárez, AGN-PGR, trib. 6, caso 31, April 12, 1980, 29).

123.  Testimony, Jaime González Almendárez, in AGN-PGR, trib. 6, caso 31, April 12, 1980, 29.

124.  In one case, Gustavo even asked local *LP* journalist Henry Vargas to serve as godfather to one of his children and offered him employment at Somo-

za's paper, *Novedades*, complete with a professional camera and paid travel to the United States. When Vargas refused, Gustavo denounced his supposed "friend" for "writing articles against the government and the GN"; Chronology of OSN denunciations (entry July 19, 1978), Testimony of Henry Vargas, AGN-PGR trib. 6, caso 31, April 12, 1980, 25–26.

125. Testimony, AGN-PGR, trib. 2, caso 83, June 18, 1980, 34.

126. "Entregan cadáver de joven del FSLN," *LP*, November 23, 1971.

127. "Pista de hombre clave del FSLN," *LP*, July 14, 1976.

128. AGN-PGR, trib. 6, caso 353, June 11, 1980, 6.

129. Guardia Nacional, Oficina de Leyes y Relaciones Públicas, "Informe Oficial," cited in *LP*, June 28, 1976.

130. Testimony, AGN-PGR, trib. 4, caso 63, May 28, 1980, 5.

131. AGN-PGR, trib. 4, caso 63, May 28, 1980, 5

132. AGN-PGR, trib. 8, caso 245, October 14, 1980, 3.

133. Ibid., 4.

134. "OSN Reporte de Informante, 15 de Octubre 1976, 09:00 horas: Actividades del FSLN en Condega, Mao Gómez," in AGN-PGR, trib. 8, caso 245, October 14, 1980, 32; OSN "Reporte de Informante, 29 de Octubre 1976, 17:30 hrs, Condega, FSLN, Mao Gómez," in trib. 8, caso 245, October 14, 1980, 33; OSN "Reporte, 7 de mayo 1979, 11:00 hrs, Mao Gómez," in trib. 8, caso 245, October 14, 1980, 25.

135. AGN-PGR, trib. 8, caso 106, August 6, 1980, 40; Document, "Comunicado de la Junta Directiva del Instituto Técnico Vocacional," August 25, 1969, trib. 8, caso 106, August 6, 1980, 45.

136. "Jaime," interview with author, Somoto, Madriz, 2010. During his interview, he professed innocence for the numerous denunciations for which he was imprisoned during the 1980s, despite the existence of ample evidence from the OSN archives and an earlier televised confession.

137. Mónica Baltodano to Tribunal Especial No. 8, in AGN-PGR, trib. 8, caso 106, August 6, 1980, 35–36, 39.

138. Mónica Baltodano to Bayardo Arce, February 4, 1977, CHM-MR E-002, C-021, 000611.

139. "Reporte de Informante: Informe de Interés," February 23, 1977, Somoto, in OSN file "Bayardo Arce," CHM-MR, E-001, C-017, 000488.

140. Mónica Baltodano to Tribunal Especial No. 8, in AGN-PGR, trib. 8, caso 106, August 6, 1980, 35–36, 39.

141. Bayardo Arce to Mónica Baltodano, February 3, 1977, CHM-MR E-002, C-021, 000611.

142. Mónica Baltodano to Bayardo Arce, "Conclusion of the meeting with Silvia, Trabajo en Mas Uno [Somoto]," October 24, 1976, Bayardo Arce to Mónica Baltodano, February 3, 1977, CHM-MR E-002, C-021, 000611; "OSN Reporte de Entrevista," Somoto, September 12, 1976; "OSN Reporte de Entrevista," Somoto, September 13, 1976, in trib. 8, caso 106, August 6, 1980, 53–56; "OSN Reporte Operacional," Managua, March 3, 1976; "OSN Reporte Operacional: Actividades Subversivas," Empalme Palacagüina, Somoto, April 29, 1976; "Reporte de Informante: Informe de Interés" February 23, 1977, Somoto in OSN file "Bayardo Arce," CHM-MR, E-001, C-017, 000488.

143. "OSN Reporte de Entrevista," September 13, 1976, in AGN-PGR, trib. 8, caso 106, August 6, 1980, 54.

144. It seems that the OSN did not attack or arrest the guerrilla leader, hoping that a functioning border route would provide them opportunities to catch or kill the FSLN's top leaders ("Reporte de Informante: Informe de Interés," February 23, 1977, Somoto in OSN file "Bayardo Arce," CHM-MR, E-001, C-017, 000488).

145. Mónica Baltodano to Tribunal Especial No. 8, in AGN-PGR, trib. 8, caso 106, August 6, 1980, 37.

146. "Patrulla en persecución," LP, August 8, 1977; Document, "La voz de denuncia en el asesinato del Ing. Raúl González A.," CHM-MR, 001, C-016, 000468. The cause of González's death drew a great deal of attention, with the deputy chief of mission at the U.S. embassy acknowledging that "on the basis of information and documents furnished by the González family it seems their version of their brother having been beaten to death rather than killed in a shootout may be true" (Irwin Rubenstein, "Human Rights: Raúl González Case," U.S. Embassy Cable 4205, September 9, 1977, PlusD). Weeks later, Ambassador Mauricio Solaún wrote that "the Embassy cannot come to a determination as to whether Mr. González was killed in a shootout with the GN or was beaten to death as his family alleges. Given the traditional lack of impartial, apolitical investigatory bodies in Nicaragua, an impartial investigation of González's death is unlikely" (Mauricio Solaún "Human Rights: Raúl González Case—Update," U.S. Embassy Cable 4452, September 26, 1977, PlusD).

147. "Captura de Doris Tijerino," LP, April 13, 1978.

148. Testimony, Doris Tijerino, AGN-PGR, trib. 8, caso 106, August 6, 1980, 31–32.

149. Testimony, Manuel Maldonado Lovo, AGN-PGR, trib. 8, caso 106, August 6, 1980, 39.

150. Mónica Baltodano to Tribunal Especial, AGN-PGR, trib. 8, caso 106, August 6, 1980, 38.

151. Jaime was later jailed and convicted in his 1980 trial following a public confession (which he later retracted).

FIVE.    "A Crime to Be Young"

1. Colonel Carlos Edmundo Vergara, "Estelí, la ciudad de mayor progreso del Norte," Acción Cívica, September 1977.

2. Communiqué, "Del Estado Mayor del Frente Norte 'Carlos Fonseca,'" November 11, 1978; published in Lucha Sandinista, January 1979.

3. On the meaning of childhood and the diverse roles of children as targets of state terror and participants in revolutionary movements, see Anna L. Peterson and Kay A. Read, "Victims, Heroes, Enemies: Children in Central American Wars," in Minor Omissions: Children in Latin American History and Society, ed. Tobias Hecht (Madison: University of Wisconsin Press, 2002), 215–31.

4. José del Carmen Araúz, interview by A. B., Santa Cruz, Estelí, 1980, IHNCA-CNA, 1A-715.714.703.

5. Bayard de Volo, *Mothers of Heroes and Martyrs*. On the most famous use of maternal identity as a protest against military dictatorship, see Marysa Navarro, "The Personal Is Political: Las Madres de Plaza de Mayo," in *Power and Popular Protest: Latin American Social Movements, Updated and Expanded Edition*, ed. Susan Eckstein (Berkeley: University of California Press, 2001), 241–58.

6. As recent literature on the Cuban Revolution has shown, female revolutionaries similarly mobilized around traditional gender identities of maternalism and moral authority (in largely unarmed roles); see Chase, *Revolution within the Revolution*; Bayard de Volo, *Women and the Cuban Insurrection*.

7. Karen Kampwirth, "Women in the Armed Struggles in Nicaragua: Sandinistas and Contras Compared," in *Radical Women in Latin America: Left and Right*, ed. Victoria González-Rivera and Karen Kampwirth (University Park: Penn State University Press, 2010), 84; Carlos M. Vilas, cited in Kampwirth, *Women and Guerrilla Movements*, 10.

8. Zimmermann, *Sandinista*, 205.

9. Mark Everingham, *Revolution and the Multiclass Coalition in Nicaragua* (Pittsburgh: University of Pittsburgh Press, 1996); Rose J. Spalding, *Capitalists and Revolution in Nicaragua: Opposition and Accommodation, 1979–1993* (Chapel Hill: University of North Carolina Press, 1994).

10. "A seis meses de la caída de dos dirigentes," *Gaceta Sandinista*, February-March 1976, 23. For more on the three tendencies, see Hodges, *Intellectual Foundations of the Nicaraguan Revolution*, 197–240; and Nolan, *The Ideology of the Sandinistas and the Nicaraguan Revolution*, 32–65.

11. Mónica Baltodano to Bayardo Arce, "Informe del Trabajo," October 24, 1976, CHM-MR, E-002, C-021, 000611.

12. Mónica Baltodano to Bayardo Arce, January 19, 1977, CHM-MR, E-002, C-021, 000611.

13. Socorro Sirias to Bayardo Arce, August 6, 1977, CHM-MR, E-002, C-021, 000611. Interestingly, Arce strongly opposed the formation of a chess club: "This so-called scientific game is alienating. The kids later will only think about this subject and forget their concrete problems. The regime and the GN support this game . . . holding tournaments and giving away boards" (Bayardo Arce to Mónica Baltodano, August 20, 1976, CHM-MR, E-002, C-021, 000611).

14. Bayardo Arce to Mónica Baltodano, August 20, 1976, CHM-MR, E-002, C-021, 000611.

15. Socorro Sirias to Bayardo Arce, August 6, 1977. E-002, C-021, 000616.

16. Bayardo Arce to Mónica Baltodano, August 20, 1976, CHM-MR, E-002, C-021, 000611.

17. Ibid.

18. Baltodano, *Memorias de la lucha sandinista*, 2:52, 56.

19. Cabezas, *Canción de amor para los hombres*, 293.

20. "Dos acciones del FSLN," *LP*, May 5, 1977; James Theberge, "Urban Attack on National Guard," U.S. Embassy Cable 2106, May 5, 1977, PlusD; "Nicaragua: Guerra Popular Sandinista," *Gaceta Sandinista*, May 1977, 21.

21. Lawrence Pezzullo and Ralph Pezzullo, *At the Fall of Somoza* (Pittsburgh: University of Pittsburgh Press, 1993), 260–61.

22. Mauricio Solaún, "FSLN Attacks: Chronology," U.S. Embassy Cable 4887, October 21, 1977, PlusD.

23. UDEL, founded in 1974, included the opposition Conservative Party, PLI, PSN, PSC, and dissident former members of Somoza's PLN; see Carlos M. Vilas, *The Sandinista Revolution: National Liberation and Social Transformation in Central America* (New York: Monthly Review Press, 1986), 132–33; Dunkerley, *Power in the Isthmus*, 236. Its influence in the Segovias was limited mostly to the small group of people involved in opposition party politics.

24. Black, *Triumph of the People*, 107–8; Booth, *The End and the Beginning*, 157–58.

25. Anonymous, interview by B. E. L., Barrio El Calvario, Estelí, 1980, IHNCA-CNA, 1A.137.

26. Salvador Maldonado, interview by L. H., San Juan de Limay, Estelí, 1980, IHNCA-CNA, 1C. 26.

27. Mauricio Solaún, "Continuing Disturbances," U.S. Embassy Cable 1724, April 13, 1978, PlusD.

28. "Toma otro colegio en Estelí," *LP*, April 8, 1978.

29. "Furia en Estelí, Asesinan a niño y hirieron a 6 más," *LP*, April 24, 1978.

30. "Convulsión en Estelí, queman casa de René Molina," *LP*, April 24, 1978; "Estelí: Paros, fogatas y lacrimógenas," *LP*, April 26, 1978; "Prudente calma llega a Estelí, manifestantes vivan a Vergara," *LP*, April 28, 1978; Equipo Pastoral de Estelí, *Camino de liberación*, 46–47.

31. Leonel Raudez, interview by S. T., Ocotal, Nueva Segovia, 1980, IHNCA-CNA, 2A-54.55.56.

32. "Convulsión en Estelí, queman casa de René Molina," *LP*, April 24, 1978. Molina was in the United States at the time, but his mother-in-law received advance warning from Padre Julio López of the potential riot to assure that René's children were nowhere nearby on that day. He remained grateful for the priest's help for the rest of his life (René Molina Valenzuela, interview with author, Ometepe, Rivas, 2010).

33. "Molina acusa al Comandante," *LP*, April 27, 1978; "Convulsión en Estelí, queman casa de René Molina," *LP*, April 24, 1978; "Estelí: Paros, fogatas y lacrimógenas," *LP*, April 26, 1978; "Prudente calma llega a Estelí," *LP*, April 28, 1978.

34. "Estelí Amotinado!" *LP*, May 25, 1978; "Cámara de Comercio: 12 millones en pérdidas," *LP*, May 26, 1978; "Estelí Responde Con Fuego," *Boletín Sandinista*, CHM-MR, fondo 2, box 8, document 49.

35. Mauricio Solaún, "Serious Disturbances in Estelí," U.S. Embassy Cable 2418, May 25, 1978, PlusD.

36. Francisco Moreno Torres to Antonio Mora Rostrán, Minister of the Interior, May 22, 1978; published in *LP*, May 27, 1978.

37. Rivera Quintero and Ramírez, *La marca del Zorro*, 174.

38. Artemio to Oscar (Bayardo Arce), June 5, 1978, CHM-MR, E-002, C-020, 000608.

39. José Benito Escobar, "Situación política de Estelí," July, 1978, 2; cited in Diócesis de Estelí, "Presencia cristiana en el proceso revolucionario," 48.

40. "AMPRONAC de Estelí protesta agresión a niños," *LP*, May 26, 1978.

41. Tanalís Padilla describes a similar dynamic at work in women's participation in the Jaramillista movement in Mexico; see Padilla, *Rural Resistance in the Land of Zapata: The Jaramillista Movement and the Myth of the Pax-Priísta, 1940–1962* (Durham, NC: Duke University Press, 2008), 161–83.

42. Francisca Dormus Zea, interview with author, Estelí, 2010.

43. Bernadero Valladares, interview by R. A. B., Somoto, Madriz, 1980, IHNCA-CNA, 3A.80.81.

44. "Padres de familia analizan desastre educativo en Estelí," *LP*, July 28, 1978.

45. Chase, *Revolution within the Revolution*, 161.

46. In early February, the elderly Bishop Monseñor Clemente Carranza y López passed away. His death likely gave freer rein to the priests identified with the popular movement ("Muere un Obispo que era todo humildad," *LP*, February 2, 1978).

47. Anonymous, interview by M. M. G., Esteli, 1980. IHNCA-CNA, 1A-33.

48. Josefa Ruíz Lorente, interview with author, El Calvario, Estelí, 2010.

49. Padre Julio López, interview with author, Estelí, 2010.

50. MPU, "¿Qué son los Comités de Defensa Civil (CDC)?," IHNCA, CDC No. 0012, 1.

51. Ibid., 2.

52. MPU, "Líneas particulares para los CDC," IHNCA, CDC No. 005.

53. Magdalena Derruti, interview by O. M. V., Barrio Milenia Hernández, Estelí, 1980, IHNCA-CNA, 1A-210.

54. The GN denounced the CDCs as an imitation of the Committees in Defense of the Revolution (CDRs) in Fidel Castro's Cuba. However, in contrast to those progovernment vigilance block committees, the CDCs had emerged directly from the ground up as oppositional Christian associations. For the role of the CDRs in squelching dissent and establishing the Castro regime in Cuba, see Lillian Guerra, *Visions of Power in Cuba: Revolution, Redemption, and Resistance, 1959–1971* (Chapel Hill: University of North Carolina Press, 2012), 207–15.

55. Bayardo Arce to Felipe Escobar, June 23, 1978, CHM-MR, E-002, C-021, 000637.

56. MPU, "¿Qué es un CDC?," IHNCA, CDC-0013, 4; Black, *Triumph of the People*, 139.

57. Bayardo Arce to Felipe Escobar, August 20, 1978, CHM-MR, E-002, C-021, 000637.

58. Florencia Mallon similarly relays the story of a young Chilean who chose to join the revolutionary movement after being slapped by his father, who opposed political activism. Of his male role models, he said: "I admired these compañeros. . . . To me, they seemed like small heroes, small gods. I think I held them up as mythical characters" (Mallon, "Barbudos, Warriors, and Rotos," 185).

59. Rivera Quintero and Ramírez, *La marca del Zorro*, 168.

60. See chapter 4 for further detail on the assassination of Escobar. "Cadáver en Estelí," *LP*, July 15, 1978; "Cae José Benito Escobar," *LP*, July 16, 1978; "Muerte de José Benito Escobar en Estelí confirma injerencia cubana,"

*Novedades*, July 17, 1978; Mauricio Solaún, "FSLN Leader Escobar Killed in Estelí," U.S. Embassy Cable 3217, July 17, 1978, PlusD; Cabestrero, *No los separó la muerte*, 137–38.

61. "Una sola consigna en Estelí: Unidad," *LP*, July 17, 1978.

62. *LP*, July 16-17, 1978.

63. "Otro estudiante muerto en Estelí," *LP*, July 20, 1978; Rubén Mairena Molina, interview by B. E. L., Estelí, 1980, IHNCA-CNA, 1A-130; Javier Benavides, interview by B. E. L., El Calvario, Estelí, 1980, IHNCA-CNA, 1A-134; Anonymous, interview by K. L. G., San Juan de Limay, Barrio Silvio Bravo, 1980, IHNCA-CNA, 1C-18; Anonymous, interview by C. V., San Juan de Río Coco, Madriz, 1980, IHNCA-CNA, 3B-3.

64. Testimony, Leonel Blandón Juárez, AGN-PGR, trib. 2, caso 83, June 18, 1980, 52; Mauricio Solaún, "General Work Stoppage of July 19," U.S. Embassy Cable 3303, July 20, 1978, PlusD.

65. Carta Pastoral de la Conferencia Episcopal de Nicaragua, "A los hombres de buena voluntad," *LP*, August 3, 1978.

66. Mauricio Solaún, "Church Reports Harassment," U.S. Embassy Cable 3800, August 16, 1978, PlusD.

67. Ibid.

68. Ibid.

69. For an account of the capture of the National Palace, see Manuel Eugarrios, *Dos . . . uno . . . Cero, comandante* (San José: Lehmann, 1979).

70. "Paro Total: Cámaras," *LP*, August 28, 1978, "Palacagüina, Pueblo Nuevo y Condega al paro," *LP*, September 2, 1978; "Estelí sitiada," *LP*, September 2, 1978; Warren Hoge, "City Faces Uncertainties after Nicaraguan War," *NY Times News Service*, August 4, 1979; Dávila Bolaños, *El interrogatorio*.

71. "Estelí: Hora por hora, muerte por muerte," *LP*, September 13, 1978.

72. "Violencia en 5 ciudades!!!" *LP*, September 10, 1978; Frente Sandinista de Liberación Nacional, "Parte de Guerra, No.1," September 10, 1978; and "Parte de Guerra, No. 4," September 10, 1978, Centro de Documentación de los Movimientos Armados (hereafter CEDEMA); "Informe de Rubén," CHM, Fondo Frentes de Guerra. Picado, a member of Northern Front leadership, was killed during the insurrection.

73. Black, *Triumph of the People*, 320.

74. "Puestos insurgentes en la carretera," *LP*, September 12, 1978.

75. No. 14, "Informe Militar," CHM-MR, fondo 2, box 6, folder 89; Frente Sandinista de Liberación Nacional-GPP, "Cómo resistió Estelí: La ciudad que asombró al mundo con su valentía," September 1978, CEDEMA; "Legalizan en Masaya y Estelí Ley Marcial," *LP*, September 11, 1978; "Estelí: Hora por hora, muerte por muerte," *LP*, September 13, 1978.

76. José del Carmen Araúz, interview by A. B., Santa Cruz, Estelí, 1980, IHNCA-CNA, 1A-715.714.703.

77. For a similar dynamic of sharing and fictive kinship among Guatemalan guerrilleros, and between guerrillas and their civilian support base in the Rebel Armed Forces (Fuerzas Armadas Rebeldes), see Silvia Posocco, *Secrecy and Insurgency: Socialities and Knowledge Practices in Guatemala* (Tuscaloosa: University of Alabama Press, 2014), 153–57.

78. Magdalena Derruti, interview by O. M. V., Barrio Milenia Hernández, Estelí, 1980, IHNCA-CNA, 1A-210.

79. Pisani, *Los muchachos*, 105, 107.

80. Josefa Ruiz Lorente, interview with author, El Calvario, Estelí, 2010.

81. Magdalena de Rodríguez R., *Estelí 79, Junio-Julio* (Estelí: Editorial Alemana, 1979), 16.

82. No. 14, "Informe Militar," CHM-MR, fondo 2, box 6, folder 89.

83. Romelia Almendárez, interview by C. P. S., Barrio Juno Rodríguez, Estelí, 1980, IHNCA-CNA, 1A-268.

84. No. 14, "Informe Militar," CHM-MR, fondo 2, box 6, folder 89.

85. Inter-American Commission on Human Rights, *Report on the Situation of Human Rights in Nicaragua: Findings of the "On-Site" Observation in the Republic of Nicaragua, October 3–12, 1978* (General Secretariat, Organization of American States, 1978), 37.

86. Leonel Raudez, interview by S. T., Ocotal, Nueva Segovia, 1980, IHNCA-CNA, 2A-54.55.56.

87. "Reconquista de la ciudad," *LP*, September 20, 1978, Mauricio Solaún, "Atrocity Summary," U.S. Embassy Cable 4541, September 22, 1978; Solaún, "n/a," U.S. Embassy Cable 5053, October 13, 1978; Solaún "Draft Nicaragua Human Rights Report," U.S. Embassy Cable 5871, November 15, 1978, PlusD; Inter-American Commission on Human Rights, *Report on the Situation of Human Rights in Nicaragua*, 43; Black, *Triumph of the People*, 132–33; Booth, *The End and the Beginning*, 173.

88. Anonymous, interview with author, Estelí, 2010.

89. Anonymous, interview with author, San Lucas, Madriz, 2010.

90. Randall, *Sandino's Daughters*, 157–58.

91. "Matanza no se detiene," *LP*, September 25, 1978; "El sacerdote católico Francisco Luis Espinoza," *LP*, September 20, 1978; Frente Sandinista de Liberación Nacional "Del Estado Mayor del Frente Norte 'Carlos Fonseca,'" November 18, 1978, CEDEMA, 25; Rooper, *Fragile Victory*, 170; Carmen Hidalgo v. de Terán, *Crónicas de Estelí* (Managua: Teranhidal, 2007), 206–7.

92. "Estelí: Hora por hora, muerte por muerte," *LP*, September 13, 1978; "Vio a Sandinistas fusilando a quince personas en Estelí," *Novedades*, September 23, 1978; Frente Sandinista de Liberación Nacional, "¡Vivan los héroes de Septiembre," October 1, 1978, CEDEMA. For the role of ajusticiamientos in the strategy of the Guatemalan guerrillas, see Carlota McAllister, "A Headlong Rush into the Future: Violence and Revolution in a Guatemalan Indigenous Village," in *A Century of Revolution: Insurgent and Counterinsurgent Violence during Latin America's Long Cold War*, ed. Gilbert M. Joseph and Greg Grandin (Durham, NC: Duke University Press, 2010), 276–308.

93. No. 14, "Informe Militar," CHM-MR, fondo 2, box 6, folder 89.

94. "Reconquista de la ciudad," *LP*, September 20, 1978.

95. "Estelí ya no existe," *LP*, September 22, 1978.

96. Bayardo Arce to "Toño," October 6, 1978, CHM-MR, E-002, C-021, 000637.

97. No. 14, "Informe Militar," CHM-MR, fondo 2, box 6, folder 89.

98. Modesto Venegas, interview by J. R. L. I., Pueblo Nuevo, Estelí, 1980, IHNCA-CNA, 1D-31.

99. Carlos José Blandón López, interview O. O. G., La Trinidad, Estelí, 1980, IHNCA-CNA, 1E-3.

100. Gregorio Talavera, interview by R. G. S., Ocotal, Nueva Segovia, July 17, 1980, IHNCA-CNA, 2A-64; Denis Alonso, interview with author, El Calvario, Estelí, 2010.

101. Comandante Francisco Rivera, CHM, Fondo Sonoteca, document 103.

102. Pisani, *Los muchachos*, 87.

103. Martha Úbeda, interview by J. T., La Trinidad, Estelí, 1980, IHNCA-CNA, 1E-15.

104. Feliciano López, interview by B. E. L., El Calvario, Estelí, 1980, IHNCA-CNA, 1A-137.

105. C.f. Mack, *Organización y movilización*, 87–88. Rosario Montoya, however, writes that the mythic vision of "the mountain . . . [as] a place where class divisions were erased to give way to male bonding, male solidarity, and the birth of the New Man . . . was in fact an expression of a homosocial love between revolutionary men and of women's exclusion from the national community" (Montoya, *Gendered Scenarios of Revolution*, 90–91).

106. Leonel Raudez, interview by S. T. Ocotal, Nueva Segovia, 1980, IHNCA-CNA, 2A-54.55.56.

107. Anonymous, interview by R. J. R., Los Potreros, Condega, August 6, 1980, IHNCA-CNA, 2B-55.54.53.

108. Juan José Aguilar, interview by J. R., Condega, Estelí, 1980, IHNCA-CNA, 1B-1.

109. Moisés Calero, interview by E. G., Condega, Estelí, 1980, IHNCA-CNA, 1B-13.14.

110. "Martha Úbeda gana medalla de oro en tira de bala," *LP*, October 22, 1975; Martha Úbeda, interview by J. T., La Trinidad, Estelí, 1980, IHNCA-CNA, 1E-15; Martha Úbeda, interview with author, Pueblo Nuevo, Estelí, 2010. Pavón was killed in combat in Estelí on June 22, 1979, less than a month before the defeat of the Somoza regime. She was three months pregnant at the time of her death (Baltodano, *Memorias de la lucha sandinista*, 2:146–47).

111. Among Karen Kampwirth's sample of female guerrillas in Nicaragua, 76 percent had some college education, compared to 3 percent of the wider public (Kampwirth, *Women and Guerrilla Movements*, 39).

112. Dietrich Ortega, "Looking Beyond Violent Militarized Masculinities," 491.

113. Kampwirth, *Women and Guerrilla Movements*, 102. Other estimates of female enlistment in the guerrilla army are found in Vilas, *The Sandinista Revolution*, 108–9; Linda L. Reif, "Women in Latin American Guerrilla Movements: A Comparative Perspective," *Comparative Politics* 18, no. 2 (1986): 158; Randall, *Sandino's Daughters Revisited*, 26.

114. Martha Úbeda, interview with author, Pueblo Nuevo, Estelí, 2010.

115. Alexander Aviña analyzes armed movements in 1960s Guerrero, Mexico, in which women similarly were in the minority and occasionally took up arms as guerrilleras, providing "glimpses of alternative visions and social rela-

tionships that challenged gender norms"; Aviña, *Specters of Revolution: Peasant Guerrillas in the Cold War Mexican Countryside* (Oxford: Oxford University Press, 2014), 64.

116. Aura Estela Talavera Pérez (Rebeca), interview with author, Estelí, 2010.

117. Justo Úbeda Altamirano, interview by B. E. L., El Tular, Estelí, 1980, IHNCA-CNA, 1A-131.

118. Some women recalled their experiences in the montaña as far more positive than the machismo that returned after the FSLN took power (Kampwirth, *Women and Guerrilla Movements*, 33–34).

SIX.    *"How Costly is Freedom!"*

1. Anonymous, interview by L. G., Los Araditos, La Montañita, Estelí, 1980, IHNCA-CNA.1A-647.

2. Frank Tucker, "Political Disturbances and Human Rights Situation: March 25–April 9," U.S. Embassy Cable 1720, April 9, 1979, PlusD.

3. Though we have little insight into the specific orders given to carry out these attacks, they seem to follow a pattern similar to that in Guatemala, in which specific communities were seen as proguerrilla ("red"), mixed proguerrilla and progovernment ("pink"), and progovernment ("green"). These communities were targeted with terror, selective violence, and surveillance, respectively; see Robert M. Carmack, ed., *Harvest of Violence: The Maya Indians and the Guatemalan Crisis* (Norman: University of Oklahoma Press, 1992).

4. While sexual violence appears to have been a weapon of war of many Latin American military dictatorships, leftist insurgencies in the hemisphere "typically [instituted] intensive socialization processes and effective command structures" that expressly aimed to prevent these atrocities; Elisabeth Jean Wood, "Variation in Sexual Violence during War," *Politics & Society* 34, no. 3 (2006): 307–42.

5. Sociologist Carlos Vilas's analysis of those killed during the insurrectionary period found that campesinos made up only 4.5 percent of the victims. In fact, only in Estelí (out of all of the departments) were campesinos the single largest group, accounting for nearly a third of those killed (Vilas, *The Sandinista Revolution*, 112, 117).

6. Geoffrey Robinson, "Mass Violence in Southeast Asia," in *Political Violence in South and Southeast Asia: Critical Perspectives*, ed. Itty Abraham, Edward Newman, and Meredith Leigh Weiss (New York: United Nations University Press, 2010), 74 (emphasis in original).

7. David Stoll, *Between Two Armies in the Ixil Towns of Guatemala* (New York: Columbia University Press, 1993); Jeffrey L. Gould and Aldo A. Lauria-Santiago, *To Rise in Darkness: Revolution, Repression, and Memory in El Salvador, 1920–1932* (Durham, NC: Duke University Press, 2009); McAllister, "A Headlong Rush into the Future."

8. On the role of discourses of martyrdom and sacrifice as mobilizing political action in El Salvador since the 1970s, see Anna L. Peterson and Brandt G.

Peterson, "Martyrdom, Sacrifice, and Political Memory in El Salvador," *Social Research* 75, no. 2 (2008): 511–42.

9. Ortega Saavedra, "La insurrección nacional victoriosa (Entrevista por Marta Harnecker)," 48.

10. Rivera Quintero and Ramírez, *La marca del Zorro*, 191.

11. Comandante Francisco Rivera, March 1979, CHM, Fondo Sonoteca 103.

12. Ibid.

13. Frente Sandinista de Liberación Nacional, "¡Ante la maniobra oportunista, la insurrección popular sandinista!," November 8, 1978, CEDEMA.

14. Urban squads were called *Los Tupamaros* in tribute to the Uruguayan urban guerrillas and were responsible for carrying several bank robberies and ambushes (Mack, *Organización y movilización*, 102; Rivera Quintero and Ramírez, *La marca del Zorro*, 190–91).

15. Frente Sandinista de Liberación Nacional, "Parte de Guerra No. 11," December 11, 1978, CEDEMA; Comandante Francisco Rivera, March 1979, CHM, Fondo Sonoteca 103; Rubén (Francisco Rivera) to Dirección Nacional del Frente Sandinista, "Evaluación del Estado Mayor del Frente Norte, Carlos Fonseca Amador, sobre la insurrección de Estelí y los combates de Condega, El Sauce y Achuapa," Abril 1979, CHM, Fondo Frentes de Guerra, folder 6.

16. Mauricio Solaún, "Impact of Nicaraguan Civil Strife in the Rural Areas," U.S. Embassy Cable 4661, September 26, 1978, PlusD.

17. In this, they differed from the Peruvian Shining Path (*Sendero Luminoso*), which seems to have relied largely on coercion and force in its relations with its peasant "base"; see Carlos Iván Degregori, *How Difficult It Is to Be God: Shining Path's Politics of War in Peru, 1980–1999* (Madison: University of Wisconsin Press, 2012).

18. Rivera Quintero and Ramírez, *La marca del Zorro*, 166–67, 176.

19. Mauricio Solaún, "GN Issues Communiques on Recent Fighting," U.S. Embassy Cable 6310, December 4, 1978, PlusD; Mauricio Solaún, "Recent FSLN Activity," U.S. Embassy Cable 43, January 4, 1979, PlusD; Mauricio Solaún, "More GN-FSLN Activities," U.S. Embassy Cable 335, January 19, 1979, PlusD.

20. Estado Mayor, "Informe de Rubén." Somoza had been publicly denied support by the CONDECA governments, but Sandinista combatants in Estelí reported finding large sums in Central American currencies, such as *quetzales*, *lempiras*, and *colones*, in GN backpacks, suggesting the presence of foreign mercenaries (Mauricio Solaún, "FSLN Claims it is Fighting CONDECA," U.S. Embassy Cable 247, January 16, 1979, PlusD).

21. Frente Sandinista de Liberación Nacional, "De la comisión exterior del FSLN al Pueblo de Nicaragua," January 8, 1979, CEDEMA; "Partes de los diferentes frentes de guerra," January 14, 1979, CEDEMA.

22. Mauricio Solaún, "Recent FSLN Activity," U.S. Embassy Cable 167, January 11, 1979, PlusD.

23. "Hallan 21 cadáveres en El Tular," *LP*, February 21, 1979; U.S. Ambassador Mauricio Solaún noted that the "spectre of GN reprisals against non-

combatants is suggested by some"; "CPDH Denounces New Human Rights Violations," U.S. Embassy Cable 662, February 6, 1979, PlusD; "Disturbances and Human Rights Situation: February 16–25," U.S. Embassy Cable 1023, February 26, 1979, PlusD.

24. "Terror y éxodo en el norte," *LP*, January 22, 1979; "Horror en el norte," *LP*, January 26, 1979.

25. Anonymous, interview with author, Estelí, 2010. A similar allegation regarding GN "trophies" of campesina rape victims in El Tular is found in "Partes de los diferentes frentes de guerra," January 14, 1979, CEDEMA.

26. Salomé García, interview by M. M. G., El Tular, Estelí, 1980, IHNCA-CNA, 1B-134.5.

27. Campesinos emphasized that Alejandro Briones, as "a good rich man" and an anti-Somocista, had offered his full encouragement to these efforts. In late March, a large cache of weapons and ammunition was discovered on the Estelí hacienda of Alcides Valenzuela Úbeda, another wealthy local. Denying torture, the U.S. embassy reported, the GN made the "incredible" claim that Valenzuela had ended up in the "hospital after suffering an attack of nerves while being questioned, which caused him to bang his head against the walls of the GN post where he was being questioned" (Frank Tucker, "GN Unearths New Arms Cache," U.S. Embassy Cable 1597, March 30, 1979, PlusD).

28. "En valles de Estelí capturas masivas de campesinos," *LP*, January 25, 1979; "Horror en el norte," *LP*, January 26, 1979; Mauricio Solaún, "CPDH Denounces New Human Rights Violations," U.S. Embassy Cable 662, February 6, 1979, PlusD.

29. Description drawn from the common description of events repeated in interviews conducted by author in La Montañita, Estelí, 2010, and also found in IHNCA-CNA, 1-A, 1980.

30. Silveria Cruz Zedilla, interview by I. Z. D., La Montañita, Estelí, 1980, IHNCA-CNA, 1A-674-675.

31. Venancia Olles Briones, interview by I. Z. D., La Montañita, Estelí, 1980, IHNCA-CNA, 1A-659.

32. Petrona Cruz Briones, interview by I. Z. D., La Montañita, Estelí, 1980, IHNCA-CNA, 1A-662.

33. Venancia Olles Briones, interview by I. Z. D., La Montañita, Estelí, 1980, IHNCA-CNA, 1A-659.

34. María González Zelaya v. de Cruz, interview by I. Z. D., El Edén, La Montañita, Estelí, 1980, IHNCA-CNA, 1A-663.

35. Julio Girón, interview by H. M., Buena Vista, Santa Cruz, Estelí, 1980, IHNCA-CNA, 1A-720.

36. Espectación Jirón Cruz to Comisión Permanente de Derechos Humanos, April 10, 1979, cited in *Gaceta Sandinista*, no. 3-4, 1979, 35.

37. Anonymous, interview with author, Buena Vista, Santa Cruz, Estelí, 2010.

38. Valentín Girón Lanuza, interview with author, Buena Vista, Santa Cruz, Estelí, 2010.

39. Marco Orozco Espinoza, interview by Y. C., Santa Cruz, Estelí, 1980, IHNCA-CNA, 1A-691.688.

40. In her discussion of the Mothers of the Heroes and Martyrs during the 1980s, Lorraine Bayard de Volo raises the question, "Why were there no Fathers of the Heroes and Martyrs?" The women replied that machista cultural codes led men to respond to their grief individually and often destructively with alcohol (Bayard de Volo, *Mothers of Heroes and Martyrs*, 59–63).

41. Filemón Moncada, interview with author, Estelí, 2008.

42. Comisión Permanente de Derechos Humanos (CPDH), "Los Desaparecidos: Un abominable crimen somocista," 14–16, Princeton University Latin American Pamphlet Collection, "Human and Civil Rights in Nicaragua," reel 2.

43. Jaime Talavera Olivas, interview with author, Estelí, 2010.

44. Hidalgo v. de Terán, *Crónicas de Estelí*, 197. Josefa Ruiz Lorente, interview with author, Estelí, 2010; Felipe Urrutia, interview with author, El Limón, Estelí, 2010; Rivera Quintero and Ramírez, *La marca del Zorro*, 205.

45. Claribel Alegría and D. J. Flakoll, *Nicaragua, la revolución sandinista: Una crónica política, 1855–1979* (Managua: Anama Ediciones Centroamericanas, 2004), 354–55.

46. "Insurrección en el norte," *LP*, April 9, 1979; Ortega Saavedra, "La insurrección nacional victoriosa (Entrevista por Marta Harnecker)," 47; Booth, *The End and the Beginning*, 173.

47. These included in El Sauce, Río Grande, Achuapa, Condega, Ducualí, Palacagüina, San Juan de Limay, San Rafael del Norte, San Nicolás, and Santa Cruz; see "Insurrección en el norte," *LP*, April 9, 1979; Rubén, "Evaluación del Frente Norte . . . "; Frank Tucker, "FSLN Attacks," U.S. Embassy Cable 1719, April 9, 1979, PlusD; Frank Tucker, "Political Disturbances and Human Rights Situation: March 25-April 9," U.S. Embassy Cable 1720, April 9, 1979, PlusD.

48. Baltodano, *Memorias de la lucha sandinista*, 2:126–27.

49. "Pelea casa por casa," *LP*, April 13, 1979; "Parte de Guerra del Frente Norte," April 4, 1979, CHM, Fondo Sonoteca 00331; Rubén, "Evaluación del Frente Norte . . . "; "Estelí liberada de las hordas comunistas," *Novedades*, April 15, 1979; Frank Tucker, "FSLN Attacks," U.S. Embassy Cable 1719, April 9, 1979, PlusD; Frank Tucker, "Security Situation in Nicaragua, April 10, 1979 – 3:30 P.M.," U.S. Embassy Cable 1754, April 10, 1979, PlusD; Frank Tucker, "Nicaraguan Situation, 11:00 A.M. April 12," U.S. Embassy Cable 1770, April 12, 1979, PlusD.

50. Hidalgo v. de Terán, *Crónicas de Estelí*, 198. The Somoza government congratulated the GN on the "professionalism and care it took to clean out the FSLN with minimum danger to civilians or private property" (Frank Tucker, "Sandinistas Virtually Cleared from Estelí," U.S. Embassy Cable 1778, April 15, 1979, PlusD).

51. Written Testimony, Mercedes Mendoza, AGN-PGR, trib. 3, case 42, April 30, 1980, 12.

52. "Urgen respuestas sobre la masacre," *LP*, May 5, 1979; Written Testimony, Juan Ramón Medrano, AGN-PGR, trib. 5, case 331, November 15, 1980, 33.

53. Frank Tucker, "Estelí Situation," U.S. Embassy Cable 1779, April 16, 1979, PlusD; Frank Tucker, "Visit to Estelí," U.S. Embassy Cable 1792, April 16,

1979, PlusD; Frank Tucker, "Further on Estelí," U.S. Embassy 1832, April 18, 1979, PlusD.

54. Testimony, Rosa Celinda Bellorín, AGN-PGR, trib. 5, case 331, November 15, 1980, 28.

55. "Testimonio de Alejandro Dávila Bolaños, 8 de abril 1979," CHM, Fondo Nuevo, box 23, no. 18.

56. Feliciano López, interview by B. E. L., El Calvario, Estelí, 1980, IHNCA-CNA, 1A-137.

57. Frente Norte Carlos Fonseca, "Parte de Guerra," April 21, 1979, CHM, Fondo Frentes de Guerra, box 15, folder 9. After the victory of the Sandinistas, Estelí's hospital was renamed after Dávila Bolaños, as was the military hospital in Managua. In homage, the three civilians were posthumously granted the rank of medical officer in the guerrilla army.

58. Frank Tucker, "Somoza Press Conference," U.S. Embassy 1824, April 18, 1979, PlusD.

59. Sara Hernández Zelaya v. de Cruz, interview by I. Z. D., El Edén, La Montañita, Estelí, 1980, IHNCA-CNA, 1A-672.

60. Silveria Cruz Zedilla, interview by I. Z. D., La Montañita, Estelí, 1980, IHNCA-CNA, 1A-674-675.

61. Interview, María González Zelaya, interview by I. Z. D., El Edén, La Montañita, Estelí, 1980, IHNCA-CNA, 1A-663.

62. The GN initially insisted that it had also killed Francisco Rivera in the operation. Debunking this claim proved a propaganda coup for the Frente Norte; see Frank Tucker, "Nicaraguan Situation, 11:00 A.M. April 13," U.S. Embassy Cable 1770, April 12, 1979, PlusD; Frank Tucker, "Nicaraguan Situation, 11:00 A.M. April 14," U.S. Embassy Cable 1777, April 14, 1979, PlusD; Frank Tucker, "GN Captures Letter from Humberto Ortega to Francisco Rivera," U.S. Embassy 1806, April 17, 1979, PlusD.

63. Rivera Quintero and Ramírez, *La marca del Zorro*, 212.

64. In the retreat, the Sandinistas claimed to lose only eight men, but the GN declared fifty guerrillas had been killed; René Rodríguez M. and Antonio Acevedo Espinoza, eds., *La Insurrección nicaragüense, 1978–1979: La lucha armada del FSLN y el pueblo contra la dictadura somocista en la prensa nacional y extranjera* (Managua: Banco Central de Nicaragua, 1979), 106.

65. This death squad was apparently patterned on the anticommunist "White Hand" formed in Guatemala in 1966 and similar groups formed in El Salvador; see Comisión para el Esclarecimiento Histórico, *Guatemala: Memoria del silencio*, Tomo II, *Las violaciones de los derechos humanos y los hechos de violencia* (Guatemala City: CEH, 1999), 111–12; Tommie Sue Montgomery, *Revolution in El Salvador: From Civil Strife to Civil Peace*, 2nd ed. (Boulder, CO: Westview, 1995), 55–56.

66. Mauricio Solaún, "Pro-Somoza Regime Terrorists?," U.S. Embassy Cable 2250, May 16, 1978. PlusD; Mauricio Solaún, "Analysis of 'White Hand' Existence," U.S. Embassy Cable 753, February 6, 1979, PlusD.

67. Anonymous, interview with author, Estelí, 2010.

68. Rosa Zeledón, interview by J. R., Barrio Mildred Centeno, Condega, Estelí, 1980, IHNCA-CNA, 1B-2.

69. Testimony, Luis Romeo González Almendárez, AGN-PGR, trib. esp. 5, caso 115, August 22, 1980, 64.

70. Written Testimony, Uriel Guillén González, AGN-PGR, trib. 5, caso 115, August 22, 1980, 32.

71. Testimony, Eduardo Guillén González, AGN-PGR, trib. 5, caso 115, August 22, 1980, 71.

72. "Lo de Condega es de hienas!," *LP*, May 4, 1979.

73. Written testimony, Luis Romeo González Almendárez, AGN-PGR, trib. 5, caso 115, August 22, 1980, 33.

74. Virginia Rivera de Moncada, "La Masacre de Condega," read in Virginia Rivera, interview by A. A. G., Estelí, 1980, IHNCA-CNA, 1A-11.

75. Testimony, AGN-PGR, trib. 3, caso 101, July 11, 1980, 5.

76. "Lo de Condega es de hienas!" *LP*, May 4, 1979. The U.S. embassy described the killers as "uniformed men wearing bandanas," while noting that the GN "denied that it had any involvement in this case" (Frank Tucker, "Political Violence and Human Rights Situation: April 22–May 6," U.S. Embassy Cable 2086, May 8, 1979, PlusD).

77. Written Testimony, Lidia Ubau, AGN-PGR, trib. 5, caso 115, August 22, 1980, 31; "Lo de Condega es de hienas!," *LP*, May 4, 1979.

78. "Urgen respuestas sobre la masacre," *LP*, May 5, 1979.

79. Testimony, AGN-PGR, trib. 3, caso 101, July 11, 1980, 5.

80. "5000 habitantes huyen de Condega," *LP*, May 6, 1979; "Matrimonio González está vivo!" *LP*, May 7, 1979.

81. Blanca Rosa Castillo Díaz, interview with author, La Trinidad, Estelí, 2010; Alfaro, *El último marine*, 70; Canuto Barreto, *Nicaragua desde Nicaragua* (Mexico City: Centro de Estudios Ecuménicos, 1984), 73.

82. Blanca Rosa Castillo Díaz, interview with author, La Trinidad, Estelí, 2010.

83. Javier Suazo, interview by O. O. G., La Trinidad, Estelí, 1980, IHNCA, CNA.1E-2.

84. Francisco Alcides Molina Miranda, interview with author, La Trinidad, Estelí, 2010.

85. Blanca Rosa Castillo Díaz, interview with author, La Trinidad, Estelí, 2010.

86. Anonymous, interview with author, San Lucas, Madriz, 2010.

87. Anonymous, interview with author, La Trinidad, Estelí, 2010.

88. Rivera Quintero and Ramírez, *La marca del Zorro*, 247.

89. Ibid.; Frank Tucker, "Estelí Situation," U.S. Embassy Cable 1779, April 16, 1979, PlusD.

90. Anonymous (town resident), interview with author, La Trinidad, Estelí, 2010.

91. Anonymous (former guerrilla), interview with author, La Trinidad, Estelí, 2010.

92. Anonymous (former guerrilla), interview by D. C., La Montañita, Estelí, 1980, IHNCA-CNA.1A-651.

93. Carlos Fonseca Amador, "La lucha por la transformación de Nicaragua (1960)," in *Bajo la bandera del sandinismo* (Managua: Editorial Nueva Nicaragua, 1982), 33.

94. Anonymous (former guerrilla), interview with author, El Zapote, Estelí, 2010.

95. Anonymous (former guerrilla), interview with author, El Calvario, Estelí, 2011.

96. Rivera Quintero and Ramírez, *La marca del Zorro*, 247; Jeffrey L. Gould, "On the Road to 'El Porvenir': Revolutionary and Counterrevolutionary Violence in El Salvador and Nicaragua," in *A Century of Revolution: Insurgent and Counterinsurgent Violence during Latin America's Long Cold War*, ed. Greg Grandin and Gilbert M. Joseph (Durham, NC: Duke University Press, 2010), 113.

97. Pezzullo and Pezzullo, *At the Fall of Somoza*, 272.

98. "Boletín de la Comisión de Prensa y Propaganda (para el exterior) del FSLN informando sobre las emboscadas efectuadas por el Frente Norte a un convoy militar y las acciones en Managua," May 24, 1979, CHM-Fondo Nuevo, box 6, folder 89.

99. Frank Tucker, "Red Cross Running into Growing Problems," U.S. Embassy Cable 2582, June 11, 1979, PlusD; José Simón Delgado, interview by C. D., Barrio Milenia Hernández, Estelí, 1980, IHNCA-CNA, 1A-265; Warren Hoge, "City Faces Uncertainties after Nicaraguan War," *NY Times News Service*, August 4, 1979; de Rodríguez R., *Estelí 79, Junio–Julio*, 8; Cabestrero, *No los separó la muerte*, 188; Rita Golden Gelman, *Inside Nicaragua: Young People's Dreams and Fears* (New York: Franklin Watts, 1988), 74–75; Hidalgo v. de Terán, *Crónicas de Estelí*, 202.

100. "Estelí, epitafio del somocismo," *Barricada*, June 22, 1980; "La toma de Estelí," *Barricada*, July 19, 1980; Rivera Quintero and Ramírez, *La marca del Zorro*, 242.

101. Rivera Quintero and Ramírez, 257; de Rodríguez R., *Estelí 79, Junio–Julio*, 23–25.

102. Rivera Quintero and Ramírez, *La marca del Zorro*, 259.

103. Jaime Talavera Olivas, interview with author, Estelí, 2010.

104. Carmen Castellón, interview by B. E. L., San Juan de Limay, Estelí, 1980, IHNCA-CNA, 1C-8.

105. Despaciano Blandón Morales, interview by L. H., La Ceibita, San Juan de Limay, Estelí, 1980, IHNCA-CNA, 1C-64.

106. Anonymous, interview with author, El Colorado, Pueblo Nuevo, Estelí, 2010.

107. Ibid.

108. Carmen Castellón, interview by B. E. L., San Juan de Limay, Estelí, 1980, IHNCA-CNA, 1C-8.

109. Marcial Torruño, interview by A. U., Somoto, Madriz, 1980, IHNCA-CNA.3A-43.44.

110. Leonel Raudez, interview by S. T., Ocotal, Nueva Segovia, 1980, IHNCA-CNA, 2A-54.55.56.

Epilogue

1. Anonymous, interview by L. H., San Juan de Limay, Barrio Silvio Bravo, 1980, IHNCA-CNA, 1C-13. Anastasio Somoza Debayle was later assassinated in Asunción, Paraguay, where he had gone into exile.

2. Feliciano López, interview by B. E. L., El Calvario, Estelí, 1980, IHNCA-CNA, 1A-137.

3. "Nicaraguan City, Shattered in War, Faces Harsh Peace," *New York Times*, August 4, 1979.

4. Leonel Raudez, interview by S. T., Ocotal, Nueva Segovia, 1980, IHNCA-CNA, 2A-54.55.56.

5. Tom O'Donnell, "GRN Begins Issuing Decrees," U.S. Embassy Cable 3293, July 21, 1979, PlusD.

6. Junta de Gobierno de Reconstrucción Nacional, "Ley sobre el mantenimiento del orden y seguridad pública," *La Gaceta*, August 22, 1979.

7. "Reagan Terms Nicaraguan Rebels 'Moral Equal of Founding Fathers,'" *New York Times*, March 2, 1985.

8. Henrik Saxgren, *Solomon's House: The Lost Children of Nicaragua* (New York: Aperture, 2000).

# BIBLIOGRAPHY

## Manuscript Collections

Archivo General de la Nación (AGN), Managua, Nicaragua
    Fondo Comunidades Indígenas
    Fondo Gobernación
        Sección Alcaldías
        Sección Jefatura Política
    Fondo Guardia Nacional
        Sección Estado Mayor
    Fondo Presidencial
        Sección Consejo Nacional de Elecciones
    Fondo Procuraduría General de la República
        Tribunales Especiales de Justicia
Centro de Documentación de los Movimientos Armados (CEDEMA), http://www.cedema.org/
Centro de Historia Militar (CHM), Managua, Nicaragua
    Fondo Frentes de Guerra
    Fondo Movimiento Revolucionario
    Fondo Nuevo
    Fondo Sonoteca
Instituto de Historia de Nicaragua y Centroamérica (IHNCA), Managua, Nicaragua
    Archivo Oral de la Cruzada Nacional de Alfabetización
    Fondo Comités de Defensa Civil
Princeton University, Latin American Pamphlet Collection. Princeton, NJ: Photographic Services, Princeton University Library, 1989, "Human and Civil Rights in Nicaragua"
Robert J. Alexander Papers. Microfilm. Leiden, Netherlands: IDC, 2002
    Interview Collection, 1947–1994
School of the Americas Watch (SOAW), Washington, DC
    School of the Americas/Western Hemisphere Institute for Security Cooperation Graduates 1946–2004 Database

Wikileaks, Public Library of U.S. Diplomacy (PlusD), http://search.wikileaks
.org/plusd/

## PERIODICALS AND MAGAZINES

*Acción Cívica*
*Barricada*
*Black Belt Magazine*
*Boletín Sandinista*
*El Infante*
*Gaceta Sandinista*
*Impacto*
*La Gaceta (Diario Oficial)*
*La Información*
*La Nación*
*La Nueva Prensa*
*La Prensa*
*La Prensa Magazine*
*Lucha Sandinista*
*New York Times*
*Novedades*
*Revista de la GN*
*Soldier of Fortune*
*Time*

## BOOKS AND ARTICLES

Ablard, Jonathan D. "'The Barracks Receives Spoiled Children and Returns
    Men': Debating Military Service, Masculinity and Nation-Building in Ar-
    gentina, 1901–1930." *The Americas* 74, no. 3 (2017): 299–329.
Alegre, Robert F. *Railroad Radicals in Cold War Mexico: Gender, Class, and
    Memory.* Lincoln: University of Nebraska Press, 2014.
Alegría, Claribel, and D. J. Flakoll. *Nicaragua, la revolución sandinista: Una
    crónica política, 1855–1979.* Managua: Anama Ediciones Centroamericanas,
    2004.
Alemán Bolaños, Gustavo. *Los pobres diablos: Segunda parte de un lombrosiano:
    Somoza: 1939–1944.* Guatemala City: Editorial Hispanía, 1947.
Alexander, Robert Jackson, and Eldon M. Parker. *A History of Organized Labor
    in Panama and Central America.* Westport, CT: Praeger, 2008.
Allodi, Federico. "Somoza's National Guard: A Study of Human Rights Abuses,
    Psychological Health and Moral Development." In *The Politics of Pain:
    Torturers and their Masters*, edited by Ronald D. Crelinsten and Alex Peter
    Schmid, 125–40. Boulder, CO: Westview, 1995.
Álvarez Arzate, María Dolores. "Relaciones sociales y de parentesco en dos fa-
    milias de Estelí, Nicaragua." In *Familia y diversidad en América Latina:*

*Estudios de casos*, edited by David Robichaux, 355–74. Buenos Aires: CLACSO, 2007.

Amnesty International. *The Republic of Nicaragua: An Amnesty International Report Including the Findings of a Mission to Nicaragua, 10–15 May 1976.* London: Amnesty International Publications, 1977.

Arias, Pilar. *Nicaragua, revolución: Relatos de combatientes del Frente Sandinista.* Mexico: Siglo Veintiuno Editores, 1988.

Asociación Latinoamericana de Educación Radiofónica. *Siempre estuvimos alerta: Testimonios de las escuelas radiofónicas de Nicaragua.* Quito: Secretaría Ejecutiva ALER, 1984.

Aviña, Alexander. *Specters of Revolution: Peasant Guerrillas in the Cold War Mexican Countryside.* Oxford: Oxford University Press, 2014.

Baltodano, Mónica. *Memorias de la lucha sandinista.* Tomo I, *De la forja de la vanguardia a la montaña.* Managua: Instituto de Historia de Nicaragua y Centroamérica, Universidad Centroamericana, 2010.

——. *Memorias de la lucha sandinista.* Tomo II, *El crisol de las insurrecciones: Las Segovias, Managua y León.* Managua: Instituto de Historia de Nicaragua y Centroamérica, Universidad Centroamericana, 2010.

Banco Central de Nicaragua-Ministerio de Economía, Industria y Comercio. *Compendio estadístico, 1965–1974.* Managua: Editorial y Litografía San José, 1976.

Barbosa, Francisco J. "July 23, 1959: Student Protest and State Violence as Myth and Memory in León, Nicaragua." *Hispanic American Historical Review* 85, no. 2 (2005): 187–222.

Barreto, Canuto. *Nicaragua desde Nicaragua.* Mexico City: Centro de Estudios Ecuménicos, 1984.

Bayard de Volo, Lorraine. *Mothers of Heroes and Martyrs: Gender Identity Politics in Nicaragua, 1979–1999.* Baltimore: Johns Hopkins University Press, 2001.

——. *Women and the Cuban Insurrection: How Gender Shaped Castro's Victory.* New York: Cambridge University Press, 2018.

Beattie, Peter M. *The Tribute of Blood: Army, Honor, Race, and Nation in Brazil, 1864–1945.* Durham, NC: Duke University Press, 2001.

Belli, Humberto. *Breaking Faith: The Sandinista Revolution and Its Impact on Freedom and Christian Faith in Nicaragua.* Westchester, IL: Puebla Institute, 1985.

Berryman, Phillip. *Liberation Theology: Essential Facts about the Revolutionary Movement in Latin America—and Beyond.* Philadelphia: Temple University Press, 1987.

Black, George. *Triumph of the People: The Sandinista Revolution in Nicaragua.* London: Zed Press, 1981.

Blandón, Chuno. *Entre Sandino y Fonseca.* Managua: Segovia Ediciones Latinoamericanas, 2008.

Bliss, Katherine Elaine. *Compromised Positions: Prostitution, Public Health, and Gender Politics in Revolutionary Mexico City.* University Park: Pennsylvania State University Press, 2010.

———. "'Guided by an Imperious, Moral Need': Prostitutes, Motherhood, and Nationalism in Revolutionary Mexico." In *Reconstructing Criminality in Latin America*, edited by Carlos Aguirre and Robert Buffington, 167–94. Lanham, MD: Rowman and Littlefield, 2000.

Bobrow-Strain, Aaron. *Intimate Enemies: Landowners, Power, and Violence in Chiapas*. Durham, NC: Duke University Press, 2007.

Booth, John A. *The End and the Beginning: The Nicaraguan Revolution*. Boulder, CO: Westview, 1985.

———. "The Somoza Regime in Nicaragua." In *Sultanistic Regimes*, edited by H. E. Chehabi and Juan José Linz, 131–52. Baltimore: Johns Hopkins University Press, 1998.

Borge, Tomás. *Carlos, el amanecer ya no es una tentación*. Managua: Editorial Nueva Nicaragua, 1982.

———. *La paciente impaciencia*. Managua: Editorial Vanguardia, 1989.

Brandes, Stanley. "Drink, Abstinence, and Male Identity in Mexico City." In *Changing Men and Masculinities in Latin America*, edited by Matthew C. Gutmann, 153–76. Durham, NC: Duke University Press, 2003.

Briceño, Henry. *Un ejército dentro de un ejército: Bajo el genocidio somocista*. San José: Imprenta Borrase, 1979.

Brock, Rita Nakashima, and Susan Brooks Thistlethwaite. *Casting Stones: Prostitution and Liberation in Asia and the United States*. Minneapolis: Fortress Press, 1996.

Brown, Timothy Charles. *The Real Contra War: Highlander Peasant Resistance in Nicaragua*. Norman: University of Oklahoma Press, 2001.

Browning, Christopher R. *Ordinary Men: Reserve Police Battalion 101 and the Final Solution in Poland*. New York: HarperCollins, 1993.

Brusco, Elizabeth E. *The Reformation of Machismo: Evangelical Conversion and Gender in Colombia*. Austin: University of Texas Press, 2011.

Burns, E. Bradford. *Patriarch and Folk: The Emergence of Nicaragua, 1798–1858*. Cambridge, MA: Harvard University Press, 1991.

Cabestrero, Teófilo. *Leonel Rugama: El delito de tomar la vida en serio*. Managua: Editorial Nueva Nicaragua, 1990.

———. *No los separó la muerte: Felipe y Mary Barreda, esposos cristianos que dieron su vida por Nicaragua*. Santander: Editorial Sal Terrae, 1985.

Cabezas, Omar. *Canción de amor para los hombres*. Managua: Editorial Nueva Nicaragua, 1988.

———. *La montaña es algo más que una inmensa estepa verde*. Mexico City: Siglo Veintiuno Editores, 1986.

Cardenal, Luis Gonzaga. *Mi rebelión: La dictadura de los Somoza*. Mexico City: Ediciones Patria y Libertad, 1961.

Carey, David, Jr. "Drunks and Dictators: Inebriation's Gendered, Ethnic, and Class Components in Guatemala, 1898–1944." In *Alcohol in Latin America: A Social and Cultural History*, edited by Gretchen Pierce and Áurea Toxqui, 131–58. Tucson: University of Arizona Press, 2014.

———. "Mayan Soldier-Citizen: Ethnic Pride in the Guatemala Military, 1925–1945." In *Military Struggle and Identity Formation in Latin America: Race,*

*Nation, and Community during the Liberal Period*, edited by Nicola Foote and René D. Harder Horst, 136–56. Gainesville: University Press of Florida, 2010.

Carmack, Robert M., ed. *Harvest of Violence: The Maya Indians and the Guatemalan Crisis*. Norman: University of Oklahoma Press, 1992.

Castillo Herrera, Beverly. *La tradición oral en la conformación de la identidad histórica-cultural del municipio de Condega: Historia, tradiciones y costumbres*. Estelí: Centro de Investigación y Comunicación Social SINSLANI, 2006.

Centro de Investigación y Estudios de la Reforma Agraria (CIERA). *Diagnóstico Socioeconómico de PRONORTE*, Managua: CIERA-MIDINRA, 1980.

———. *Nicaragua, y por eso defendemos la frontera*. Managua: CIERA-MIDINRA, 1984.

Chamorro, Emiliano. *El último caudillo: Autobiografía*. Managua: Ediciones del Partido Conservador Demócrata, 1983.

Charlip, Julie A. *Cultivating Coffee: The Farmers of Carazo, Nicaragua, 1880–1930*. Athens: Ohio University Press, 2003.

Chase, Michelle. *Revolution within the Revolution: Women and Gender Politics in Cuba, 1952–1962*. Chapel Hill: University of North Carolina Press, 2015.

Ching, Erik. *Authoritarian El Salvador: Politics and the Origins of the Military Regimes, 1880–1940*. Notre Dame, IN: University of Notre Dame Press, 2014.

Christian, Shirley. *Nicaragua, Revolution in the Family*. New York: Random House, 1985.

Comisión para el Esclarecimiento Histórico. *Guatemala: Memoria del silencio. Tomo II, Las violaciones de los derechos humanos y los hechos de violencia*. Guatemala: CEH, 1999.

Consejo de Estado. *Primera legislatura, 1980: 4 mayo, 1927–1980, día de la dignidad nacional, instauración del Consejo de Estado*. Managua: Asesoría Jurídica y Divulgación y Prensa del Consejo de Estado, 1980.

Coronado, Rosa María Pochet, and Abelino Martínez. *Nicaragua—Iglesia: Manipulación o profecía?* San José: Departamento Ecuménico de Investigaciones, 1987.

Cowan, Benjamin A. *Securing Sex: Morality and Repression in the Making of Cold War Brazil*. Chapel Hill: University of North Carolina Press, 2016.

Cuadra Pasos, Carlos. *Posibilidades de existencia del comunismo en Nicaragua*. Granada: Tipografía El Centro Americano, 1937.

Dávila Bolaños, Alejandro. *El interrogatorio: Escrito en la cuarta semana de diciembre de 1978*. Estelí: Loaisiga, 1979.

Dawley, William. "From Wrestling with Monsters to Wrestling with God: Masculinities, 'Spirituality,' and the Group-Ization of Religious Life in Northern Costa Rica." *Anthropological Quarterly* 91, no. 1 (2018): 79–131.

*De cara al futuro de la Iglesia en Nicaragua*. Managua: Ediciones Fichero Pastoral Centroamericano, 1968.

Degregori, Carlos Iván. *How Difficult It Is to Be God: Shining Path's Politics of War in Peru, 1980–1999*. Madison: University of Wisconsin Press, 2012.

Derby, Lauren. "In the Shadow of the State: The Politics of Denunciation and Panegyric during the Trujillo Regime in the Dominican Republic, 1940–1958." *Hispanic American Historical Review* 83, no. 2 (2003): 295–344.

———. *The Dictator's Seduction: Politics and the Popular Imagination in the Era of Trujillo*. Durham, NC: Duke University Press, 2009.

Díaz Rodríguez, Miriam, Ruth Aguilar Pérez, and María Auxiliadora Chiong Gutiérrez. "La herencia colonial en los minifeudos de Santa Cruz (Estelí)." In *El universo de la tierra: Las culturas campesinas en el Pacífico y centro de Nicaragua: Una investigación socio-antropológica de la Universidad Nacional Autónoma de Nicaragua*, edited by Leo Gabriel. Managua: Editorial Universitaria, 1993.

Dietrich Ortega, Luisa María. "Looking Beyond Violent Militarized Masculinities: Guerrilla Gender Regimes in Latin America." *International Feminist Journal of Politics* 14, no. 4 (2012): 489–507.

Diócesis de Estelí. "Presencia cristiana en el proceso revolucionario." In *Apuntes para una teología nicaragüense: Encuentro de teología: 8–14 de septiembre de 1980*, 45–50. San José: Departamento Ecuménico de Investigaciones, 1981.

Dodson, Michael, and Laura Nuzzi O'Shaughnessy. *Nicaragua's Other Revolution: Religious Faith and Political Struggle*. Chapel Hill: University of North Carolina Press, 1990.

Dore, Elizabeth. *Myths of Modernity: Peonage and Patriarchy in Nicaragua*. Durham, NC: Duke University Press, 2006.

———. "The 'Holy Family': Imagined Households in Latin American History." In *Gender Politics in Latin America: Debates in Theory and Practice*, edited by Elizabeth Dore, 101–17. New York: Monthly Review Press, 1997.

Dore, Elizabeth, and John Weeks. *The Red and Black: The Sandinistas and the Nicaraguan Revolution*. London: Institute of Latin American Studies, 1992.

Duncan, Walter Raymond. *Latin American Politics: A Developmental Approach*. New York: Praeger, 1976.

Dunkerley, James. *Power in the Isthmus: A Political History of Modern Central America*. London: Verso, 1988.

Eber, Christine. "'Take My Water': Liberation through Prohibition in San Pedro Chenalhó, Chiapas, Mexico." *Social Science & Medicine* 53, no. 2 (2001): 251–62.

Equipo Pastoral de Estelí. *Camino de liberación*. Managua: Equipo Pastoral de Estelí, 1980.

Estelí (Nicaragua). *Alcaldía Municipal de Estelí: Censo general año 1971*. Estelí, Nicaragua, 1972.

Eugarrios, Manuel. *Dos . . . uno . . . Cero, comandante*. San José: Lehmann, 1979.

Everingham, Mark. *Revolution and the Multiclass Coalition in Nicaragua*. Pittsburgh: University of Pittsburgh Press, 1996.

Fajardo, José Floripe. *Estelí en retazos*. Estelí: Editorial Letras, 2004.

Fauné, Angélica. *Cooperación y subordinación en las familias campesinas*. Centro para la Promoción, Investigación y el Desarrollo Rural y Social, 1990.

Fernández de la Villa, Isaac. *El pequeño gigante: La vida de Manuelito Maldonado Lovo*. Managua: Amerrisque, 2009.

Fiallos Oyanguren, Mariano. "The Nicaraguan Political System: The Flow of Demands and the Reactions of the Regime." PhD diss., University of Kansas, 1968.

Findlay, Eileen. *Imposing Decency: The Politics of Sexuality and Race in Puerto Rico, 1870–1920*. Durham, NC: Duke University Press, 1999.

Fitzpatrick, Sheila, and Robert Gellately. "Introduction to the Practices of Denunciation in Modern European History." *The Journal of Modern History* 68, no. 4 (1996): 747–67.

Fonseca Amador, Carlos. *Ideario político de Augusto César Sandino*. Managua: Departamento de Propaganda y Educación Política del FSLN, 1984.

——. "La lucha por la transformación de Nicaragua (1960)." In *Bajo la bandera del sandinismo*, 25–38. Managua: Editorial Nueva Nicaragua, 1982.

——. "Mensaje del FSLN a los estudiantes revolucionarios (April 1968)." In *Bajo la bandera del sandinismo*, 55–72. Managua: Editorial Nueva Nicaragua, 1982.

——. "Sandino, guerrillero proletario." In *Obras*, 1:368–84. Managua: Nueva Nicaragua, 1982.

Foote, Nicola, and René Harder Horst. *Military Struggle and Identity Formation in Latin America: Race, Nation, and Community during the Liberal Period*. Gainesville: University Press of Florida, 2010.

Francis, Hilary. "¡Que Se Rinda Tu Madre! Leonel Rugama and Nicaragua's Changing Politics of Memory." *Journal of Latin American Cultural Studies* 21, no. 2 (2012): 235–52.

French, William. "Moralizing the Masses." In *Latin America's Middle Class: Unsettled Debates and New Histories*, edited by David Stuart Parker and Louise E. Walker, 79–104. Lanham, MD: Lexington Books, 2012.

Frente Sandinista de Liberación Nacional, Comando Juan José Quezada. *Frente Sandinista: Diciembre victorioso*. Mexico City: Editorial Diógenes, 1976.

Fuller, Norma. "The Social Constitution of Gender Identity among Peruvian Men." In *Changing Men and Masculinities in Latin America*, edited by Matthew C. Gutmann, 316–31. Durham, NC: Duke University Press, 2003.

Garza, James Alex. *The Imagined Underworld: Sex, Crime, and Vice in Porfirian Mexico City*. Lincoln: University of Nebraska Press, 2007.

Gelman, Rita Golden. *Inside Nicaragua: Young People's Dreams and Fears*. New York: Franklin Watts, 1988.

Gilbert, Dennis. *Sandinistas: The Party and the Revolution*. New York: Basil Blackwell, 1988.

Gill, Lesley. "Creating Citizens, Making Men: The Military and Masculinity in Bolivia." *Cultural Anthropology* 12, no. 4 (1997): 527–50.

——. *The School of the Americas: Military Training and Political Violence in the Americas*. Durham, NC: Duke University Press, 2004.

Glover, Jonathan. *Humanity: A Moral History of the Twentieth Century*. 2nd ed. New Haven, CT: Yale University Press, 2012.

Gobat, Michel. *Confronting the American Dream: Nicaragua under U.S. Imperial Rule*. Durham, NC: Duke University Press, 2005.

González-Rivera, Victoria. *Before the Revolution: Women's Rights and Right-Wing Politics in Nicaragua, 1821–1979*. University Park: Pennsylvania State University Press, 2011.

Goodwin, Jeff. *No Other Way Out: States and Revolutionary Movements, 1945–1991*. Cambridge: Cambridge University Press, 2001.

Gould, Jeffrey L. "'For an Organized Nicaragua': Somoza and the Labour Movement, 1944–1948." *Journal of Latin American Studies* 19, no. 2 (1987): 353–87.

———. "On the Road to 'El Porvenir': Revolutionary and Counterrevolutionary Violence in El Salvador and Nicaragua." In *A Century of Revolution: Insurgent and Counterinsurgent Violence during Latin America's Long Cold War*, edited by Greg Grandin and Gilbert M. Joseph, 88–120. Durham, NC: Duke University Press, 2010.

———. *To Die in This Way: Nicaraguan Indians and the Myth of Mestizaje, 1880–1965*. Durham, NC: Duke University Press, 1998.

———. *To Lead as Equals: Rural Protest and Political Consciousness in Chinandega, Nicaragua, 1912–1979*. Chapel Hill: University of North Carolina Press, 1990.

Gould, Jeffrey L., and Aldo A. Lauria-Santiago. *To Rise in Darkness: Revolution, Repression, and Memory in El Salvador, 1920–1932*. Durham, NC: Duke University Press, 2009.

Grandin, Greg. *The Last Colonial Massacre: Latin America in the Cold War*. Chicago: University of Chicago Press, 2004.

Grossman, Richard. "'Hermanos en La Patria': Nationalism, Honor, and Rebellion: Augusto Sandino and the Army in Defense of the National Sovereignty of Nicaragua, 1927–1934." PhD diss., University of Chicago, 1996.

———. "'The Blood of the People': The Guardia Nacional's Fifty-Year War against the People of Nicaragua, 1927–1979." In *When States Kill: Latin America, the U.S., and Technologies of Terror*, edited by Cecilia Menjívar and Néstor Rodríguez, 59–84. Austin: University of Texas Press, 2005.

Grubbe, Peter. "Nicaragua vista por un alemán." *Revista Conservadora* 1, no. 10 (1962): 23–25.

Guerra, Lillian. *Visions of Power in Cuba: Revolution, Redemption, and Resistance, 1959–1971*. Chapel Hill: University of North Carolina Press, 2012.

Guerrero Castillo, Julián N., and Lola Soriano de Guerrero. *Estelí (Monografía)*. Managua: Artes Gráficas, 1967.

———. *Madriz (Monografía)*. Managua: Artes Gráficas, 1971.

Guevara, Ernesto. *El socialismo y el hombre nuevo*. Mexico City: Siglo Veintiuno Editores, 1979.

———. "La guerra de guerrillas." In *Obras, 1957–1967*, 24–149. Havana: Casa de las Américas, 1970.

Guider, Margaret Eletta. *Daughters of Rahab: Prostitution and the Church of Liberation in Brazil*. Minneapolis: Fortress Press, 1995.

Gutiérrez, Rafael. "El alcoholismo." *Revista Conservadora* 4, no. 21 (1962): 26–28.

Gutiérrez Pimentel, Rodolfo. *Alcohol y alcoholismo en Centroamérica: Informe de un estudio*. San Salvador: Secretaría General de la Organización de Estados Centroamericanos, 1970.

Guy, Donna J. *Sex and Danger in Buenos Aires: Prostitution, Family, and Nation in Argentina*. Lincoln: University of Nebraska Press, 1991.

Hart, John Mason. *Revolutionary Mexico: The Coming and Process of the Mexican Revolution*. Berkeley: University of California Press, 1987.

Herrera Chavarría, Jaime. *Estampas de mi tierra*. Estelí: Impresiones ISNAYA, 2009.

Hervas, Juan. *Manual de dirigentes de cursillos de cristiandad*. Madrid: Euramérica, 1968.

Hidalgo v. de Terán, Carmen. *Crónicas de Estelí*. Managua: Teranhidal, 2007.

Hodges, Donald. *Intellectual Foundations of the Nicaraguan Revolution*. Austin: University of Texas Press, 1986.

Holden, Robert H. "Securing Central America against Communism: The United States and the Modernization of Surveillance in the Cold War." *Journal of Interamerican Studies and World Affairs* 41, no. 1 (1999): 1–30.

Horton, Lynn. *Peasants in Arms: War and Peace in the Mountains of Nicaragua, 1979–1994*. Athens: Ohio University Press, 1998.

Huggins, Martha Knisely. *Political Policing: The United States and Latin America*. Durham, NC: Duke University Press, 1998.

Hynson, Rachel. "'Count, Capture, and Reeducate': The Campaign to Rehabilitate Cuba's Female Sex Workers, 1959–1966." *Journal of the History of Sexuality* 24, no. 1 (2015): 125–53.

Instituto Centroamericano de Administración de Empresas, Centro de Asesoramiento. *Estudio de las municipalidades en Nicaragua*. Managua: INCAE, 1973.

Instituto de Estudio del Sandinismo. *Y se armó la runga . . .! Testimonios de la insurrección popular sandinista en Masaya*. Managua: Editorial Nueva Nicaragua, 1982.

Inter-American Commission on Human Rights. *Report on the Situation of Human Rights in Nicaragua: Findings of the "On-Site" Observation in the Republic of Nicaragua, October 3–12, 1978*. General Secretariat, Organization of American States, 1978.

Irarrázaval, Diego. "Nicaragua: Una sorprendente religiosidad." In *Religión y política en América Central: Hacia una nueva interpretación de la religiosidad popular*, edited by Pablo Richard and Diego Irarrázaval, 35–52. San José: Departamento Ecuménico de Investigaciones, 1981.

Johnson, Lyman L. "Dangerous Words, Provocative Gestures, and Violent Acts: The Disputed Hierarchies of Plebeian Life in Colonial Buenos Aires." In *The Faces of Honor: Sex, Shame, and Violence in Colonial Latin America*, edited by Lyman L. Johnson and Sonya Lipsett-Rivera, 127–51. Albuquerque: University of New Mexico Press, 1998.

Joseph, Gilbert M. "What We Now Know and Should Know: Bringing Latin America More Meaningfully into Cold War Studies." In *In from the Cold: Latin America's New Encounter with the Cold War*, edited by Gilbert M. Joseph and Daniela Spenser, 3–46. Durham, NC: Duke University Press, 2008.

Juárez, Orient Bolívar. *La catedral de Estelí: Historia y arquitectura*. Managua: Editorial Hispamer, 1993.

Kampwirth, Karen. *Feminism and the Legacy of Revolution: Nicaragua, El Salvador, Chiapas*. Athens: Ohio University Press, 2004.

———. *Women and Guerrilla Movements: Nicaragua, El Salvador, Chiapas, Cuba.* University Park: Pennsylvania State University Press, 2002.

———. "Women in the Armed Struggles in Nicaragua: Sandinistas and Contras Compared." In *Radical Women in Latin America: Left and Right,* edited by Victoria González-Rivera and Karen Kampwirth, 79–110. University Park: Pennsylvania State University Press, 2010.

Kleiner, Karol C. *Labor Law and Practice in Nicaragua.* Washington, DC: U.S. Department of Labor, Bureau of Labor Statistics, 1964.

Knight, Alan. "The United States and the Mexican Peasantry, circa 1880–1940." In *Rural Revolt in Mexico: U.S. Intervention and the Domain of Subaltern Politics,* edited by Daniel Nugent, 25–63. Durham, NC: Duke University Press, 1998.

Krehm, William. *Democracia y tiranías en el Caribe.* Buenos Aires: Editorial Parnaso, 1957.

Kruijt, Dirk. *Guerrillas: War and Peace in Central America.* London: Zed Books, 2008.

Lancaster, Roger N. *Life Is Hard: Machismo, Danger, and the Intimacy of Power in Nicaragua.* Berkeley: University of California Press, 1994.

———. *Thanks to God and the Revolution: Popular Religion and Class Consciousness in the New Nicaragua.* New York: Columbia University Press, 1988.

*Leonel Rugama: Datos biográficos.* Managua: Secretaría Nacional de Propaganda y Educación Política del F.S.L.N., 1980.

Levine, Daniel H. "How Not to Understand Liberation Theology, Nicaragua, or Both." *Journal of Interamerican Studies and World Affairs* 32, no. 3 (1990): 229–45.

Lowy, Michael. *The War of Gods: Religion and Politics in Latin America.* London: Verso, 1996.

Loza, Salvador, and Mario Rizo. *Mística y coraje: Testimonio del guerrillero Salvador Loza.* Managua: Amerrisque, 2009.

Luciak, Ilja A. *After the Revolution: Gender and Democracy in El Salvador, Nicaragua, and Guatemala.* Baltimore: Johns Hopkins University Press, 2003.

Mack, Myrna. *Organización y movilización: La propuesta nicaragüense de los '80 para Centroamérica.* Guatemala City: AVANCSO, Fundación Myrna Mack, 1995.

Mallon, Florencia E. "Barbudos, Warriors, and Rotos: The MIR, Masculinity, and Power in the Chilean Agrarian Reform, 1965–1974." In *Changing Men and Masculinities in Latin America,* edited by Matthew C. Gutmann, 179–215. Durham, NC: Duke University Press, 2002.

Mantica, Carlos. "Ubicación del método de cursillos dentro de la Pastoral de Conjunto." In *De cara al futuro de la Iglesia en Nicaragua,* 188–212. Managua: Ediciones Fichero Pastoral Centroamericano, 1968.

Manzano, Valeria. "Sex, Gender and the Making of the 'Enemy Within' in Cold War Argentina." *Journal of Latin American Studies* 47, no. 1 (2015): 1–29.

McAllister, Carlota. "A Headlong Rush into the Future: Violence and Revolution in a Guatemalan Indigenous Village." In *A Century of Revolution: In-*

*surgent and Counterinsurgent Violence during Latin America's Long Cold War*, edited by Gilbert M. Joseph and Greg Grandin, 276–308. Durham, NC: Duke University Press, 2010.

Mejía Salcedo, Ramón. "Organization of the Administrative Phase of a Public Health Department in Nicaragua." Master's in Public Health, University of Michigan, 1945.

*Memorias del V Congreso de la Federación de Trabajadores de Managua*. Managua: Imprenta Democrática, 1962.

Mendieta Alfaro, Róger. *El último marine: 1980, año de la alfabetización*. Managua: Editorial Unión Cardoza, 1980.

Milanich, Nara. "Whither Family History? A Road Map from Latin America." *American Historical Review* 112, no. 2 (2007): 439–58.

Millett, Richard. *Guardians of the Dynasty*. Maryknoll, NY: Orbis, 1977.

Ministerio de Economía, Dirección General de Estadística y Censo. *Censo 1963, Cifras provisionales, Boletín 1*. Managua: DGEC, 1963.

——. *Censos nacionales, 1963*. Vol. 2. Managua: DGEC, 1964.

——. *Censos nacionales, 1963*. Vol. 5, *Población*. Managua: DGEC, 1964.

Ministerio de Gobernación y Anexos. *Manual del juez de mesta*. Managua: Talleres Nacionales, 1952.

Molyneux, Maxine. "Mobilization without Emancipation? Women's Interests, the State, and Revolution in Nicaragua." *Feminist Studies* 11, no. 2 (1985): 227–54.

Montgomery, Tommie Sue. *Revolution in El Salvador: From Civil Strife to Civil Peace*. 2nd ed. Boulder, CO: Westview, 1995.

Montoya, Rosario. *Gendered Scenarios of Revolution: Making New Men and New Women in Nicaragua, 1975–2000*. Tucson: University of Arizona Press, 2012.

Navarro, Marysa. "The Personal Is Political: Las Madres de Plaza de Mayo." In *Power and Popular Protest: Latin American Social Movements, Updated and Expanded Edition*, edited by Susan Eckstein, 241–58. Berkeley: University of California Press, 2001.

Neufeld, Stephen B. *The Blood Contingent: The Military and the Making of Modern Mexico, 1876–1911*. Albuquerque: University of New Mexico Press, 2017.

Nicaragua. *Constitución política de Nicaragua y leyes constitutivas de Nicaragua*. Managua: Talleres Nacionales, 1948.

——. *Constitución política, ley de amparo y ley marcial de Nicaragua*. Managua: Talleres Nacionales, 1951.

——. *Constitución política y leyes constitutivas de Nicaragua*. Managua: Talleres Nacionales, 1939.

——. *Reglamento de policia de la República de Nicaragua*. 8th ed. Managua: Tipografía Nacional, 1951.

Nickson, R. Andrew. *Local Government in Latin America*. Boulder, CO: Lynne Rienner, 1995.

Nolan, David. *The Ideology of the Sandinistas and the Nicaraguan Revolution*. Coral Gables, FL: Institute of Interamerican Studies, Graduate School of International Studies, University of Miami, 1984.

O'Leary-Macias, Geraldine. *Lighting My Fire: Memoirs between Two Worlds: The Passionate Journey of a Young American Woman.* Bloomington, IN: Trafford, 2013.

Ortega Hegg, Manuel, and Marcelina Castillo. *Religión y política: La experiencia de Nicaragua.* Managua: Ruth Casa Editorial, 2006.

Ortega Saavedra, Humberto. *La epopeya de la insurrección: Nicaragua siglo XX: Pensamiento y acción, análisis histórico, narración inédita.* Managua: Lea Grupo Editorial, 2004.

———. "La insurrección nacional victoriosa (Entrevista por Marta Harnecker)." *Nicaráuac* 1 (May–June 1980): 26–57.

Ozouf, Mona. "Regeneration." In *A Critical Dictionary of the French Revolution,* edited by François Furet and Mona Ozouf, 778–91. Cambridge, MA: Harvard University Press, 1989.

Padilla, Tanalís. *Rural Resistance in the Land of Zapata: The Jaramillista Movement and the Myth of the Pax-Priísta, 1940–1962.* Durham, NC: Duke University Press, 2008.

Palmer, Steven. "Carlos Fonseca and the Construction of Sandinismo in Nicaragua." *Latin American Research Review* 23, no. 1 (1988): 91–109.

Palmer, Stuart Hunter. *The Violent Society.* New Haven, CT: College & University Press, 1972.

Partido Conservador de Nicaragua. *Programa de gobierno del Dr. Fernando Agüero Rocha candidato a la presidencia de la República por el Partido Conservador de Nicaragua y bases de acción para un gobierno de unidad nacional.* Unión Cardoza, Managua, 1966.

Passmore, Leith. *The Wars inside Chile's Barracks: Remembering Military Service under Pinochet.* Madison: University of Wisconsin Press, 2017.

Paz, Demócrito. *Apuntes de viaje.* Buenos Aires: Editorial Prometeo, 1975.

Pearce, Jenny. *Promised Land: Peasant Rebellion in Chalatenango, El Salvador.* London: Latin America Bureau, 1986.

Peña-Pérez, Enrique. *Secretos de la revolución sandinista.* New York: Book-Mart Press, 2004.

Pérez, Justiniano. *EEBI: Los Quijotes Del Ocaso.* Miami, FL: Orbis, 2008.

———. *Los mitos de la Guardia Nacional de Nicaragua.* Miami, FL: Orbis, 2007.

———. *Semper fidelis: El secuestro de la Guardia Nacional de Nicaragua.* Miami, FL: Orbis, 2005.

Pérez Baltodano, Andrés. *Entre el Estado Conquistador y el Estado Nación: Providencialismo, pensamiento político y estructuras de poder en el desarrollo histórico de Nicaragua.* Managua: Instituto de Historia de Nicaragua y Centroamérica, Universidad Centroamericana, 2003.

Pérez Bermúdez, Carlos, and Onofre Guevara López. *El movimiento obrero en Nicaragua: Apuntes para el conocimiento de su historia.* Managua: Editorial El Amanecer, 1980.

Peterson, Anna L. *Martyrdom and the Politics of Religion: Progressive Catholicism in El Salvador's Civil War.* Albany: State University of New York Press, 1997.

Peterson, Anna L., and Brandt G. Peterson. "Martyrdom, Sacrifice, and Political Memory in El Salvador." *Social Research* 75, no. 2 (2008): 511–42.

Peterson, Anna L., and Kay A. Read. "Victims, Heroes, Enemies: Children in Central American Wars." In *Minor Omissions: Children in Latin American History and Society*, edited by Tobias Hecht, 215–31. Madison: University of Wisconsin Press, 2002.

Pezzullo, Lawrence, and Ralph Pezzullo. *At the Fall of Somoza*. Pittsburgh: University of Pittsburgh Press, 1993.

Pierce, Gretchen. "Fighting Bacteria, the Bible, and the Bottle: Projects to Create New Men, Women, and Children, 1910–1940." In *A Companion to Mexican History and Culture*, edited by William H. Beezley, 505–17. Malden, MA: John Wiley & Sons, 2011.

———. "Pulqueros, Cerveceros, and Mezcaleros: Small Alcohol Producers and Popular Resistance to Mexico's Anti-Alcohol Campaigns, 1910–1940," in *Alcohol in Latin America: A Social and Cultural History*, edited by Gretchen Pierce and Áurea Toxqui, 161–84. Tucson: University of Arizona Press, 2014.

Pisani, Francis. *Los muchachos*. Managua: Editorial Vanguardia, 1989.

Posocco, Silvia. *Secrecy and Insurgency: Socialities and Knowledge Practices in Guatemala*. Tuscaloosa: University of Alabama Press, 2014.

Powell, David R., and Kevin B. Youngs. *Report of the Public Safety Program and the Nicaragua National Guard, June 1970*. Washington, DC: Agency for International Development, 1971.

*Programa histórico del FSLN*. Managua: Departamento de Propaganda y Educación Política del FSLN, 1984.

Putnam, Lara. "Sex and Standing on the Streets of Port Limón, Costa Rica, 1890–1910." In *Honor, Status, and Law in Modern Latin America*, edited by Sueann Caulfield, Sarah C. Chambers, and Lara Putnam, 155–75. Durham, NC: Duke University Press, 2005.

Quinlan, Sean. "Physical and Moral Regeneration after the Terror: Medical Culture, Sensibility and Family Politics in France, 1794–1804." *Social History* 29, no. 2 (2004): 139–64.

Radu, Michael. "The Nature of the Insurgency." In *The Continuing Crisis: U.S. Policy in Central America and the Caribbean*, edited by Mark Falcoff and Robert Royal, 409–32. Washington, DC: Ethics and Public Policy Center, 1987.

Ramírez, Sergio. *Adiós muchachos: Una memoria de la revolución sandinista*. Mexico City: Aguilar, 1999.

Randall, Margaret. *Sandino's Daughters: Testimonies of Nicaraguan Women in Struggle*. New Brunswick, NJ: Rutgers University Press, 1981.

———. *Sandino's Daughters Revisited: Feminism in Nicaragua*. New Brunswick, NJ: Rutgers University Press, 1994.

Reed, Jean-Pierre. "Emotions in Context: Revolutionary Accelerators, Hope, Moral Outrage, and Other Emotions in the Making of Nicaragua's Revolution." *Theory and Society* 33, no. 6 (2004): 653–703.

Reif, Linda L. "Women in Latin American Guerrilla Movements: A Comparative Perspective." *Comparative Politics* 18, no. 2 (1986): 147–69.

Rivera Quintero, Francisco, and Sergio Ramírez. *La marca del Zorro: Hazañas del comandante Francisco Rivera Quintero*. Managua: Editorial Nueva Nicaragua, 1989.

Rizo, Mario. *Historia del pueblo indígena de Telpaneca.* Managua: UNICEF, 2009.

Robinson, Geoffrey. "Mass Violence in Southeast Asia." In *Political Violence in South and Southeast Asia: Critical Perspectives,* edited by Itty Abraham, Edward Newman, and Meredith Leigh Weiss, 69–90. New York: United Nations University Press, 2010.

Rodríguez M., René, and Antonio Acevedo Espinoza, eds. *La Insurrección nicaragüense, 1978–1979: La lucha armada del FSLN y el pueblo contra la dictadura somocista en la prensa nacional y extranjera.* Managua: Banco Central de Nicaragua, 1979.

Rodríguez R., Magdalena de. *Estelí 79, Junio–Julio.* Estelí: Editorial Alemana, 1979.

Rodríguez Rosales, Isolda. *Anécdotas nicaragüenses: Estelí, Matagalpa, Chontales, Managua, Granada, Rivas.* Managua: Fondo Editorial CIRA, 2004.

Rodríguez y Palacios, Ciriaco. *Cuando el ayer es hoy: ¡Viva Estelí, que es mi pueblo!* Hollywood, CA: Orbe Publications, 1973.

Rooper, Alison. *Fragile Victory: A Nicaraguan Community at War.* London: Weidenfeld and Nicolson, 1987.

Rosemblatt, Karin Alejandra. *Gendered Compromises: Political Cultures and the State in Chile, 1920–1950.* Chapel Hill: University of North Carolina Press, 2000.

Rugama, Leonel. *The Earth Is a Satellite of the Moon.* Translated by Sara Miles, Richard Schaaf, and Nancy Weisberg. Willimantic, CT: Curbstone Press, 1985.

Ryan, John Morris, Robert N. Anderson, Harry R. Bradley, Carl E. Nesus, Robert B. Johnson, Charles W. Hanks, Gerald F. Croteau, and Cathy C. Council. *Area Handbook for Nicaragua.* Washington, DC: U.S. Government Printing Office, 1970.

Sabia, Debra. *Contradiction and Conflict: The Popular Church in Nicaragua.* Tuscaloosa: University of Alabama Press, 1997.

Saxgren, Henrik. *Solomon's House: The Lost Children of Nicaragua.* New York: Aperture, 2000.

Schroeder, Michael J. "Horse Thieves to Rebels to Dogs: Political Gang Violence and the State in the Western Segovias, Nicaragua, in the Time of Sandino, 1926–1934." *Journal of Latin American Studies* 28, no. 2 (1996): 383–434.

———. "The Sandino Rebellion Revisited: Civil War, Imperialism, Popular Nationalism, and State Formation Muddied Up Together in the Segovias of Nicaragua, 1926–1934." In *Close Encounters of Empire: Writing the Cultural History of U.S.–Latin American Relations,* edited by Gilbert M. Joseph, Catherine LeGrand, and Ricardo D. Salvatore. Durham, NC: Duke University Press, 1998.

Segovia, Pablo. "For a National Democratic Front." *World Marxist Review* 8 (1965): 51–54.

Sequeira Arellano, Adán. "El Abigeato." *Revista Conservadora* 2, no. 13 (1962): 30.

Sippial, Tiffany A. *Prostitution, Modernity, and the Making of the Cuban Republic, 1840–1920.* Chapel Hill: University of North Carolina Press, 2013.

Skocpol, Theda. *States and Social Revolutions: A Comparative Analysis of France, Russia, and China.* Cambridge: Cambridge University Press, 1979.

Smith, Christian. *The Emergence of Liberation Theology: Radical Religion and Social Movement Theory.* Chicago: University of Chicago Press, 1991.

Smith, Marshall. "One More Somoza in Nicaragua." *Life,* April 28, 1967.

Smith, Peter H. "Development and Dictatorship in Nicaragua: 1950–1960." *The American Economist* 7, no. 1 (1963): 24–32.

Somoza Debayle, Anastasio. *Primer mensaje al Congreso Nacional.* Managua: Imprenta Nacional, 1968.

Somoza García, Anastasio. *El verdadero Sandino: o, El calvario de las Segovias.* Managua: Tipografía Robelo, 1936.

Spalding, Rose J. *Capitalists and Revolution in Nicaragua: Opposition and Accommodation, 1979–1993.* Chapel Hill: University of North Carolina Press, 1994.

Stern, Steve J. *The Secret History of Gender: Women, Men, and Power in Late Colonial Mexico.* Chapel Hill: University of North Carolina Press, 2000.

Stoll, David. *Between Two Armies in the Ixil Towns of Guatemala.* New York: Columbia University Press, 1993.

Suárez, Luis. *Entre el fusil y la palabra.* Universidad Nacional Autónoma de México, 1980.

Tatar, Bradley. "Emergence of Nationalist Identity in Armed Insurrections: A Comparison of Iraq and Nicaragua." *Anthropological Quarterly* 78, no. 1 (2005): 179–95.

Taylor, James Robert. *Agricultural Settlement and Development in Eastern Nicaragua.* Madison: Land Tenure Center, University of Wisconsin, 1969.

Thomas, Gwynn. *Contesting Legitimacy in Chile: Familial Ideals, Citizenship, and Political Struggle, 1970–1990.* University Park: Pennsylvania State University Press, 2011.

Transchel, Kate. *Under the Influence: Working-Class Drinking, Temperance, and Cultural Revolution in Russia, 1895–1932.* Pittsburgh: University of Pittsburgh Press, 2006.

Trujillo Bolio, Mario A. *Historia de los trabajadores en el capitalismo nicaragüense (1850–1950).* Mexico City: Centro de Estudios Latinoamericanos-UNAM, 1992.

United Nations, Statistical Office. *Demographic Yearbook 1960.* New York: UN, 1960.

———. *Demographic Yearbook 1966.* New York: UN, 1967.

———. *Demographic Yearbook 1967.* New York: UN, 1968.

Upham, William Kennedy. "A Sociological Analysis of Man–Land Relations in Central America." Ph.D. diss., University of Florida, 1969.

Vargas, Oscar-René. *Floreció al filo de la espada: El movimiento de Sandino, 1926–1939. Once ensayos de interpretación.* Managua: Centro de Estudios de la Realidad Nacional, 1995.

Vilas, Carlos M. "Family Affairs: Class, Lineage and Politics in Contemporary Nicaragua." *Journal of Latin American Studies* 24, no. 2 (1992): 309–41.

———. *The Sandinista Revolution: National Liberation and Social Transformation in Central America.* New York: Monthly Review Press, 1986.

Walker, Thomas W. *The Christian Democratic Movement in Nicaragua*. Tucson: University of Arizona Press, 1970.

Walter, Knut. *The Regime of Anastasio Somoza, 1936–1956*. Chapel Hill: University of North Carolina Press, 1993.

Wheelock, Jaime. *Imperialismo y dictadura: Crisis de una formación social*. Mexico City: Siglo Veintiuno Editores, 1976.

Wickham-Crowley, Timothy P. *Guerrillas and Revolution in Latin America: A Comparative Study of Insurgents and Regimes since 1956*. Princeton, NJ: Princeton University Press, 1992.

Williams, Philip. *The Catholic Church and Politics in Nicaragua and Costa Rica*. Pittsburgh: University of Pittsburgh Press, 1989.

Wolfe, Justin. *The Everyday Nation-State: Community and Ethnicity in Nineteenth-Century Nicaragua*. Lincoln: University of Nebraska Press, 2007.

Wood, Elisabeth Jean. "Variation in Sexual Violence during War." *Politics & Society* 34, no. 3 (2006): 307–42.

Wright, Thomas C. *Latin America in the Era of the Cuban Revolution*. 2nd ed. Westport, CT: Praeger, 2001.

Yongming, Zhou. "Nationalism, Identity, and State-Building: The Antidrug Crusade in the People's Republic, 1949–1952." In *Opium Regimes: China, Britain, and Japan, 1839–1952*, edited by Timothy Brook and Bob Tadashi Wakabayashi, 380–403. Berkeley: University of California Press, 2000.

Zimmermann, Matilde. *Sandinista: Carlos Fonseca and the Nicaraguan Revolution*. Durham, NC: Duke University Press, 2000.

## INDEX

ROBERT SIERAKOWSKI is a history teacher and advisor in the Department of History, Trevor Day School. He is a former lecturer in the Department of History and Archaeology at the University of the West Indies.